SEÁN O'CASEY: POLITICAL ACTIVIST AND WRITER

By the same author

Shelley and Revolutionary Ireland
The 1913 Lockout
Shelley's Revolutionary Year

Seán O'Casey

Political activist and writer

PAUL O'BRIEN

CORK UNIVERSITY PRESS

First published in 2023 by
Cork University Press
Boole Library
University College Cork
CORK
T12 ND89
Ireland
Reprinted 2023

Library of Congress Control Number: 2023932128
Distribution in the USA: Longleaf Services, Chapel Hill, NC, USA

British Library Cataloguing in Publication Data
A CIP record for this book is available from the British Library.

ISBN: 978-1-78205-341-5

Printed by BZ Graf in Poland
Print origination & design by Carrigboy Typesetting Services
www.carrigboy.co.uk

COVER IMAGE – Portrait of Seán O'Casey, © courtesy Alamy Limited

www.corkuniversitypress.com

For my mother

Eilish O'Brien

1919–2014

Contents

PART 5

List of Abbreviations

ASRS	Amalgamated Society of Railway Servants
Autobiographies	Sean O'Casey, *Autobiographies*, vols 1–6 (London: Pan Books, 1971–3)
Berg	Berg Collection of English and American Literature, New York Public Library
CPGB	Communist Party of Great Britain
CPI	Communist Party of Ireland
GNR	Great Northern Railway
HUAC	House Un-American Activities Committee
ICA	Irish Citizen Army
ICTU	Irish Congress of Trade Unions
IRA	Irish Republican Army
IRB	Irish Republican Brotherhood
ITGWU	Irish Transport and General Workers' Union
IWDC	Irish Workers' Dramatic Company
IWL	Irish Workers' League
IWWU	Irish Women Workers' Union
Letters	*The Letters of Sean O'Casey*, David Krause (ed.), 4 vols (1975–92)
NLI	National Library of Ireland
NUDL	National Union of Dock Labourers
OSFC	Order of Saint Francis, Capuchin
RAF	Royal Air Force
RUC	Royal Ulster Constabulary
SIPTU	Services Industrial Professional and Technical Union
SJ	Society of Jesus
SLOT	St Laurence O'Toole [Club]
SPI	Socialist Party of Ireland
TD	Teachta Dála (Member of Parliament)
TUC	Trades Union Congress
USSR	Union of Soviet Socialist Republics
WUI	Workers' Union of Ireland

Foreword

Regarding my father and politics, my brother Breon wrote in *Sean O'Casey: A portrait*: 'He could be happier in the company of a Tory than a socialist, or a Catholic priest than an agnostic, if he liked them better as men.' It has taken a long time for a book to be written on my father's political and ethical beliefs and how they come through in his work for the theatre. Professor Ronald Ayling was going to do this, but it never materialised. Now Paul O'Brien has taken on the mammoth task and produced a book that is minutely archived and dense with information. He writes with a love of Seán's work, but also takes the academic freedom to make many critical evaluations of the work and of Seán as a man. It is not for me to defend my father – all that he wrote does that for me. My own feeling is that one should avoid reading too deeply into his texts and his productions as an extension of his politics. His priority as an artist was to structure his plays as a musician might a sonata or a symphony. And as to what makes a play – such as those of Strindberg and Ibsen – great, his answer was, 'They are human.'

I enjoy the way in which Paul O'Brien opens his study with an account of Seán's early life as a worker and activist, writing articles and pamphlets and lyrics to Irish airs, all before *The Shadow of a Gunman* was finally accepted by the Abbey Theatre in 1923. In these early pages, I found old friends like Jack and Mina Carney, George Gilmore and Barney Conway, with whom I spent unforgettable hours one day back in 1964.

As I read on, some of Ireland's harsh critical responses to Sean's post-Abbey plays start to resound in my ears – those I first heard during my visit to Dublin to see the production of *The Bishop's Bonfire* in 1955. Of course, there were many in Ireland who enjoyed Seán's work, unlike Quidnunc (Séamus Kelly) and Gabriel Fallon who disliked his plays. Then, over the years, the early naysayers were joined by the voices of some younger critics with yet other objections. In Britain, the negative criticism was more subdued, and in the United States there was a much more sympathetic reception to the new work. Seán's response to hostility was of course defiant: 'I have met with a good deal of opposition, mainly due to my political judgements. However, I am not worried in the least about the way they think of my judgements, for, since I believe them to be honest and true to me, they are not to be changed because some dislike them.'

Of the works after the early Abbey successes, which were seen – I think often mistakenly – as distorted by their overtly political message, I managed to catch in 1958 Paul Shyre's off-Broadway production of *Purple Dust* at the Cherry Lane Theatre, which ran for over a year. I also saw Shyre's produced readings of Seán's autobiographies, *I Knock at the Door* and *Pictures in the Hallway*, which were well received. In Britain, Seán and Eileen were at the 1959 Royal Court Theatre premiere of *Cock-a-Doodle Dandy*, directed by George Devine. It went from London to the Edinburgh Festival where it won the Earl of Harwood prize for best play.

Of the later plays, a number of productions from abroad are of special interest. The celebrated German actor Otto Sander, when asked in 1975 to choose any play to perform in, decided on the short farce *The End of the Beginning*. This seeded productions all over eastern Europe, one in Romania's National Theatre playing to an audience of some 1,000 every night. The Czech Republic is still performing *Bedtime Story*, which gained country-wide recognition after a popular film version directed by Jiří Krejčík. But while I hugely admire the later plays, and regret that they are too much neglected by theatre producers devoted to the early work, the most recent productions which have meant a lot to me are three of these early plays, presented by London's Royal National Theatre. *Juno and the Paycock* and *The Silver Tassie* were directed by Howard Davies, who was too ill to direct his planned production of *The Plough and the Stars*, but this still came through in a fine representation by Jeremy Herrin, to whom Howard had given his directorial notes.

The debate will continue on whether Seán the playwright became too much the polemicist. But I think he was just continuing to be the man he always was – a socialist, an atheist and an ardent opponent of civic violence. These principles made him, for me, the kind and compassionate man and loving father that he always was, and made all of his plays, early and late, simply – and in his chosen word – 'human'.

Shivaun O'Casey

Acknowledgements

I am grateful to Maria O'Donovan, Michael Collins and their colleagues at Cork University Press for their help and support in completing this project, also Alison Burns of Studio 10 Design for her wonderful cover, and my copy-editor, Aonghus Meaney. I would like to acknowledge the anonymous reviewers whose comments helped shape the final draft.

The book has been a long time in the making, and I want to thank all my family, friends, comrades, individuals, universities and institutions in Ireland, Britain and America for their patience, helpfulness and generosity. No work of this nature is independent of the libraries and institutions that preserve the books, manuscripts and ephemera that are the bedrock of scholarship. I owe a debt to the courteous assistance of the staff of the many libraries holding O'Casey material, and in particular to the staff and volunteers of the working-class and socialist libraries, who unearthed the sometimes obscure political documents and publications that contain letters, articles or references to O'Casey. They are too many to list individually, but I am grateful to all of them.

I cannot let this acknowledgement pass without a few notable mentions. Firstly, my thanks to all the O'Casey scholars who went before me and who have helped another follow in their footsteps. Also, my thanks to Shivaun O'Casey, Christopher Murray, Robert Lowery and the East Wall community for their thoughtful answers and suggestions to my many queries. I would also like to thank Mary Ryder, William Cumming, Niamh Morris and Simon Coury for their advice and assistance in editing the various drafts that led to the final manuscript.

And lastly, my debt to my late parents, Peter and Eilish O'Brien, who indulged and encouraged my youthful interest in books on our weekly visit to the local library, which sparked my interest in theatre and O'Casey all those years ago.

Introduction

Seán O'Casey was a man of immense contradictions who refused to conform to the image created for him by the literary and political elites in Ireland or elsewhere. O'Casey gave a voice to those who are rarely heard: the poor, the dispossessed, the tenement-dweller, whose lives he shaped into works of art. Their very presence on the stage is a claim to justice and a better future. He was a socialist, a humanist and a great writer who put politics at the centre of his work; he asserted the role of the writer as a transformative force in society. An exile in England at the age of forty-six, he sent his blasts and benedictions across the world for the rest of his life. O'Casey was always a fighter and never suffered from the cruelty of low ambition. He was an angry man capable of great rages long before John Osborne and his generation gave birth to the concept in the 1950s. However, as Richard Watts has pointed out, 'his anger was based, not on his dislike for mankind, but on his love for it. When O'Casey scourges Ireland, it is because he feels it is betraying the ideals he cherishes for the native land he loves so fiercely'.[1]

Perhaps this was the reason why Irish critics were sometimes provisional or uncertain in their attitude to O'Casey. Despite this, he lived to witness the birth of a new generation of scholars, young American academics who had a love for and understanding of his work. By the 1960s, the 'O'Casey industry' was thriving; Robert Lowery, writing in 1976, believed that O'Casey's reputation was 'alive and well'. David Krause, friend, biographer and editor of O'Casey's *Collected Letters*, felt that the publication of the four volumes of letters 'will open up an O'Casey industry in Ireland and among outside scholars, at least as great as the Joyce industry'.[2] However, by the end of the 1980s, O'Casey's reputation was in decline – a sickly relative of the 'Joyce industry' – the Dublin plays fell out of the repertoire, and the later plays were rarely produced.

Nevertheless, O'Casey is too good a writer to be left languishing in the second division for very long; new material, particularly the acquisition of a significant archive of O'Casey's papers by the National Library of Ireland in 2002, opened up new insights into the man and his work. The centenary of the Abbey Theatre in 2004 demanded an appraisal of his career and his place in Irish theatre. Shivaun O'Casey's documentary film *Sean O'Casey: Under a coloured cap* (2004) showed a softer side of O'Casey, the family man, the artist at work, and Christopher Murray's *Seán O'Casey: Writer at work* (2004) will surely stand as the definitive biography for years to come.[3] If there were intellectual giants who recognised O'Casey's genius, there were also those who tried to impugn it. This had nothing to do with literary merit or historical accuracy, but rather a dislike of his politics and his critical comments on the role of the Catholic Church in Ireland. O'Casey was a divisive figure right from the beginning of his career. 'People get it all wrong about why my own countrymen dislike me and some hate me. It has to do with Irish politics, with world politics, but as often as not with religion'.[4] He was a fierce battler, never afraid to enter into a dispute, even if it was to his detriment. However, as Rónán McDonald has suggested, it is 'an appropriate tribute to O'Casey that the spirit of dispute lives on amongst his critics'.[5]

The emphasis that modern biography places on childhood, married life and so forth often displaces the work, ideas and social context of the artist or writer. We do O'Casey no favours by softening or dismissing his political beliefs; they go to the heart of the man and writer. O'Casey was one of the most political writers of his generation, constantly exploring the frontiers between literature and politics. Like his friend Bernard Shaw, he wrote for a purpose. His life reflects the history of the early twentieth century, a period shaped by two great ideas: nationalism and socialism. History and politics are woven into the fabric of his life. Maureen Malone and Bernice Schrank are among a minority of scholars who fully understood O'Casey's commitment to both the political and artistic aspects of his life. Schrank lamented: 'While there is growing acceptance of O'Casey's radical reinvention of the stage, there is less willingness to deal with O'Casey's ideological commitments'.[6]

Great drama or literature has a political aspect because of the way it involves complexity, contradiction, difficulty and beauty. However, we must take heed of Walter Benjamin's warning against 'having a message in readiness'[7] and the danger of being over-reductive in linking politics and literature. However, a sympathetic reading of O'Casey's drama illustrates how his life experiences animated his concerns with political, social and moral issues. James Larkin, the Irish labour leader, had a profound effect on O'Casey. Larkin, who came to Dublin in 1907 on his 'divine mission of discontent',[8] inspired O'Casey to use words as weapons in the fight against poverty and oppression. John Newsinger and Mary E. Papke have described O'Casey's Dublin plays as 'Larkinite stage parables'.[9] But it was his experience as a labourer, underfed and exploited, that heightened his interest in socialism. O'Casey believed that his participation in the Dublin lockout of 1913 ranked as his finest moment. Class was 'a key motivation dynamic to rouse the young O'Casey to creative endeavour'.[10]

His daughter Shivaun described him as 'a politician who couldn't help being a writer'.[11] My aim is to extend our understanding of the way his politics influenced his drama, and in doing so, throw some light on the ongoing debate on the relationship between politics and literature. However, this is not to insist that O'Casey's dramas are propaganda, as understood in the usual sense. Most of his plays are open-ended, without a resolution, trusting the audience to draw their own conclusions. My object here is not an exclusive critical or literary analysis of his work, but an exploration of the interplay between the political and historical context of O'Casey's life and its representation in his drama and prose and the way O'Casey negotiated the interplay between politics and aesthetics. My aim here is threefold: firstly, to identify the key political themes in O'Casey's life and their importance in understanding his drama and prose. Secondly, to locate O'Casey's politics in the context of his time and to explore the way this shaped his work. And lastly, to suggest ways that O'Casey's work might shed some light on the ongoing debate about the relationship between literature and politics. O'Casey came of age at the beginning of the twentieth century and lived through what the German historian Heinrich Winkler called 'The Age Of Catastrophe',[12] a period dominated by war and revolution. I also had in mind when writing this book Fredric Jameson's point, which emphasises the need to judge a literary or artistic work in the context of its time and place.[13] This is not a standard account of his life; it is a combination of biographical and thematic chapters that are not strictly chronological. O'Casey's life and work raise questions about the relationship between culture and politics, art and society, enjoyment and thinking, and this discussion is developed across all of the chapters. The plays I have selected for attention are mainly his better-known works, but elements in this exploration carry over into his lesser-known works.

I am grateful to the East Wall History Group for their work in recovering information about O'Casey's early life. I have also drawn on unpublished material in the National Library of Ireland collection and the many radical and socialist newspapers in Ireland and Britain, which shed light on the development of O'Casey's political thought and how that influenced his writing. Given the diverse nature of his work over his lifetime, no single methodology informs this study. While I have relied on the work of Marxists, post-colonial theorists, the debates within the Frankfurt School on realism and modernism, and feminist critics to back up my study of his work, I have concentrated on a political reading of O'Casey on his terms. Postcriticism theorists have influenced both the style and methodology of the book in the way that they argue for a style of writing and a language that breaks down the supposed divide between a detached academic reading and a lay reading for pleasure or enlightenment.

The first section of the book (1880–1905) covers his early life and family background and the importance of the East Wall district of Dublin as a factor in shaping O'Casey's life and work. The O'Casey family were Protestant, and his father's books, along with the Bible and other religious tracts, provided the intellectual core of Seán's education. I explore the influence of Charles Stewart Parnell, Michael Davitt, and the Young Ireland writers James Fintan Lalor and John Mitchel on the development of O'Casey's nationalist politics and writing style. Chapter three deals with his time in the Gaelic League, the Irish Republican Brotherhood and the St Laurence O'Toole Club, where he spent ten years promoting the Irish language and culture.

The second section (1905–22) examines O'Casey's relationship with James Larkin and the 1913 lockout, the one truly transformative event in his life, which had a profound effect on his political outlook, and his development as a writer. Chapters 6 and 7 deal with the 1916 Rising and O'Casey's differences with James Connolly and the nationalists regarding the rising and its aftermath.

The third section is mainly thematic and deals with the 'new drama' – an urban working-class drama that arose alongside a radical socialist and trade union consciousness that paved the way for O'Casey, and with Bernard Shaw, who was an important early influence who transformed O'Casey's view of drama and politics. Chapters 9 and 10 deal with the Dublin plays. They look back at a country in crisis in the years following independence. O'Casey refused to either deify or vilify the 1916 rebels, but instead he projected the reality of the Free State that emerged, for all the talk of sacrifice and heroes. It was clear to him that the new state aimed to advance business interests rather than the ambitions of the poor or the dispossessed, and for this he was never forgiven by some sections of society.

The fourth section opens with his departure to London in 1926. The rejection of *The Silver Tassie* by the Abbey Theatre in 1928 profoundly affected both O'Casey and the Abbey, who as a result lost its most successful writer. A turning point in O'Casey's political life was the Spanish Civil War in 1936, which re-energised his enthusiasm for socialist politics and his support for the Soviet Union. The following three chapters are thematic and outline his attitude to Stalin and the USSR, the Hungarian Revolution in 1956, and the influence of communist politics on his writing. Lastly, I consider his attitude to religion in Irish society. I also examine the way O'Casey's work is constantly critiqued in terms of the differences between men and women in their attitude to violence. Given the development of feminist theory, it is surprising how few critics have moved beyond this analysis and explored the role of women in his later plays, where a far more developed dynamic exists. Here, women are stronger, bolder, more sensual, and have a determined independence.

The final section is devoted to an assessment of the post-war period where O'Casey turned his attention to what he perceived to be an oppressive Catholic theocracy that was stifling Irish society. This was a theme that O'Casey explored in his major plays, from *Cock-a-Doodle Dandy* in 1949 to *The Drums of Father Ned* in 1958. Unfortunately, audiences did not want to believe or even hear what he had to say about the reactionary role of the Catholic church in Ireland. This led to a conflict with the organisers of the 1958 An Tóstal festival and the church authorities that ended with O'Casey banning all productions of his work in Ireland. I assess the critical and political response to the six volumes of his *Autobiography* and the four volumes of his *Collected Letters*. In the last chapter, I review his dramatic legacy and the implications for the ongoing and contentious debate about the relationship between literature and politics.

I would like to acknowledge the scholarship of those that went before me. There is a rich heritage from Brooks Atkinson and George Jean Nathan in the 1920s and '30s, to David Krause, Bernard Benstock, Robert Lowery, Robert Hogan, Michael Durkin and Ronald Ayling from the 1960s onwards, up to Christopher Murray today, and I am grateful to all of them. Christopher Murray's biography of O'Casey has left few stones unturned and, in the process, settled most of the contentious issues surrounding O'Casey's early life that have marred O'Casey studies over the last four decades. I have also drawn on the work of a new generation of scholars who have added to and expanded our understanding of O'Casey's work. Therefore, I do not intend to dwell at any great length on the biographical details of O'Casey's life, except where they impact on the development of his political and dramatic outlook. Throughout the book, I have engaged with those topics where they support the book's primary focus – the social and political geography of O'Casey's drama. I do not claim to see further, only to look in a different direction. In the past, his critics have often been too rigorously academic or exclusive in accusing O'Casey of politicising art; few acknowledge his contribution to the aestheticisation of politics.

I have retained O'Casey's spelling in direct quotes throughout the book. He often abbreviated or misspelt words for alliterative effect or to reproduce on the page local idioms. He was christened John Casey, but used the Irish version Sean O'Cathasaigh, which was then shortened to the more manageable Sean O'Casey, after he joined the Gaelic League. I have used Sean or Seán where it is appropriate. O'Casey never used the accented 'a' in his writings and it is never used in the titles of his books. I have used 'Seán' throughout to distinguish the person from the 'Sean' in the autobiographies and other writing.

PART 1

CHAPTER 1

The Shake of the Bag

Seán O'Casey was born in Dublin on 30 March 1880 at 85 Upper Dorset Street and lived in a small enclave just north of the River Liffey for the first forty-six years of his life. The survival of a child born in Dublin near the end of the nineteenth century depended on luck and the relative prosperity of their parents. O'Casey had both. He described himself as 'the shake of the bag'; he was the eighth child of Susan and Michael Casey, of whom five survived.[1] He was a sickly child, and his devout parents challenged providence by naming him John; the two dead boys who had gone before him were also christened John.[2] O'Casey's account of his family background is sketchy and controversial, and we know relatively little about his parents. They were probably no different from many other families in the way they glossed over the gaps and discrepancies in their background. The family history handed down to the young John Casey was most likely a polished-up version of reality. His father, Michael Casey, was born *c.*1838 in Limerick. Michael's father was a Catholic who had married a Protestant, and the children were reared up 'in the thick of the Catholic religion'. His father died when Michael was an infant, and according to O'Casey, 'his mother [took] the chance to bring up her last born in the true Protestant faith'.[3] Arguments simmered over religion, which became quite bitter after the death of Michael's mother. Sometime in the late 1850s, he shook the dust of Limerick and his Catholic family from his shoes and set out for Dublin. Michael Casey settled in the Coombe district of the Liberties and married Susan Archer in 1863; he died aged forty-eight when Seán was just six years old. He probably never knew the full story of his father's background, and as a result, his account in the autobiographies is rather sketchy and unconvincing. However, these kinds of fabrications usually grow into myths that families live by and carry emotional truths that can be as valid as documented facts.

Michael Casey would have been seven or eight years old at the time of the Famine in the mid-1840s. His childhood coincided with the arrival of Protestant proselytising evangelists in the west of Ireland; they believed that God had sent the Famine to punish the Irish for their 'ignorance and superstition and slavish adherence to Rome'.[4] The starving poor were ready to clutch at anything that would help them survive. The evangelical missionaries served up stirabout with Bible classes, and the Catholic poor and destitute were only too willing to avail of their charity. Over a hundred years later, poor Protestants in Ireland were often assumed to be 'soupers' or 'jumpers': Catholics who had converted during the Famine as the price of survival. Christopher Murray relates a story current in Dublin in the 1950s that 'the whole Casey family had turned "soupers" at some point'.[5] We will probably never know the truth as those terrible times are buried deep in people's memory, not willingly recalled, and official records are rarely concerned with the life and death struggles of the poor. Michael Casey lived at 22 Chamber Street, near the Coombe on the south side of Dublin, in a shabby two-storey house long since demolished like so much of the inner city. We do not know whether Michael encountered the Protestant evangelical movement in Limerick, but they had been active in the Coombe since 1853. The Protestant Irish Church Missions (ICM) built schools and orphanages across the city. Their central office was in Townsend Street, where Michael Casey worked as an assistant clerk.

The East Wall area of the city where Seán O'Casey lived is now almost lost to us forever. A postmodern city of steel, cement and glass has transformed the north-side docklands in a way that would have been unimaginable to O'Casey. Following the Act of Union in 1801 and the abolition of the Irish parliament, Ireland was ruled directly from London. Subsequently, the Irish nobility and landed gentry withdrew to their country estates or to England and left their houses in Dublin to fall into decay and ruin, as Dublin slowly took on the appearance of a provincial slum. By the 1930s, the Dublin tenements were probably 'the worst slums in Europe'.[6] In 1880, the year Seán O'Casey was born, the Royal Sanitary Commission documented the severe overcrowding, lack of sanitation, poor diet, damp and cold conditions, and the foul air that conspired against the health of the tenement dwellers. Tuberculosis was twice as prevalent in Dublin as in London, and children under the age of one accounted for one-fifth of all deaths in the city, the majority from the poorer classes.[7] O'Casey's portrayal of the young Mollser, who in *The Plough and the Stars* is dying of tuberculosis, was a reality on the streets of Dublin, rather than a 'Little Nell' character tugging at the heartstrings.[8] A government inquiry into housing conditions in Dublin in November 1913 reported that 5,322 tenement houses accommodated 25,882 families with a total population of 87,305. The worst of the slums, 1,518 tenements 'unfit for human habitation and incapable of being rendered fit for human habitation', were occupied by 22,701 people.[9] A recruiting officer for the British army during the First World War encouraged young men from the slums of Dublin to enlist because they had a better chance of survival on the Western Front than in the disease-ridden hovels of Dublin.[10] In the tenements, one man in five was unemployed, few had full-time work, and unemployment was a constant companion. Prostitution and alcoholism were rampant in the city; 'Monto' was one of Europe's most notorious red-light districts. In the area around Montgomery Street, up to 1,300 women plied their trade;[11] prostitutes like Rosie Redmond from *The Plough and the Stars* were a familiar sight on the streets of Dublin. On Sackville Street (now O'Connell Street), 'respectable people' walked only on one side of the street because the other was a promenading ground for prostitutes.

O'Casey, like Bernard Shaw, was outraged at the conditions in the slums. After he left Dublin, Shaw, in his bitter satire on slum landlords, *Widowers' Houses* (1892), drew upon the years he had spent in the 1870s working as a clerk in a Dublin real estate office. In the preface, he wrote, 'I have shown middle-class respectability and younger son gentility fattening on the poverty of the slum, as flies fatten on filth'.[12] O'Casey was no less forceful in his condemnation:

> Frequently he wandered, hurt with anger, through these cancerous streets that were incensed into resigned woe by the rotting houses, a desperate and dying humanity, garbage and shit in the roadway; where all the worst diseases were the only nobility present ... Many times, as he wandered there, the tears of rage would flow into his eyes, and thoughts of bitter astonishment made him wonder why the poor worm-eaten souls there couldn't rise in furious activity and tear the guts out of those who kept them as they were.[13]

Dublin was saturated with drink; O'Casey, along with James Larkin and Bernard Shaw, had an abiding hatred for the destructive effects of alcohol on working-class communities. The temperance movement was supported by the progressive elements in the trade union and socialist movement. James Connolly in 1911 noted that 'the Irish Transport and General Workers' Union contingent in the Temperance Demonstration was the talk of the City, though the Press did not refer to it at all'.[14] O'Casey had no time for public house culture and was more likely to be found in the Broadway Soda Fountain on O'Connell Street – where many of the Abbey Theatre people gathered to drink tea and socialise – than in any of the public houses, literary or otherwise. His brothers Mick and Tom were heavy drinkers, while his other brother Isaac lost one good job after another and died young because of his alcoholism. His attitude to drink is spelt out in *The Star Turns Red* (1940), where, in the course of the revolution, Red Jim implores Brannigan to give up the booze:

> RED JIM: I can't trust you if you drink – sober, I'd trust you with my life eternal!
> BRANNIGAN: I'll do it Jim; no drink; not once; no more; never again – so help me God![15]

When James Larkin arrived in Ireland in 1907, he was determined that 'Christ will not be crucified any longer in Dublin by these men'.[16] More than anyone else, it was Larkin who inspired O'Casey to use words as weapons in the fight against the gombeen men and the exploiters of the Dublin poor. In Larkin's paper the *Irish Worker*, and later in the autobiographies, O'Casey lacerated the corruption and ineptitude of Dublin Corporation to alleviate the terrible living conditions of the city's poor.

SCHOOL OR THE LACK OF IT?

His parents, Michael and Susan Casey, moved across the Liffey to Wellington Street, where Isabella (Bella), the first of the five children that survived, was born in 1865.[17] As the family increased, they moved house several times but remained in the same general neighbourhood on the city's north side. A year later, Michael (Mick) was born, followed by Tom in 1869 and Isaac in 1873. Seven years later, John (Seán) was born, by which time the family had moved to 85 Upper Dorset Street. The house was subsequently demolished during redevelopment and rebuilt as a branch of the Bank of Ireland. A plaque on the wall is all that is left to commemorate O'Casey's birthplace. Here the Casey family enjoyed a comfortable lower-middle-class existence. In 1882, shortly after John Casey's birth, the family moved around the corner to Innisfallen Parade, a small, terraced cottage with a hall, scullery and back bedroom. This was a small step down the social ladder for the Casey family, but it was clean, comfortable, and far removed from the slum conditions of the adjacent tenements.

Michael Casey was determined that his children would get the best education his means would allow. Bella and the three elder boys attended the Central Model School in Marlborough Street, 'where small fees were paid by parents' and 'books were dearer and superior to most of the others used in the ordinary National Schools'.[18] The Model School catered for ambitious parents of the lower middle classes. For the Casey family, the expense of private education for their children was a necessity to improve or at least maintain their position in a petty, class-conscious society. The three elder Casey boys rarely missed a day at school, but they were poor students, though Tom and Mick obtained certificates and considered teaching a career at one time. Only Bella applied herself, winning prizes along the way. In 1882 she was awarded a scholarship to train as a teacher at the college in the Model School complex. The scholarship paid for her fees and accommodation in the college, which eased the pressure on the family in the little cottage on Innisfallen Parade. In 1884, at the end of the two-year course, she obtained a position as a teacher in St Mary's Infant School, Dominick Street. After leaving school, Mick and Tom took up clerical positions in the Post Office. The salary scales at the time indicate that they earned as much as their father. Still, Michael Casey was probably disappointed, having harboured ambitions that the boys might aspire to the professions. Isaac never completed his education; his father had died before his final year, and he left school to take up work as an office boy with the *Dublin Daily Express*.

John was born into a world where illness was a constant companion. He was 'delicately and physically undecided', but 'God was good' and 'he crept along' with his mother watching over him 'with ever-verdant care'.[19] When he was five, he contracted trachoma, an infectious eye disease that in later life left him blind in one eye and partially sighted in the other. His doctor insisted that school was out of the question as his eyes must have absolute rest. Reflecting on those dark-filled days, O'Casey maintained that as a result of his eye infection, he could 'not go to school, and in later years when I was fifteen or more, I pinned myself down to learn the fundamentals of the English language, geography, arithmetic, and general knowledge; I became a life-long student, and am a student still'.[20] Unlike his siblings, he did not attend the fee-paying Central Model School; perhaps his father bridled at the cost, afraid that because of his eyes, John 'would grow up to be a dunce'.[21] More likely, he went to St Mary's National School to be under the watchful eye of his sister Bella; he attended St Mary's on an irregular basis until he was nine years old.

At the beginning of 1886, following a fall from a ladder at work that injured his spine, Michael Casey resigned from his position with the Irish

Church Missions. The February minutes of the ICM record paying Michael Casey £17-10*s*-0*d*, which amounted to three months' wages, in recognition of his service in the Dublin office.[22] Within nine months, Michael Casey was dead. His death foreshadowed a decline in the family's position and the start of a gradual slide into relative poverty. The following year Seán's brothers Mick and Tom left their jobs in the Post Office and enlisted in the British army. While the family was glad of the extra space around the house, this must have been a blow to Susan Casey. Not only had her sons thrown over well-paid jobs, but enlisting as privates in the army also represented a loss of standing in the local Protestant community. Despite the death of his father and the loss of his brothers' company, the next two years were probably the happiest of John's childhood. Both Susan and Bella indulged and, at times, spoiled him. Bella was a second mother to him, and if he missed school, as he frequently did, Bella taught him his lessons at home. In March 1889, Bella married Nicholas Beaver, a lance corporal in the British army. Her mother, who did not approve of her choice or attend the wedding, warned her that 'you will sup sorrow if you marry him'.[23] Marriage may also have been a way to escape the strict Protestant attitudes of her mother and life at home; whatever her reasons, Bella had no choice as she was seven months pregnant at the time. Catholic or Protestant, Dublin was no place for an unwed mother: 'Banished as "shameless hussies", no mothers were more pitiable than those unwed and unwanted. Disowned by parents, lashed by fathers, expelled from home, virtually imprisoned in convents, shipped off to Liverpool, or simply thrown into the streets to fend for themselves'.[24]

While O'Casey refers to the row between Bella and his mother over her relationship with Beaver, he never refers to Bella's pregnancy in the autobiographies. Given his age, he may not have been aware of it, but he most likely resented Beaver's intrusion into his life. Bella was gone from him; 'she'd sing, now, only for her drummer boy'.[25] He disliked Beaver and depicted him many years later as a vain good-for-nothing. Whatever misgivings her mother may have had, pregnancy outside marriage was unforgivable for a national schoolteacher. However, Bella was not sacked but was allowed to resign from her position at the school; as a result, she was evicted from her teacher's accommodation in Dominick Street. Beaver still had five years' service to complete, and he returned to his regiment in England. Shortly after the birth of her child, she moved in with her own family at the Caseys' new home in Hawthorn Terrace, in the East Wall district of Dublin.

Alan Simpson has identified the East Wall area, where O'Casey lived from 1889 to 1920, as a key factor in shaping O'Casey's life and work.[26] East Wall contained a Protestant enclave of working-class families, traditionally and emotionally linked to Britain and yet fiercely proud of their Irish heritage.[27] Many had a Northern Irish and unionist background and worked for the Great Northern Railway. The inhabitants clung tenaciously to the hard old religious traditions and values of Protestantism. East Wall was not an exclusively Protestant area. The Halpins, who lived a few doors up in Hawthorn Terrace, were Catholic. Edwin Halpin was well known for his nationalist, trade union and socialist views and, according to local tradition, influenced the young Seán O'Casey both dramatically and politically.[28] Edwin's son William, who was a few years younger than O'Casey, was a member of the Irish Transport and General Workers' Union during the lockout in 1913. Halpin, along with O'Casey and several neighbours, including Paddy Lennon from Abercorn Place, Daniel Courtney of Merchant's Road, and the Carpenter family of Caledon Road, were also members of the Irish Citizen Army. Walter Carpenter, who was originally from England, was an organiser for the Socialist Party of Ireland and later became an official with the Irish Transport and General Workers' Union. His two sons fought in the 1916 Rising in the ranks of the ICA. In 1911 Carpenter was jailed for insulting the king, and shortly after his release he was the main speaker at the launch of the Sligo branch of the union, leading the bishop of Sligo to describe him as an imported mischief-maker. Desmond Ryan reported that at a public meeting, O'Casey had made a similar accusation against Carpenter. Ryan claimed that O'Casey had left the meeting, refusing to listen to any Englishman, namely Walter Carpenter.[29] In a letter to Robert Hogan in 1962, O'Casey denied that accusation:

> I did Not leave the meeting, and I did Not use the words attributed to me. It was the chairman of the meeting, Arthur Griffith, who declared he would not allow any Englishman to speak at an Irish meeting; and the speaker in question was not Walter Carpenter, but a man named Edwards.[30]

O'Casey went on to describe Carpenter as 'a bit of a cod … who never sacrificed anything for Socialism' and in later life was 'a lick-spittle to every priest and nun he happened to meet'.[31] We know very little about the politics and ideas that were current in the East Wall area that might have influenced the young O'Casey. In recent years, the East Wall History Group, inspired by the concept of history from below, have managed to partially recover the diverse history of the area and, in the process, uncover information about some of the events and the people that made an impact on O'Casey's early life.[32]

LEARNING

The move to Hawthorn Terrace meant a new school for the nine-year-old John Casey. The school was attached to the St Barnabas parish church, now demolished, and stood adjacent to the North Wall railway depot. The parishioners were mainly working-class Protestants from the Great Northern Railway. The national school was situated at the rear of the church, and here, for the next four years, John Casey 'had a brief and final fling at formal education'.[33] Bella was no longer there to support and nurture him, and the sensitive and stubborn child recoiled at the brutal teaching methods of his teacher, a west of Ireland man with little aptitude for the profession. The school principal and vicar of St Barnabas, the Reverend J.S. Fletcher, terrorised the child and hounded his mother because of John's irregular attendance. He was more interested in the capitation fee than young Casey's health or education and threatened to stop the parish supply of coal to the family if John's attendance didn't improve. The punishment John received at school show that Catholic educators were not alone in mistreating children in their care. After a severe beating and a visit from the Reverend Fletcher, his mother refused to send him back there: 'The harsh hand that fell on him today shall not fall on him tomorrow, or the next day, and its dark shadow shall he never see again'.[34]

School was like a prison rather than a place of learning, and it left a bitter memory that scarred his mind. In later life, reform of the education system was always close to his heart; the first article that O'Casey managed to have published, 'Sound the Loud Trumpet' (1907), criticised the educational policy of the British government in Ireland. He never saw a distinction between the fight for better wages and conditions for working men and women and their right to education, literature and art: 'Why should the docker reading Anatole France, or the carter reading Yeats, be a laughter-provoking conception? Have they then a claim in the Unemployment Exchange, but not in the upward progress of man?'[35] He was determined that his children would have all the educational advantages that were denied to him, which was one of the reasons why the O'Casey family moved from

London to Devon in 1938. On Bernard Shaw's advice, their children were enrolled in Dartington Hall School, a liberal, child-centred, co-educational school with few rules and which prohibited corporal punishment. Writing to the headmaster of Dartington Hall in 1944, O'Casey recommended Patrick Pearse's curriculum from St Enda's School in Dublin, which taught:

> Modern languages orally; which should be bi-lingual in method; which should aim at a wider and humaner culture than other Irish Secondary schools; which should set its face like iron against 'cramming' and against all the evils of the competitive examination system, which should work at fostering the growth of the personality of each of its pupils rather than at forcing all into a predetermined groove.[36]

His father was well-read and a lover of books. According to O'Casey, he read Latin, which was unusual for a Protestant from an evangelical background, given its status in Catholic liturgy. His father's legacy, a bookcase with a 'regiment of theological controversial books', formed the basic reading and education for the young O'Casey:

> d'Aubigné's *History of the Reformation*, Milner's *End of Controversy*, Chillingworth's *Protestantism*, holding forth that the bible, and the bible alone, is the religion of Protestants ... Foxe's *Book of Martyrs*, full of fire and blood and brimstone, *Popery Practical Paganism*, *Was St. Peter Ever in Rome?* ... Like inspection officers, the English Bible, the Latin Vulgate, and the Douai Testament stood pompously together, and to the right, *Cruden's Concordance* acting as orderly officer; a neatly uniformed company of Dickens', Scott's, George Eliot's, Meredith's, and Thackeray's novels; Shakespeare's Works; Burns', Keats', Milton's, Gray's, and Pope's poetry; on the top shelf, six or seven huge volumes, like podgy generals, of *The Decline and Fall of the Roman Empire*; and leaning idly by their side was Locke's *Essay on the Human Understanding*.[37]

These books were the intellectual core of O'Casey's education, and their influence, along with the daily Bible readings that he shared with his devout mother and the experience of teaching Sunday school classes in his parish church, can be found in all his work. In O'Casey's alternate world, the workers are all young vibrant men and women who are full of the joys of life and enjoy books, songs and poetry. In *Juno and the Paycock*, Mary Boyle is reading the plays of Ibsen. In the later plays, The Dreamer and the Young Whore (*Within the Gates*, 1934), Drishogue (*Oak Leaves and Lavender*, 1946), O'Killigain (*Purple Dust*, 1940) and Ayamonn Breydon (*Red Roses for Me*, 1942) read Shakespeare, Milton, Ruskin, Darwin and the classics. By 1949 Loreleen Marthraun (*Cock-a-Doodle Dandy*) is reading James Joyce's *Ulysses* and a book about Voltaire. John Jordan, taking a realistic view rather than allowing O'Casey any artistic licence, has described these characters as 'for the most part, paste-board people [who] are the progeny of an imagination entirely in revolt against the actual world, the dream children of an autodidact'.[38]

O'Casey developed a lifelong attachment to reading; he describes sitting down with his copy of Shelley's 'Prometheus Unbound' and Walker's dictionary side-by-side, working his way through it until he understood it completely. He learnt of the world and the nature of things from his father's books and the books he bought or occasionally stole from the second-hand stalls along the quays with the few pennies he managed to save each week. However, there was another dynamic at work that introduced John Casey to a world beyond books: that of work, love, politics and Irish music and culture. Seán O'Casey was not an alter ego for John Casey in the way other writers take on pseudonyms; rather, it was an evolution grounded in his personal and political development. His involvement with the Irish language and the nationalist movement in his early twenties saw John Casey dive in at one end, and through a process of linguistic and political evolution, the Gaelicised Seán O'Casey swam ashore at the other end. The shy, awkward Seán O'Casey was almost ready to take on the world: 'He'd learnt poethry and had kissed a girl. If he hadn' gone to school, he'd met the scholars; if he hadn' gone into the house, he had knocked at the door'.[39]

CHAPTER 2

Twenty Years A-Growing

The fall of Charles Stewart Parnell in 1890, or at least the myth surrounding his life and death, was part of the process that transformed Irish life in the years subsequent to his death. Any hope for a peaceful evolution of Anglo-Irish relations, along the lines of dominion status enjoyed by Canada and Australia, receded at that time. What Parnell's downfall meant to the young O'Casey is difficult to gauge. As a ten-year-old, he would have had little perception of the events that surrounded Parnell's fall from office and his premature death a year later at the age of forty-five. Yet, almost sixty years after that event in a eulogy for the late Jim Larkin, O'Casey described Larkin as 'the greatest Irishman since Parnell'.[1] He described Dr Michael O'Hickey, who was dismissed from his teaching post in Maynooth College because of his support for the Irish language, as 'A Parnell with a Roman White choker round his neck fighting the battle of Banba's language'.[2] Many years later, the Scottish poet Hugh MacDiarmid recalled that O'Casey was 'positively electrified' when he quoted some lines from the poet Francis Adams' sonnet 'To Charles Parnell'.[3] Here, as in nearly all of O'Casey's political assessments, Parnell is the touchstone by which individuals were judged.[4] In O'Casey's pantheon of political heroes, Parnell and Larkin were deemed equal to Marx and Lenin – perhaps even superior. Decency, humanity and even personal frailty were always more important to O'Casey than the correct political line. During the riots that greeted *The Plough and the Stars*, he raged at Cathleen ni Houlihan who had 'hounded Parnell to his death', yelled and torn at Yeats and Synge and 'now was doing the same to him'.[5]

Charles Stewart Parnell (1846–91) is, simultaneously one of the best-known and least understood figures in Irish history. On the surface, he is an iconic figure, part of a political and cultural tradition that stretches back to Wolfe Tone, Robert Emmet and Lord Edward FitzGerald. Parnell remains an elusive and enigmatic figure who baffled his contemporaries and has puzzled posterity ever since. Even today, it isn't easy to separate the myth of Parnell from reality. This inscrutable leader never advocated anything more than a limited form of home rule for Ireland, yet he is remembered for his speech that defined Irish nationalism: 'No man has a right to fix the boundary of the march of a nation.'[6] How was it that O'Casey held him in such high regard? The ambivalence that O'Casey condemned in James Connolly and many other political figures, he overlooked in Parnell.

Parnell won a seat representing County Meath for the Irish Parliamentary Party in a by-election in April 1875. Within a few years, he was the leader of the party, which he transformed into a formidable, disciplined group that dominated British and Irish politics until his downfall in 1890. What emerges from F.S.L. Lyons' biography is a conservative Parnell who managed, almost to the very end, to harness the revolutionary tradition of the Fenians and the Land League with the constitutionalists in pursuit of home rule for Ireland.[7] After Michael Davitt's release from prison in 1877, Parnell and Davitt began to explore the possibility of joint action between the Fenians and the Home Rule Party. In the process, they created the most dynamic political partnership in modern Irish history. Despite the failure of the first home rule bill in 1886, the alliance of the Irish Parliamentary Party and the Liberal Party would have delivered home rule had it not been for the crisis concerning Parnell's involvement in the divorce proceeding instituted by Captain O'Shea. In the ensuing scandal, the Irish Parliamentary Party had to choose between Parnell and the policy he had brought to the brink of success. In the infamous meeting in committee room fifteen, the 'Chief' was thrown aside, and within a year, he was dead.[8]

THE ENIGMA OF PARNELL

It is difficult to precisely ascertain the attitude of the Casey family to Parnell and Irish politics during the first twenty years of O'Casey's life. Perhaps it was Parnell's enigmatic personality, his emotional frailty, alongside his political bravery that made him so appealing to O'Casey. By the beginning of the twentieth century, Parnell's legacy was all-pervasive. Patrick Pearse numbered Parnell, along with Thomas Davis, James Fintan Lalor and John Mitchel, among the founding fathers of Irish nationalism in a way that takes on an almost charismatic quality.[9] James Connolly seized upon the fact that Parnell had turned to the Irish working class for support in his final struggle for survival.[10] For James Joyce, the fall of Parnell represented social paralysis, moral cowardice and a deadening Catholic hypocrisy.[11]

Lady Gregory, Lennox Robinson, Seán O'Faoláin and Frank O'Connor wrote about Parnell as a messianic figure and as 'a touchstone for various kinds of disenchantment'.[12] F.S.L. Lyons locates O'Casey's disenchantment with Irish constitutional politics with the downfall of Parnell. O'Casey never wholly resisted the messianic tone that permeates Irish writing about Parnell; nevertheless, he summoned up something that contemporary writers and historians generally neglected: 'the irrelevance of the public drama of politics to the poor whose struggle for survival occupies them to the exclusion of all else'.[13] O'Casey contrasted the poverty and nobility of the poor, Parnell's staunchest supporters, with the baseness of the politicians, priests and hypocrites who laid him low.

Parnell is the pivotal political figure in the first two volumes of O'Casey's autobiography. He utilises the public events and family discussions surrounding the rise and fall of Parnell to describe his political awakening and his political journey from a Protestant unionist family background to revolutionary Irish nationalism. He recalled the discussion with his mother on the way home from his father's funeral as to whether it was Parnell's involvement with a married woman or 'the guttermen' and the priests 'preaching against Parnell from off the althars' who were responsible for his ruin,[14] and that 'his father had said that Parnell was a great Protestant, a great Irishman, and a grand man; and it was a good thing there was someone, anyway, fit to hinder the English from walking over the Irish people'.[15] Towards the end of the first volume, in a chapter titled 'The Red above the Green', O'Casey explores the dilemma he faced as a poor Protestant growing up in a predominantly Catholic city; the 'Red' in this case, is not for socialism, as we would expect, but for Britain. He describes the bewilderment of the young John Casey as he deals with his confusion over the distinctions between being Irish or British, Protestant or Catholic, orange or green. During the public celebrations for Queen Victoria's birthday in Dublin, Johnny and his mother were caught up in the crush. They were saved from injury by the conductor of a passing tram, who pulled them on board. When they had settled on the upper deck 'giving them a grand view of everything' his mother said: 'Your poor father often said that Fenians were all honest, outspoken men. One of them lived in our house before he had to fly the country, ere you were born; an' he an' your father were great friends ... besides some of the Fenians were Protestants too'.[16] The procession ended in a riot between the Trinity College boys carrying a large Union Jack and the nationalists with their green banners. O'Casey ended the chapter with a very poignant description of an unconscious nationalist demonstrator 'lying still in the street, midway between the bank and the college, almost hidden in the folds of a gay green banner'.[17] The 'gay green banner' caught the attention of the young John Casey that day, and he remained faithful to that banner in one form or another for the rest of his life. However, we have to accept that O'Casey wrote these fragmented recollections at a distance of over forty years from the events he describes, and they cannot possibly be a detailed account of the conversations that took place. Undoubtedly, there is an element of post-rationalisation; nonetheless, he catches the mood of the different ideas and influences from his childhood that opened his eyes to other possibilities.

The second volume of his autobiography opens with the funeral of Parnell, who died on 6 October 1891 in England. His body was returned to Ireland the following Sunday, the day on which Parnell had promised to return to address his critics. A far greater crowd turned out to march in the funeral procession than had ever attended the 'Chief' when he was alive. O'Casey describes the day of the funeral in a style that is almost Joycean and recounts how his brother Archie took a fine crayon drawing of Parnell, done by his older brother Michael, down from the wall. The picture was placed on the sideboard facing out the window, draped in black crepe, and:

> on a white piece of cardboard, Archie, in beautifully-formed letters, wrote down, Give My Love To My Colleagues And To The Irish Race and fixed it firmly to the bottom of the frame. ... There he is now, said Archie, with defiant sorrow in his voice, lookin' out on the people who first denied, an' then bethrayed him.[18]

The prospect of home rule may have revived the ghost of the 1782 settlement that terrified the more backward elements of the ascendancy class.[19] For the more forward-looking elements, Parnell was viewed as the saviour of the landlords who accepted that change was necessary in Ireland. They did not fear a settlement on the lines of 1782, including equality for the Catholic majority, which they believed was inevitable. The alternative, as far as they were concerned, was a revolutionary settlement that would exclude them from economic and political power. Even to someone like Michael Casey, a lower-middle-class Protestant with some education, a reader of books and newspapers, it must have seemed obvious that some form of home rule for Ireland was only a matter of time. Parnell offered the only hope for Michael Casey's class that home rule would not mean Rome rule. The options for many forward-thinking Irish Protestants during the Land League agitation were Parnell or 'Captain Moonlight'.[20] O'Casey's family probably identified with the politically conservative side of Parnell: the man who had kept in check the revolutionary forces inherent in the

Land League agitation in the late 1880s; the Parnell who defied the Catholic clergy and offered the best hope for independence that did not substantially challenge the position of the Protestant minority in Ireland.

When Parnell's long love affair with Kitty O'Shea, the wife of a fellow member of parliament, became public in 1890, Gladstone and the British Liberals turned against him. The Catholic bishops withdrew their support, and, following that fateful meeting at Westminster, the Irish Parliamentary Party split into two factions, creating rival Parnellite and anti-Parnellite parties. That Parnell was laid low by his fellow countrymen rather than the English and that the Catholic clergy had turned against him was another reason why the Casey family might have admired him. Parnell was the yardstick by which the inadequacies of Catholic Ireland could be judged:

> The Bishops and the Party
> That tragic story made,[21]

Conversely, Parnell's flirtation with revolutionary Fenianism, his nationalist rhetoric, his anti-English outbursts and stubbornness of spirit appealed to the older O'Casey. Parnell, for him, became the symbol of independence that could only be achieved by revolutionary means. He managed to live with this contradictory interpretation and remained faithful to the myth of Parnell to the end of his life. In 1955, nearing his seventy-fifth birthday, O'Casey recorded several broadcasts for Radio Éireann. In the third broadcast looking back on Irish history, he sang a few verses from a ballad he remembered from his childhood, 'The Late Lamented Charles Stewart Parnell'. Even Larkin never surpassed the martyred Parnell; he was merely the new 'Chief' who had replaced him.[22]

THE FORGOTTEN HERO

Michael Davitt (1846–1906), the socialist and agrarian activist, is the person closest in time and beliefs to O'Casey, but if Parnell dominates the first two volumes of his autobiography, the absence of Michael Davitt is glaringly obvious. Davitt was the son of a small peasant leaseholder in County Mayo.[23] The family survived the Famine but experienced hard times as almost everything they possessed was sold to procure the necessities of life. In 1851 they were thrown on the side of the road as the 'crowbar brigade' demolished their cabin for failing to pay rent arrears. The family left for Manchester to work in the cotton mills, where the eleven-year-old

Michael lost an arm in an industrial accident. In his mind, the degradation of the English industrial worker was forever linked with the servitude of the agricultural worker in Ireland.

In later life, Davitt had all the qualities that O'Casey had come to admire in working-class leaders; his love of literature and the clarity of his journalism and political writing were all factors that should have endeared him to O'Casey. Jim Larkin's use of the sympathy strike in 1913 owed much to Davitt's tactic of the boycott during the land war. O'Casey certainly had some interest in Davitt. In 1953 an American journalist, Robert Emmett Ginna, visited O'Casey's old room on the North Circular Road, where Jim Kavanagh showed him some books that O'Casey had left behind after he departed for London.[24] They included Michael Davitt's *The Fall of Feudalism in Ireland, or The Story of the Land League Revolution*. Davitt only features in O'Casey's thinking and writing to any great extent after he settled in England and engaged with the Communist Party. A typical example from this period is a letter where he defends Davitt from St John Ervine's character assassination: 'Ervine is wrong about him. Davitt was a revolutionary ... he was a Socialist long before his time'.[25] In another letter written in 1949, O'Casey claims that he became a socialist because of the influence of Parnell and Davitt, and that the great Jim Larkin 'settled the question of Social Science for me'.[26] There is no evidence that this was O'Casey's view of Davitt during his early years. For the Casey family, Davitt was a threat: a Catholic, a revolutionary, a Fenian, and perhaps most of all, he was perceived as a betrayer of Parnell. In the immediate aftermath of the split in the Irish Parliamentary Party, Davitt did not support the Parnellite faction. In the parliamentary election of 1892, he stood as an anti-Parnellite candidate.

Davitt was still alive during O'Casey's formative years, and a more sympathetic reading of Davitt's politics might have provided O'Casey with a better understanding of how the national question and the socialist question could be fused into a mass movement. In later life, in an article in the *Irish Democrat*, he acknowledged Davitt's position in the roll call of the great and the good in the socialist movement: 'The Gael will have a hosting of his own, Lalor, Mitchel, Davitt, and William Thompson ... Goldsmith and a cloud of poets, sages, saints, and soldiers'.[27]

THE PROPHET OF REVOLUTION

Parnell and Davitt are perhaps the best known of a number of nationalists and socialists who influenced the young O'Casey. However, the publisher James Duffy (1809–71) is little known today. Nonetheless, his association with the Young Ireland movement in the 1840s contributed to the political and literary revival at the end of the century. Ernie O'Malley recalled that during the revolutionary period (1920), a Volunteer like himself 'could find in many a house in a remote mountain, or on a wide tract of bogland, a number of well-worn books'.[28] These were the cheap editions of popular historical and literary books, including the works of John Mitchel, James Clarence Mangan, James Fintan Lalor and Thomas Davis, published by James Duffy. They sold in great numbers, and even a peasant farmer or a common labourer like O'Casey could afford to buy them.

In early 1847 a series of letters appeared in the pages of *The Nation* newspaper, signed by the relatively unknown James Fintan Lalor (1807–49). He was a member of the Young Ireland movement and played an active part in the rebellion of 1848. His writings influenced Irish politicians and writers, including Michael Davitt, James Connolly, Patrick Pearse and Seán O'Casey. Lalor, according to Davitt, was the prophet of revolutionary land reform; he believed that 'the ideas and proposals which were published in the columns of *The Felon* were seeds sown for another generation of land reformers'.[29] Lalor, in a series of letters in the pages of the *Irish Felon*, the paper of the Young Ireland movement, set out his principles for the reconquest of Ireland: 'Years ago I saw that the conquest consisted of two parts, the conquest of our liberties and the conquest of our land ... I saw clearly that the reconquest of our liberties would be incomplete and worthless without the reconquest of our land'.[30] Lalor was a product of the Enlightenment, following in the footsteps of Tom Paine[31] 'in his appeal to popular sovereignty, in his anti-aristocratic sentiments, and in his use of the principle of government by consent of the governed'.[32] Lalor maintained that if independence meant anything, it was necessary to undo the economic and social aspects of the conquest as well as the union with Britain. This demand found an echo in the political writings of Seán O'Casey and James Connolly. In 1896 Connolly wrote a preface for a pamphlet of Lalor's writings in which he claimed that: 'The Socialist Party of Ireland is the only political party in Ireland which fully accepts Fintan Lalor's teaching, from his declaration of principles to his system of insurrection'.[33] In 1911, Larkin republished a series of articles from 1847 by Lalor in the *Irish Worker* that

O'Casey would have read.[34] Lalor had posed the question regarding what sort of Ireland would emerge after independence – individual or communal – a question that O'Casey himself posed almost seventy years after Lalor's demise. His unproduced satirical play on the newly independent Free State, *The Cooing of the Doves* (1923), harks back to Lalor's proposition: 'But the day of the common people'll come when the workers'll stand on the principles enunciated by Fintan Lalor'.[35]

Lalor was a great essayist, and O'Casey's prose style owes something to him, particularly in his articles for the *Irish Worker*. O'Casey shared Lalor's penchant for 'long explanatory sentences' and 'glowing enkindling phrases' but lacked the 'curt emotional ones' and 'the slow deliberate statements of fact' that are so powerful in Lalor's work.[36] Lalor pointed out that nationality was not freedom, that Europe was full of nationalities, but not all nations were free. His critique of nationalism permeates the politics and work of O'Casey. Lalor's position was 'not to repeal the Union, then, but to repeal the Conquest – not to disturb or dismantle the empire, but to abolish it forever'.[37] In the Dublin plays, the underlying political message is that the 1916 Rising, and the subsequent War of Independence, did not repeal the conquest; it merely changed those at the top of society and left untouched the mass of people. By 1918, O'Casey's regard for Lalor led him to suggest to his publisher that they should publish a collection of his works with an introduction by O'Casey.[38]

THE BIBLE OF IRISH NATIONALISM

John Mitchel (1815–75) was born in County Derry. His best-known and most enduring work, the *Jail Journal*, is the *Odyssey* of Irish historical writing, and in O'Casey's time it was known as the 'Bible of Irish nationalism'. James Connolly maintained that Mitchel's insistence upon 'a social revolution as the only possible basis for a national revolution'[39] was the key to Mitchel's continued influence on the radical and socialist movement. This strand in Mitchel's politics appealed to O'Casey and found its fullest expression in *The Plough and the Stars*. Mitchel was one of the most capable journalists of his day, a great stylist in the tradition of Swift, Carlyle and Emerson. He was a Northern Presbyterian who took his views from the Old rather than the New Testament and utilised its idioms in his writings and journalism.[40] Mitchel was a man of many contradictions, and in many ways O'Casey was shaped from the same mould. Mitchel and O'Casey were gentle in private life, but in public they were uncompromising, unbending and stern. Both set out to provoke the world into a response, confident that their command of words would put them on an equal footing with their enemy. Many writers associated with the Young Ireland movement were literary rather than scientific, idealist rather than realist, which may be the reason why the youthful O'Casey was attracted to them.

The fact that O'Casey's nationalism had its intellectual base in the works of Lalor and Mitchel led him in time to look for a socialist solution to the Irish question. But, like so much in O'Casey's life, his attitude to Lalor and Mitchel appears at times to be contradictory. He admired their style and the anti-British sentiments in their writings, but he was also capable of criticising them unmercifully. In an article in *Irish Freedom* as late as March 1913, he lashes out, complaining that 'England's suckled socialists' had nothing to teach Irish workers. Then he vents his anger at Ireland's prophets of revolution, declaring that 'there is nothing new under Ireland's sun in Mitchel's or Lalor's doctrines'.[41] A year later, in the pages of the *Irish Worker* in February 1914, we hear a different register:

> I am chided for using the name of Mitchel. I quote Mitchel because I am a Republican in principle and practice; because he denounced tyranny everywhere he found it, in the English parliament, in the Irish convention; because he stood for the Irish worker against the English Lord and the Irish aristocrats.[42]

A month later, we hear the voice of Fintan Lalor in the background, in terms of both style and politics, as O'Casey strives to develop a synthesis between his long-held views on republicanism and his emerging socialist convictions:

> Our work is not alone to drive far from us our connection with England, but to enter into our inheritance; not to repeal the Union, but to overthrow the conquest; not alone to end our subjection to England, but to labour that we may have life and have it more abundantly.[43]

What accounts for this fundamental change in his attitude and views was his experience of the eight-month-long lockout in Dublin, which began in August 1913 and which, O'Casey maintained, was the most important event in his life.[44]

In an essay written for *International Literature*, published in the USSR in December 1939, O'Casey acknowledged the literary skills of Lalor and

Mitchel. He described 'the fiery denunciations of John Mitchel in a paper called *The Nation*, read by all who could read, and listened to by all who could not ... here, at this time too, wrote Fintan Lalor, the Lenin of his day, the most advanced thinker of his period with his Irish Communistic Manifesto of the time – *The Rights of Ireland*'.[45] Desmond Ryan describes O'Casey speaking at the Sinn Féin club in Drumcondra, where his speeches were peppered with 'bitter phrases from Mitchel and Lalor's most urgent calls for revolt on the eve of Forty-Eight'.[46]

O'Casey's understanding of the relationship between the individual and society was a development of Lalor's pamphlet *A New Nation* (1848), which was written as a warning to the landlords of Ireland if they did not change their ways. In a letter to David Krause, he quotes Lalor's pamphlet:

> You are far less important to the people than the people are to you. You cannot stand or act alone, but they can. You cannot act against them, you cannot act without them. A clear original right returns and reverts to the people – the right of establishing and entering into a new social arrangement. The right is in them because the power is in them.[47]

Lalor published his pamphlet in 1848, the same year that Karl Marx and Friedrich Engels published the *Communist Manifesto*. His summary of class relations and the potential power of the masses to transform their world has an affinity with the work of Marx and Engels and was one of the reasons why it made such a deep impression on O'Casey. However, it would be a mistake to imagine that O'Casey's political development consisted of a series of epiphanies that transformed his thinking in an instant. Parnell dominated the political landscape of his early life. If Parnell gave the Irish people back their self-respect, he also provided a vision of Ireland where the Protestant tradition of the Casey family had a future. The Protestant tradition that he inherited, and his father's books, introduced him to the radical poetry of John Milton and Percy Bysshe Shelley, William Shakespeare and Dickens' novels of social conscience. These books were part of a tradition that saw no conflict between the Protestant religion and the principles of freedom, which had a democratic and libertarian impulse rooted in the English revolutionary period of the seventeenth century. However, other political currents would sweep O'Casey a long way from his family and church background.

THE TRAM CONDUCTOR AND THE ACTOR

The writers from the Irish literary revival era provided a vision of Ireland with a glorious past and a promising future. They were part of a mass social movement where the Gaelic League, the Co-operative Movement, the Gaelic Athletic Association, the Irish Republican Brotherhood and Sinn Féin could flourish. In these movements, O'Casey, as a young man, found some of the answers he was seeking. Between 1894 and 1905, his formative years intellectually, two figures from the world beyond his family and church background stand out: the tram conductor Ayamonn O'Farrel, and Seán Connolly, the Abbey actor and member of the Irish Citizen Army, who was killed during the 1916 Rising. O'Casey identified them in his autobiography as the two people who introduced him to the Irish language and nationalist politics. Sometime about 1897, he refers to the tram conductor:

> He slipped Part One of O'Growney's *Simple Lessons in Irish* into his breast pocket, hoping to get an odd squint at it in some quiet corner while he worked. The tram-conductor he had heard singing about Wolfe Tone, the night of the illuminations, had given it to him during a theatrical night in the stable of Hill Street.[48]

The tram conductor lent him copies of Wolfe Tone's autobiography and reprints of speeches from the dock by Irish rebels, and nationalist songs such as 'The Felons of our Land' and 'Who Fears to Speak of Ninety-Eight'. He was the person who first invited O'Casey to Bodenstown for the annual Wolfe Tone commemoration.[49] As he departed O'Casey's house one evening, he whispered to Johnny that the Fenians were still active.

> Th' Sword of Light is flamin' still!
> What sword of light?
> Th' Fenians! And without another word, he hurried off.[50]

The tram conductor is omnipresent whenever these politically transformative moments occur in O'Casey's early life. O'Casey credits this moment as the time when John Casey became Sean O'Cathasaigh.[51] In 1899 the tram conductor invited O'Casey along to heckle Yeats' play *The Countess Cathleen*. He is by O'Casey's side during the Boer War riots in 1900, the lockout in 1913, and again in 1921 when the truce ending the War of Independence is declared.[52] O'Farrel is a constant foil for O'Casey's thoughts and speculations on Irish history and politics. In *Red Roses for*

Me (1942), the tram conductor is given flesh in the character of Roory O'Balacaun.

There were also other factors and people who influenced the young O'Casey. In 1897, his friend and curate of St Barnabas, Reverend Henry Fletcher, provided a reference for a job in Eason & Son, the wholesale newspaper distributor. The work was hard, especially for a young man not yet physically developed. O'Casey started work at 4.15 a.m. and did not finish until 6 p.m. O'Casey lasted a week. He maintained he lost his job because he refused to doff his cap to the management when collecting his wages. The chapter detailing this incident, 'The Cap in the Counting House', is typical of how the autobiography operates on a number of different levels. It is both a set-piece narrative of his life story, an account of the harsh working conditions in Easons, and a symbolic or imaginative outline of his growing political awareness. He describes three leaflets that mysteriously 'fluttered down before his face' as he worked at his bench in the basement of Easons – the first a leaflet inviting him to a Christian revival meeting, the second to a meeting of James Connolly's Irish Socialist Republican Party, and the third to a nationalist meeting commemorating the rebellion of 1798. O'Casey uses this incident to outline the political choices that faced him: 'Three appeals to him, the humblest Roman of them all: for God, for Man, and for Country; three so different from each other, yet all alike in so far that each was made in the dimness, silently, and in fear.'[53]

Seán Connolly (1883–1916) was an Abbey actor of real potential. He was a member of the Irish Citizen Army (ICA) and was involved in the 1913 lockout. O'Casey recalls working with Seán Connolly in Easons, where he noticed the badge of the Gaelic League on the lapel of Connolly's coat. Connolly is portrayed as a heroic figure, youthful yet manly, a Fenian, and a worker who was not afraid to stand up to the foreman: 'creeping about like black-beetles, he murmured; all afraid, bar Sean Connolly'.[54] O'Casey next encountered Seán Connolly in the Irish Transport and General Workers' Union and the ICA during the Howth gun-running episode in July 1914.[55] On the morning of Easter Monday 1916, Seán Connolly led out the second company of the ICA from Liberty Hall and was one of the first rebels killed during the attack on Dublin Castle. O'Casey remembered Seán Connolly as 'a natural actor, and one of the handsomest and truest young Irishmen then living. He, too, was a sad loss to Ireland.'[56] Lady Gregory, who admired him as an actor and friend, wrote a moving eulogy on hearing of his death.[57]

We have to read these incidents in the way O'Casey intended, as metaphors or as symbolic ways of explaining the different ideas and political currents he encountered and tried to come to terms with. So far, no one has been able to trace the tram-conductor, Ayamonn O'Farrel, whose republican views influenced O'Casey's thinking.[58] It is questionable whether he was at O'Casey's shoulder to lend an ear or explain the complexities of Irish politics during almost every significant event from 1897 to 1923. His claim that O'Farrel gave him a copy of O'Growney's *Simple Lessons in Irish* in 1897 seems doubtful, although, in a letter in 1958, he claimed that he was interested in the Irish language as early as the late 1890s. Perhaps, in O'Farrel, O'Casey created a composite figure, an 'everyman' representative of the many nationalist working men and women who influenced him. O'Casey describes the cauldron of personalities, ideas, debates and political arguments that gripped Ireland in the late 1890s. Forty years later, in his autobiographies, he recreates those heroic figures in the guise of O'Farrel and Connolly to give expression to the debates and arguments that were troubling him.

O'Casey could rarely afford to buy the magazines and journals that charted the political and literary development of the country, such as *The Nation*, *The Irish Homestead*, *Dana*, and a host of others that provided successive generations with their village square club and debating society rolled into one. Whether the Casey family could afford a regular newspaper is unknown, and O'Casey does not refer to this one way or another. Most likely, they only had access to the *Dublin Daily Express*, where O'Casey's brother Archie started work as an office boy, sometime around 1888.[59]

Whatever about newspapers and magazines, O'Casey was an avid reader of plays, especially those of Shakespeare and Boucicault. His brother Archie had over 100 copies of the threepenny edition of *Dicks' Standard Plays* bound into one volume, which the young John Casey passionately read. This experience exposed him to a view of the world that was quite different from the unionist and British-centred history he had absorbed at school, at church and at home. In their little theatre in Hill Street,[60] O'Casey and his brother Archie acted out scenes from *Julius Caesar* and *Henry VI*; but he also admired the works of the Irish playwright Dion Boucicault (1820–90), whose work he knew 'as well as Shakespeare'.[61] O'Casey performed in extracts from Boucicault's *The Octoroon* and *The Shaughraun* in the Hill Street theatre. In 1899 he played the part of Father Dolan in *The Shaughraun* at the Mechanics' Theatre, which became the Abbey Theatre in 1904.[62] Boucicault had a profound impact on O'Casey's work, especially in his use of song, music, and the way he used comedy to lighten the tragedy. While Boucicault's plays are conventional melodramas, there is also a political ambivalence that challenged the stereotypical image of the stage-Irishman of his day. Both *Arrah-na-Pogue* and *Peep O' Day* are about the 1798 rebellion. They do not end in victory or defeat but in compromise and a resolution of the political antagonisms they portray. *Peep O' Day* ends with a pardon for the rebels, who are revealed not to have been rebels at all. Chris Morash points out that 'by bringing together adversaries', Boucicault's plays became 'a parable for reconciliation', capable of being performed as a command performance for the lord lieutenant in Dublin or before a predominantly Fenian audience in Boston or New York.[63] To our eyes, Boucicault's plays may appear dated or even offensive in their portrayal of Irish people. Nevertheless, in the late nineteenth century, when the stage-Irishman was usually portrayed as a drunkard, a fool, or wild and ignorant, they were a revelation. Boucicault created a more trustworthy and heroic image of the Irish people that replaced the racist stereotype in English literature, which was finally killed off twenty years later by Bernard Shaw in the figure of Larry Doyle in *John Bull's Other Island*.[64] Boucicault did not set out to challenge British authority in Ireland, but he did expose its shortcomings.

For John Casey, the sight of Irish rebels as heroic figures challenged his perception of the past and exposed him to a view of Irish history that was significantly different from the received British history that dominated his early life. Wolfe Tone, Lord Edward FitzGerald and Robert Emmet came to life as credible figures who were acceptable to polite society, but also as representatives of a glorious hidden past that contained the possibilities of a heroic future. In Boucicault's plays, Irish nationalism becomes a virtue, to which he gave 'a romantic whiff of Fenian charm', rather than an accusation.[65] Despite this, there are problems with Boucicault's representation of the Irish on the stage. The cleavage between the educated and well-mannered ascendancy class and the crafty peasant is never far from the surface, and his portrayal of the Irish peasantry, while a real advance on what went before, was a far cry from the reality of their situation.

In some respects, Boucicault anticipates Synge, Yeats and the Abbey peasant play, despite these shortcomings. We do not have to interrogate Boucicault's work to any great extent to find the antecedent of Christy Mahon from Synge's *The Playboy of the Western World* or that of Dan Burke from *The Shadow of the Glen*. W.B. Yeats' early play *Cathleen ni Houlihan* (1902) has a classic Boucicault-style ending:

> Did you see an old woman going down the path?
> I did not,
> But I saw a young girl, and she had the walk of a queen.[66]

The Queen's Theatre, where O'Casey saw his first play, and at that time his only experience of professional theatre, was the home of Irish melodrama. Here, the plays, especially those of P.J. Bourke, J.W. Whitbread and Hubert O'Grady, had a decidedly political edge, exposing the audience and O'Casey to works such as *Lord Edward, Insurgent Chief, Sarsfield, Wolfe Tone, Fenian* and a host of Irish historical dramas. The impact of these nationalist dramas on public consciousness is rarely acknowledged. In addition to the Queen's Theatre, they were seen all over Ireland in the J. Kennedy Miller touring company productions.[67] Séamus de Búrca maintained that they had a far greater influence on nationalist and proletarian opinion than the Abbey Theatre productions: 'They're inclined to think that the Abbey was national all the time. But the real national theatre – certainly up to 1916 and I would suggest up to about 1923 – was the Queen's Theatre'.[68]

If, as O'Casey claims, at the age of twelve or so, Shakespeare tapped on the window,[69] by the time he was twenty, Boucicault and the Queen's tradition had walked in the front door.[70] Fluther Good and Captain Boyle are the direct descendants of the free-spirited Conn and Myles from Boucicault's *The Shaughraun* and *The Colleen Bawn*, who are alert to their limitations and failings but demand and receive the indulgence of the audience. O'Casey draws on Boucicault's technique in the way that he weaves his comedy and political themes together to give depth and colour to his characters. In his drama, O'Casey draws on the tradition of Shakespeare's history plays, Boucicault's melodramas and Shaw's discussion plays to create a unique synthesis. He created a drama with opposing characters who do not find a resolution in the course of the play. His conclusions are politically open-ended, which continues to frustrate many of his critics. Moreover, he was never afraid of offending any section of society or political grouping.

James Joyce may have believed that at the end of the nineteenth century, Dublin was 'the centre of paralysis', but for many others, this was a time of momentous intellectual and political turbulence.[71] Several events came together, which Roy Foster has argued 'focused much moderate Irish opinion into an anti-imperial mould, and provided a mobilising "cause" against the government'.[72] Two events that influenced O'Casey's developing political awareness were the centenary celebrations of the 1798 rebellion and the outbreak of the Boer War in 1899. In a key chapter, 'I Strike a

Blow for You, Dear Land', O'Casey describes how his 'whole world was divided against himself'.[73] Irish nationalists and socialists also utilised the resentment over Queen Victoria's jubilee celebrations in 1897 and the Boer War two years later to organise and extend anti-British feeling. At the outbreak of the Boer War in 1899, O'Casey's brother Tom was recalled to the army. The family, like most of the Protestant community in Ireland, supported the British intervention in South Africa. O'Casey recalled carrying his brother's rifle with pride as Tom marched through Dublin and off to war. Dublin was alive with controversy over the war – meetings, demonstrations, riots, ribbons and flags of all descriptions: Irish, Transvaal, socialist, in every window and street, and pro-Boer buttons on every lapel.

The anti-jubilee agitation in 1897, and the 1798 centenary celebrations the following year, was the springboard that helped unite the Home Rule Party and heal the wounds created by the Parnell split in 1890. This political upsurge was a transformative moment when O'Casey's family and church beliefs conflicted with his experience of the outside world. In his autobiography, O'Casey conflates these events into a description of the riots that followed a pro-Boer meeting in the Mansion House in Dublin on 1 March 1900. He describes his involvement in the riots alongside Ayamonn O'Farrel, where he unseated a mounted policeman who was hacking his way through the crowd with his sabre 'gleaming sourly in the grey air'. Here we also meet a prototype for Bessie Burgess from *The Plough and the Stars*, shouting at the rioters:

> It 'ud be fitter for yous to work to help yourselves than to set yourselves dhreamin' of help for the Boers; for listen to me – in about as much time as it 'ud take a clever hand and a sharp knife to peel an apple, England'll put the sign o' death on Kruger an' his gang![74]

The chapter ends with a sensual, sexual encounter with the lovely and alluring Daisy Battles. The first volume of the autobiographies ends at the age of twelve, with O'Casey kissing a girl and learning about the pleasure of books. The second ends at the age of twenty, with O'Casey participating in a riot and sleeping with a young woman; he was now ready to take on the world. At the turn of the century, O'Casey put his 'twenty years a-growing' behind him. He was facing a decisive time in his own life and in Ireland's history. 'God' had not yet let go of him, 'Man' was an appeal that he could not ignore, but 'Country' was to have his loyalty, affection and energy for some time to come. It seemed as if his whole world was divided against itself.[75]

CHAPTER 3

The Gaelic League and Other Matters

What constitutes a nation and the problem of 'nation-building' was a question that agitated the minds of the political class in Ireland for much of the nineteenth century.[1] The belief that the Irish nation had existed since time immemorial, even if it had gone through prolonged periods of slumber, was a central tenet of Irish nationalism.[2] However, the concept of nationhood is a relatively modern phenomenon in world history. In England, this concept began as early as the mid-seventeenth century, and in Europe and America about one hundred years later. The origins and history of nation-states are a contested and controversial subject, and scholars continue to debate a number of possible concepts. Caoimhín De Barra, in his book on the Irish language, points out that what constitutes a 'nation' is a loose concept and ultimately an 'imagined social concept'.[3] Nation-building can best be described as a process whereby people transfer their loyalty from the local village, area, tribe or clan to a central political system or unit. A nation is defined not just geographically, but also culturally and politically. The 'nation state' embodied the sovereign people, a written constitution and the abolition of aristocratic prerogative. Across Europe, industrialisation also saw a shift in power from the countryside to the urban centres. Allied to this was a shift in literary taste, now generally referred to as Romanticism,[4] which highlighted the link between language and national identity.[5] Thomas Davis, in the 1840s, gave voice to a similar philosophy that would energise the Gaelic revival fifty years later: 'A people without a language of its own is only half a nation ... To lose your native tongue and learn that of an alien, is the worst badge of conquest',[6] a concept echoed by Ernest Blythe in his 1949 pamphlet *The State and the Language*: 'Ireland as a nation will disappear if language is lost.'[7] Given that proposition and the colonial relationship between Britain and Ireland, it was inevitable that the question of identity in Ireland would be posed very sharply in cultural and linguistic terms. Up to the time of the Famine of 1845–52, Irish was the daily language of over half the Irish population; in its aftermath, the language declined dramatically.[8] The rate of linguistic change has almost no parallel anywhere else in the world. It became clear to a large section of the Irish peasantry that if they wished to make a place for themselves in the community or the wider world, they must first 'bow to the language of their masters' and discard that 'infirm language, hiding it from the sight of strangers'.[9] Very few were literate in Irish, which became more and more a language of the home, while English was the language of public discourse.

The launch of the *Gaelic Journal* in 1882 brought together a number of personalities who formed the Gaelic League in July 1893. Prominent among them were Douglas Hyde and Father Eugene O'Growney, with whom the Gaelic League became synonymous.[10] Shortly after O'Casey joined in 1903, there were over 500 branches and a membership approaching 50,000. In addition to the language, the league fostered a modern Gaelic literature. In 1901, the Irish Literary Theatre produced Hyde's play *Casadh an tSúgáin* (The Twisting of the Rope) in what was both a literary and a political statement.[11] During the first three decades of its existence, the league 'exercised a great and growing influence over contemporary society' and was substantially responsible for a 'social revolution' in Irish society.[12] A movement that mobilised such numbers inevitably raised political questions, but this was a development that the founders of the league had never envisaged. Their insistence that the movement should be non-political encouraged significant numbers of Protestants and unionists to join in the early years, a factor that undoubtedly influenced O'Casey.

Seán O'Casey was an unlikely member of the Gaelic League as few working-class Protestants joined. He described his first faltering attempts at learning Irish, using the copy of Father O'Growney's *Simple Lessons in Irish*[13] that O'Farrel had given to him in the Hill Street theatre some time previously:

> He sat down on the shafts for a rest, taking out his little Irish book, bending carefully over it, so that the snow couldn't damage it, and tried to learn a few more words. Atá an sneachta a tuitim síos, he murmured, coining little sentences from what he saw around him ... When I earn enough in the week, I must join the Gaelic League.[14]

Like the great scholar that he was, he soon became proficient and, over time, a first-rate Irish speaker. The autobiographies are full of conversations and conflicts that O'Casey sets in a dialectical framework that allows us to understand the tensions that shaped his political thinking. In this extract, he describes a workplace conversation where he asks a fellow worker if he is interested in learning Irish. The worker replies:

> A full pot an' the fire to boil it is what I want.
> But, insisted Johnny, a full pot and a fire to boil it isn't the be-all and end-all of life.
> It is to me with a wife an' three kids, an' fifteen shillin's a week, an' a house in Merrion Square to keep goin'.[15]

The dilemma confronting O'Casey during his time in the Gaelic League and the Irish Republican Brotherhood (IRB) was how to hitch the plough to the stars or, at a more basic level, put a loaf of bread on the worker's table as well as a vase of flowers.

ACTIVIST

As with everything he was interested in, he threw himself headlong into the Gaelic League and all things Irish. In 1901, O'Casey started work as a bricklayer's assistant on the Great Northern Railway, where he was known to his fellow workers as Irish Jack. On occasions, he paraded the streets of Dublin in his kilt, all seven yards of Irish woven tartan. O'Casey also took up hurling, which he played with more gusto than skill. The league was a turning point in his life; his intellectual and political education changed from the solitary, that of books, to the communal. He quickly progressed from student to teacher, travelling all over north Dublin, extending the reach and influence of the Gaelic League. He held classes every second evening in Drumcondra and on Sundays in Moyvalley in County Meath. He was never a paid organiser or teacher but devoted the next ten years of his life to the Irish language. He describes his life at the time: 'Up every morning at five, bar Sunday, home again at six in the evening, after a hard day's work with hack, shovel, sledgehammer, or hod; out again at seven to work even harder for the Gaelic League or the Republican Brotherhood'.[16]

O'Casey was a member of the Drumcondra branch of the league and was elected secretary in 1908. Drumcondra was a working-class branch that none of the more respectable Gaelic Leaguers of the area would attend. Their premises was a shed in Seery's Lane beside a working-men's club that they occasionally used for an all-night céilidh. He was centrally involved both as a teacher and membership secretary. They published a monthly magazine in manuscript form, *An Lámh Dhearg* (The Red Hand),

and the contributions were read aloud on the first Sunday of the month. According to Ernest Blythe, O'Casey's contributions were always the most popular. O'Casey's stories dealt with the antics of 'the brother' Adolphus Ó Cadhsaí, an inveterate social climber, 'always thinking up plans to impress his betters and advance himself socially'.[17] These Sunday meetings were very popular, and people came just to hear the latest adventure of 'the brother'. Unfortunately, no copies of these stories seem to have survived. Proinsias Mac Aonghusa has suggested that 'O'Casey began his writing career in Irish and not in English, as is usually taken for granted'.[18]

In 1907, O'Casey cut his teeth on the first of many campaigns he embarked upon over the following fifty years. Some Protestant members of the Gaelic League came together to persuade the Church of Ireland to conduct some religious services through Irish, and thus began the Gaelic League's 'mission to Protestants'.[19] The campaign comprised two groups, one centred on the Craobh na gCúig Cúigí (the Branch of the Five Provinces) or, as it was affectionately known, the Branch of the Five Protestants. The other strand, mainly from the Drumcondra branch, consisted of O'Casey, George Irvine, Séamus Deakin and Ernest Blythe, but most of the work was carried out by the Drumcondra members. All of the Drumcondra men were members of the Irish Republican Brotherhood and went on to make important contributions to Irish political life. The ambition of the 'mission to Protestants' was threefold: firstly, to have a service in Irish at least once a month in one of the Dublin churches; secondly, to obtain the use of Protestant parochial halls for Irish cultural activities; and lastly, to introduce the Irish language and history into all Protestant schools. O'Casey was an active and committed member of the committee, but he was difficult to work with – a trait that would manifest itself on many occasions in the future. He took exception to the formal, middle-class attire worn by the committee and insisted on wearing his workmen's clothes rather than a collar and tie, and as he said himself: 'he wasn't the one to germinate into unaccustomed grandeur of clothing so that Gaelic snobs of school teachers, civil servants, and customs officers shouldn't shiver with shame when he was near them'.[20] O'Casey worked harder than most to have the Irish language as part of Protestant church services: collecting money, gathering support, writing letters. In religious matters, O'Casey was High Church and was still active in church affairs. His High Church views led to several unfortunate rows and misunderstandings with clergymen who were willing to allow services in Irish but were not prepared to accept O'Casey's opinion as to how they should conduct Holy Service. In 1941, in a letter to *The Irish Times*, he wrote about a delegation from the Gaelic League who went to see the dean of St Patrick's about the possibility of a religious service in Irish in the cathedral on St Patrick's Day: 'I was not respectable looking enough then to go with the deputation, but I heard all about it.'[21] More likely, they excluded O'Casey because they could not be sure what he might say. In his autobiography, he took the opportunity to settle some old scores, and few of his many enemies were left unscathed. He ridiculed the dean for refusing to allow services in Irish: 'What! Have a service in Erse and in St. Patrick's? ... We don't want our church filled with Conn the Shaughrauns, like a Wicklow wedding, besides Heaven is used by now to the English language and it would be a nuisance for them to have to become bilingual'.[22] In time, the different strands of the campaign came together and, in April 1914, formed Cumann Gaelach na hEaglaise. Shortly afterwards, the dean of St Patrick's Cathedral gave permission to use a side chapel for a monthly service in Irish. Problems arose in the aftermath of the 1916 Rising when the bishop of Tuam insisted that any meeting of Cumann Gaelach na hEaglaise must condemn the rising as an attack on law and order. The organisation split over the issue, but it survived and is still active in the Church of Ireland.[23]

DR MICHAEL O'HICKEY

O'Casey dedicated the third volume of his autobiography to Dr Michael O'Hickey: 'A Gael of Gaels, one-time professor of Irish in Maynooth College. In a fight for the Irish [language], he collided with arrogant Irish bishops and was summarily dismissed without a chance of defending himself'.[24] O'Hickey was a former vice-president of the Gaelic League and an ardent nationalist whose love of the Irish language drove him to defy the bishops and the Vatican. O'Hickey was not a particularly brilliant scholar, but he instilled a love of the language and was partially responsible for turning out 'what was probably the most nationally-minded generation of priests ever turned out by Maynooth'.[25] O'Hickey's pamphlet *The True National Idea* (1902) opened the eyes of thousands to the link between the Irish language and Irish nationalism: 'The problem which the Irish people are now called upon to solve is the most important that could confront any people; it is the problem of their distinct existence as a nation'.[26]

His dismissal from his position in Maynooth in 1909 became a *cause célèbre* in Gaelic League circles. Most of the public controversies in which the Gaelic League was involved centred on the place of the language in Irish education. When the National University of Ireland opened in 1908, the Gaelic League insisted that Irish should be an essential subject for enrolment in the new university. However, Father Delaney, the president of the old Catholic University College, announced that he could not support the league's policy because Catholic students who did not know Irish were left with no choice except Trinity College with its Protestant ethos. Delaney was a member of the Gaelic League but drew a distinction between the Irish of the fair or the common people and the Irish of scholars.[27] His announcement outraged members of the league. O'Hickey replied to Delaney's pronouncement in forceful terms: 'To be opposed by the colonists is a thing we are accustomed to; to be opposed by a section of our own, no matter how worthless and degenerate, is not to be tolerated'.[28] In a series of letters and pamphlets, O'Hickey roused the country on the issue, following which Maynooth College demanded his resignation, and when he refused, they dismissed him. The dispute over O'Hickey's dismissal added fuel to the political tensions emerging in the Gaelic League. His image as a man who refused to be silenced, who took risks, 'a nationalist defending the Irish language; a priest who was defying the Catholic Church',[29] transformed him into a heroic figure who had redrawn the boundaries of Irish culture. In many ways, O'Hickey was similar to O'Casey – he was a difficult man to deal with, he lacked diplomacy – but his iron will and his fighting spirit, regardless of the damage he might inflict on himself, must have appealed to O'Casey. He contributed 15*s*., practically a week's wages, to a fund to support O'Hickey, and threw himself into the campaign. He lobbied all the nationalist leaders and parties, demanding that they support O'Hickey, but to little effect: 'What do you expect us to do over a question that is plainly one for ecclesiastical juridicity? asked a Sinn Feiner who had plussed himself into a Republican, while the massive-minded Griffith robed himself in the stillness of the strong, silent man'.[30]

In a chapter in his autobiography called 'Lost Leader', O'Casey almost bestows the laurel last worn by Parnell on O'Hickey's head.[31] What O'Casey instinctively understood, even though he could not have been aware of the long-term importance of the issue at that time, was that the O'Hickey case was a pivotal moment in nationalist politics. This was a fight between the Catholic Church and the broad nationalist, literary and cultural movement over the future social and moral direction of Irish society. On the surface, it was a debate about education policy with O'Hickey caught in the crossfire. At another level, it was 'a struggle to determine whether the Irish language or the Catholic religion were to be the most important markers of national identity'.[32] O'Casey, like W.B. Yeats and many Protestant nationalists, hoped for an Ireland that was not defined by Catholicism and would join with them in encouraging their fellow Protestants to identify with the nationalist project.

O'Casey spent the best part of ten years working tirelessly to promote the Irish language and culture, but his frustrations with the pace of change were evident in a letter he wrote regarding the Robert Emmet commemoration concert on St Patrick's Day in 1910. He complained that the speeches were in English, which insulted 'the language of our Motherland ... This after fifteen years' work on the part of the Gaelic League in the capital of Ireland'.[33] O'Casey was never just a hurler on the ditch shouting the odds and letting others do the work. He earned his right to criticise the league, and in 1907, in his second published article, he put forward a constructive plan of reorganisation to revitalise the movement and make it 'a great power' in Dublin.[34] By 1918 he had given up all hope that the Gaelic League could turn the situation around. In a piece written for *Irish Opinion*, his arguments regarding the teaching of Irish are as relevant today as they were then:

> The teaching of it must be happiness to the teachers, and the learning of it must be a joy for our children. At present, wherever it may be taught, the children hate it, for it is not taught, but administered as a noxious medicine. If we hope to restore the Irish language through the schools, then the whole system of Irish Popular Education will have to be revolutionised. The teachers must be lifted to a plane of elevated citizenship, free from economical worry of every description, so that they may teach, and our children must be comfortably clad, and fully fed, so they may be able to learn.[35]

In 1924, in the *Irish Statesman*, O'Casey described how, in the newly independent state, the middle classes had received all the benefits, leaving the working class with the consolation that their children, though starving, had the joy of learning Irish in school. His article 'Irish in the Schools' is the story of an unemployed worker who is refused the dole by an overbearing official of the Free State. In the course of a heated discussion, Jack, who is plainly speaking for O'Casey, says:

> The problem of havin' enough food to eat is of more importance than that of havin' a little Irish to speak. The Gaelic spoken by the Ard-

> Breitheamh [High Judge] is very different to the Gaelic spoken in the labour exchange. It makes me mad to think of those who are shoutin' we've nothin' to do but learn Irish if we want to enter into the joy of the Lord. And then, to think of our over-worked teachers, underfed children, hardly one of whom is sound in body.[36]

Even though the Gaelic League lost some of its most dynamic members during the Easter Rising and the War of Independence, it is difficult to comprehend the near-collapse of the organisation in the aftermath of the Civil War. One factor in this decline was the belief that the newly independent Irish state would take responsibility for the revival of the language. In reality, the Gaeltacht areas were allowed to wither away, and restoring the language became an aspiration rather than an active policy.[37]

The petty-bourgeois character of the Gaelic League clashed with O'Casey's experience of the world as a worker. His attitude to the league in 1924 was not much different from that of James Connolly. In the *Workers' Republic* in October 1898, Connolly wrote that 'you cannot teach starving men Gaelic' and went on to say that 'the chief enemy of a Celtic revival today is the crushing force of capitalism'.[38] It is unlikely that twenty-five years later O'Casey was aware of Connolly's article, but the similarities are striking. Because he had a far better grasp of Marxist theory than O'Casey ever aspired to, Connolly was able to synthesise his thinking in a way that did not alienate him from the best elements in the Gaelic League and nationalist politics. Connolly tried to make socialists see the importance of the anti-imperialist struggle and nationalists see that they must tie their anti-imperialism to the broader struggle for a socialist republic. O'Casey always struggled with this concept. At this time in his life, he tended to see politics as a series of dichotomies or contradictions – nationalism or socialism, the Irish language or the abolition of poverty – but he could rarely fuse them into a coherent theory or practice that allowed him to make a radical contribution to the political problems confronting the movement.

By 1924, O'Casey had concluded that attempting to restore the Irish language this side of a socialist society was futile. We do not know if O'Casey formally resigned from the Gaelic League; most likely, he just drifted away. His life in the tenements, at work, and on the streets of Dublin educated him politically, but in the Gaelic League he learned how to write. O'Growney's *Irish Grammar* gave his writing a structure and a set of rules the self-taught sometimes lack. The league provided him with the opportunity to try out his literary skills, but he could never escape the contradiction that his life in the tenements and on the railways threw up – the tension between socialist and nationalist politics – and that unresolved tension eventually led him in a different direction. O'Casey lost faith in the motivation and ability of the Gaelic League and the nationalist movement, not alone to restore the Irish language but also to transform the lives of the poor and the dispossessed. Despite his frustrations and political differences with the movement, O'Casey never lost his love for the Irish language. After his move to Devon in 1938, he subscribed to the Irish-language newspaper *Inniú* and the Gaelic Book Club. He tuned in most evenings to Radio Éireann: 'it is grand at times to lean one's hand on the set and listen to the old songs sung. At times, I have to break away and go; it moves me too much.'[39] O'Casey based the one-act play *End of the Beginning* (1953) on an old Irish storybook, *An baile seo 'gainn-ne* by An Seabhac.[40] Among the Irish-language books O'Casey read and liked were Seosamh Mac Grianna's *Mo Bhealach Féin* (1940) and Mac Grianna's *Dá mBíodh Ruball ar an Éan* (1940), a satire on General O'Duffy's fascist Blueshirt movement.[41] While critical of the leadership of the Gaelic League, O'Casey was always supportive of the Irish language. In a letter to Walter Macken in 1942 acknowledging the receipt of £14 for the production of an Irish translation of *The Plough and the Stars* in Galway, he lamented the fact that 'Jim Larkin wasn't an Irish speaker; and what a pity Pearse died in Easter Week'. He was incredulous that the Gaelic League had to survive on £400 a year and that it appears 'it has lost its sparkle and its punch'.[42]

The English language allowed Yeats and his friends to reach an international audience and put forward a claim for cultural independence. But if they were to weaken the bulwark of English cultural hegemony in Ireland, then it had to be 'in an English powerfully remoulded by the syntactical energies of Irish, an English that would be as Irish as it is possible for that language to be'.[43] The hybrid Hiberno-English pioneered by the Anglo-Irish Yeats, Synge and Lady Gregory had a vibrancy that went beyond either Standard Irish or Standard English from which it emerged. Yeats and his friends propagated the image of the dignified and cultured peasant in his mud cabin as an expression of the Irish nation. O'Casey was from the city, a tenement-dweller, whose occasional forays into the country beyond Finglas were his only contact with the peasantry. Labouring with pick and shovel on the Great Northern Railway offers a different perspective on the world from that of the Anglo-Irish ascendancy. What O'Casey uniquely added to this linguistic melange of the Anglo-Irish Protestant and the overwhelmingly Catholic Irish peasantry was the voice of the urban poor.

He helped complete a process that allowed subsequent post-colonial writers to remodel English as a global literary language, irrespective of whether they were from a peasant or urban background.[44]

IRISH REPUBLICAN BROTHERHOOD

The Irish Republican Brotherhood (IRB) was founded in 1858 to keep alive the physical force tradition in Irish politics; the IRB's constitution declared that it was the 'sole government' of the Irish republic.[45] The abject failure of the Fenian Rising in 1867 and the constant disputes in the leadership marginalised the role of the IRB in Irish politics, and by the 1890s it appeared to be in terminal decline. However, the growth of a number of organisations in the last years of the century, and in particular the foundation of the Gaelic Athletic Association in 1884, helped to give a new vitality and character not only to the nationalist and parliamentary parties, but also to the clandestine IRB. We do not know for sure when O'Casey joined the IRB, but it may have been sometime in 1905. O'Casey refers to the tram-conductor Ayamonn O'Farrel as the person who introduced him to the IRB, but there were other avenues that might have led O'Casey to its inner sanctum. Despite its Northern and Protestant associations, a remnant of the radical Protestant tradition from the time of the United Irishmen of 1798 still existed among some of the employees of the Great Northern Railway. Fred Allen, a Methodist from a unionist background, recounted how in the late 1880s he was introduced to the writings of John Mitchel and Michael Davitt by his fellow employees in the Great Northern Railway (GNR) in Dublin.[46] Allen went on to become a leading member of the IRB. Whether any of this radical tradition survived into O'Casey's time in the GNR is not known.[47] Another Protestant, Ernest Blythe, recounts in his autobiography how O'Casey, on the way home from a hurling match in the Phoenix Park, mentioned the Fenians and how he regretted the fact that there was no militant organisation capable of confronting the British in Ireland. When Blythe agreed with him and lamented the disappearance of the Fenians, O'Casey told him about the IRB and how they were always looking for likely recruits and asked if he would care to join. After being assured that the IRB was not engaged in assassination plots, Blythe agreed to sign up.[48] O'Casey was a member of the Teeling circle of the IRB, which in the opinion of Bulmer Hobson was 'the largest and about the intellectually toughest circle in Dublin and included many members of the

Gaelic League'.[49] When O'Casey joined, the IRB was relatively inactive; membership mainly consisted of attending the monthly meeting, listening to reports of the various committees or raising money for the arms fund. The irregular activities of the IRB did not impact on his time to any great extent during the first few years of his membership.

The return to Ireland of the Fenian Tom Clarke in 1908 was one of the factors that revitalised the IRB, whose membership at that stage had fallen to about one thousand, mainly in the Dublin area.[50] He had served fifteen years in an English prison for his part in the 1883 bombing campaign. Clarke had purchased a tobacconist shop on the corner of Parnell Street and Sackville Street, which soon became a meeting place for the more militant members of the IRB, where they exchanged news and made plans for the future. O'Casey was secretary of the Wolfe Tone Memorial Committee, a front organisation for the IRB, which revived the annual pilgrimage to Wolfe Tone's grave in Bodenstown in June 1912. The St Laurence O'Toole Pipe Band and the Fianna boy scouts accompanied the parade. O'Casey, who had a good eye for publicity, arranged for the parade to be filmed and shown in cinemas around Dublin. He also introduced the ceremonial saluting of the republican flag as part of the ceremony to give it a theatrical flair.

At O'Casey's instigation, a committee was formed to develop a closer working relationship between the IRB and the labour movement. Seán MacDermott and O'Casey were delegated to meet with James Larkin to discuss whether the *Irish Worker* would report on the meetings and activities of the IRB. Larkin agreed and, in turn, suggested that *Irish Freedom* should do the same for the labour movement. The next meeting of the committee was in the *Irish Freedom* office; when O'Casey got there:

> He found Tom Clarke sitting on the counter, waiting for the others to come. None of the rest [arrived] ... Nor did any send a reason for their absence. They just ignored the whole thing. Both Sean [O'Casey] and Tom Clarke waited for some time. Tom Clarke slid from the counter saying, they can't be coming. I must go back to the shop.[51]

O'Casey suspected that Clarke was aware that the others had no intention of showing up. O'Casey's growing involvement in the labour movement and the activities of the ITGWU distanced him from the IRB: 'I became critical of pure nationalism. But, still more I was critical of the working of the IRB. It was making no progress, & appealed only to clerks and artisans – the great body of the workers was set aside'.[52]

The response of the IRB to the lockout in 1913 strained O'Casey's relationship with the organisation to breaking point. Tom Clarke was one of several IRB leaders who were sympathetic to the working class. Bulmer Hobson was also personally favourable to the labour movement. However, Hobson's 'friendly but neutral attitude' may have alienated O'Casey, and he resigned from the IRB in 1913 over their refusal to take the workers' side. The catalyst for his resignation was a general meeting of the IRB in Dublin. O'Casey was incensed at Hobson's assertion that the IRB could not intervene on the side of the workers because it was supportive of all Irish citizens. A few of those present supported O'Casey, but he was howled down by most of the audience. In the commotion that followed, O'Casey alleged that Hobson drew a gun to restore order.[53] That was the final straw, as far as O'Casey was concerned:

> So, afterwards, with some others, I left the IRB & flung myself into the Labour Movement, though still doing all I could for the National Movement, & for P.H. Pearse's School St. Enda, & St. Laurence O'Toole's Hurling & Football Club & Pipers Band, which I founded & brought to a fine band.[54]

SLOT

The St Laurence O'Toole Club (SLOT) has existed since 1901. In 1910 O'Casey attended a meeting called by Frank Cahill in the Christian Brothers' school in Seville Place in the north inner city, where it was proposed to start a pipe band. Also present were Tom Clarke and Seán MacDermott of the IRB, Arthur Griffith of Sinn Féin, and Patrick Pearse and Douglas Hyde of the Gaelic League. From the beginning, it was clear that the pipe band was bound up with both the Gaelic League and the IRB. O'Casey had joined the club through the influence of Frank Cahill, a fellow member of the Gaelic League and the IRB. He transferred to the SLOT branch of the Gaelic League, and it became his cultural home for the next ten years or so. O'Casey was known for his organising skills and was elected secretary. He scheduled public appearances, took charge of publicity and was, in effect, chief organiser and general factotum for the band. O'Casey also designed and organised the procurement of the uniforms – a crimson shawl, green kilt and Balmoral cap. O'Casey played the bagpipes about as well as he played hurling and seldom participated in the band's performances. SLOT was part of the cultural upheaval that gripped Dublin in the early days of the literary revival, with a minimal division between politics and culture. The pipe band played on the streets of Dublin in 1913 in support of the locked-out workers. On one occasion, as they made their way to Liberty Hall, they were caught up in a baton charge by the Dublin Metropolitan Police, and many of their instruments were destroyed. They played at the funeral of O'Donovan Rossa in Glasnevin in 1915 and Thomas Ashe's funeral in 1917. During the War of Independence, the British army attacked their premises on several occasions and their equipment was severely damaged. Despite this harassment, they survived and are still in existence today, the oldest pipe band in Ireland.

O'Casey was much more at ease in the SLOT branch of the Gaelic League; it was adjacent to where he lived, and most afternoons he would meet up with Frank Cahill or other members of the club and roam the streets of north Dublin talking about the affairs of the club, books and politics. His friend Paddy McDonnell remembers O'Casey expounding with great enthusiasm on the works of Bernard Shaw, Robbie Burns and Jack London.[55] Surprisingly, Frank Cahill does not feature in O'Casey's autobiography. Cahill took the pro-treaty side in the Civil War in 1922, which may account for the omission, but there were personal reasons as well. When O'Casey criticised the SLOT players for aping the Abbey Theatre style, Cahill suggested that he should write a play for the drama group. The result was *The Frost in the Flower* (1918), for which O'Casey used an episode from Cahill's life as the basis for the play. Cahill was portrayed as a weak individual afraid to apply for a promotion in the local school. Although the drama society liked the play, they refused to produce it because of the offence it might cause to Cahill and his family. Cahill was offended by the hurtful way O'Casey portrayed him, and their friendship ended. O'Casey had enough confidence in his ability to submit the play to the Abbey Theatre for consideration, but it was deemed unsuitable for production. Unfortunately, the text has not survived.

O'Casey persevered, and ten months later, in October 1919, he had completed a new play intended for the Abbey Theatre, *The Harvest Festival*; but this met a similar fate. In the meantime, there were battles to be fought; the workers of Dublin 'still waited for a Prometheus to bring down a brand of the divine fire and set the leaden hearts of the poor aflame from one end of Ireland to the other'.[56]

PART 2

CHAPTER 4

A Prometheus in Dublin

On a cold winter's day, Seán O'Casey strode down to the Custom House, where Parnell had once stood, to hear the man God had sent 'into their midst whose name was Larkin'.[1] James Larkin came to Ireland in 1907 to organise the workers in their fight for better wages and conditions and raise the working class from their knees so they might inherit the earth. Larkin had an almost messianic quality, and his ascendancy over the workers in Dublin came from his ability to identify with them. He spoke to the slum dweller as a human being, 'degraded, yet capable of nobility, capable even of music and literature'.[2] He was one of them, a man who demanded as much of them as he did of himself: 'We are going to rouse the working class out of their slough of despond ... out of the mire of poverty and misery – and lift them to a place higher ... that is the claim we are making today'.[3] Larkin was an agitator rather than a theorist or bureaucrat. He was a difficult man to work with; he could be cruel and unmerciful to those who disagreed with him, yet capable of great acts of kindness. He never saw workers as economic units, rather as men and women capable of nobility – a trait that made him so attractive to someone like O'Casey. Larkin set out his stall in the Irish Transport and General Workers' Union (ITGWU) rule book in 1909, possibly the nearest thing we have to a manifesto of his political stance. Not much of it is original, and in many cases the rules were cobbled together from the rule books of existing unions. They were a combination of socialist demands, nationalist rhetoric, anti-British sentiments, and warnings against sectional interests that divide the skilled and general worker.[4]

Occasionally, Larkin's grammar may have let him down, but here was a man who could use words as weapons. His style was literary, rhetorical and biblical, and it touched the soul of the Irish working class. This was the template that O'Casey was looking for. The literary tradition of John Mitchel, James Fintan Lalor, Shakespeare and the King James Bible fused with the hard-edged demands of the socialist movement. O'Casey refined and shaped this way of writing into a weapon of class warfare. If the Gaelic League had educated O'Casey in grammar and syntax, Larkin gave him his subject. O'Casey instinctively understood that Larkin had a real sense of the pain of life and that it was better to starve fighting than to starve working. O'Casey described Larkin as a living Prometheus:

> He is tall and strongly built. His eyes are grey and brilliant. His hair is raven black. His nose is long, thick, and combative. He walks with a slight seaman's lurch. He is dressed in a dark-green coat, faded blue trousers, and his head is covered by a wide-brimmed black slouch hat. When he speaks one hears a touch of hoarseness in his voice, due to constant speaking in the open to large crowds.[5]

By 1911 O'Casey was 'ripe for someone with Larkin's magnetism and class outlook'.[6] His disenchantment with the Gaelic League and the Irish Republican Brotherhood caused him to look in other directions: 'Following afar off for a while, Sean had come to hear Larkin speak, to stand under a red flag, rather than the green banner'.[7]

Jim Larkin was born to Irish parents in Liverpool in 1874. He arrived in Belfast on 20 January 1907, the same week that John Millington Synge's play *The Playboy of the Western World* opened at the Abbey Theatre in Dublin. The two events were unconnected, but they transformed Irish politics and culture forever. Larkin established his reputation as an organiser for the National Union of Dock Labourers (NUDL) during the five-month transport strike in Belfast.[8] The strike ended with a bureaucratic compromise, but for a few months, socialists and trade unionists from both sides of the sectarian divide overcame the traditional political and religious bigotry associated with the city in a fight for better wages and conditions. At the end of the strike, he refused to go to Scotland as instructed by the NUDL, claiming that an opportunity existed to organise all workers, including the unskilled, in Ireland. A few weeks later, on 28 December 1909, Larkin launched a breakaway union, the Irish Transport and General Workers' Union (ITGWU): 'In a room of a tenement in Townsend Street, with a candle in a bottle for a torch and a billycan for tea ... the Irish Transport and General Workers' Union was founded, a tiny speck of flame now, but soon to become a pillar of fire'.[9]

The ITGWU represented a new style of trade unionism that reached out to the unskilled worker. The new unions preached class warfare and tried to break down the traditional hostility of craft workers towards the unskilled. The ITGWU was organised on the basis of 'One Big Union', and its philosophy was 'an injury to one is an injury to all'. What came to be known as Larkinism was part of an international wave of militancy, representing an Irish variant of syndicalism, and this concept would exert a formative impact on Irish labour from 1909 to 1923. Syndicalism originated in France as a response to the failure of the existing socialist parties to represent the economic or political interests of the unskilled worker. The syndicalist movement emphasised direct action, militancy and strikes to build workers' consciousness, culminating in a general strike where workers could take control of industry and organise production for the benefit of all.[10] In all his plays about the labour movement, *The Harvest Festival, Red Roses for Me* and *The Star Turns Red*, O'Casey 'responded to the moral and spiritual appeal of syndicalism' espoused by Larkin and the ITGWU.[11] Larkin succeeded in making Dublin one of the best union-organised cities in Europe. The ITGWU's use of the sympathetic strike and the doctrine of 'tainted goods' was the cornerstone of its strategy to force employers to recognise the union and negotiate for better wages and conditions. The *Freeman's Journal* gave a flavour of the period when in March 1913 it warned of 'grave industrial unrest' and that the working class 'threatens to become its own doctor and use its own remedies, which may or may not involve the rest of us in disaster ... the poor are clamouring not for doles but for justice'. The editorial went on to say, 'there was a whiff of revolution in the air, and there was no point in just blaming Larkin, who articulated the cry of the poor and the oppressed for better wages and conditions'.[12]

RAIL STRIKE

The 'Great Unrest' of 1910–14 was one of the most prolonged and sustained rebellions in British working-class history. Leon Trotsky was not alone in suggesting that 'during those days a dim spectre of revolution hung over Britain'.[13] In August 1911, labour unrest in the British docks spread to the railways, and they joined the strike for better pay and a reduction in the working week. The strike spread to Dublin, and the Amalgamated Society of Railway Servants (ASRS) put out a dramatic call to action: 'Your Liberty is at stake. All railwaymen must strike at once. The loyalty of each means victory for all'.[14] On 18 August, a national strike across the Irish network closed down the railways. O'Casey must have been involved, as 'almost every man at the Great Northern Railway (GNR) terminus ... struck work, including signalmen, porters, and the whole of the goods and traffic employees'.[15] After three days, the strike ended following talks in London between the ASRS and the employers. Increases of between 1*s*. and 4*s*. a week were won, but the sixty-hour week remained.

The second rail strike in Ireland, which began on 15 September, was a far more significant and substantial affair. When the first rail strike ended in August, the employees of the Dublin timber merchants who were locked out because they supported the strike refused to return to work without a pay rise. The employers inflamed the situation by sending a consignment of timber to Kingsbridge (Heuston) train station. The railway workers blacked the consignment in support of the striking timbermen. The strike spread to the rail workers; the focus had now moved beyond the blacking of 'tainted goods' to the issue of union recognition and better pay. The ASRS responded by calling a national strike of rail workers in Ireland. While Irish rail workers had supported the strike in Britain just a month earlier, the ASRS now refused to call out its members in Britain in support of their colleagues in Ireland. The rail companies, sensing weakness, refused all offers of compromise, which forced the ASRS to call off the dispute. Whether O'Casey was a member of the ASRS or any other union leading up to the strikes in 1911 is unknown, but during the dispute, he joined the Irish Transport and General Workers' Union. In the immediate aftermath, the ASRS lost a quarter of their membership in Ireland, partially as a result of victimisation, but also because of real anger at the failure of the British-based union to support their Irish colleagues. The most militant workers, including O'Casey, joined the ITGWU, inspired by Larkin's ability to articulate their hopes and aspirations. The rise in nationalist feeling was also an important factor in the development of Irish-based unions.[16] By the end of 1911, the ITGWU had increased its membership from 5,000 to 18,000. The launch of Larkin's paper the *Irish Worker* in May 1911 meant that there was now a powerful voice for the 'new unionism' and working-class republicanism.

About 10 per cent of the men on strike were not re-hired at the end of the dispute. O'Casey was not victimised on that occasion and returned to work in early October. However, a few months later, on 8 December, he was told his services were no longer required. The GNR never thought highly of O'Casey, as he was known to be difficult, and they certainly were not going to tolerate him now. The GNR claimed his work was 'unsatisfactory'. O'Casey was a known troublemaker; most likely, he was dismissed for attacking the working conditions on the railway and praising Jim Larkin and the ITGWU. According to his friend Jim Kavanagh, the GNR dismissed O'Casey because he refused to sign a loyal address from the railway workers to King George and Queen Mary to celebrate their visit to Ireland. The foreman insisted that 'everyone must sign it'. Seán replied, 'I'd like to meet the man between here and Belfast who'd get me to sign a paper like that'.[17] O'Casey retaliated by publishing the correspondence with the GNR regarding his dismissal in the pages of the *Irish Worker*.[18] The editor, James Larkin, was always prepared to open the pages of the paper to a victimised worker like O'Casey, who wanted to tell his story. In all, O'Casey wrote six articles about his sacking, exposing the incompetence of the GNR management, the fraud and wastefulness, and disregard for their employees that was endemic in the company:

> I saw one man threatened with dismissal one day because he stopped to give a drayman a lift with a bag of flour which had fallen off his cart. Space is not ample enough to enumerate all the mean, cowardly efforts to make the workmen feel that they are dust, and to dust they shall return.[19]

These articles are significant because they signify for the first time his public engagement with the ITGWU and the syndicalist politics of James Larkin. O'Casey's articles are generally too detailed about the inner workings of the GNR. When he moved beyond the specifics of his case, we see a writer who could use irony and humour to underline his point. O'Casey exposed the terrible working conditions endured by the 'slaves' of the GNR. Reporting a conversation with a porter employed by the company, he asked him how much he paid for his lodgings:

> 'Eleven shillings a week', he told me.
> 'How much does the railway give you?' I asked.
> 'Ten bob a week', was the reply.
> 'How on earth, then, do you pay 11*s*. a week for your lodgings?'
> 'You see,' said this poor slave, 'I work every Sunday and get 2*s*.
> for it, and so I have a shilling a week for myself.'[20]

THE RED AND GREEN BANNER

O'Casey was thirty-one years old, and except for occasional or casual work, he never again obtained secure employment. He was entitled to unemployment benefit of 10*s*. a week which lasted for six months. After that ended, he depended on his mother's meagre old age pension of 5*s*. a week. Unemployment suited O'Casey as he had few needs and appeared to live on endless cups of strong tea and the occasional scrap of food. He had more than enough interests to fill his day. He wrote articles for the *Irish Worker* and *Irish Freedom* and was active in the Gaelic League, the St Laurence O'Toole Club, the pipe band, the drama club and the ITGWU. The 1911 strike was not a Saint Paul moment on the road to Liberty Hall. Despite what he wrote in his autobiography some thirty years later, he had not stepped out entirely from under the 'green banner'. Even though Liberty Hall, the headquarters of the ITGWU, was an important part of his life, he moved easily between the red and the green banners.

Larkin and the ITGWU's support for republicanism and separatism reflected a deep-seated tradition held by the most political section of the working class in Dublin. Working-class republicanism was an essential component of Larkin's politics, and this stance was taken by the ITGWU independently of James Connolly. There is a tendency among Connolly's biographers to discuss this aspect of the ITGWU's position on the national question 'as if Connolly was the lone advocate of republicanism within the labour movement'.[21] In the first issue of the *Irish Worker*, Larkin outlined a statement of principles that gave almost equal weight to the nationalist and socialist ideals of the ITGWU:

> By freedom we mean that ... [w]e owe no allegiance to any other nations, nor the king, governors, or representatives of any other nation. That all such persons are interlopers and trespassers on this our land, and that we are determined to accomplish not only National Freedom, but a greater thing – Individual Freedom – Freedom from military and political slavery, such as we suffer under at present, but also from a more degraded slavery, economic or wage slavery.[22]

Therefore, it did not require a great leap of faith on O'Casey's part to embrace the red banner fluttering over Liberty Hall. The position of Larkin and the ITGWU on the national question was not significantly different from that outlined by O'Casey in the *Irish Worker* and *Irish Freedom* between 1912 and 1913. If the red banner was flying over one corner of Liberty Hall, the green banner was flying just as prominently over the other. In *Irish Freedom*, the paper of the IRB, writing for a republican audience in early 1913, O'Casey suggested that:

> There should be a union between the Separatists and the railway labourer, the factory hand, and the transport worker ... The men who are linked to Wolfe Tone's soul are mainly toilers and their condition must be better in a Republican Ireland ... We will have a Brotherhood

> and Equality in a Free Ireland; not merely cringing equality based on modern English socialistic ideals.[23]

O'Casey's dislike of English socialists was not just an anti-British feeling, but resentment at their failure to support the strike movement in 1911 and the refusal of the British Trades Union Congress to support the Dublin workers during the lockout in 1913. In a series of articles over the following two years, he set out how the red and the green could unite to win a republic based on the ideals of Tone, Mitchel and Lalor:

> Wolfe Tone turned away from the Ascendancy gang, and laboured to unite Dissenter and Catholic to fight for a free Ireland. It is up to us now to turn away from the self-satisfied gentry and the soulless controllers of commerce, and to unite the Separatist ranks with the forces of Labour and the social advancement of the people.[24]

While O'Casey canvassed for the Larkinite candidates in the January 1914 municipal elections, he was also a regular reader of the Sinn Féin newspaper.

O'Casey was not at this time a Marxist, nor had he developed an analysis of Irish politics that placed it in an international context. He was still thinking in Irish terms only. In contrast, James Connolly was steeped in the tradition of the Second Socialist International and had worked as a socialist organiser in Britain, America and Ireland.[25] However, despite his Marxist background, nowhere in Connolly's writing is there a fundamental critique of republican ideology: 'At most, there is tactical advice offered to the republicans about the need to engage in open political activity'.[26] In effect, Connolly incorporated republicanism into the socialist tradition. Up to 1913, O'Casey, Larkin and Connolly shared the belief that republicanism was the natural ally of the working-class movement and that they should work together. O'Casey's critique of Connolly and the republicans hardened in the aftermath of the 1913 lockout. He expressed his resentment in the pages of the *Irish Worker* at the failure of the nationalists to support the workers during the lockout. Drawing on the Protestant tradition and the language of Cromwell and the King James Bible, he raged at the nationalists:

> To-day to the workers, Nationalism is a gospel without hope; it does not signify life to them. National leaders of to-day, if ye cannot sanctify your Nationalism with the breath of humanity, cease shouting at us, and in the name of God, leave us alone.[27]

O'Casey's socialism was a work in progress. His thinking lacked clarity, and rhetoric substituted for theoretical exactness. In a controversy that developed in the pages of the *Irish Worker* in February and March 1913, O'Casey crossed swords with A. Patrick Wilson, the journalist and playwright. Wilson wrote a regular column for the *Irish Worker* under the pseudonym Euchan. In his column, 'The Rebel Movement: Labour and its relation to home rule',[28] Euchan argued that the coming of home rule would bring Ireland into line with its commercial neighbours and that Irish workers must prepare instead for the battle between capital and labour.

> Ireland can never again be the glorious nation it was. The present age is a commercial one, and all that the British political bosses desire is that Ireland will become a cohesive, active and willing part of the British commercial empire, and Ireland will undoubtedly become so after home rule is established.[29]

Euchan's arguments in favour of Labour were not terribly complex or even well written, but they had some currency on the left in the trade union movement. James Larkin put forward a similar position, suggesting that the national question, which had been 'used to divide us in the past', would be settled 'once and for all' by the forthcoming home rule bill.[30] O'Casey jumped headlong into the argument with Euchan, defending the ideals of Gaelic Ireland over those of Labour in a series of articles that were rhetorical, intellectually weak and imprecise:

> What does he know about Ireland's past? Can he see further than the soldiers, the saints, and the sages of Eireann? ... The delivery of Ireland is not in the Labour Manifesto, good and salutary as it may be, but in the strength, beauty, nobility and imagination of the Gaelic ideal.[31]

In the heat of the dispute, O'Casey put forward a series of arguments that conflicted with his own publicly stated beliefs on the relationship between labour and nationalism:

> He [Euchan] still holds the "Labour Movement is the only Rebel Movement in Ireland" ... I suppose he is still content to arm his "Rebels" with votes! ... It was the rifle on Bunker Hill, not the VOTES of the American Representatives, that won American Independence. It was the same power that overthrew the French Monarchy.[32]

Euchan accused O'Casey of being a dreamer, of proposing a way of life that was no longer possible. Euchan believed that the offer of home rule in 1912 had settled the 'Irish question', and from now on, only the class issue mattered. O'Casey challenged him to a debate, offering to refute the core propositions put forward by Euchan, but he declined, and the correspondence degenerated into personal abuse. In later life, O'Casey would have had no trouble homing in on the fundamental weaknesses in Euchan's position. His final reply is interesting because it contains his first known reference to James Connolly. O'Casey insisted that it is not possible to separate economic and political history and suggested to Euchan that 'James Connolly could give you some valuable information on this question'[33] – advice he might have heeded himself in the years following the 1916 Rising.

O'Casey had written for the journals and newspapers of the Gaelic League, *Irish Homestead* and *Irish Freedom*, but he developed as a writer in the pages of the *Irish Worker*. In the first issue of the *Irish Worker*, Larkin declared, in a phrase taken almost directly from William Wordsworth, 'the *Irish Worker* will be a lamp to guide your feet in the hours of impending struggle'.[34] The paper ran for 189 issues before the British authorities suppressed it in 1915. Larkin's ability to find the exact phrase or word that could electrify the moment derived from the fact that he had immersed himself in the great writers of the past. According to John de Courcy Ireland: 'If Larkin was not attending a meeting, he would retire to bed at ten o'clock with a bundle of books; Keats, Shelley, and Tennyson were his favourites, and announce that he would be finished reading them by the morning'.[35] He could articulate the anger, frustration and rage of the Dublin working class, but more than that, he gave expression to their hopes and longings for a better world. When Larkin died in 1947, O'Casey's tribute appeared in *The Irish Times*: 'He fought for the loaf of bread as no man has ever fought; but, with the loaf of bread, he also brought the flask of wine and the book of verse'.[36]

The *Irish Worker* had a circulation of 20,000 at its peak and an estimated readership of 'more than twice its print run', giving Larkin access to practically the entire working class in Dublin.[37] Larkin's extravagant personality set the tone for the paper. Between 1911 and 1914, he wrote over 400 articles in which he thundered against poverty and injustice. Contributors included James Connolly, Delia Larkin, William Partridge, A. Patrick Wilson, Standish O'Grady and many others. Over two years, starting in March 1912, O'Casey contributed sixty-two articles to the *Irish Worker*, including poems, songs and translations from the Irish.[38] He was never afraid to use poetry or song to soften the harshness of the prose.

He also wrote press releases for the many campaigns and organisations he supported. As secretary of the ICA, he contributed a series of 'Citizen Army Notes', outlining the upcoming activities of the army.[39]

THE 1913 LOCKOUT

Seán O'Casey's dismissal from the GNR in 1911 was a turning point in his life. His freedom from the necessity of a twelve-hour shift labouring on the railway gave him time for reflection. His encounter with Charles Darwin's *On the Origin of Species* challenged his religious beliefs,[40] even if, as many of his admirers have suggested, in later life he was the most religious atheist they ever encountered. The books and articles of John Ruskin, the art critic and social reformer, introduced him to the literature of reform,[41] but it was the works of Bernard Shaw that opened his eyes to socialist ideas. Liberty Hall, where Larkin had made such a dramatic impact on the city's life, transformed O'Casey's politics and his life from that time on. Liberty Hall was the political and social centre of Dublin's working-class life; a meeting place for strikers and agitators, a venue for plays and music, the nerve centre of the 1913 lockout and a place of refuge for working-class men, women and children.[42] The 'hidden Ireland began to show herself ... disturbing those engaged in the exciting job of buying cheap and selling dear'.[43] O'Casey never rejected the idea of a free independent Ireland, but his support was now conditional on the nationalists' ability to deliver material advantages for the working class of Ireland. Despite the influence of Larkin and his growing disillusionment with the Gaelic League,[44] O'Casey remained active in the St Laurence O'Toole Club, his hurling team, the pipers' club and the drama group. He marched to Bodenstown for the Wolfe Tone commemoration every June with the SLOT contingent. In the *Irish Worker* in June 1913, O'Casey called for a large turnout of ITGWU members, and there is a photograph of him marching alongside the SLOT pipe band.[45]

During the 'Great Unrest', it became clear to the employers that they would have to break Larkin, or he would break them. Many employers were prepared to tolerate what they described as an 'ordinary combination of workers', but Larkin and his militant syndicalist doctrines were another matter. Larkin, in the employers' eyes, was the devil incarnate and they were determined to destroy him. This was class war, and in William Martin Murphy the employers had found an uncompromising general.[46] It was a role Murphy willingly took on, threatening his staff that if they heeded Larkin's call to strike, 'it will be the Waterloo of Mr. Larkin'.[47] On 15 August

1913, Murphy, who owned the *Irish Independent*, entered the dispatch department and informed the workers that they must choose between Larkin and their jobs. Murphy sacked forty employees who refused to resign from the union. Within hours, the street newsboys refused to sell the *Evening Herald*, which Murphy also owned; they had not forgotten Larkin's support for them during their dispute in 1911. The next day the van drivers in Easons, the newspaper distributor, refused to handle any Independent Group newspapers, and they were locked out. Murphy, the majority shareholder in the Dublin United Tram Company, retaliated by sacking 200 tram workers who refused to resign from the ITGWU. Events were hurtling towards a showdown. Larkin and the tram workers had no choice; at 10 a.m. on 26 August, the tram drivers and conductors switched off the motors and left the trams where they stood. The Employers' Federation responded by locking out any worker who supported the ITGWU or refused to resign their membership.[48]

On Saturday, 30 August, disturbances broke out across the city as strikers laid siege to the tramway electrical station in Ringsend and attacked delivery vans belonging to Independent Group newspapers. The police were at breaking point and retaliated by attacking strikers and their families in the city centre tenements. In a brutal attack, the police injured over two hundred and killed two workers, James Nolan and John Byrne, both members of the ITGWU. O'Casey went to the wake and funeral of James Nolan, and in a very moving passage he described the scene in a simple lyrical style that, in a few paragraphs, portrays life in the tenements in a way that few others have managed:

> There he was between two comrades who were carrying a round wreath to one of their Union who had been battered to death by many police batons ... The now slumbering fire in the grate, the kettle and saucepans on the hob, with a galvanised bath in a corner, showed Sean where the family fed, washed, and slept ... In this one room, they are born, they live, they grow old, and then they die.[49]

By the middle of September, 25,000 workers were locked out, affecting almost the entire working-class population of Dublin. O'Casey, in the *Irish Worker*, appealed to the workers to stand by the union:

> That ancient swelling and desire for liberty is again stirring in our souls. The workers have lifted up their eyes unto the hills. They have no friends but themselves; but in their own strength they can conquer.

> Their only hope is their Union. 'Sacrifice the Union', say the employers, 'and all is gained'. Sacrifice the Union – all is lost.[50]

With no end in sight, the dispute became a war of attrition, and given their resources, this was a war the employers were bound to win. A special conference of the TUC in Britain to discuss the situation in Dublin took place on 9 December. The delegates rejected the motion by Jack Jones of the Gasworkers' and General Labourers' Union to blockade Dublin and black all goods. *The Irish Times* trumpeted the news that the TUC in Britain had 'absolutely and emphatically repudiated' Larkinism and that even Ben Tillet, a well-known socialist, had turned against the 'folly and violence of the Celtic syndicalists'.[51] This was a devastating blow that effectively ended any hopes of victory. By the middle of January 1914, the trickle of workers returning to work on the employer's terms turned into a torrent. The ITGWU advised its members to return to work wherever possible without signing the employer's document. In the end, workers returned on any terms they could get, while the more militant members and their families faced blacklisting or the emigrant ship.

Up to 1913, O'Casey's politics had developed as 'a progressive growth within a consistent framework of values' rather than a series of epiphanies.[52] His hatred of the rack-renters and the sweatshop owners who squeezed the very life out of people distanced him from the nationalists who had no understanding of the conditions that the poor of Dublin endured. How it must have rankled with O'Casey to hear, in the afternoon at Liberty Hall, about a worker sacked, or a family evicted, and later that evening to be in the company of the offending employer or landlord at some nationalist event as they loudly denounced the British presence in Ireland. Nearly all of O'Casey's biographers agree that the lockout was the one genuinely transformative event in his life. Robert Hogan can speak for all of them in his summary of this dramatic shift in O'Casey's politics:

> To O'Casey, who was in the middle of it all, these facts must have made one point indelibly clear: the real battle in Ireland was not as he had suggested a few months before, for Irish freedom but against Irish poverty; the real struggle was not between the English Imperialist and the Irish Republican, but between international capitalism and the workers of the world.[53]

However, O'Casey did not entirely throw over the republican and the egalitarian tradition of Tone and Lalor. He always recognised that the British presence in Ireland was part of the problem.

It is difficult to piece together precisely what role O'Casey played in the lockout. There are few contemporary accounts of O'Casey's activities during that time; what we know is mainly from second-hand sources. In his autobiography, he is relatively silent about his day-to-day activities. In fact, the chapter 'Prometheus Hibernica',[54] which deals with the strike, is one of the least satisfactory chapters in the autobiographies; the allegorical style he adopts, with a few exceptions, fails to convey any sense of the revolutionary events that transformed his life and politics. In his 1960 biography, David Krause devotes no more than a few pages to the lockout, while Christopher Murray in 2004 was not much more forthcoming, and little of substance has been revealed by anyone else. The fact that *The Toiler*, a vicious anti-union paper funded by the employers, saw fit to slander O'Casey by accusing him of misappropriating funds during the dispute is an indication of the prominent role he played during the lockout:

> Shaun Casey, head of Larkin's souper pipers' band, Seville Place. Well, Shaun, my Irish-speaking bowsie, you were afraid of the *Toiler* scout to bring the band to the runaway army's Swords march out. How much of the collection did you collar?[55]

In the early months of 1913, O'Casey was in many ways a contented man; he had time to read and had an outlet for his articles and poems in the nationalist and labour press. Money or material matters were of little interest to him, and as always, he worked tirelessly, unpaid and sometimes unappreciated, for the many organisations he was involved with. In the office of *Irish Freedom*, Kathleen Clarke remembered 'with gratitude his willingness to hump parcels on his back and perform other unpaid duties'.[56] In the pages of the *Irish Worker*, he attempted to unite the national and labour movements by urging workers to support nationalist events. In 1913, he publicised the Irish pageant organised by Patrick Pearse to raise funds for St Enda's school and reported on the fundraising efforts of the Wolfe Tone Committee. As late as October 1913, he still hoped that the nationalists would support the workers. In a letter to the *Irish Worker*, he reported that: 'Evidences are everywhere manifesting themselves of the Gael's determination to stand by the workers in their magnificent fight to vindicate the liberties of man. The GAA has nobly taken its stand with the workers'.[57] Sometime around July 1913, Seán T. O'Kelly, a councillor in Dublin Corporation and a member of the IRB, obtained a temporary position for O'Casey as a labourer with one of the Dublin building firms. O'Casey maintained that he lost this job for refusing to sign the employer's pledge not to join the ITGWU.[58] If that was the case, then O'Casey was most likely locked out on 9 September 1913, when Murphy demanded the building employers should lock their men out.

As was usual with O'Casey, he threw himself wholeheartedly into the work of the ITGWU, speaking at public meetings in Finglas, Loughshinney and Ballisk. He was not a paid official but spent most of his days in Liberty Hall, working in the kitchen or around the office. Here he met Hanna and Francis Sheehy Skeffington, both of whom he came to admire and who, along with countless others, worked tirelessly to feed the bodies and spirits of the locked-out workers and their families. O'Casey never saw any reason to publicise his work for the ITGWU during the lockout; most of it was routine or mundane work that every other volunteer was happy to do. The fact that he was literate, numerate and trustworthy meant that he spent much of his time in the less glamorous work of correspondence, fundraising and accounting, work that is soon forgotten and rarely acknowledged. He was the joint honorary secretary of the Women and Children's Relief Fund. He must have issued hundreds of receipts and letters during the lockout, but it is unlikely that any have survived as a testament to his work.[59] O'Casey worked long hours, ensuring workers' families had at least one meal every day. His co-secretary was Patrick Lennon, a horse and cart driver and a neighbour in East Wall, who was one of the strikers hospitalised when the police attacked the workers on Bloody Sunday.[60] They travelled all over Dublin, collecting the sizeable sum of around £70 a week for the strike fund.[61] O'Casey's report in the *Irish Worker* gives some idea of the scale of the problems faced by the ITGWU in sustaining the strike:

> 1,335 children of the locked-out workers have been fully dressed with serviceable warm clothing ... In eighty maternity cases the mothers and babies have also been fully dressed ... on average between 2,500 and 3,000 children get breakfast of cocoa and bread, and about 75 women and their babies get dinner daily.[62]

During the strike, O'Casey worked himself into a state of exhaustion. Most likely, Lennon's horse was better fed than O'Casey. His health was broken by months of sacrifice, but his pride would not allow him to accept any help. He refused the offer of a pair of boots and a warm coat from the Liberty Hall store, even when Jim Larkin pressed him to take them. By the end of the strike, he was in a state of collapse and confined to bed. O'Casey only managed to recover through the generosity of his good friends from his time in the IRB and the Laurence O'Toole Club.

PROMETHEUS RETURNS

Following his departure from Ireland in 1914 to the USA, James Larkin became an organiser for the Industrial Workers of the World and the Socialist Party of America. In 1919, at the height of the red scare, Larkin was arrested, charged with 'criminal anarchy', and sentenced to five-to-ten years in prison. Mass meetings and demonstrations took place across the United States, and a 'Larkin Defence Committee' was established to demand his release. O'Casey's old friend from the ITGWU, Jack Carney, and his wife Mina were the leading lights in the campaign in the United States. O'Casey, Barney Conway, Micheál Ó Maoláin and Delia Larkin set up the Release Jim Larkin Committee and the Jim Larkin Correspondence Committee in Ireland. As secretary, O'Casey organised letters of support and petitions for his release. In June 1920, 2,000 dockworkers in Dublin came out on strike for two hours, demanding Larkin's release. In November 1920, O'Casey drafted an appeal on behalf of Larkin. Unfortunately, only the second page of the draft survives:

> … materially, by an improvement in their conditions; morally by a fuller and saner appreciation of their endless importance, and intellectually by the encouragement of all things in art literature and science among the workers of Ireland. Through the lectures held in Liberty Hall, the concerts organised in the same place, the Dramas performed there, the Festivals, Sports and General Summer Entertainments held in the workers' Suburban Recreation Park in Dublin, Jim demonstrated that culture, national enjoyment of leisure hours, refinement of taste and Artistic Desire were not the monopoly of the leisured aristocracy, or the affluent capitalists but were through the natural law of life in the upward tendency of evolution, the inalienable heritage of all men. We, the Irish workers, still struggling for the attainment of these things, anxiously watch for the return of our beloved Leader that he may continue to the end the good work that he has begun in us.[63]

The following year O'Casey designed a Christmas card costing one penny to raise funds for the campaign. He encouraged the buyers to post the card to Larkin, 'who loved you, worked for you, and is now in jail for you'. If the message was a bit sentimental, the drawing by O'Casey on the front of the card was not. He provided a militaristic embellishment to the traditional communist symbol of the hammer and sickle by adding a rifle, with all three symbols entwined as one and coloured green, white and orange.[64] In early November 1921, O'Casey wrote a formal letter to William O'Brien asking for support from the ITGWU for the campaign. O'Casey appealed to labour and republican activists who he said are 'united in the bonds of admiration and affection for the great Irish Labour Leader who fearlessly did so much for Irish Labour and the cause of Irish Freedom'.[65] O'Brien and his friends in Liberty Hall were not in any hurry to welcome back the 'great Irish Leader', and O'Casey's appeal fell on deaf ears. He went to the office on several occasions but failed to meet with O'Brien. However, he put his pride aside and sent a grovelling letter requesting just 'ten minutes' to make his case:

> You will surely remember Sean O'Cathasaigh & he is confident that, on account of past efforts in the Irish Labour Movement, you will readily grant the favour he requests of you. He is willing to suit your own convenience, any hour between the 'rising of the sun & the going down of the same' – or after.[66]

The meeting never took place, and O'Casey and his friends got short shrift from O'Brien, who remembered O'Casey as a troublemaker and a supporter of Larkin agitating on the steps of Liberty Hall. The ITGWU leadership, anticipating trouble when Larkin returned, wanted nothing to do with 'the freak release committee' headed by O'Casey.[67] Nevertheless, he persisted, sending out appeals for support. During the Dáil treaty debates in 1922, O'Casey attempted to lobby the delegates with a request that they issue a statement demanding Larkin's release. A young acquaintance from the SLOT club, on guard duty at the meeting, agreed to send in O'Casey's request to Constance Markievicz, Austin Stack and Tom Hunter, delegates known to be sympathetic to Larkin's cause. But there were far more divisive issues facing the delegates than Larkin's imprisonment, and O'Casey's request received scant attention.[68]

In 1922, O'Casey befriended a young English socialist, R.M. Fox, who later wrote a history of the ICA and a biography of James Larkin. While Fox was in Dublin, he wrote an article calling for Larkin's release from prison. O'Casey knocked the material into shape with substantial additions of his own and had it published in *The Gael* under Fox's name.[69] In the United States, Jack and Mina Carney worked tirelessly for Larkin's release. The victory of Al Smith as governor of New York in 1922 was an indicator that the 'red scare' had abated. Smith pardoned Larkin; on 17 January 1923, Larkin was released, and he returned to Ireland at the end of April. However, the Ireland he returned to had changed dramatically, as had the ITGWU. A special conference in April 1923 was intended to clip Larkin's wings. The general secretary's duties were redefined, and a five-person collective leadership was proposed and endorsed.[70] In June, Larkin launched a scathing attack on the ITGWU leadership, complaining that the old militancy was forgotten and that his achievements in building the union were ignored.

The Russian Revolution had transformed Larkin's political thinking. Influenced by socialists such as John Reed and Joe Hill, Larkin helped establish the American Communist Party.[71] While in prison, he expressed his support for the anti-treaty position in Ireland and the Russian Revolution. After his release and return to Ireland, it was assumed that Larkin would play a leading role in the Communist Party of Ireland (CPI). However, he was dismissive of the CPI and announced that he would not be joining or associated with the party, which may be one of the reasons why O'Casey never joined. The Communist Party strategists in Moscow and Britain believed that a mass party based on the experience and popularity of Larkin was now possible in Ireland. Moscow ordered the CPI to dissolve and instructed its members to join Larkin's new party, the Irish Worker League (IWL). The launch of the IWL took place at a large public meeting in the Mansion House in September 1923, with Jim Larkin and Bob Stewart of the Communist Party of Great Britain as the main speakers. Larkin revived the *Irish Worker* as a weekly paper, both as the voice of the IWL and Larkin's new union, the Workers' Union of Ireland (WUI), which had split from the ITGWU. Larkin received an invitation to represent Ireland at the Fifth World Congress of the Communist International in Moscow in June 1924. He spoke on a number of issues, and at the closing session was elected to the ruling body of the Communist International.[72] The IWL had every chance of success; it was recognised as the Irish section of the Communist International and had the financial and practical support of the Communist Party of Great Britain. Larkin's historical and political stature provided a platform for the IWL to grow into a significant left-wing revolutionary party.

Despite the problems of organising the IWL in the immediate aftermath of the Civil War, 500 members signed up at the inaugural meeting. Over 16,000 members of the ITGWU had defected to Larkin's new union. The republican movement, disorganised and demoralised after its defeat by the Free State forces, looked leftwards to the social and economic struggles to rebuild the movement. Inspired by the writings of Liam Mellows, a new generation of republican leaders such as Peadar O'Donnell,

George Gilmore and Frank Ryan argued for a more radical and political direction if the republican movement was to succeed.[73] There was now a real possibility of uniting the republican and socialist traditions in a radical challenge to the establishment, North and South. However, this was not to be. The immaturity of the movement, combined with personal and sectarian differences, allied to a deep-rooted political intransigence on all sides, meant that the parties ended up going their separate ways. Confusion reigned in the IWL from the beginning. Larkin never made clear what type of party or organisation he envisaged. In the *Irish Worker* in September 1923, he defined the IWL as a 'social rather than a political or economic organisation'.[74] The IWL never really functioned as a political party, but Larkin used the title as the occasion required, either for electoral purposes or as a platform for his pronouncements.

O'Casey was aware of the difficulties surrounding Larkin's attempt to launch the new party and the problems with Larkin's temperament. In *The Star Turns Red* (1940), O'Casey portrays the Larkinite figure 'Red Jim' in a heroic fashion, but he also points to the fatal weakness in his character: his need to dominate every organisation he was part of. In the play, when Red Jim is challenged by the committee to conform to the rules, he replies, 'I'm the Committee; I'm the Union'.[75] According to Lady Gregory, O'Casey said that he avoided contact with Larkin after his return to Dublin, 'Because I love the man and am afraid he would bring me into the movement. And I do not believe that it will succeed on its present lines'.[76] Despite this assertion, O'Casey was in touch with Larkin after he returned to Ireland, as a letter to Lady Gregory in September 1925 makes clear: 'Jim Larkin had a great meeting here on Wednesday night. His men were jubilant, for five boats laden with coal, purchased by the Union, had berthed in the Liffey, and some of the food ships are expected too'.[77]

Shortly after his return to Dublin, Larkin separated from his wife and lived with his sister, Delia, in Gardiner Place. Here, Larkin held court, and almost every evening a succession of workers, the unemployed, and socialists such as Seán O'Casey, Peadar O'Donnell, R.M. Fox or Liam O'Flaherty would discuss the issues of the day.[78] In January 1925, O'Casey typed up an article by the artist William Orpen to give to Larkin, which was an account of Orpen's friendship with Larkin, including some drawings Orpen had made during the 1913 lockout. O'Casey also refers to a dinner with Larkin and a communist organiser in a letter to Lady Gregory.[79] Larkin and O'Casey remained friends but at a distance. There are no known extant letters to Larkin, although they did correspond after O'Casey's departure to England.[80] The fact that Jim Larkin refused to make a public stand in support of the republican forces in 1936 during the civil war in Spain did not seem to affect their relationship. However, their mutual friend Jack Carney resigned his position in Larkin's union over this issue and left for London to work as a journalist.[81] This was just another sad stop on the political journey of Jim Larkin as he drifted away from left-wing politics, ultimately finding a home in the Labour Party that had done so much to bring him down over the previous twenty years.[82]

In a letter to Jack Carney in 1946, O'Casey said that he wrote to Larkin suggesting that he contact Peadar O'Donnell, editor of *The Bell*, who wanted to write a feature piece on Larkin.[83] Throughout the four volumes of O'Casey's letters to his friends and correspondents across the world, his admiration and unwavering support for Larkin stands out. In 1942, he took issue with William O'Brien of the ITGWU, who, in *Plebs*, a Scottish monthly, had denigrated the roles played by both Larkin and O'Casey in the formation of the Irish Citizen Army.[84] Their friendship continued after O'Casey departed for England. While he was in England, Larkin visited O'Casey at his home in Devon, where they talked over old times and the battles they had fought together. In Larkin's last years, all the old energy and enthusiasm had drained away, even if there were occasional flashes of the former street fighter. He was by now a Prometheus whose fire had diminished to little more than the flicker of a candle. O'Casey's eulogy for Larkin in *The Irish Times* in January 1947 was a moving testament to the 'lion of the Labour movement':

> It is hard to believe that this great man is dead, for all thoughts and all activities surged in the soul of this labour leader. He was far and away above the orthodox labour leader, for he combined within himself the imagination of the artist, with the fire and determination of a leader of a downtrodden class.[85]

Despite his sorrow at the passing of Larkin, O'Casey wrote to his old comrade, Jack Carney, complaining about the church funeral for Larkin: 'I don't like that [the presence] of Church and State at Jim's funeral. Imagine S.T. O'Kelly praying for Jim's soul! And the slimey McQuaid. The Church has horned in on the Labour Movement'.[86]

O'Casey's persistent attacks on James Connolly, fuelled by his anger at the way sections of the left and the ITGWU treated Larkin, were unfair and demeaning. O'Casey wrote to the *Irish Democrat* in 1946 replying to a review of *Drums Under the Windows*, where the reviewer had suggested that

O'Casey was not helping the Irish labour movement by extolling Larkin at the expense of Connolly, especially at a time when William O'Brien of the ITGWU was trying to split the movement. O'Casey defended his position by claiming that Larkin 'was the outstanding figure in the Irish Labour Movement, it was he, and he only, who created it'. O'Casey went on to say, 'it was the excessive devotion to Connolly, at the expense of Larkin, that gave O'Brien his chance; a thing I warned the Labour Movement about fifteen years ago'.[87] The following year, in a letter to Jack Carney, he hit out in the most extreme manner at R.M. Fox's book on James Connolly.[88] He lashes Fox, calling him a 'little lowser' for lauding the virtues of Connolly and totally underplaying Larkin's role in the 1913 lockout and the ICA. O'Casey's anger at Fox and his misrepresentation of Larkin spilt over into an unjustified attack on Connolly:

> Connolly had that weakness – he passionately wanted fame, & did everything he consistently could to achieve it – the parading of the ICA; the natty green uniform he had made specially for himself; the hoisting of the 'Green Flag' over Liberty Hall; the companionship of the Countess; the writing of a play ... and all the rest of it, photographed & ready for such serving shits as Fox. And as for military skill – well, Connolly showed how little he had of it.[89]

This was a private letter where O'Casey expressed his anger and frustration at the treatment of Larkin in a way that he would never have done publicly. Despite these outbursts, O'Casey admired Connolly; that much is clear from any examination of his writings from 1913 up to the time of his death in 1964. A letter from 1945 to a comrade in America is one of the many instances where O'Casey praised him: 'Connolly was a great fellow, too, dogged, true and incorruptible.'[90] However, O'Casey never forgave Connolly 'for mixing the struggle for national liberation with the struggle of the working class'.[91] He also disliked the way Connolly was honoured in Ireland at the expense of Larkin. O'Casey rarely forgave those who slighted him or offended those he admired. He was right to defend Larkin's status in Irish politics and history. However, it was not necessary to denigrate Connolly in order to do so. The Connolly that the Irish Free State and the labour movement had elevated to the status of political sainthood had little to do with the reality of what Connolly stood for. O'Casey could have stood by Connolly, linking his name with that of Larkin in the fight against capitalist exploitation and exposing the sham politics of William O'Brien and his friends in the Labour Party who claimed to speak in Connolly's name. Connolly was safely dead and could not reply, but Larkin was a living reminder of what might have been and therefore was denounced by the bureaucrats and the reformists and reduced to the second rate.

POLITICS AS DRAMA

As the 1913 strike came to its bitter conclusion, O'Casey was now a marked man due to his active support for Larkin and the ITGWU and was unlikely to find work again. Writing had become a necessity as much as a pleasure if he was to earn a living. His love of drama found expression in his sketches and recitals performed by the Gaelic League and the St Laurence O'Toole Club. Building on this experience, he submitted five plays between 1916 and 1922 to the Abbey Theatre in Dublin; none were accepted, but the rejection slips were encouraging.

One such play was *The Harvest Festival* (1919), a reflection in a literary and heroic form on the events during the labour unrest of 1911–13. The play deals with the efforts of the more militant members of the unskilled unions to put some backbone into the trade union movement in its fight for better pay and conditions. The action takes place during the preparations for the annual religious celebration of the harvest festival, which allows O'Casey to make the point that 'thanking God for nature's bounty at a time of widespread starvation is hollow and hypocritical'.[92] O'Casey also cuts against the stereotypes of working-class Catholics and upper-class Protestants. Jack Rocliffe,[93] a labourer and strike leader, is a Protestant, a characterisation used in many of O'Casey's later plays to emphasise the fact that class is more important than religion. He sent the play to the Abbey Theatre, but they returned the script as unsuitable for production, and it remained unpublished until 1979. However, O'Casey never gave up on *The Harvest Festival*, and he re-used the concept in 1942 as the basis for *Red Roses for Me*. In 1925 O'Casey contemplated writing a play called *The Scab* based on these events. In a letter to a Russian comrade, he revealed that he intended to write several plays 'dealing with the activities of Labour, for instance I am thinking of one to be called "The Scab", a term used by workers for one who takes the place of a man (or a woman) who is on strike'.[94] He utilised this concept in the script for *Red Roses for Me.* In the last act, the crowd flings stones at two 'scabs' running down the road. The crowd are marching behind a red flag and singing:

> If we can't fire a gun, we can fire a hard stone,
> Till th' life of a scab shrivels into a moan.[95]

Red Roses for Me was perhaps his most autobiographical play, where he reflects on those great days in 1913, when 'the workers, were on the march! [and] the eloquent roaring voice of the great Jim Larkin became the trumpet of the Irish workers'.[96] Ayamonn Breydon, a railway worker, is an idealised version of the younger O'Casey, and Mrs Breydon is a loving tribute to his mother, Susan. He outlines the alternatives inherent in Irish history that could be recognised and developed in contemporary conditions. O'Casey takes the religious festival and symbolism of Easter and transforms it into an earthly vision of sacrifice and hope for the future.

O'Casey paints a 'vision of a city, of Dublin as it existed in the life of the people ... in its despair and in its moment of glory, its deep tragedy and the permanence of its heroic endeavour'.[97] O'Casey's play shares the same festive spirit of a great city coming alive in a new millennium with Bertolt Brecht's *The Days of the Commune*.[98] Both writers paint a picture of a new age of learning and a bright future for humankind. Both plays are based on historical facts revealing the process of history through the struggle of the masses. *Red Roses for Me* is a portrait of the artist as a young socialist. The play strikes a more collective note than is usual in O'Casey's work. Typically, his protagonists are tragic figures who reveal rather than overthrow the laws of society. However, Ayamonn is not shown explicitly as a communist; he represents O'Casey's understanding of the communist ideal that is every bit as heroic as that of the Communards in Brecht's play. Ayamonn represents the reality and aspirations of a working-class person hoping for a better life for himself and his class. O'Casey sets forth a vision of people changing under the impact of tragic events, in the course of which his characters have to confront the realities of capitalist society. Ayamonn is also the personification of the anonymous 'mob' who make their own history and refuse to have their destinies determined by events happening elsewhere. Ayamonn is killed during the strike by the police, and the police inspector considers him a fool for sacrificing his life for a paltry shilling pay rise:

> INSPECTOR: It wasn't a very noble thing to die for a single shilling.
> SHEILA: Maybe he saw the shilling in the shape of a new world.[99]

John Brannigan has suggested that O'Casey in *Red Roses for Me* was painting a picture of a new world 'glimpsed in the struggle for better pay or working conditions [which] is both a political and aesthetic experience'.[100] At the heart of O'Casey's writing at this period is his concern over the relationship between aesthetics and politics and how workers acquire consciousness or intellectual capital that will allow them to confront and overturn the conditions that oppress them.

CHAPTER 5

The Road to 1916

In April 1912, Lloyd George's home rule bill was put before parliament. Despite the setback created by the defeat of the bill in the House of Lords, it began its torturous three-year cycle through the British parliamentary system, at the end of which it would become law. Fatally, at least for Ireland, Bonar Law and Churchill chose to play the 'Orange card'.[1] The Ulster unionists declared their total opposition, symbolised by the launch of a Solemn League and Covenant signed by 400,000 unionists to resist home rule by any means necessary. The Ulster Volunteer Force, a unionist militia, was founded in late 1912 and organised and armed on military lines. The developments in Ulster had not gone unnoticed by nationalists in the south, and many felt that the time was right to train and equip in a similar manner. An article, 'The North Began', in *An Claidheamh Soluis* in November 1913, by the politically moderate Professor Eoin MacNeill, suggesting such an organisation took everyone by surprise.[2] MacNeill organised the launch of the Irish Volunteers at a mass rally at the Rotunda ring in Dublin at the end of November. The rally was a great success, despite the failure to invite Jim Larkin or representatives of the ITGWU onto the platform. Members of the ITGWU, armed with hurley sticks, demanded that Larkin be allowed to speak, resulting in 'an unpleasant scene' that was instigated by an organised crowd from Liberty Hall.[3] In the forefront of that 'unpleasant scene' was Seán O'Casey. Despite the tumult, up to 3,000 recruits enrolled on the night, and within six months the Irish Volunteers numbered 75,000. The IRB saw the possibilities of realising the Fenian ideals of 1867, but this time with substantial forces at their command.

The outbreak of the First World War on 4 August 1914 engulfed Britain in a crisis that dwarfed its problems in Ireland. Prime Minister Asquith shelved the problem by putting the home rule bill on the statute books but postponed its implementation until after the war ended. The unionist leader, Edward Carson, promised unionist support for the war effort. Following Carson's example, John Redmond pledged Ireland's support and suggested that the defence of Ireland should be entrusted to the Irish and Ulster Volunteers. His impromptu speech, on 20 September in

County Wexford, offering the Irish Volunteers for service in France caused a crisis within the Volunteers.[4] As a result, the organisation split into two factions. The majority, about 140,000 strong, stayed with Redmond and was renamed the National Volunteers, their sole function being to supply a stream of recruits for the war in Europe. The minority, about 12,000, comprising the most militant and republican sections, split off to form a new organisation while retaining the name of the Irish Volunteers. In the aftermath of the split, the IRB held five of the eight positions on the executive committee of the Irish Volunteers. In effect, they now controlled the movement, although the more conservative elements in the leadership of the Irish Volunteers still commanded considerable support. Both factions in the Irish Volunteers hoped to profit from the war on the continent. The IRB faction of Clarke, Pearse and MacDonagh was determined to organise a rebellion while Britain was otherwise occupied. The MacNeill and Hobson group wanted to build up the Volunteers into an effective army that would then be in a position to demand Irish independence. Both sides believed the war with Germany would be over within the year. In the meantime, they were prepared to fight if the British tried to suppress the Volunteers or introduce conscription in Ireland.

Despite these developments, O'Casey underestimated the change in the political situation following the defeat in the lockout and the outbreak of the war. He understood that 'there is, in Ireland, the murmur of men marching',[5] but he had little concept of how to connect the socialist and labour movement with the anti-war and anti-conscription feeling that was being exploited by the nationalists. O'Casey had not taken into consideration how the mood of the country had turned against the home rule bill, especially among the young militant members of the Volunteers. Redmond's acceptance of partition, the shelving of the home rule bill and his support for the Allied war effort had weakened his political base. Nationalist sentiment in Ireland was moving towards the more radical separatist elements in the country; the question for socialists was how to respond to this shift. As far as O'Casey was concerned, the political options amounted to a choice between the syndicalist policies of James Larkin or the narrow nationalist politics of Arthur Griffith and his supporters in the Employers' Federation. O'Casey believed that the labour movement had departed from Larkin's class-based politics, and, under Connolly's leadership, Liberty Hall was 'no longer the headquarters of the Irish Labour movement but the centre of Irish national disaffection'.[6] He disagreed with Connolly because he believed the relationship between the Irish Citizen

Army and the Irish Volunteers had changed from one of opposition to one of active unity and co-operation. The war in Europe was one of the decisive factors that pushed Connolly and the nationalists into an armed conflict with the British state. In doing so, Connolly hoped to win a place for the working class in the emerging struggle for Irish independence.

A CITIZEN ARMY

The attack by the police on striking workers on 'Bloody Sunday', 31 August 1913, convinced both Larkin and Connolly that workers needed an organisation of their own to protect the picket lines and union meetings from assault by the police and the hired thugs of the employers. On the eve of the lockout, Larkin's declaration that workers had the right to arm may have been rhetorical, but it was understandable that once planted, the concept would take root. Shortly after, at a rally to welcome Larkin home after his release from jail, James Connolly told the assembled crowd that they were in a 'state of war' and 'The next time we go out for a march, I want to be accompanied by four battalions of our own men. I want them to have their own corporals and sergeants and men who will be able to form fours'.[7] In *The Story of the Irish Citizen Army* (1919), O'Casey attributes this speech, or at least a version of it, to Jim Larkin rather than Connolly.[8] However, Larkin could not have made the speech as he was too ill to attend the rally. Within a fortnight, the world's first 'Red Army' was mobilised. Over 1,000 enrolled, and drilling commenced under the command of Captain James White in Croydon Park. The difference between those who joined and the numbers who turned up for training was substantial. In truth, the Irish Citizen Army (ICA) was not exactly a 'Red Army'; perhaps a 'Red Guard' is a more apt description.[9] The ICA were not central to the dispute, even if it made the police more circumspect about attacking the workers. O'Casey had initially looked to the Irish Republican Brotherhood to supply a force that could defend workers during the lockout. In the pages of the *Irish Worker*, he urged the newly formed Irish Volunteers to give their support and protect their meetings and pickets. O'Casey hoped to unite the red and green in the fight for a new Ireland based on the principles of Tone, Mitchel and Lalor with a colouration of the socialist ideals of Larkin, Shaw and Connolly. However, the leadership of the Volunteers feared that support for the strike would cause divisions in the movement; others, who were employers themselves, were openly hostile to the ITGWU. O'Casey's attempt to fuse the political teaching of Wolfe Tone with the socialist politics of James Larkin had reached breaking point, and sometime in late 1913 or early 1914 he severed his links with the IRB and 'took several others with him'.[10]

In late January 1914, as the strike petered out, it seemed to a number of activists that the ICA had ceased to be relevant. In the changed circumstances, several workers transferred their support from the ICA to the Irish Volunteers. The active membership had fallen to about fifty. Whether Larkin prompted him, or it was on his own initiative, O'Casey published 'An Open Letter to the Workers in the Volunteers' in the *Irish Worker*, appealing for them to remain within the ranks of the ICA:

> Many of you have been tempted to join this much talked about movement [Irish Volunteers] ... You have momentarily forgotten that there can be no interests outside of those identified with your own class ... and yield allegiance to no movement that does not avow the ultimate destiny of the workers.[11]

James MacGowan, a member of the ITGWU and the Volunteers, replied, and over the following six weeks they exchanged views in a series of letters. O'Casey appealed to the workers of Ireland to stand by the ICA and not to be taken in by the 'chattering well-fed aristocrats' who run the Volunteers and not to 'drill or train for anything less than complete enfranchisement' and for 'the utter alteration of the present social system'.[12] MacGowan's reply mirrors in some respects the position that O'Casey himself had held and articulated in his dispute with Euchan just twelve months earlier. MacGowan suggested that the:

> Volunteer movement provides a common meeting ground for the best and most progressive elements in Irish life. It is a movement that will enable different sections to come to a better understanding with each other ... the fact that men like Pearse, Macken, and honest Tom Kelly are identified with the organisation is sufficient guarantee that the workers will not be trampled on.[13]

O'Casey's reply contains a clear statement of his political thinking at the time and the embryo of his ensuing disagreement with Connolly over the latter's support for the nationalists during the 1916 Rising:

> Personally, I hold the workers are beside themselves with foolishness to support any movement that does not stand to make the workers

> supreme, for these are the people, and without them there can be no life nor power. The time is passing, and soon all workers shall realise that it is good to die for one's friend, but foolish to die for one's enemy.[14]

'Honest Tom Kelly' got short shrift from O'Casey, who pointed out that Kelly held a high position in Sinn Féin during the lockout while their paper 'slashed unmercifully at the workers'. His anger at Patrick Pearse was palpable: 'Pearse is worse than all. When the workers of Dublin were waging a life and death struggle to preserve some of the "liberties" which ought to be common to all Irishmen, this leader of democratic opinion consistently used the trams on every occasion'.[15] Whether Pearse ever used the trams on any occasion during the lockout is unclear. However, O'Casey was mistaken in the way he accused Pearse of not supporting the striking workers. Pearse, as has been well documented, was supportive both in public and in private of the locked-out workers, which O'Casey acknowledged many years later. In his reply MacGowan made one last attempt to refute O'Casey's position:

> National Freedom is essential to the social and intellectual emancipation of our people ... In other words, the interests of the country overshadow the interests of any section or class ... The evils of capitalism were unknown in free Gaelic Ireland, but they shall remain to blight our country, and her people until the day when a revivified Ireland shall rise from the ashes of the past glorious, immortal and free.[16]

A politically resurgent O'Casey had no problems swatting aside such arguments; an appeal to a glorious Gaelic past cut no ice with him. The lockout had hardened him both politically and personally, and the idea of Cú Chulainn or Ferdia galloping to the rescue of the poverty-stricken workers of Ireland held little appeal. In O'Casey's mind, the 'Rights of Man' had supplanted, or at least deserved an equal place with, the 'Rights of Ireland'. O'Casey ended his response with a rhetorical, if convoluted, flourish that dismissed the nationalists and illustrated just how far he had strayed from the nationalist camp since the beginning of the lockout:

> Who were they that caused the Castle Authorities to imagine that they saw recently in the streets of Dublin the Birth of a Revolution? Who were they who were charged with sedition and conspiracy to

> disturb the Peace of His Majesty's subject? Were they the leaders of the Volunteers? Dublin Castle again sleeps in peace. The revolution was stillborn.[17]

The working class had arrived on the stage of history, and, as far as O'Casey was concerned, they were there to stay. The lockout had forced him to rethink his political philosophy, and the events in Russia in 1917 reinforced his political faith in the ability of and the necessity for workers to carve out their own future.

The decimation of the ITGWU during the lockout took its toll on the union and its leaders. The political ground had shifted; the outbreak of the war in August 1914 ended the strike wave in Britain. In Ireland, workers had little fight left in them and for the next period rebuilding the ITGWU was the main priority of the union. Larkin was physically and mentally exhausted; the terrible defeat had left him in the position of a working-class general without an army. Never a man to stand still, and drawing on his last reserves of strength, he threw himself into rebuilding the ICA. Syndicalism and republicanism were at the core of Larkin's politics. However, given the dearth of working-class militancy, his republican politics came to the fore. The labour movement issued *A Manifesto to the Workers of Ireland* protesting about the proposed exclusion of the North in the home rule bill. Larkin claimed that 'if it is lawful for Carson to arm, it is lawful for us – the workers – to arm', and he called on the workers of Ireland to protest at 'The suggested amputation of Ireland's right hand, the exclusion of Ulster and the criminal and traitorous conduct of a class-conscious group masquerading as Army Officers, who have set themselves up as a military Junta evidently determined to thwart the will of the people'.[18] By this time, the ICA was in bad shape. The penalty of dismissal, which the employers held over the heads of workers associated with the ITGWU, frightened hundreds into abandoning their connection with the ICA. Most likely, it was Larkin who asked O'Casey to take the re-organisation of the ICA in hand. At O'Casey's suggestion, a constitution was drafted and submitted to a general meeting for approval. He recommended that recruitment and drilling should recommence, and a fund instituted to raise money for equipment. Uniforms were purchased to infuse the recruits with a sense of dignity, and tents were acquired so that training camps could take place in Croydon Park.

At a meeting on 22 March 1914, O'Casey read out his proposal for a new ICA constitution. He records that it was discussed 'clause by clause, and unanimously accepted by the vote of all those present'. What is significant is the absence of class politics in the constitution put forward by O'Casey:

- That the first and last principle of the Irish Citizen Army is the avowal that the ownership of Ireland, moral and material, is vested of right in the people of Ireland.
- That the Irish Citizen Army shall stand for the absolute unity of Irish nationhood, and shall support the rights and liberties of the democracies of all other nations.
- That one of its objects shall be to sink all differences of birth, property and creed under the common name of the Irish people.
- That the Citizen Army shall be open to all who accept the principle of equal rights and opportunities for the Irish people.

The first clause draws on the position of James Fintan Lalor from 1848. Lalor maintained that if independence meant anything, it was necessary to undo the economic and social aspects of the conquest and that the land should be vested in the people.[19] Clause two of O'Casey's original draft was amended to include the following: 'to arm and train all Irishmen capable of bearing arms to defend and enforce its first principle'.[20] A fifth clause, added at Larkin's suggestion, at least nods towards the working-class ethos of the ICA:

- Every enrolled member must be, if possible, a member of a Trades Union recognised by the Irish Trades Union Congress.[21]

The original draft, which O'Casey put to the meeting, hardly represents the views of the man who had polemicised so vehemently against James MacGowan a few weeks earlier. Not once is the working class mentioned; instead, vague generalities about the 'people of Ireland' and 'Irish nationhood' that would not be out of place in the constitution of the most conservative nationalist organisation dominate the document. If the constitution as adopted by the meeting represented O'Casey's political convictions, he could hardly have had any problems with the political direction in which Connolly took the ICA from 1915 onwards, nor with Constance Markievicz's dual membership of the ICA and the Volunteers.

O'Casey claimed that he drafted a few sentences that could 'easily fit into the simplest mind as no sentences in a catechism could': the words of Fintan Lalor and John Mitchel at prayer, and 'here was O'Casside to say amen'.[22] The style is all O'Casey, but whether the content is his or that of the organising committee is another matter. However, the draft constitution, even as amended, failed to reflect the political differences between the ICA and the Irish Volunteers. The difference between the constitution and a handbill issued by O'Casey on behalf of the ICA a short time later is startling. Under 'Reasons Why the Workers Should Join the Irish Citizen Army', it lists the following:

- Because it is controlled by Leaders of your own class.
- Because it stands for Labour and the principles of Wolfe Tone, John Mitchel, and Fintan Lalor.
- Because it has the sympathy and support of the Dublin Trades Council.
- Because it refuses to allow in its ranks those who have proved untrue to Labour.[23]

This handbill reiterates almost word for word O'Casey's position as outlined in his articles in the *Irish Worker*, defending the independence of the ICA and its role as the defender of working-class interests. On the other hand, a recruiting poster for the ICA, which was designed and issued by O'Casey, highlights the ICA's efforts to unite the red and the green in a fight for an Irish Co-operative Commonwealth and reflects the political contradictions that would lead to O'Casey's break with the ICA:

> This organisation embraces the full principles of Republican Democracy; its aim is to sink the differences of Birth, Privilege and Creed under the common name of the Irish People. It stands for a Union of Progressive Nationalism with the Democratic forces of Ireland, and its policy is to achieve that for which Theobald Wolfe Tone died and John Mitchel suffered – AN INDEPENDENT IRELAND. Irishmen! Join the Citizen Army NOW and help us build up an Irish Co-operative Commonwealth.[24]

Whether this reflected O'Casey's views, those of Connolly, or the collective views of the leadership, it is impossible to say. In his articles for the *Irish Worker* and his political work for the ICA, O'Casey wrestles with the problem, but he cannot find a way of resolving it. By the end of 1914, he believed the ICA had to choose between the red and the green.

Despite his bad health, O'Casey was in the thick of it, issuing manifestoes, writing to labour movement organisations around the country, and organising public meetings to recruit for the ICA. He recounts how on several occasions, with a few other committee members, he was out until 3 or 4 a.m. sticking up posters for an event to raise money for uniforms. He travelled all over the greater Dublin area and beyond – Lucan, Clondalkin, Coolock, Kinsealy, Kingstown and Bray – speaking on public platforms in an attempt to set up new battalions. Difficulties with the Volunteers made it difficult to build or recruit outside the city centre. The ICA remained essentially a Dublin-based organisation, unable to challenge the hegemony of the Irish Volunteers in the rest of the country. Starting with the issue of 4 April 1914, O'Casey began a regular column in the *Irish Worker* under the title 'By the Camp Fire', which reported news about the ICA. Here, he reports on a meeting in Finglas to form a new company of the ICA: 'Sean O Cathasaigh [O'Casey] spoke and those present declared themselves in accord with the advice given to join no movement that had not the full confidence of the Leaders of Irish Organised Labour'.[25]

The ICA ordered fifty uniforms of dark green serge from Arnotts outfitters. The battalion looked smart and military; the new uniform was topped off with the famous slouch hat, worn in the same style as the South African Boers, with one side pinned up with the union red hand badge engraved with the initials ICA. The first consignment of uniforms engendered a sense of pride among the citizen soldiers. Parading in their new uniforms demonstrated that they were, in fact, a real army that could stand comparison with the Volunteers at the Bodenstown parade or on any other public occasion. There was real pressure to kit out the rest of the army, as a report by O'Casey of an ICA meeting in Kingstown (Dún Laoghaire) reveals: 'A strong desire exists for a number of uniforms as soon as possible. Some of the men have already paid off same. Think this would aid in getting recruits'.[26] His detractors have advanced the existence of this report, co-signed by Lieutenant J. Byrne and Seán O'Casey, as further evidence of the unreliability of O'Casey's version of events surrounding the founding of the ICA and the political and tactical differences within the organisation.[27] However, it is clear from the report that O'Casey and Byrne were merely reporting the opinions of the men in Kingstown rather than their own personal views. Despite the Kingstown report, O'Casey disagreed with the concept of the ICA as a regular uniformed army. Whatever about uniforms for parades or commemorative marches, he had little faith in the British army respecting their rights under the Hague Convention in the event of a war against the British. He believed that in British eyes, the ICA would be 'no more than decorated rebels',[28] and would be dealt with as such. O'Casey argued that in urban warfare, a rebel in uniform would instantly reveal themselves as a target; better to be in civilian clothes, to use hit-and-run tactics and fade into the crowd or the countryside after an ambush. Many years later, he reflected on the hit-and-run tactics employed by Thomas Ashe at Ashbourne during the 1916 Rising, quoting Bernard Shaw, who compared Ireland's fight with England 'as a perambulator up against a Pickford van'.[29]

The resurgence of the ICA coincided with an upturn in the political situation. Opposition to the war in Europe was growing, especially with the threat of conscription in Ireland. The IRB was preparing to strike against the old enemy, a hint of rebellion was in the air, and Connolly, in the pages of the *Workers' Republic*, fanned the flames of revolt. In a series of articles beginning in May 1915, Connolly set out the basis for a 'people's warfare', based on the experience of the revolutionary upheavals over the previous fifty years. He wanted to develop a strategy for urban warfare suitable for the ICA's limited forces. The Irish Volunteers were also refining their tactics; Bulmer Hobson argued that given their numbers, they could not hope to put a conventional army in the field. He suggested that guerrilla warfare was 'the only method by which resistance could be maintained over any length of time or with any prospect of success'.[30] Hobson and O'Casey shared the same position regarding military tactics. Thirty years later, O'Casey wrote, 'Sean knew that Connolly's men would fight, and the Irish volunteers would stand by them; but he knew in his soul that they were going the wrong way about it'.[31] According to O'Casey, he wrote an article on guerrilla tactics for *The Volunteer*, but it was not published. He also wrote to both Pearse and Connolly suggesting a debate on military strategy, but they never replied. He claims that he argued against concentrating their forces in static positions and pointed to the example of the Boers' use of mobile forces and the hit-and-run tactics that were so effective.[32]

O'CASEY RESIGNS FROM THE ICA

Captain White and Constance Markievicz tried to smooth the strained relationship between the ICA and the Volunteers. White was ambitious for the ICA to play a more prominent role in Irish politics and was dissatisfied with the limited growth and ambitions of the organisation.[33] In May 1914, he resigned as chairman, and Jim Larkin was elected to take his place. White's resignation indicated the tensions within the ICA between those who believed it should be a 'Red Guard' to defend the labour movement and the republican current who wanted the ICA to play a part in the broader nationalist movement.

In 1915, the ITGWU published Connolly's pamphlet *The Re-Conquest of Ireland*. Here, Connolly laid out the path that would lead to the executioner's yard in Kilmainham Gaol just over a year later. Given the crisis thrown up by the war in Europe, Connolly wanted to unite the ICA and the nationalist movement in a revolutionary fight against the British presence in Ireland while maintaining the political independence of the ICA within the broader movement. A few weeks before the 1916 Rising, in an article in the *Workers' Republic*, he stated: 'The Irish working class ... [is] the only secure foundation upon which a free nation can be reared'.[34] This was a difficult position for Connolly to sustain. The danger of liquidating the labour movement into the broader nationalist camp was always present, or of making political concessions that marginalised the labour programme in the name of unity. That, in essence, was the source of their political differences and why O'Casey was so critical of Connolly in the years to come. He believed Connolly had lowered the red flag in favour of the green and that 'Labour had laid its precious gift of Independence on the altar of Irish Nationalism'.[35] Like so many of the personal and political ruptures in O'Casey's life, his break with the ICA was sudden and final.

Constance Gore-Booth (1868–1927) came from a Protestant ascendancy family and grew up in Lissadell, the family estate in County Sligo.[36] The family were artistic, liberal and tolerant. Constance was influenced by the political and literary ideals of W.B. Yeats, who was a frequent visitor to the Lissadell estate. She moved to Paris, where she met Count Casimir Markievicz of Poland, and they married in 1900. On her return to Ireland, Countess Markievicz joined Sinn Féin and Inghinidhe na hÉireann (Daughters of Ireland), a revolutionary women's movement founded by Maud Gonne. She was also a member of the Volunteers and the ICA. For whatever reason, O'Casey and the countess intensely disliked each other. During the lockout, O'Casey claimed that he had 'never seen the Countess do anything anyone could call a spot of work', but that if a reporter strayed into Liberty Hall, the countess was behind the counter ladling out soup in her spotless bib.[37] Over twenty-five years later, in *The Star Turns Red*, he settled an old score in a cutting remark that probably refers to Markievicz: 'I can never understand why some workers are ready to fall on their knees the minute a well-dressed cow flits in front of them'.[38] Despite this, O'Casey admitted that the one thing she had in abundance was physical courage:

'with that she was clothed as with a garment'.[39] Regardless of O'Casey's personal experience of working with Markievicz during the lockout, his visceral dislike of madam was certainly political. He believed that she 'whirled into a meeting and then whirled out again, a spluttering Catherine-wheel of irresponsibility' and that 'no part of her melted into the cause of Ireland, nor did she ever set foot on the threshold of Socialism'.[40] O'Casey was not alone in believing that she was a Trojan horse or spy for the Volunteers. Mick Mullen, an associate of O'Casey on the council, accused her of being 'a spy and an informer' and offered to provide evidence against her.[41]

Tensions increased between the ICA and the Volunteers as 'day by day it became evident that in aim and objects the two forces were marching towards opposite poles'.[42] In these changed circumstances, and taking his lead from Larkin, O'Casey called a special council meeting in late August 1914 to discuss whether members of the ICA council should also be allowed to hold membership of the Irish Volunteers. O'Casey had deliberately aimed this thrust at Countess Markievicz. He disliked her upper-class manner, but his motion to effectively expel her from the ICA was political. Markievicz was a member of Cumann na mBan, the women's section of the Volunteers, and the joint treasurer of the ICA. O'Casey demanded that she choose between the two organisations, and it would appear that he assumed he had the support of Larkin for his motion, although Larkin was not present at the meeting. After a heated discussion, a vote of confidence in the countess was proposed by those opposed to O'Casey's motion, which was carried by seven votes to six. The meeting then supported a proposal that the secretary should tender an apology to Countess Markievicz; O'Casey said he could not apologise for saying what he believed to be the truth and tendered his resignation. His political naivety was evident in this situation, for he was not without significant support for his position. O'Casey lost the argument because he lacked the tactical and personal skills to mobilise his support. If O'Casey had argued his case and built his support among members of the council who were sympathetic to his position, or if he had amended it to secure Larkin's support, it certainly would have been passed. O'Casey naively abstained in the vote of confidence, while Markievicz voted for the motion, ensuring it passed by a single vote. A few days later, in an attempt to defuse the situation, Larkin called a general meeting of the ICA to discuss the question. He appealed to O'Casey to withdraw anything he had said and 'allow everything in the army to proceed smoothly without friction or unnecessary contention'.[43] O'Casey refused to do so, and the meeting accepted his resignation. As so often with O'Casey, he found himself in a political straitjacket of his own making. He constantly elevated tactical questions into matters of principle and would seldom take a pragmatic or tactical position. Instead, he rushed headlong into one dispute after another in a way that damaged his own position and alienated his political friends.

A WRITER AT LAST

Maunsel & Co. published O'Casey's seventy-two-page booklet *The Story of the Irish Citizen Army* in 1919. O'Casey was very modest in his claims for the book; he hoped that the materials gathered together and 'recorded during the organising period of the Army' would be of use for 'incorporation into whatever history may be subsequently written', and that it was 'a simple and concise narration of the facts as they occurred'.[44] However, as Robert Hogan points out, the book, 'like all of O'Casey's work is saturated with opinion'.[45] The book lacked balance in that nine of the eleven chapters deal with the founding of the ICA, its role in the lockout, and the ICA's difficulties with the National Volunteers. The rapprochement with the Volunteers under Connolly's leadership, the role of the ICA in the 1916 Rising, and its subsequent history received scant attention. There were two reasons for this. Firstly, O'Casey was centrally involved in the launch of the ICA and its subsequent reorganisation in March 1914. He was familiar with this period and, as the former secretary, had various letters and documents in his possession up to the time of his resignation in October 1914. The other reason was the British authorities' censorship, particularly in the last two chapters, which dealt with the post-1916 situation. The manuscript was scored in red, green and blue pencil as it was passed from bureaucrat to bureaucrat until the British authorities were satisfied that nothing in the book would reflect badly on the administration. O'Casey virtually disowned the book, claiming that it was not the book he had written because of the extreme level of censorship. In a letter to Ronald Ayling in 1963, O'Casey explained that his book was not intended to be an 'official' history of the ICA, but part of a series of popular 'stories' that he planned to write for his publisher, Fergus O'Connor. He had already published *The Story of Thomas Ashe* in 1917, and O'Casey proposed to continue the series with the 'stories' of Wolfe Tone, John Mitchel and so on.

O'Casey's little book had few pretensions either as history or theory; it was a polemic which attempted to reinstate the centrality of class into the ongoing debates after the 1916 Rising. His core argument was that nationalism gained and labour lost as a result of the ICA's participation in the rising. Despite the problems with the book, and there are many, O'Casey was practically a lone voice in trying to analyse the dynamic of Irish history from a working-class perspective, which saw the revolutionary potential of the 1913 period subsumed into the nationalist struggle for independence. He set out his position in the opening pages of the *Citizen Army* book: 'The people of Ireland were not ripe enough to be shaken from the green tree of Nationalism into the wide basket of an Irish Labour Army'.[46] In the period immediately after 1916, nationalist interpretations dominated the political debate. Bulmer Hobson's *History of the Irish Volunteers*,[47] published a year earlier, does not contain a single reference to the ICA or the significance of the lockout in Irish politics. Éamon de Valera is famously supposed to have suggested in 1918 that 'Labour must wait' in order to give Sinn Féin a free run in the upcoming Westminster election. Whether he used that exact phrase is not the point – but that is what Sinn Féin demanded and got. In his polemics and pamphlets, O'Casey was trying to come to terms with the new political landscape that had emerged. W.P. Ryan, in his history of *The Irish Labour Movement*, also published in 1919, was the only other writer at that time who dared dispute this orthodoxy.[48] It took until 1936 when in his book *Easter Week* the socialist and republican Brian O'Neill put in perspective the social parameters of the period that led up to that eventful week.[49] The ICA was not impressed by O'Casey's book, and at a council meeting they decided not to sell or distribute it. A subsequent council meeting described the book as 'inaccurate in many points' and 'not a true history'.[50] In the *Irish Statesman*, Eimar O'Duffy wrote disapprovingly but insightfully that:

> The actions and attitudes of the national movement are judged, or misjudged, entirely in reference to their bearing on the labouring section of the nation. And the worth of each and every prominent Nationalist is estimated from his attitude towards the social and economic views of Mr O Cathasaigh.[51]

The ICA had 340 active members leading up to the 1916 Rising, and about 220 mustered for action on Easter Monday. James Connolly and Michael Mallin were executed after the surrender, and eleven ICA members were killed in action.[52] The ICA fought in the War of Independence and on the republican side in the Civil War. They struggled on until 1935 before dissolving to form the nucleus of the left wing of the Labour Party. The historical significance of the ICA, its 'heroic period', occurred between 1913 and 1916, and there were considerable changes, both tactical and strategic, in the composition and strategy of the ICA in that period. Only five of the original twenty-four members of the Army Council mobilised on Easter Monday 1916, and the two senior commandants, Connolly and Mallin, had not been on the earlier body.[53] This shift, both in strategy and its leading personnel, lends credibility to O'Casey's critique of the ICA. Frank Robbins, who was close to Connolly politically, wrote about the problems in the ICA in 1919. He described how many of the old working-class members had resigned, and the newer recruits had little or no loyalty to the union.[54] His book lends credence to the problems in the ICA that O'Casey had highlighted.

CHAPTER 6

The 1916 Rising

The year 1914 was perhaps the most troublesome one of O'Casey's life. Defeat piled upon defeat, as the workers of Dublin were starved into submission by the employers. O'Casey's resignation from the ICA had left him politically isolated. In July, the partition of Ireland became a virtual certainty when the leaders of the Home Rule Party entered negotiations with the unionists; in August, the opening shots of the First World War led to the collapse of the Socialist International. Within days, with a few honourable exceptions, the leaders of the Socialist International marched behind their respective governments in a rush to war. In Ireland, the Independent Labour Party was split over their attitude to the war. The Belfast branch supported the British war effort and suspended all activities for the duration of the war; however, James Connolly, one of the few socialists in Europe who held firm to his beliefs, wrote: 'To me, the socialist of another country is a fellow patriot as the capitalist of my own is a natural enemy'.[1]

In January 1916, the *Workers' Republic* published one of O'Casey's best-known ballads, 'The Grand Oul' Dame Britannia', which he wrote in response to the proposal to introduce conscription in England. Ireland was exempted, at least for the time being, but the threat was always there:

> John Redmond to the throne is bowed
> 'Mid a frantic cheering crowd –
> Sure it's like the days of Shane the Proud
> Ses the Grand Oul' Dame Britannia.[2]

O'Casey published it under his old pen-name, An Gall Fada, from his Gaelic League days. Given his rift with the ICA and the ITGWU, it was unlikely they would have published the song under his own name. When he asked Seamus Hughes, who worked in Liberty Hall, to set another of his ballads, 'The Call of the Tribe', to music, Hughes returned it a week later, saying he had orders from the top not to have anything to do with O'Casey. Larkin's departure for America and his resignation from the ICA meant that O'Casey was no longer welcome in Liberty Hall. He was a well-known and indeed prominent member of the 'steps committee', a group of disgruntled members who hung around the front door of Liberty Hall. As far as O'Casey was concerned, Liberty Hall was by now no more than 'a hatchway for the payment of dues'.[3] He was part of a coterie of dissidents who were critical of Connolly and the ICA's courtship of the Volunteers. These included Delia Larkin and Michael Mullen, who worked in the insurance section. However, the William O'Brien and Thomas Foran faction of the union were firmly in control, and busy isolating supporters of James Larkin. This was a difficult time for O'Casey, but it provided time and space to explore other avenues. He relates how he sat quietly on the steps of the General Post Office:

> Reading the new catechism of the *Communist Manifesto* with its great commandment of Workers of all lands unite! And in all the shouting and the tumult and the misery around, he heard the roll of new drums, blowing of new bugles, and the sound of millions of men marching.[4]

REBELLION

The split in the Volunteers in September 1914 strengthened the position of those in the leadership who favoured a rebellion. However, there were divisions between the MacNeill, Hobson and O'Rahilly group, who advocated using the Irish Volunteers as a powerful lever for independence if provoked by the British authorities, and the Supreme Council of the IRB, who were determined to seize the opportunity to strike while Britain was engaged in the war. James Connolly and the ICA, coming from a socialist perspective, were equally determined to fight. The IRB was fearful that Connolly's strident demands for a rebellion would alarm the British authorities and undermine its own plans. The tone of his demands for military action was apparent from the pages of the *Workers' Republic*, where Connolly issued a ringing call for action: 'the time for Ireland's battle is NOW, the place for Ireland's battle is here'.[5] On 19 January 1916, the IRB arranged a meeting with Connolly and, over the following three days, set in place the plans for the rebellion. Connolly was co-opted onto the Military Council, cementing the military alliance between the Volunteers and the ICA.[6]

On Sunday, 16 April, just a week before the Easter Rising, thousands gathered to see the green republican flag hoisted over Liberty Hall. Connolly, who appeared for the first time in his ICA uniform, was there to see a young Citizen Army woman unfurl the flag on the roof of the building.

A symbolic act, perhaps, but O'Casey saw it as an indication that Connolly had stepped out from the shadow of the red flag and embraced the green. On the following Wednesday, Pearse and Plunkett tried to convince MacNeill to support the rising by showing him a Dublin Castle document that implied a crackdown on the Volunteers was imminent and alerting him to the fact that a shipment of arms from Germany would arrive. MacNeill reluctantly agreed to the mobilisation that Sunday. However, the plans for a full mobilisation were thrown into disarray when the German arms ship was intercepted and scuttled off the south coast. As these events unfolded, it became clear that the inner coterie of IRB members in the Volunteer leadership had deceived MacNeill. On Easter Saturday night, he issued an order rescinding the planned mobilisation for the next day. Given that situation and their plans in disarray, the Military Council had no option but to postpone the mobilisation until the following day. Once MacNeill's order to stand down was published, the rising was doomed to defeat. The prospects of success for the insurgents were always limited, but with a full mobilisation and the additional arms from Germany, a revolt that managed to hold the major cities and towns for a few days could have been the catalyst for a general uprising across the country.

The insurgents marched out to 'the uncertain glory of an April day'[7] and took up fixed positions in several buildings throughout Dublin. Because of MacNeill's actions, the rebels could only muster about 220 members of the ICA and 1,200 Irish Volunteers. The GPO was occupied for its symbolic nature as much as for its military significance. The Tricolour, which came to symbolise the nascent republic, flew over the GPO. Connolly ensured that the flag of the ICA, the Plough and the Stars, was hoisted over the Imperial Hotel, which was owned by his old adversary, William Martin Murphy. Connolly may also have ordered the occupation of Jacob's biscuit factory, though it had little strategic or military value, in retribution for the owner's conduct during the 1913 lockout. Connolly and the ICA were putting down a marker that the revolution also had social and economic objectives. On the eve of the rising, Connolly had instructed his comrades in the ICA that 'in the event of victory, hold on to your rifles, as those with whom we are fighting may stop before our goal is reached. We are for economic as well as political liberty.'[8] The 1916 Rising was a down-payment by Connolly and the ICA for a socialist future that was never realised.[9]

On Easter Monday, Pearse read out the Proclamation of Independence, which contained the political objectives of the rising, to the bemused passers-by outside the GPO:

> The Republic guarantees religious and civil liberty, equal rights and equal opportunities for all its citizens, and declares its resolve to pursue the happiness and prosperity of the whole nation and all its parts, cherishing all the children of the nation equally.[10]

Who stood by Pearse's shoulder as he read out the proclamation that Easter Monday? Cú Chulainn, Tone, Emmett, Mitchel – the heroic past made flesh by the rebels who marched out that morning. However, the heroic past buttered no parsnips for the workers of Dublin and their families. No one had consulted them or asked for their support, which was the principal reason why the working class and the tenement dwellers of Dublin did not rally to the flag as the rebels had hoped. Once the rebellion commenced, they looted the shops and public houses in a personal revolt against a society that had impoverished and excluded them. Paradoxically, the ICA members took a harsher view of the looters than the Irish Volunteers, possibly because they felt it reflected badly on the working class of Dublin, in whose name and interest they had marched out to fight. The rebels held out for a week. After the surrender, 160 prisoners were tried by military courts-martial. Most of the trials lasted less than twenty minutes, and fifteen of the leaders, including the seven signatories of the proclamation, were executed by firing squad. The executions started on 3 May with Pearse, Clarke and MacDonagh, and ended with MacDermott and Connolly on 12 May.[11]

O'CASEY AND CONNOLLY

O'Casey's antipathy to James Connolly was both personal and political. Despite Connolly's ongoing frustration at Larkin's lack of organisational skills and fiery temper, Connolly was not responsible for side-lining Larkin from the structures of the ITGWU in the aftermath of the lockout. After Larkin's departure for America, the process by which the ITGWU fell into the hands of the most conservative elements, such as William O'Brien – whom O'Casey compared to a 'most respectable clerk at home in a secure job' – was not of Connolly's making.[12]

Connolly was one of the first socialists to try and come to grips with the problem of fighting against capitalism in a country dominated by imperialism.[13] He believed that socialists should oppose imperialism in Ireland for two fundamental reasons. Firstly, because capitalism had imposed a system of private land ownership in Ireland, which led to the development of the landlord–tenant system of tenure. Secondly, Connolly argued that colonialism held back the development of capitalism in Ireland and retarded the growth of the working class. Consequently, he believed that the fight against imperialism in Ireland was not just about switching flags from Union Jack to Tricolour, but about stirring up revolutionary forces that could go beyond basic bourgeois nationalist demands and unleash a challenge to capitalism. Connolly hoped that the revolution in Ireland would 'set the torch to a European conflagration' that would sweep away capitalist and bondholder.[14] In the months leading up to the rebellion, however, his writing took on a more nationalist and militaristic tone; this was the price he had to pay to cajole and push the leadership of the IRB towards rebellion. Connolly would have preferred to do it differently, but after the defeat of 1913 he had little choice but to fight on nationalists' terms. Connolly had grasped the importance of the united front, which is a matter of strategy and tactics, and how socialists should operate, taking into account the balance of class forces available rather than political principles alone. O'Casey had argued for unity between the 'green' and the 'red' during the lockout in 1913, but he never acknowledged Connolly's attempt to unite labour and the nationalists in a fight against Britain and the wider anti-imperialist project in the period leading up to the 1916 Rising. In later life, O'Casey did acknowledge Connolly's contribution and his standing in the international socialist movement. Nevertheless, when the occasion arose, he could never resist the opportunity of denigrating Connolly in order to defend Larkin's reputation.[15] O'Casey did not comprehend the revolutionary dynamic that developed in those few years that led up to the rebellion. He may have read the *Communist Manifesto*, but in terms of practice, he had much to learn. He was a disgruntled outsider, a hurler on the ditch, shouting the odds as history passed him by.

Despite O'Casey's acrimonious resignation from the ICA, he was concerned for his friends who had turned out on Easter Monday and for the outcome of the rebellion. He must have known nearly all the men and women from SLOT and the ICA who had fought that week. Notwithstanding the imposition of martial law, during the rising O'Casey was out and about in the city surveying the situation. On the Thursday of Easter week, the British army raided the O'Casey household; he was taken prisoner and held overnight in St Barnabas Church, where he had often worshipped. The next day, he was taken with about 100 other men suspected of republican sympathies and held in the Merchant Warehousing granary store until his release a day later. Critics have suggested that

O'Casey felt guilty or ashamed over his failure to participate in the rising and that he suffered from 'survivor guilt', which is why he was so critical of the rising in *The Plough and the Stars*. One of his friends from SLOT, who had fought in the rising, recounted that it broke O'Casey's heart that he was not with the 'boys' in 1916 and that he would never openly discuss the matter.[16] He never mentioned or referred to his own feelings on the subject in the autobiographies or any of his letters. We do not know how he felt at the time about that fateful week or whether he had any doubts or uncertainties concerning the events that led up to it. However, there is no evidence that he suffered from 'survivor guilt', or any other traumatic consequences because he had not been 'out in Easter Week'. O'Casey was not a member of the ICA at the time of the rebellion and had taken no part in the discussions or events leading up to it. His eyesight was poor, and he had no training in the use of firearms. His participation would have been no more than a token gesture in those circumstances.

O'Casey was not indifferent to the fate of his comrades. In the aftermath of the rising, when the insurgents were jeered on the streets of Dublin as they marched off to an internment camp in Wales, O'Casey did not forget them. He wrote to them often, mainly to Jimmy Shields and Johnny MacDonald of SLOT. His letters are full of news and cartoon caricatures of O'Casey and Frank Cahill to cheer up the inmates. One letter has a drawing of a bemused policeman standing outside a shop in the slums during the 1916 Rising. A poor shabbily dressed man enters the store and emerges a little later dressed like a gentleman. He used this image in a slightly altered form in the looting scene in act three of *The Plough and the Stars*:

> MRS GOGAN: I don't remember ever havin' seen such lovely pairs as them with th' pointed toes an th' Cuban heels.
> BESSIE: They'll go grand with th' dhresses we're afther liftin', when we've stitched a sthray bit o' silk to lift the bodices up a little bit higher, so as to shake th' shame out o' them.[17]

Despite his sustained attacks on the IRB in the trade union press over the previous few years, he remained friends with many of his former comrades. That summer, Frank Cahill and about ten of the rebels who had evaded capture in the aftermath of the rising set up camp in County Meath to avoid the police raids. O'Casey accompanied them as he had no job or commitments to keep him in Dublin. He sent a cartoon to MacDonald in the internment camp in Wales depicting himself and Cahill as hobos sitting around the campfire.[18] He never abandoned his republican comrades. In 1922 he donated £1, nearly a week's wages, to the Irish Republican Prisoners' Dependants' Fund. Even after he moved to England, he lobbied and wrote letters on behalf of republican prisoners in English jails in the aftermath of the IRA bombing campaign in England in the 1930s and '40s.[19] He could always be relied on to write a piece for an Irish republican newspaper, if requested. In March 1940 he was invited to speak alongside T.A. Jackson, Hugh Delargy and Krishna Menon at an Easter week commemoration in the Holborn Hall in London organised by the Connolly Association.[20] These were not the actions of a man hostile to the republican movement. In 1957, O'Casey wrote a favourable review of Seán O'Callaghan's book *The Easter Lily* in *Tribune*, a newspaper associated with the British Labour Party. O'Callaghan, a former member of the IRA, was critical of the bombing campaign in Britain in the late 1930s and the disastrous 'border campaign' in the 1950s. O'Casey hoped the book would make an impact in Ireland so that 'we can make an honest effort to be better and wiser than we are'.[21] Despite his disapproval of the 'border campaign', he was still writing letters in 1963 in support of an amnesty for Irish political prisoners in British jails caught up in those events:

> There are many young Irish people imprisoned in the jails of Belfast and one in the dismal, horrifying jail called Dartmoor, who have long ago paid a fair price for what they have done, but who are still behind bars keeping them from the love of their people and the warmth of friendship with their fellow Irishmen and Irishwomen.[22]

Following the release of the prisoners from internment in Wales in early 1917, O'Casey and his friend Paddy McDonnell organised the SLOT Dramatic Society in Seville Place. As usual, O'Casey took on the role of secretary and organiser. The following November, the drama club organised a benefit evening at the Empire Theatre to provide 'Meals for Necessitous Children and the Poor'. The *Dublin Saturday Post* reported that O'Casey's satirical song 'The Constitutional Movement Must Go On' was a great hit, but they were less enthusiastic about his acting abilities in Thomas Moylan's one-act play *Naboclish*.[23] As he handed over the money raised for the penny dinners to the Sisters of Charity, he thought 'that no one needed a penny dinner more than his mother and himself; but pride kept the two of them miles away from one'.[24]

After the 1916 Rising, several of O'Casey's old friends in SLOT were interned, and some of the younger and newer activists, who had little time for O'Casey, were drawn towards the Irish Republican Army. Military matters and tactics were now at the centre of their lives, rather than trade union affairs, the Irish language, music and culture, which were so important to O'Casey. After the general amnesty in 1917 and the return of his old friends from internment, O'Casey could sense that the atmosphere had changed. He drifted away from the club, and by 1920 it had ceased to be an important part of his life.

FRANCIS SHEEHY SKEFFINGTON

In *The Story of the Citizen Army*, O'Casey's statement that 'in Sheehy-Skeffington, and not in Connolly, fell the first martyr to Irish Socialism'[25] was perceived as a slight, and by some a slur, on the memory of Connolly. Sheehy Skeffington was a socialist, a pacifist, and a friend of Bernard Shaw, which was another reason why O'Casey admired him. Sheehy Skeffington had also used the same phrase to describe the death of the suffragist Marjorie Hasler in 1913. The headline on the front page of the *Citizen* called her 'The First Martyr of the Irish Women's Franchise League'.[26] Sheehy Skeffington was a founding member of the ICA but did not participate in the rising. During Easter week, he tried to organise a citizens' committee to prevent civil disorder and the looting that was taking place. As he returned home on Tuesday, 25 April he was arrested and taken to Portobello barracks. The next morning Sheehy Skeffington and two other prisoners were summarily executed in the yard of Portobello barracks by a British army officer. Public opinion in Ireland and Britain was outraged at this cold-blooded murder and the subsequent inquiry, which resulted in a cover-up. O'Casey knew and respected Sheehy Skeffington both politically and personally and wrote that he was:

> the living antithesis of the Easter Insurrection: a spirit of peace enveloped in the flame and rage and hatred of the contending elements, absolutely free from all its terrifying madness; and yet he was the purified soul of revolt against not only one nation's injustice to another, but he was also the soul of revolt against man's inhumanity to man.[27]

Sheehy Skeffington has almost faded from public memory, while Connolly remains one of the dominant figures from that period in Irish history. O'Casey's remark, referring to Sheehy Skeffington as Ireland's first socialist martyr, was not aimed at Connolly, as many of his detractors claim. O'Casey's target was the leaders of the ITGWU who, in October 1916, had reissued Connolly's *The Re-Conquest of Ireland* with a new introduction by Robert Lynd, the writer and polemicist. In the first sentence, Lynd stated that 'James Connolly is Ireland's first Socialist martyr'.[28] Connolly would have hated to be described in that manner. The clay had hardly settled on the graves of those executed in the aftermath of the rebellion before the mythmakers set to work, transforming them into martyrs and plaster saints. O'Casey was one of the few who stood out against this apotheosis. His little book attempted to put working-class politics back on the political agenda. He was still hopeful that the working class would reassert themselves and take back the leadership of the fight for a workers' republic:

> While the ultimate destiny of Ireland will be in the hands of Labour, it would be foolish to deny that the present is practically in the hands of the Sinn Fein Organisation ... Labour leaders, sooner or later, will be forced to realise that they must become Irish if they expect to win the confidence and support of the Irish working class ... Labour must build the future state; democratising the national movement and Irishising itself. Labour will probably have to fight Sinn Fein – indeed the challenge seems to have been thrown down already.[29]

In those few pages, O'Casey comes closest to a synthesis of the class question and the national question that had impelled James Connolly to lead his forces into battle in 1916. From late 1917 onwards, despite his trenchant criticism of Connolly, O'Casey's core argument was not substantially different from Connolly's position leading up to the 1916 Rising. O'Casey, in a letter to the *Dublin Saturday Post* in September 1917, maintained that labour must lead the fight against imperialism: 'The Labour movement ought to make the workers, by education and propaganda, a power in all those organisations, particularly in those that appeal to the national sentiments of the people.'[30]

O'Casey's position on the Easter Rising built on his experience of the 1913 lockout. He understood the nature of British imperialism in Ireland and how it held back the country's economic development. Nevertheless, he believed that a successful revolution on nationalist terms would only empower the Irish ruling class, the very people who had reduced the workers of Dublin to abject poverty in 1913 in order to protect their own class interests. O'Casey argued that it was irrational to rely for liberation on a class whose own position depended on exploiting Irish workers.

Because the revolution was presented in purely nationalist terms, as far as O'Casey was concerned it held little appeal for the working class. The 1916 Proclamation was more of a gesture towards social change – an ideal of freedom rather than a blueprint to transform Irish society. What could have energised the working class to join the revolution was a fight against imperialism on their terms, one that put working-class interests, allied to those of the small farmers and the landless labourers, at the centre of the struggle.

Internationally, the most explicit support for the rising came from the revolutionary left. The Russian revolutionary Vladimir Lenin's support arose from a general opposition to the narrow and formalistic politics that judged every struggle on the basis of the purity of its socialist programme. While sounding very left-wing, in reality this leads to a form of passivity. When writing about the 1916 Rising, Lenin pointed out that unless socialists sided with those who wanted to fight imperialism, even if the nationalists held prejudiced or reactionary ideas, they could never hope to shape events or the political outcome of the struggle. Lenin's support was not predicated on the radical content of the 1916 Proclamation, but rather on his belief that it was the right of people in an oppressed country to fight for their freedom and that socialists should support them.[31]

Connolly was correct about the 1916 Rising being a blow against British imperialism and war. However, his political tactics leading up to the rising were more problematic. O'Casey suggested that Connolly's approach to the rising disguised the left's distinctive position. Even though he was acting general secretary of the ITGWU, Connolly did not substantially campaign or agitate among the membership or organise within the advanced sections of the working class in the months leading up to the rising.[32] Instead, in January 1916 he embraced the conspiratorial tactics of the IRB to promote the rebellion. O'Casey, however, was mistaken in believing that Connolly abandoned socialism entirely and fought exclusively on nationalist terms. Unlike Lenin and Connolly, he failed to appreciate that revolutionaries must use every movement available to them if they are to defeat imperialism.

Writers who have characterised the 1916 Rising as a blood sacrifice rely heavily on the mystical and spiritual elements in Pearse's writing, which are also present in the poetry of Plunkett and MacDonagh.[33] The accounts by the participants, held in the Military Archives, indicate that the vast majority of the rebels did not deliberately set out to make a sacrifice of their lives.[34] They marched out to fight for a republic that guaranteed equality and justice for all its citizens. Shortly before the rising, Pearse had warned against the emergence of a new elite:

> in this Volunteer movement, as I understand it, the people are to be master; and it will be for the people to say when and against whom the Volunteers shall draw the sword or point the rifle ... The Volunteers themselves, the people themselves, must keep control of this movement. Any man or any group of men that seeks to establish an ascendancy should be dealt with summarily.[35]

After independence, the new 'ascendancy' won out and elevated Pearse into a plaster saint, emptied of all radical thought and content. Almost alone, O'Casey stood out against this sanctification of the rebels. He tried to give them back their humanity – he painted them as real people made of flesh and blood with all the strengths and weaknesses that go with the human condition. More importantly, O'Casey wanted to give the revolution back to the people, to get rid of the elite and, in Pearse's words, to ensure that 'the people are to be master' of their destiny. In his assessment of Connolly and the Easter Rising, O'Casey glossed over Larkin's republicanism and his role in instilling a republican ethos in both the ICA and the ITGWU. There was little difference between Connolly and Larkin on the national question. With the outbreak of the war, both leaders had concluded that a rebellion was a possibility, even a necessity. While in the United States, Larkin repeatedly called for action in Ireland. In September 1915, Kuno Meyer 'found him reassuring on preparations for the Rising'.[36]

His critics condemned O'Casey's Dublin plays for failing to acknowledge the bravery of the insurgents and the impact of the rising in transforming Irish politics. O'Casey was not a member of any political organisation or movement that could influence events when he wrote the plays. All he had was the Abbey stage, where he challenged the audience to re-evaluate the events of the previous ten years and to question whether all that death and destruction had radically transformed the social conditions of Irish society. As an artist, he could do no more.

CHAPTER 7

A Writer at Last: 1917–22

The journeyman playwright was determined that a play of his would be performed on the Abbey stage. By the end of 1919, the Abbey directorate was well aware of his talents and encouraged him to persevere. But O'Casey had not given up on politics. Between January and March 1918 he wrote three articles for *Irish Opinion*, a left-wing weekly produced in Dublin. In the *Evening Telegraph* he defended P.T. Daly from the gossipmongering and rumours circulating that Daly, a few years previously, had been accused of dishonesty by the ITGWU. Daly was a supporter of Larkin, and the accusations were an attempt to get rid of him and tarnish Larkin by association. O'Casey wrote that Daly always had the confidence of Tom Clarke and Seán MacDermott, two of the executed leaders of the 1916 Rising. In a letter to the *Evening Telegraph* he outlined his friendship with Tom Clarke and Seán MacDermott: 'I speak out not as an acquaintance of a few months, but an intimate friendship of many years, which I am glad to say, notwithstanding differences of opinion, endured cordially to the end'.[1] Kathleen Clarke, the widow of Tom Clarke, replied to his letter, contradicting O'Casey's claim and insisting that her husband and Seán MacDermott had broken with both P.T. Daly and O'Casey some years prior to 1916. O'Casey replied that on several public occasions, Clarke had shown support for Daly and that when Daly stood in the council elections in 1915, Clarke had voted for him. O'Casey ended his letter with a plea to end the sectarian bitterness and public debates that make 'martyrs of its own flesh and blood'.[2]

In March 1918, O'Casey wrote to Fergus O'Connor, asking him to publish his edited collection of the poems of John Boyle O'Reilly[3] and a pamphlet on James Connolly. The Boyle O'Reilly collection and the Connolly pamphlet were never published, and the original drafts, if ever completed, have not survived. O'Casey believed his pamphlets would find an audience among the advanced sections of Sinn Féin. He told O'Connor that he was prepared to debate his views with leading members of the party: 'Take [Darrell] Figgis or [Seán] Milroy, ay, or even [Arthur] Griffith and give me one-half hour with each of them on the same platform, and let those who are present judge as to the force, fire and originality of each'.[4] The debates did not take place, and none of the projects came to fruition.

In February 1918, two friends and political acquaintances, William Kelly and a Mr King, proposed setting up a publishing company to print O'Casey's work. Not alone would this give him an outlet for his polemics, but they also agreed to share the profits with him with a guarantee of £2 for each piece. He needed the money, as his mother's pension hardly kept them alive, but more importantly, he believed he had something to say concerning Labour and Sinn Féin. In a letter to his then-current publisher Fergus O'Connor, he outlined his position: 'I believe my opinions concerning Labour and Sinn Féin are pregnant with truth and foreknowledge.' O'Casey also mentioned the *Griffith and English Labour* pamphlet, which Kelly and King were anxious to publish.[5] Unfortunately, the publishing firm of Kelly and King never got off the ground. The political tracts would have to wait for another day, and the O'Casey household would have to survive on bread and tea for a while yet.

The death of his mother during the influenza epidemic in November 1918 forced him to consider his future. O'Connor had lost interest in publishing his political pamphlets as he believed that O'Casey was out of step with the reality of politics in Ireland. By November 1919, O'Casey had compiled a book of essays, *Three Shouts on a Hill*. The book was never published, but he reused sections of it for a number of articles in *Irish Opinion* and the Dublin newspapers. Meanwhile, he was working on his plays *The Harvest Festival* and *The Frost in the Flower*, both of which were rejected by the Abbey Theatre.

O'Casey's ballads and poetry are one element of his work that is largely ignored. His poetry was a means to appeal to the masses, particularly during the great political upheavals between 1913 and 1923, and his anger at the world can be read in every line. His style leans towards the romantic tradition, heavily influenced by his reading of Shelley, Keats and Tennyson, and the old Dublin ballad tradition. At their best, the poems have a lyrical quality, but they hardly bear comparison with the work of his contemporaries:

> When, stung to Rage by Pity, eloquent men
> Have roused with pealing voice the unnumbered tribes
> That toil and groan and bleed, hungry and blind.[6]

He had far more success commercially with a series of ballads and poems that O'Connor published as eight-page songbooks, *Songs of the Wren* (1918).

These were popular satirical street ballads commenting on the political situation in Ireland. They seem to have been popular, as O'Connor printed 10,000 copies of the second edition. O'Casey, like Connolly, was opposed to the First World War. *Songs of the Wren* were mostly satires on the war, or in opposition to the proposed introduction of conscription in Ireland, with titles such as 'The Man from the Daily Mail' and 'If the Germans Came to Ireland in the Mornin'':

> To capture, sure, they're eager, each United Irish Leaguer,
> In Home Rule Sauce to give them all a cornin';
> An' the men that serve king Billy, they'd be fed on Popish skilly,
> If the Germans came to Ireland in the mornin'!

A few lines from his anti-conscription song 'The Devil's Recruiting Song' give a flavour of his style:

> A public meeting was held there not very long ago,
> Too all tooral, ooral, ooral, ooo!
> 'Twas the Devil that presided, and soon it was decided
> That the only way to see the matter through,
> An' to keep the British Nation at its present elevation,
> Was to hasten on Conscription, tooral ooo![7]

Several of O'Casey's plays, particularly *Red Roses for Me*, include songs. In 1980 Paul Brady and John Kavanagh issued a fine record of his songs and ballads on the EMI label, however it is rarely referenced today.[8] He never realised his potential as a poet, though it found expression in the wonderful lyrical quality of the language and the songs in his plays. Like John Millington Synge, he was more poetic in prose than in poetry.

THOMAS ASHE

Although Sinn Féin had played almost no part in the 1916 Rising, they were the primary beneficiaries; the 'Sinn Féin Rebellion' was a label that stuck in the absence of any other organisation claiming responsibility. The victory of Sinn Féin in 1917 in the Roscommon and Longford by-elections transformed the movement into a coherent organisation that picked up support across the country.[9] In September 1917, O'Casey's friend, and

Sinn Féin member, Thomas Ashe, died in jail as a result of force feeding. His funeral was a national event that electrified the country. However, his death was also a political tragedy for the radical and socialist-minded supporters of Sinn Féin. Ashe, the hero of Ashbourne and head of the IRB, had the status and reputation to possibly challenge de Valera for the leadership of the movement. Whether Ashe could have combined a more radical socialist programme with the nationalist ethos and conservative economic programme of Sinn Féin was another matter. Thomas Ashe was born in Kerry in 1885. He trained as a teacher and worked in a school in north County Dublin. He was an active member of the teachers' union, a member of the Gaelic League and a founder member of the Black Raven Pipe Band. He was a friend of O'Casey's and a strong supporter of the workers during the lockout. In a letter, Ashe refers to the events connected with the lockout:

> I suppose you know by this that Jem Larkin was sent to jail ... The Government got afraid of a general strike in England which the Englishmen were organising in his favour. So they let him out ... He'll beat hell out of the snobbish, mean, seoinin employers yet, and more power to him.[10]

Ashe championed the landless rural worker and shared with O'Casey an abiding hatred of the conditions that the tenement dwellers had to endure in the slums of Dublin. Their shared concerns led to a close personal friendship, which also included Mícheál Ó Foghludha, an Irish-language activist who also fought in the 1916 Rising. They discussed the issues of the day during their long walks along the Dublin quays. Ashe's sister Nora said that 'Tomás thought the world of him', and O'Casey felt the same about Ashe.[11]

O'Casey wrote a lament for his old friend and fellow piper, which Fergus O'Connor published almost immediately after Ashe's death. The thousands who had gathered outside the gates of Mountjoy jail to pay tribute to Ashe were moved to tears as O'Connor recited O'Casey's lament for his dead friend:

> Why gathers the gloom in a manner appalling –
> What causes the sunshine in terror to flee?
> The Mountains of Erin are plaintively calling –
> Thomas Ashe, Thomas Ashe, we are mourning for thee[12]

He followed this up in November with a sixteen-page pamphlet, *The Story of Thomas Ashe*, where he took the opportunity to pay full tribute to his friend. He also took the opportunity to claim Ashe as a champion of the unity between labour and republicanism:

> His principles are surging into stronger life within the minds of the Irish Proletariat, the Irish Scholar, and the Irish Worker. Death has won a poor victory! Labour has lost a champion; Irish-Ireland has lost a son; Militant Ireland has lost a soldier; but all have gained a mighty and enduring inspiration. Ashe died that Human Liberty might be vindicated and that Ireland might live.[13]

In a letter to the *Dublin Evening Post* headed 'Republican and Internationalist', O'Casey spelt out Ashe's commitment to the 'working classes of all countries' and that the 'Red Flag', the symbol of the Brotherhood of Man, should have been draped on his coffin alongside the Irish republican flag. He went on to outline Ashe's 'inexhaustible sympathy' for the locked-out workers in 1913 and that 'it would be well if every Sinn Feiner followed in his steps'.[14] Ashe embodied the fusion of socialist and republican ideals that O'Casey was trying to achieve. At the start of the 1916 Rising, Ashe had assembled his men at Knocksedan in north County Dublin. In *The Shadow of a Gunman*, perhaps as a tribute to his friend, Knocksedan was the setting where Maguire, the IRA gunman, meets his death.

THE SOCIALIST PARTY OF IRELAND

The 1916 Rising and the anti-conscription campaign transformed the political atmosphere in the country. There was a vibrancy about politics, a sense that something dramatic was about to happen. Most of this enthusiasm and interest coalesced around a revitalised Sinn Féin. Nevertheless, a resurgent socialist and trade union movement also had a significant following. In the aftermath of the Russian Revolution and the victorious general strike against conscription, the Socialist Party of Ireland (SPI) was reorganised to take advantage of the rising mood of class militancy. In late 1917 O'Casey joined the SPI, inspired by its enthusiasm for the Russian Revolution that had brought the Bolsheviks to power. The SPI pamphlet *New Russia: Anniversary bulletin of Bolshevik Revolution November 1917–1918* was indicative of the level of support for the revolution within the organisation. In later life, O'Casey referred to his interest in the Russian Revolution at that time and seemed to imply that he was well informed about events in Russia. The first mention of O'Casey's participation in the activities of the SPI is in December 1917, speaking at a public meeting organised by the party in the Trades Hall in Capel Street. His topic was 'Labour, Bread and Sinn Féin'. According to the magazine *Irish Opinion*, those present took part in a 'keen discussion', but it noted that the attendance was rather sparse.[15] O'Casey later made use of this or a similar experience in *Juno and the Paycock*:

> MARY: Do you remember, Jerry, the verses you read when you gave the lecture in the Socialist Rooms some time ago, on Humanity's Strife with Nature?[16]

Irish Opinion was launched in December 1917. The front-page banner proclaimed it as 'A Weekly Journal of Industrial and Political Democracy'. The magazine supported the fight for independence; it had a left-wing ethos, supporting trade union and working-class action. The first edition reprinted an article by James Connolly, 'We Are a Great People', and in the following issue, it promoted support for a 'democratically controlled Labour Party' independent of Sinn Féin.[17] Under the editorship of Andrew Malone, the magazine's political position was in line with O'Casey's thinking. An editorial in March 1918 welcomed the Russian Revolution, reported on 'the great demonstration at the Mansion House to welcome the Revolution',[18] and suggested that the revolution had:

> cheered Ireland and we rejoice that Ireland has risen to the time. The great demonstration at the Mansion House to welcome the Revolution and to show the revolutionaries that they have our sympathy was an inspiring gathering.[19]

During this radical period under Malone's editorship, O'Casey contributed three articles, two on the Gaelic League and another on the proposed affiliation of the Irish National Teachers' Organisation to the Dublin Trades Council. The magazine had financial problems and in March 1918 came under the control of Tom Johnson and William O'Brien. The tone of the magazine shifted, and it effectively came to reflect the political views of the Johnson and O'Brien faction in the ITGWU and the SPI. O'Casey was identified with the Larkinite faction, and as a result, the pages of *Irish Opinion* were no longer welcoming as a vehicle for his polemics.

The Dublin newspapers published several of his letters on political matters during this time. In a letter to the *Dublin Evening Telegraph*, he highlighted the case of Patrick Higgins, who was given a ten-year prison sentence during the 1913 lockout:

> His comrades of the coal trade have not forgotten him, and are determined that the measure of pity meted out to others, because presumably, they occupy an influential position in the social scale, shall be extended to their comrade, Higgins. Why the law must always take its course with a coal heaver, when it can be set aside for the sake of others.[20]

O'Casey's membership of the SPI was brief, lasting about as long as the party's enthusiasm for the Russian Revolution. The SPI's support for the Bolsheviks was a worrying development for the more conservative elements of the party. The bishops were also concerned about the direction the left was taking, and they informed the leadership that this ambiguity should be cleared up. Whether O'Casey ever formally resigned from the SPI or when he left is unknown, but by early 1919 he had severed his ties with the party. Sinn Féin was now the dominant force in Irish politics, and the opening shots in the War of Independence reinforced their position. In those circumstances, there were few opportunities for O'Casey to argue his position on the relationship between labour and republicanism.

In the first decades of the century, O'Casey had developed as a classic worker intellectual, a participant and agitator in the working-class and socialist movement while educating himself on the finer points of socialist and Marxist theory. In addition to Shaw, Marx and Darwin, O'Casey had access to a range of socialist literature from Ireland, Britain and America in the reading room of the Socialist Party.[21]

THE WAR OF INDEPENDENCE

The 1916 Rising and its aftermath hammered the first nails into the coffin of the Irish Parliamentary Party, but the conscription crisis in April 1918 killed it off almost entirely. However, Sinn Féin was not the only possible beneficiary of the militant opposition to the extension of conscription to Ireland and the realignment of the political landscape. The conscription crisis revealed to everyone the potential power of the Irish working class, and its ability to shape the future of Irish society. The organised labour movement was the leading light in the campaign. Even *The Irish Times* acknowledged that the one-day general strike against conscription revealed that 'April 23rd will be chiefly remembered as the day on which Irish Labour realised its strength'.[22]

However, Labour failed to build on its success. It stood aside in the 1918 general election under pressure from Sinn Féin. In the election, the Irish Parliamentary Party, the party of Parnell, was annihilated, winning only six seats compared to seventy-three for Sinn Féin. The people had discarded the old home rulers in favour of the separatists. On the strength of this victory, Sinn Féin set about building a shadow state apparatus that functioned in opposition to the British state. As part of that strategy, republican courts were established across the country in an attempt to bypass the British legal system. In 1921, O'Casey wrote to the court on behalf of a neighbour who was being abused by his neighbours. Austin Stack, the minister for home affairs, replied that if the court found in favour of his neighbour, 'such an order will be handed to the Republican Police whose duty it will be to see that the Order is obeyed'.[23] In 1922, O'Casey utilised this incident in *The Shadow of a Gunman*. However, this was a short-lived experiment in popular justice. In the aftermath of the truce, the republican courts were dismantled, and the British legal system was reintroduced; the harp replaced the crown over the door, but any concept of a democratic and local justice system was firmly squashed.

The standard histories of the War of Independence emphasise two aspects of the war: firstly, a detailed analysis of the military campaign waged by the IRA from January 1919 until the truce in July 1921, and secondly, the political campaign by Sinn Féin to build alternative state structures to undermine British rule in Ireland. There were, however, other political forces at work. Between 1919 and 1921, there were over a hundred occupations or 'soviets' in workplaces across the country. The decision in May 1920 by Irish rail workers to refuse to drive trains that transported British troops or munitions for the army could have been a decisive factor in the war. Working-class rank and file militancy aided the political and military campaign of Sinn Féin by undermining the authority of the British state in Ireland. Charles Townshend has suggested that if 'the [rail] embargo had been made total in scope and indefinite in duration, it is hard to see how a functional military presence in the hinterland could have been maintained'.[24] That may or may not be the case, but it reinforces the view that O'Casey was correct in the way that he called attention to the failure of the labour bureaucracy to give a lead or engage in militant political action during the 1919–21 period.[25] The execution of James Connolly and Jim Larkin's exile had decimated what was already a very thin layer on the socialist left. They were replaced by more moderate leaders who talked left but acted in a more conservative and conciliatory manner.

O'Casey was not a lone voice arguing for the primacy of class over nation. Peadar O'Donnell, a socialist, also saw these events as a fight between the rabble and the wealthy, with the republicans, in O'Donnell's view, the champions of the dispossessed and the small farmers.[26] This was also the view of Ernie O'Malley, who during the Civil War acknowledged the need to get the workers to support the republicans: 'The need for a Democratic Republican Constitution is felt and I believe that it would get the workers' to support the republicans.'[27] In the course of the War of Independence, it was apparent even to a conservative like Aodh de Blácam that the social situation needed to be reformed and 'it must be either by revolution or evolution', and he went on to say that 'we need the idealism that has kept alive the desire for freedom to be given now to fostering a desire for a fair as well as a free Ireland'.[28] However, this was not to be – the closing stages of the revolution descended into a divisive and bloody civil war that obscured economic and social demands. The real inheritors of the revolution were the conservative middle class and the petty shopkeeper class, who mobilised the church to attack any individual or movement that might offer an alternative progressive outcome.

In hindsight, it is clear that O'Casey was correct in the way that he argued for other possibilities in the fight against the British presence in Ireland, a point he makes very forcefully in his early polemical plays such as *The Harvest Festival* and *Kathleen Listens In*. The social or class question was always an issue that simmered below the surface during those troubled years. Gavin Foster, in the *Atlas of the Irish Revolution*, points to the fact that: 'A growing body of research demonstrates that the lines of fracture in the Civil War invariably interacted with economic structures, class hierarchies, and other special forces in important, if complex, ways.' However, Foster also points to the fact that the Labour Party's acceptance of the treaty and the ambiguous role played by the trade unions can frustrate efforts to explain the Civil War in 'straightforward economic terms'.[29] Also of significance is that, despite differing views on the treaty, both sides in the civil war shared common assumptions 'about how people should not be "diverted from the struggle for freedom by a class war"'.[30]

Many years later, in his autobiography, O'Casey recalled that at the time, it was clear to him and his neighbours that 'The Dublin slums were at war with the British empire' and that this was 'an unequal fight ... but the slums would win'.[31] He spent the rest of his life trying to understand why the outcome of the War of Independence felt like a terrible defeat. However, we get no sense in the autobiographies of O'Casey's views on the war or the effectiveness of the political or military strategy carried out by Sinn Féin and the IRA. All we have to indicate how he felt at the time are a few comments in his letters to Fergus O'Connor. In April 1918, he noted de Valera's acknowledgement of Labour's support for Sinn Féin and went on to say that 'It indicates strongly the growing power of Labour opinions'.[32]

Once the military campaign kicked off, O'Casey was clear about which side he supported. This was not the time to shout about the differences between Labour and Sinn Féin. He had lost that battle; all he could do was add his voice to those looking for a more radical outcome. From the beginning of the IRA's military campaign in 1919 to the truce in 1921, there are no articles or letters from O'Casey criticising Sinn Féin or the conduct of the war. He proposed writing a pamphlet, *England's Atrocities in Ireland*, but his publisher did not take up the offer.[33] In January 1918, he wrote a Sinn Féin election ballad, 'Hurrah for Ireland and Sinn Féin'. O'Casey never sold himself short politically, either then or later in life, so we can assume that this represented, at least in a populist version, his position regarding Sinn Féin:

> Now or never is the call!
> March we with the true and brave,
> For the freedom of the slave,
> And for Ireland, blessed Ireland over all![34]

Following the truce in July 1921, negotiations began between Sinn Féin and the British government. Under immense pressure from the British government, including the threat of all-out war, the Irish delegation signed the treaty that granted dominion status to the new state in December 1921. The incipient Free State government had to accept the partition of Ireland and pay off a portion of the British national debt. Britain would retain control of a number of naval bases, and the members of the Free State parliament would have to swear allegiance to the British crown. The treaty that was agreed upon was never going to be acceptable to the die-hard republicans. De Valera tried to bridge the divide by submitting Document No. 2, in which he proposed an 'external association' with Britain rather than dominion status, which would eliminate the necessity for members of the Irish parliament to swear an oath of allegiance to the British crown. In reality, there was very little difference between the two positions. Except for the oath, de Valera's document offered nothing of substance, either on the North of Ireland or the other contentious issues that divided the movement. When it was clear that Document No. 2 would not command any substantial support, it was withdrawn by de Valera. Looking back many years later on the Civil War and the terrible events that took place, O'Casey questioned the distinction between the two positions that led to the Civil War and wondered what the Civil War was actually about: 'For Document No. 2! Not to abolish poverty. No; just for a spate of words that Alice in Wonderland wouldn't understand'.[35] The treaty tore the country apart. The 'terrible beauty' born out of the sacrifice of 1916 was in danger of losing her good looks as the country descended into an ugly internecine war that split friends and families. O'Casey summed up the situation in his autobiography:

> Then those who were to become the rulers of Ireland separated into two parties. Most of the coming middle class followed Griffith, and the rest hallooed for freedom around the disappointed De Valera. The clergy stood quiet on the right; the Labour officials watched as quiet on the left; both waiting to see which would prove the stronger, hoping that some good things could be gathered from the fragments.[36]

The threatening civil war erupted on 28 June 1922 when the Free State army shelled the Four Courts, the headquarters of the anti-treaty faction of the IRA, using artillery borrowed from the British army. Within three days, the Four Courts was reduced to rubble, and the garrison surrendered. By the end of the first week, resistance in Dublin had collapsed. Following the fall of Waterford, Limerick and Cork, the IRA, or the Irregulars as they were known, fell back into a defensive guerrilla war that was relentless in its execution. Reprisals, executions and the burning of houses were common as the new state 'spiralled into an agony of self-destruction'.[37] The war ended on 24 May 1923 when de Valera issued an order to dump arms. O'Casey's sympathies in the Civil War were with the republican forces and against the Free State army, whom he referred to as the 'Green and Tans', but this did not compromise his criticism of the republicans' politics.[38]

PART 3

CHAPTER 8

The New Drama

As a young man, O'Casey had absorbed vast quantities of Shakespeare, Dickens and Boucicault: 'the first serious book I bought was a shilling copy of the Globe edition of Shakespeare and I learnt *Hamlet, Macbeth* and *Julius Caesar* by heart'.[1] If the Abbey Theatre was financially beyond him, amateur drama, which was all the rage in Dublin at the turn of the century, fired his enthusiasm for the stage. Sometime in the late 1890s, his brother Isaac, with Seán's help, had constructed a small stage in the living room of Hawthorn Terrace. Here, they performed extracts from Shakespeare and Boucicault with the help of the neighbours. The Halpin family lived up the road from the O'Casey house. The family consisted of Edwin and Marianne and their four children. Edwin would have been about fifteen years older than O'Casey and was a 'socialist in his outlook and a Gaelic revival enthusiast'.[2] He encouraged his children to speak both Irish and English. The family have a recollection that:

> Edwin was an influence on O'Casey – apparently Edwin and Marianne conducted little theatricals in their home, which were attended by everyone on the street. O'Casey attended and sometimes took part and after the shows were over, stayed behind with others to listen to Edwin talk radical politics.[3]

The Halpins' account confirms O'Casey's recollection of the importance of drama in his early years, and it was shared by several of his working-class neighbours. Cecil, one of the Halpin children, became a professional entertainer, specialising in song and dance routines and eventually became a bit player in the British film industry. O'Casey's youthful enthusiasm for drama developed on a more formal basis when his brother Isaac formed the Townsend Dramatic Society and converted an unused stable in Hill Street into a little theatre:

> Sketches were given to audiences of forty or fifty, who paid tuppence a head to get in, to see Archie [Isaac] playing the Duke of Gloucester, to

> Johnny's [O'Casey] Henry the Sixth; or to see Johnny playing Brutus in the forum scene, followed by Archie as Mark Antony, friends in the audience shouting the exclamations of the crowd for them.[4]

Isaac was acquainted with Frank Dalton, a professional actor with the Sullivan Irish Combination Theatre Group. They played Irish classic melodramas at the Mechanics' Theatre, and through him, Seán enjoyed a free pass for a front bench in the pit. A drama club developed in the St Laurence O'Toole Club, and O'Casey used his talent for singing and storytelling to sustain it during the difficult months after the 1916 Rising. O'Casey said that he wrote his first play 'for my own Drama Club attached to the National movement – about 1911 or so'.[5] This may have been a sketch for the entertainments the Gaelic League or the St Laurence O'Toole Club produced as fundraisers. The historian R.M. Fox noted that O'Casey 'had done some writing, including a strike play for Liberty Hall in 1913'.[6] Despite Fox's suggestion, Christopher Murray is doubtful if O'Casey wrote a play before 1916, when he submitted *Profit and Loss* to the Abbey Theatre. The play was rejected and returned to O'Casey within a few days. Unfortunately, no text or summary of the play exists.[7]

WORKING-CLASS DRAMA

O'Casey's interest in drama coincided with the development of working-class drama allied to the rising militancy of the trade union movement in Ireland. The decision by James Larkin to form the Irish Transport and General Workers' Union (ITGWU) in 1909 laid the foundation stone for the modern Irish labour movement. To do so, he needed to break the domination of British unions in Ireland. Larkin set out 'to decolonise labour consciousness, arguing that Irish workers should rely on their own resources and build a movement geared to tackling native conditions'.[8] In this endeavour, culture would play an important ideological role. Larkin and Connolly may have employed culture as an ideological weapon, but they also believed in its intrinsic value in enriching the lives of working-class people. Instead of holding a narrow political conception of culture, James Connolly, Jim Larkin, and especially his sister Delia Larkin, had a broader democratic concept. Culture was a mechanism that enabled Irish workers, both individually and collectively, to gain a greater sense of their dignity, humanity and worth as Irish men and women. In a speech to the

Irish Trades Union Congress in 1914, Larkin emphasised the breadth of his aspirations:

> The working class have as much right as any section or class in the community to enjoy all the advantages of science, art, and literature. No field of knowledge, no outlook on life, no book should be closed against the workers. They should demand their share in the effulgence of life and all that was created for the enjoyment of mankind.[9]

The 'new drama', 'the theatre of revolt' that emerged at the end of the nineteenth century, lacerated the bourgeoisie: 'Chekhov for their lack of culture, Shaw for their complacency, Strindberg for their cowardice, and O'Neill for their philistinism'.[10] A distinct urban working-class drama arose alongside a radical socialist and trade unionist consciousness that stretched from Marx and Shaw in England in the 1880s to Larkin and O'Casey in Ireland in the 1920s.[11]

The production of W.B. Yeats' *Cathleen ni Houlihan* in April 1902 brought the Irish National Theatre into popular view.[12] Yeats and Lady Gregory set out to create not only an Irish theatre but also a 'distinctly Irish theatrical aesthetic'[13] based on a rural ideal. Yeats and Lady Gregory elevated just one aspect of Ireland – rustic, mystical and primitive – above all others. However, this concept was not to everyone's taste. The theatre's patrons were mainly urban with little experience of rural life. They wanted an Irish theatre, but one modelled on the European realism of Ibsen and Shaw. Fred Ryan and Frank Fay contended that a new dramatic style was needed to represent the reality of modern urban life, one that could deal with the issues of class and nationalism in an Irish context. Ryan staked a claim for a drama where the urban and social are dominant.

Fred Ryan is one of the more interesting and neglected figures of the early twentieth century.[14] He was a pioneer in the struggle for women's rights and in 1909 was a founder member, along with James Larkin, of the Socialist Party of Ireland. Ryan was one of the first dramatists to challenge Yeats and Lady Gregory's rural aesthetic with his only play, *The Laying of the Foundations*, produced in the Ancient Concert Rooms in October 1902.[15] Ryan's play was modelled on Ibsen's drama *An Enemy of the People*, but with a socialist slant. The title can also stand as a metaphor for the advent of class and socialist ideas in Irish drama. For the first time, the spectre of the working class, in a Marxist sense, appeared on an Irish stage. O'Casey, like many others, was running to catch up with Ryan and later expressed his disappointment that he could never afford to purchase Ryan's political monthly, *Dana* (1904). In 1907, Ryan and Francis Sheehy Skeffington published the short-lived *National Democrat* that promised to fight against the twin tyrannies that oppressed Ireland: 'the British government and the Catholic hierarchy'. These were issues that resonated with O'Casey, and their stance was one of the many reasons why he was an admirer of both Ryan and Sheehy Skeffington.

What Ryan put on the agenda was soon followed by a number of plays with an urban or working-class setting produced in Ireland long before O'Casey's work appeared on stage.[16] The theatre of Ibsen and Shaw inspired a working-class drama infused with Boucicault's melodrama and the music hall tradition of Dublin's Queen's Theatre.[17] In 1909 the Cork Dramatic Society contained a group of actors, producers and playwrights known as the Cork Realists. They moved the dramatic action from the farmhouse kitchen to the city parlour. Terence MacSwiney's *The Holocaust* is a poignant depiction of slum life, unemployment, hunger and misery. MacSwiney draws attention to the poverty of his characters – not by grand gestures, but by convincingly observed details. Despite this, *The Holocaust* remains a 'drama of conscience' rather than one of class conflict; the working class only register in passing.[18] Daniel Corkery's *The Onus of Ownership*, also produced by the Cork Dramatic Society, explored the problems caused by slum landlords who refuse to look after their property. While in Belfast in 1911, the Ulster Literary Theatre presented William Paul's *The Jerrybuilders*, a drama that started from the premise that the city streets could be as interesting as the open field. In June 1913, just two months before the start of the lockout, William de Lacey's touring company presented *From Mill to Mansion: Or, the story of a great strike*. The posters carried the slogan: 'All we ask is a fair day's wage for a fair day's work, but the masters grudge us even that'.[19]

If in *The Laying of the Foundations* the spectre of the working class was glimpsed on the Irish stage, *Victims* by A. Patrick Wilson, a one-act play set in the tenements and produced by the Irish Workers' Dramatic Company (IWDC) at Liberty Hall in Dublin in December 1912, was the first to take the Dublin working class as its subject.[20] We get a sense that Wilson and the IWDC understood that the rising militancy of the Dublin working class provided a space where drama could give expression to the political and social aspirations of workers and their families. The play implies that a way forward for the 'victims' of society was in the resurgent trade union movement and membership of Jim Larkin's 'One Big Union'.

The Slough, Wilson's most notable work, is a three-act play about the Dublin working class produced at the Abbey in November 1914. The play has as its subject the 1913 lockout of Dublin workers. Wilson was well equipped to write about the strike and wanted to explore the reasons for the defeat. He was acquainted with Larkin and Connolly and was a prominent contributor to the *Irish Worker*, the weekly newspaper of the ITGWU. Wilson and O'Casey had previously clashed in an extended debate in the pages of the *Irish Worker* on the question of nationalism and socialism. The setting is the tenement of Peter Hanlon, a Dublin dock worker. Wilson played the part of Jake Allen, a dramatic version of Jim Larkin. *The Irish Times* reviewed the play favourably:

> Next to a war it is probable that nothing holds so much that is tragic and dramatic as a strike. *The Slough*, a new three-act play by A. Patrick Wilson, is a drama dealing, under a thin disguise, with the Dublin strike of last year, and the point of view is that of the under-dog.[21]

Wilson's play has not been published, but a copy of the text exists in the British Museum Library.[22] A summary by Robert Hogan shows a striking resemblance to Seán O'Casey's *Juno and the Paycock* and, to a lesser extent, *The Plough and the Stars*. The parallels with *Juno* are evident: the play revolves around the worn-out mother trying to keep the family together. Her husband, like Captain Boyle, is a ne'er do well, her daughter loses her virtue, another dies of consumption, and a young man is mentally broken by the violence that erupts during the strike.[23]

Blight: The tragedy of Dublin (1917) was one of only four plays that O'Casey claimed to have seen at the Abbey before 1920. *Blight* depicted the slum conditions in Dublin and was an exception to the Abbey's usual productions. The authors were Oliver St John Gogarty, a well-known surgeon, and the journalist Joseph O'Connor. *The Irish Times* gave the play an extensive and serious review: 'It was, therefore, gratifying to find that *Blight* ... reveals the horrors of slumdom in the naked light of truth, and gives an insight into the results of tenement life, which is not at all unwholesome, though it is given in a brutally realistic way'.[24] *Blight* was well received, but the play spoke with the voice of middle-class reformers rather than the people who lived in some of the worst slums not ten yards from the Abbey's front door. It was almost inevitable that *Blight* would be compared to the Dublin plays. *Blight* bears a passing resemblance to *Juno and the Paycock*, but no more than any other play of the period set in a tenement. A family racked by poverty, unemployment, drunkenness and prostitution was the staple of such productions. Gogarty and O'Connor wrote the play to expose the horror of the slums. In this regard, *Blight* partially fulfilled Yeats' concept of the role of a national theatre – to act as a forum for public debate. This format, however, is also the weakness of *Blight*; it lacks the dramatic tension that is needed to transform reportage into great drama.

NEW UNIONISM, NEW DRAMA

Larkin and Connolly were products of the new unionism in Britain and America. A sense of virtue, and a belief in the moral grandeur of the working-class family, imbued much of their politics. Along with their fierce socialist belief, or perhaps because of it, they had a strong sense of community and tried to make the ITGWU the focus of social and cultural life for working-class families. Larkin drew on his experience of the Clarion Fellowship in England to expand, with the help of his sister Delia, the cultural role of the union.[25] Connolly was equally enthusiastic about the role of poetry and drama in the socialist movement: 'no revolutionary movement is complete without a poetical expression', without which 'it is a dogma of the few, not the faith of the multitude'.[26] Jim Larkin used drama and myth to inculcate a sense of class-consciousness among Dublin workers and as a means of political mobilisation. Emmet O'Connor illustrates the way Larkin:

> demonstrated the value of using imagery which crystallised anti-capitalist sentiment, and presented in a clear, simple way the significance of each act of revolt as part of the general 'rise of the underman'. He turned strikes into battles and projected the worker as a hero. The *élan* of the 'risen people' in the 1913 lockout is the lasting monument to Larkin's style.[27]

This description exemplifies the Larkin that O'Casey portrayed in the autobiographies as 'Prometheus Hibernica' and as the heroic figure in *The Star Turns Red*. Croydon Park in Fairview, which the ITGWU purchased as a recreation centre for the members, was the crowning glory of Larkin's social programme. Larkin set the tone from the very beginning: Croydon Park opened with a Grand Temperance Fête and Children's Carnival. The union organised choral singing, dancing classes, painting and drama classes for the members and families. In an interview in the *Irish Worker*, Delia Larkin outlined her reasons for setting up the IWDC:

> Wages in Dublin are so low that the only place the workers could afford was the music hall. I do not object to the music halls, but I thought that if it was possible to provide them with a more elevating and interesting form of recreation it should be done. I started a little elocution class at Liberty Hall and discovered that some of the workers had a natural gift for acting. I trained them myself, having a great deal of interest in dramatic work, and we produced plays, learning our stage craft as we went along, and even getting our own scenery painted.[28]

Delia Larkin and the IWDC played an important role in developing O'Casey's enthusiasm for drama. Delia Larkin, born into an Irish working-class family in Liverpool in 1878, first became involved with the Irish trade union movement in 1911. She was a founder member of the ITGWU women's section, which evolved into the Irish Women Workers' Union (IWWU). Delia was a product of the new trade unionism and embraced the potential of learning and drama to enrich the lives of working-class people. She organised the construction of a small theatre in Liberty Hall, which the ITGWU had purchased in 1911. O'Casey was one of a group of union members, including his brother Isaac, who helped construct the stage and auditorium. Delia, who had a great passion for theatre, organised and trained the actors in the IWDC. In the pages of the *Irish Worker*, although she complained about the snobbery of the Abbey Theatre audience, she encouraged members of the ITGWU and the IWDC 'to pay their shilling or sixpence, and capture their seats' in order to learn from the array of plays produced by the Abbey, and added, 'for my own part I would sooner go to the Abbey once than go a dozen times to any of the other theatres'.[29] Many years later, O'Casey noted, in a letter to Lady Gregory, 'how many coal-heavers, dockers, carters and labourers have been in the Abbey and good is sure to come of their visits'.[30] The IWDC made their debut on St Stephen's night, 1912. Their ambitious programme consisted of four one-act plays: *Victims* by A. Patrick Wilson, *The Troth* by Rutherford Mayne, *The Bishop's Candlesticks* by Norman McKinnel and *The Matchmakers* by Seamus O'Kelly. The Abbey actor and playwright A. Patrick Wilson was recruited by Delia Larkin as manager and director of the IWDC.

At the end of the Dublin lockout thousands of workers were victimised and faced starvation. Delia Larkin and Jack Carney organised a tour for the IWDC in Liverpool, Manchester and London to raise funds for the Dublin Relief Committee. Given the hardship and demoralisation following the defeat of the strike, the IWDC had difficulty sustaining the group. The factional differences in the union added to their problems. After the departure of Delia Larkin in 1915, the group went into abeyance. In February 1916, James Connolly reopened the theatre in Liberty Hall – this time with a more avowedly political purpose. His announcement in the *Workers' Republic* that 'next to the revolution the greatest event of 1916 will be the opening of The New Theatre in Liberty Hall'[31] may seem excessive, but it should be read as a firm acknowledgement by Connolly and the ITGWU of the importance of culture in the labour movement. He aimed to combine culture and drama with revolutionary zeal. After one of the Sunday performances, Connolly made an appearance and told the assembled members about the activities of the ITGWU and the ICA: 'he gave those present the alternative of getting out or joining in social and dramatic activities connected with these aims'.[32] For Connolly and the reformed IWDC Players, the stage was a rehearsal place for a revolution that would spill out onto the streets of Dublin in a few short weeks.

In the months preceding the 1916 Rising, James Connolly found time to write and stage *Under Which Flag?* a play set during the Fenian insurrection of 1867.[33] The script deals sympathetically with Irish nationalism and the Fenian cause. Given the practice of urban realism fostered by the IWDC, their director A. Patrick Wilson and Connolly's trade union and socialist background, it is surprising that the setting for *Under Which Flag?* is a country cottage with a traditional rural Abbey Theatre setting and structure. The play centres on the O'Donnell family, whose son is persuaded for financial reasons to join the British army, while his girlfriend is tempted to become an informer. In the best tradition of Irish melodrama, they are saved from destruction by a realisation that their political future lies with the Irish nationalists. The plot owes a debt to Boucicault's *The Shaughraun*, and Connolly even lifted a number of expressions, songs and phrases from Boucicault's work.[34] The play has some merit, but it is very much of its time. In his review, Francis Sheehy Skeffington was supportive of Connolly's effort, in that the production 'breathes the true spirit of patriotism' and that Connolly had correctly resisted the temptation to allow his revolutionary zeal to override his aesthetic judgement. However, Sheehy Skeffington condemned Connolly's use of soliloquies, among other weaknesses, as 'dramatically inartistic'.[35]

Connolly wrote *Under Which Flag?* to counter the effect of British army recruitment drives in Ireland. By the end of 1915, 86,000 Irishmen had enlisted to fight in the war.[36] As an ex-British serviceman, he understood why working men took the king's shilling, though his anger and frustration at those who enlisted was evident in the pages of the *Workers' Republic*: 'for the sake of a few paltry shillings Irish workers have sold their country in the hour of their country's need and greatest hope'.[37] He wrote the play to incite rebellion and to politically prepare Dublin audiences for the revolution, whose plans were well advanced. In the weeks leading up to Easter, Dublin was rife with rumours of an uprising. In a provocation to the British authorities, Connolly boldly raised the green flag over Liberty Hall and stepped up his call for revolt in the pages of the *Workers' Republic*. In this tense atmosphere, the Liberty Hall Players gathered to perform *Under Which Flag?* A few weeks later, Connolly's words were made flesh. During the Easter Rising, Seán Connolly (no relation to James Connolly) of the ICA, and O'Casey's old friend from his time in Easons, was the first rebel casualty. He was an exciting young actor with the Abbey Theatre, and played the leading role in *Under Which Flag?* Seán Connolly died in the rebellion's first hours, leading the attack on City Hall. In that poignant moment, theatre stepped into the pages of history. O'Casey was outraged at the way James Connolly had appropriated the IWDC for nationalist politics. He argued that Connolly had elevated the green over the red: '*Under Which Flag?* blundered a sentimental way over a stage in the Hall in a green limelight, shot with tinsel stars ... a terrible silly, sentimental thing, because Connolly hadn't a glimmer of the artist in his whole make-up'.[38] O'Casey's objections to Connolly's play were mainly political rather than aesthetic. He believed that in 1916 the ICA fought under the wrong flag. Ten years later, he would answer Connolly's rhetorical question – 'under which flag?' – with a play of his own, *The Plough and the Stars*, which takes its title from the flag of the Irish Citizen Army.[39]

Despite the best efforts of the IWDC, the prospects for a working-class 'theatre of revolt' in Ireland were limited by the backwardness of the political and economic structures and the dominance of nationalism in Irish politics. Unlike revolutionary Germany, Russia, or even Britain to a lesser extent, Ireland lacked a large-scale industrial working class with a developed labour and socialist movement that could have provided an audience and the resources for a workers' theatre. Whatever limited possibilities the Irish Workers' Dramatic Company or the many working-class amateur theatre groups had to develop the nucleus of an audience that could respond to and support such a theatre, it evaporated with the defeat of the great strike in 1913 and the demoralisation in its aftermath. Working-class theatre ended up in a side-channel that rarely challenged nationalist theatre. The workers' movement took over a decade to recover and rebuild its strength and confidence. By the time O'Casey submitted his first play for consideration to the Abbey in 1916, the possibilities of a vibrant reciprocal relationship between writers and working-class theatre groups had disappeared.

SHAW AND O'CASEY

If Shakespeare and Boucicault had inspired the young O'Casey, Bernard Shaw transformed his view of drama and politics. In 1912, Kevin O'Loughlin, a member of the St Laurence O'Toole Club, urged O'Casey to read Bernard Shaw's *John Bull's Other Island*, insisting that the play would 'make a new man' of him.[40] Shaw wrote the play to challenge the misrepresentations of the Irish on the English stage. The play inverts the image of the stage Irishman and challenges the English audience's assumptions about Ireland. Shaw projects Larry Doyle as a real Irishman whom Shaw hopes 'will take over the job of stage interpreter of the Irish'.[41] In this scene, Doyle denounces assumptions about the Irish:

> Don't you know that all this top-o-the-morning and broth-of-a-boy and more-power-to-your-elbow business is got up in England to fool you, like the Albert Hall concerts of Irish music? No Irishman ever talks like that in Ireland, or ever did, or ever will.[42]

At that time, O'Casey's knowledge of Shaw did not extend much beyond *John Bull's Other Island*. Despite his limited reading of Shaw at this stage of his life, Shaw's writings helped O'Casey clarify his thinking on the national question and socialism during the momentous events in 1913. The Dublin lockout transformed Shaw's view of Ireland as no other Irish event had before. In his speech at the Royal Albert Hall in London in support of the locked-out workers, Shaw called on them to set up an armed section; he declared that he would like to be prosecuted for sedition so he could explain to the public that the situation was extraordinary.[43]

Initially, Shaw had little sympathy for the Irish rebels in 1916. His attitude changed when he heard of the murder of his friend, the pacifist Sheehy Skeffington, by a British army officer. He was outraged by the execution of the leaders in the aftermath of the rebellion. As the executions dragged on, Shaw wrote a letter to the *Daily News* in London.

He defended the rebels and the right of any Irishman to take up arms to achieve independence for his country, and went on to say that the Irish were only doing 'what Englishmen will do if it be their misfortune to be invaded and conquered by the Germans in the course of the present war'.[44] He warned the government that they were 'canonising their prisoners'. Shaw's letter added to the disgust many felt in Ireland and England about the almost daily executions in Dublin. Two days later, following the death of James Connolly, the executions were halted. The ninety-seven prisoners awaiting execution had their sentences commuted to life imprisonment. Undoubtedly, Shaw's letter was influential in shifting opinion in British government circles. To his credit, he also contributed a substantial sum to the fund for the wife and children of James Connolly.[45] In the wake of the failed rising, Shaw's sympathies for Irish freedom and his identity as an Irishman were transformed.

By the time O'Casey attended his first play by Shaw, *Androcles and the Lion* at the Abbey in 1919, he would have been aware of Shaw's standing as a dramatist, a socialist and an Irish nationalist, and Shaw's popularity in Ireland. O'Casey never wavered in his admiration for Shaw. He was the one person O'Casey rarely contradicted or quarrelled with throughout his life. In a letter to Horace Reynolds in 1938, he said it was 'the preaching of Jim Larkin and the books of Bernard Shaw' that swung him over to the left.[46] O'Casey's letter to Ronald Ayling in 1957 defended his friendship with Shaw against the allegations of St John Irvine, who had stated that O'Casey was 'not one of Shaw's friends'. The letter is a statement of O'Casey's admiration for, and identification with, Shaw's politics, and a manifesto of O'Casey's political and personal beliefs:

> Shaw was mainly a self-educated man, so was I; Shaw hated poverty in all its forms, so do I; Shaw fought against it most of his life, so do I, and still do; Shaw thought Stalin a great man, so do I, and so do still; Shaw was passionately devoted to the USSR and all the USSR did and was doing, so was I; Shaw hated British Imperialism, so do I; Shaw rejected the Christian beliefs, so do I; Shaw saw through the Romantic idea of Irish nationalism, so did I; Shaw was a fighter, and he knew I was one too.[47]

O'Casey wrote to Bernard Shaw in November 1919 asking if he would write a preface to his book of essays, *Three Shouts on a Hill*: 'a shout at the Gaelic League, a shout at Sinn Fein, and a shout at Labour', with a closing chapter called 'Descending the Hill'.[48] However, Shaw declined his request, telling O'Casey that he must go through the mill like every other writer and publish on his merit rather than trying to use Shaw as a shortcut to success. Shaw was the supreme polemicist and recognised the problems with O'Casey's book. In his reply, he said that 'he liked the foreword and the afterword much better than the shouts, which are prodigiously overwritten'. He went on to say that he was afraid 'the National question will insist on getting settled before the Labour question. That's why the National question is a nuisance.' He suggested that O'Casey ought 'to work out his position positively and definitely' and that shouting and objecting to everyone was useless.[49] With Shaw's preface, O'Casey had hoped to get £25 for the book, enough to keep him for a year. In light of Shaw's reply, O'Casey put aside the book and never again attempted to have it published. However, he reused and updated some of the material in his articles in *Irish Opinion*.

In 1912 O'Casey was far more interested in the ideas advanced by Shaw in his plays rather than their qualities as theatre.[50] He had read *John Bull's Other Island* as a synthesis of the conflicting ideologies confronting Ireland and understood the play to be both anti-imperialist and anti-capitalist. The spoilt priest Keegan represents the wonderful but hopeless dream of a Gaelic Ireland, where the church, the state and the people become one: 'torturing itself with an unrealisable dream'.[51] Nevertheless, he recognised that Keegan's idealistic dream was being 'hitched to a power and a will that could face the facts'.[52] With his provocative analysis of the 'Irish question', Shaw stripped away the dreams and opened O'Casey's eyes to other possibilities.

He was also reading Charles Darwin on evolution. Shaw's emphasis on human agency as the motor of history was tempered by the biological and historical determinism he took from Darwin. Shaw added some intellectual steel to the humanity at the heart of O'Casey's politics. Shaw wrote for a purpose; he attached as much importance to the preface as he did to the text in the published version of each play. In these philosophical introductions, Shaw set out, sometimes at great length, his theories on everything from atheism to vegetarianism. In his autobiography, it is Shaw's prefaces that O'Casey quotes. The emphasis is on Shaw's ideas rather than his skill as a playwright. Despite his reverence for Shaw, O'Casey did understand the limits of Shaw's socialist politics. His summary of Shaw's Fabian politics in an article written for the *New York Times* in 1946 is as good as anything written since:

> Though Shaw spoke many times to meetings of the workers, influencing them powerfully and making them feel proud of having such a fine mind as friend and leader, it was the solid, respectable, serene middle class that Shaw reached and affected most, by preface and play, by puzzling them, by teasing them, and laughing at them, even by frightening them; but eventually convincing influential numbers of them that Socialism was not only not dangerous, but acceptable to fine and intelligent minds, and a movement to be supported by intelligent and conscientious men and women.[53]

Harvest Festival, written in 1919, is the nearest O'Casey came to writing a complete Shavian drama. But at that stage of his career, he lacked Shaw's ability to translate propaganda into dramatic action. His characters are just spokespersons for his opinions. However, Shaw was always there in the background, ready to emerge when O'Casey had perfected his craft. Shaw could combine forceful intelligence with comic invention. Not all of Shaw's drama is didactic or discursive. What O'Casey picks up on in plays such as *Man and Superman* and *Arms and the Man* is Shaw's ability to use comedy and irony so effectively. Shaw's use of gentle mocking humour to undercut the seriousness of John Tanner in *Man and Superman* is also a feature of the later plays of O'Casey.

Shaw believed that the human race was a failure and that progress was impossible until humanity had developed the ability to evolve intellectually at some indeterminate date in the future. This concept of a 'life force' or creative evolution dominates much of Shaw's drama and his polemics.[54] O'Casey showed little interest in Shaw's more outlandish philosophical speculations, but the concept of a 'life force' is present primarily in O'Casey's plays written after 1945. There are, however, some disturbing elements from the neo-Darwinian theories that were popular in the 1930s in *The Silver Tassie* and *Within the Gates*. They end with a plea to leave behind the broken and the crippled and a demand that those who have survived 'must go on living'.[55] In an article for *The Daily Princetonian* headed 'Author Interprets *Within the Gates*', O'Casey concluded the piece by saying: 'Today an imbecile gets greater care than a healthy and intelligent child. The weak oppress the strong. This must end'.[56] We can read far too much into a few lines in an article or a play, but it does illustrate what currency these reactionary ideas had in the 1930s. Neither O'Casey nor Shaw ever envisaged that these dangerous ideas would gain a foothold and have an outcome in the perverted ideology of fascism which led to the Holocaust of the Second World War. O'Casey never referred to them again. Unlike Shaw, O'Casey's 'life force' is not some pseudo-scientific formula to transform the nature of humankind; rather, it is the fighting spirit within all of us. In O'Casey's view, everyone can change themselves and the world about them, but only if they throw off the dogmatism of the church and society that holds them back and live life to the full.

CHAPTER 9

Dismantling the Myth

Most nation states develop a 'creation myth' that binds the population to the state or creates a sense of identity with the new state. In the United States of America, it was the story of the Boston Tea Party that awoke the citizens to the evils of British colonial rule. In Ireland, the story of the 1916 Rising served the same purpose: 'A few hundred brave men and some women are supposed to have marched into the GPO, knowing that they were going to their deaths. Their sacrifice was thought to have awakened the Irish nation from its slumbers'.[1] In a similar vein, but writing about the War of Independence, Ernie O'Malley said, 'Many of us could hardly see ourselves for the legends built up around us ... I resented the legend. It made me other than myself and attuned to act to standards that were not my own'.[2]

The 1916 martyrs could be celebrated by the new state because they were safely dead. O'Casey portrayed working-class characters who were inconveniently alive. He refused to either deify or vilify the 1916 rebels, but instead he projected the reality of the Free State that emerged for all the talk of sacrifice and heroes. It was clear to him that the new state aimed to advance commercial interests, not the ambitions of the poor or the disadvantaged. Introducing the 2010 production of *The Plough and the Stars*, the historian Diarmaid Ferriter said that O'Casey refused to simplify or romanticise what was a painful and challenging time and that he 'refused to be pious or reverential or indulge those craving glory and gratitude, and in doing so, he had the clarity of the historian fifty years before professional historians managed it'.[3]

The Queen's Theatre melodramas at the beginning of the century paved the way for O'Casey in several ways. In addition to the nationalist dramas, the works of P.J. Bourke were popular with Dublin working-class audiences. Desmond Slowey notes how Bourke focused his plays 'on the lives of working-class urban or labouring country people'. Bourke also broke new ground 'by making a woman the hero and central character of *For the Land She Loved*'.[4] For the first time, the urban working class could see their lives on the stage 'transformed and ennobled by the aspirations to freedom'.[5] These plays were both an entertainment and propaganda in their romantic portrayal of revolutionary action. Nevertheless, despite Bourke's productions, nationalist drama was dominant on the Queen's stage. While the Queen's style is evident in O'Casey's drama, he set out to subvert the nationalist myths surrounding the 1916 Rising and the War of Independence, and in the process he overturned the heroic conventions of the Queen's dramatic style and the nationalist sentiments that gave rise to it. In *The Plough and the Stars*, O'Casey turned the conventions of the historic play inside out in a way that went beyond formal innovation. He summoned his characters from the margins of history and placed them in the spotlight while the great men and women of history were confined to the wings.

O'Casey had already tried his hand at a number of plays when he wrote *The Harvest Festival* during the first months of 1919. The hard-edged action of the play is set during the railway strike of 1911, although it also incorporates a series of events that took place during the lockout in 1913. The central character, Jack Rocliffe, is shot by one of the strike-breakers during the dispute. As they carry away his dead body, his comrades sing 'We'll Keep the Red Flag Flying Here' – a statement perhaps that in the future, a different outcome is possible.[6] *The Harvest Festival* has many faults, particularly in the way that it lectures the audience. O'Casey's protagonists lack credibility as representatives of their respective political interests. Jack Rocliffe is not just an idealised version of O'Casey, but also an idealised version of the heroic worker. Here is Rocliffe explaining the difference between the new type of worker and the old grovelling worker of the past:

> None of you seems to know that there are two types of workers. The one an old poisonous growth of what is called the Capitalist System, the other a new vigorous growth that is rapidly extinguishing the older one; the one satisfied with the least that the employing-class will give; the other dissatisfied with the least that the employing class can bestow; the one content to remain a slave, the other determined to become a man ... the one willing to submit to any kind of life to avoid death; the other prepared to meet any form of death that he may have life.[7]

O'Casey was making a statement regarding his attitude to socialism and violence in the aftermath of the 1916 Rising and labour's capitulation to nationalism. While the action takes place in the past, the issues that

O'Casey was addressing are those taking place at the time of writing. We hear the voice of O'Casey in the guise of Jack Rocliffe:

> I am not so eager that the men should gain the right towards a living wage as I am that they should overthrow the wage system altogether. But the time for that is not yet. The Leaders of Labour are as yet like children that have been born out of due season. Sometimes the rank and file are ahead of the leaders; sometimes the leaders are ahead of the rank and file. When the advanced thought of the leaders is fused with the advanced action of the men – then will come the Revolution.[8]

The Harvest Festival is a play about the potential of social revolution. O'Casey states the classic Marxist position: 'Where the chains of capitalism are forged, there they must be broken'.[9] There is no ambiguity in O'Casey's position; if industrial action fails, then force is justified if the circumstances warrant it.

Even before the Abbey returned the script of *The Harvest Festival*, O'Casey had started on his next project, *The Crimson in the Tricolour*, which he completed in 1921. The text has not survived, and we only know the form and content from the letters and notes of O'Casey, Lady Gregory and Lennox Robinson. O'Casey described *The Crimson in the Tricolour* as 'essentially a futurist work, evolved from the passions, ideas & activities of the present'.[10] The play was O'Casey's statement on the struggle between labour and Sinn Féin. His roommate in Mountjoy Square, Micheál Ó Maoláin, who had read the play, described it as 'about the Nationalist movement and how Labour interacted with that movement' and at the same time, it took a swipe at the 'well-off women who found out for the first time that they had a country to save'.[11] It seemed that O'Casey would never forgive Constance Markievicz and her well-off friends from Rathmines. In this Shavian-style debate, the nationalist position is represented by a character based on Arthur Griffith, while the union leader was an obvious parody of a sell-out bureaucrat based on William O'Brien of the ITGWU. An O'Casey figure called Kevin O'Regan, not unlike Jack Rocliffe from the earlier play, becomes a socialist as a result of his immersion in poetry and philosophy. Colbert Kearney has suggested that:

> There is substantial evidence to establish an intellectual morality play in the Shavian manner but with Dublin accents. The key movement is the change in the central character from a contemptuous dismissal of all political parties to an acceptance of his destiny as a Labour leader.[12]

The 'Crimson' that O'Casey wanted to inject into the 'Tricolour' was that of the Russian Revolution of 1917. O'Casey described it as a 'play of ideas moulded on Shaw's style' and it contained two characters that were reincarnated later as 'the Covey' and 'Fluther' in *The Plough and the Stars*.[13]

W.B. Yeats was never impressed by discursive plays, but he also objected on the grounds that it would generate political passions and reactions of the kind he disliked so much. He criticised the structure of the play because he believed that any action necessary to the dramatic development of a play should not be performed by a character that never appears on stage. O'Casey replied in typical fashion. He intended to write a play, *The Red Star*, in which Larkin would never appear, but would be responsible for all the action. This was a device that obviously appealed to O'Casey. In *The Plough and the Stars*, the 'figure in the window' never appears on stage, but his speech from off-stage sets the political tone of the play and provides the dramatic tension between the ideals of the revolutionaries and the reality of life in the tenements. He also used this device many years later in *The Drums of Father Ned*. Lady Gregory was also hesitant about the proposed production because of the political position in the country at the time:

> It is the expression of ideas that makes it interesting ... But we could not put it on while the Revolution is unaccomplished – it might hasten the Labour attack on Sinn Féin, which ought to be kept back till the fight with England is over and the new Government has had time to show what it can do.[14]

O'Casey's early unproduced plays were a direct intervention in the debate between labour and Sinn Féin that bordered on agitprop, heavily influenced by Shaw's discursive style, but with an underlying comic and ironic content that was to become his trademark. These early plays were a direct statement of O'Casey's socialist politics. His shift to a more nuanced presentation of his politics, commencing with *The Shadow of a Gunman* in 1923, pleased his more adventurous literary critics. However, his political admirers were baffled as to precisely what O'Casey had to say beyond a general disillusionment at the outcome of the War of Independence.

POLITICAL SHADOWS

After his mother's death in 1918, O'Casey left Abercorn Road and moved into a tenement in Mountjoy Square, where he shared a room with Micheál

Ó Maoláin, an Aran Islander and an old friend of Jim Larkin. O'Casey used several incidents from his time in Mountjoy Square in *The Shadow of a Gunman* (1923). The house was under surveillance, and the two IRA men who lived in an upstairs room were subjected to several raids by the military and the Black and Tans. Ó Maoláin had obtained a job for O'Casey with Delia Larkin as the caretaker in the Old Foresters' Hall in Langrishe Place. His work in the hall kept him occupied most of the day, the nights he spent writing. He did not mix with his neighbours in the tenement, and they assumed he was an IRA gunman on the run. O'Casey was caught up in a raid when the British army arrested one of his neighbours in the tenement following the discovery of a cache of arms in an outside shed. O'Casey had the Citizen Army minutes in his room, and Ó Maoláin suggested that he should slip out and hide them in the Foresters' Hall. This incident became the nucleus of *The Shadow of a Gunman* and a chapter headed 'The Raid' in the fourth volume of his autobiography. The play is set in a one-room tenement at the height of the War of Independence. *The Shadow of a Gunman* opened on 12 April 1923, near the end of the Civil War. The Abbey was under armed guard as they were threatened by the anti-treaty forces for refusing to shut, as a mark of respect, following the execution of republican prisoners by the Free State.

The title of Ernie O'Malley's compelling memoir of the War of Independence is derived from an old Ulster proverb about those who live 'on another man's wound'.[15] This was a cutting remark by O'Malley about the carpetbaggers who had taken power in the Free State on the back of other people's efforts and sacrifices. Donal Davoren in *The Shadow of a Gunman* is such a man. Davoren is not after money or position but the admiration of his neighbours and especially that of the attractive Minnie Powell, who lives across the hall. Minnie's admiration for Davoren is partly because of his way with words, but also because of a romantic attachment to the idea of Davoren as a 'gunman on the run', a misconception of which Davoren does nothing to disabuse her. Donal Davoren, the poet and dreamer, belongs to Shaw's world, where the word 'poet' is nearly always a playful term of abuse. In Shaw's work, the poet often appears as a bohemian who passes the time, vainly weaving illusions about the unbearable reality of truth. Davoren is such a man; he is both a 'shadow' of a poet and a 'shadow' of a gunman. This is a drama ridiculing hypocrisy, self-deceit and reckless bravado rather than exalting the lofty ideals of patriotism.

The Shadow of a Gunman is a study of human weakness, of disillusionment rather than heroic action. Maguire is a pedlar of knick-knacks who occasionally works in the same line of business with Davoren's roommate, Seumas Shields. Maguire is a shadowy figure, but an actual gunman, who leaves his pedlar's bag with Shields for safekeeping while he is away for a few days. Shields and Davoren are not aware that the bag contains munitions. When the news reaches them that Maguire was killed while taking part in an IRA ambush, panic ensues in the tenement, particularly when they discover the actual contents of his bag. During a raid on the house, Minnie Powell, believing that Davoren is in danger, takes Maguire's bag into her room. As a result, she is arrested, and in the confusion that follows Minnie is killed as she is led away during an exchange of fire between the British army and the IRA.

In *The Shadow of a Gunman*, words and illusions have tragic consequences. Donal Davoren, Tommy Owens and Seumas Shields live in a world of words, while Minnie Powell and Maguire live in a world of action. Seumas Shields uses language to deflate the pretensions of others while being blind to his own failings. Minnie Powell, in her speech, is matter-of-fact without the flights of empty rhetoric that afflict Davoren, Owens or Shields. Despite her limitations, she is the only character with a positive outlook. She is the bridge between words and actions, but her character lacks depth; she is not allowed to explain herself; all that remains is the image of a brave, but essentially foolish, young woman. Minnie Powell, however, is caught in the crossfire of their delusions and the war raging beyond the four walls of a Dublin tenement. The rhetoric of romantic nationalism had consequences for the inhabitants, regardless of whether they embraced such ideals. The outside world intrudes into their lives with little regard for their safety or aspirations.

The Shadow of a Gunman is, perhaps, O'Casey's most pessimistic play, with few signs of hope that either they or external political forces can change their circumstances. Joe Cleary is one of several of O'Casey's critics who suggest that the dramatic tension in the Dublin plays 'is not intellectually worked through', and this is the case with *The Shadow of a Gunman*.[16] O'Casey does not attempt to portray the heroic side of the struggle or get to grips with what motivated Maguire. The fleeting appearance of Maguire with a few lines of dialogue is not enough to provide a contrast or intellectual counterpoint against which the pretensions of Davoren, Shields and Owens can be judged. Maguire is portrayed as reckless and unthinking in the way that he places the inhabitants of the tenement in danger without any background explanation as to his nationalist convictions or why he did it. Davoren is a false hero who struts about the tenement living off the reflected glory of other men's wounds, not unlike Synge's *Playboy*, Christy Mahon, who swaggered across the Abbey stage sixteen years earlier, boasting that he had killed his brute of a father.[17] Nevertheless, their deceptions and lies have consequences. Christy loses Pegeen, the woman he has come to love, because of a lie, even as he finds personal redemption. There is no redemption, however, for Davoren. He lets Minnie Powell die for his vain conceits and remains the same cowardly, abject figure he always was. Christy Mahon and Donal Davoren exist in a hostile world not of their own making. Davoren is a self-deceiving coward, allowing people to believe in his status as a gunman in order to seduce Minnie Powell while comforting himself with the thought: 'and what danger can there be in being the shadow of a gunman?'[18]

In *The Shadow of a Gunman*, his characters have an existence independent of O'Casey's own views. In all the Dublin plays, outside forces govern the lives of O'Casey's characters, and they are overwhelmed by events they cannot control. It is only in the later plays, after O'Casey left Ireland, that they begin to shape their own fate. O'Casey does not attempt to portray the heroic side of the struggle, but he does portray how it looked to those whose world never extended a great deal further than a two-room tenement in the slums of Dublin. A contemporary review in 1924, shortly after the end of the Civil War, reflects the excitement the play generated in the way it caught the popular mood of the people:

> It tells everybody what they thought while the two armies shot up each other and made life hideous for people who wanted to go about their business and live a normal human life. It gets back at the heroes. It is a play of disillusion for a people who have been disillusioned, and can take their disillusionment without bitterness.[19]

In 1980, to mark the centenary of O'Casey's birth, two productions of *The Shadow of a Gunman*, one in Ireland and the other in England, emphasised the tragic aspect of the play over the comic. The reviews in the Irish and English papers 'remarked on the play's terrifying applicability to the current troubles in Northern Ireland'.[20]

O'Casey began writing *The Shadow of a Gunman* in 1922, the same year Joyce's *Ulysses* and T.S. Eliot's *The Waste Land* shattered the old literary concepts and instituted the modernist era in English literature. *The Shadow of a Gunman* hardly ranks beside them. However, all the elements that came to fruition in *The Silver Tassie* and *Within the Gates* were present in this early work:

> Its grotesque admixture of disparate styles, its profoundly disturbing atmosphere and shock effects presaged its creator's unobtrusive but assured admission to the ranks of modernist authors.[21]

The Shadow of a Gunman does not have a conventional ending that can provide closure or catharsis for the audience. They were left to reflect on the outcome of the decade of revolution that was drawing to a close. However, as in all of his work, 'the social significance of the play is just as important as its historical aspects, and the locality is chosen with as much care as the date of the action'. In a short scene in act two, O'Casey captures the brutality of the Black and Tans and the abject terror they inflicted on the local population. During the War of Independence, British soldiers and the Black and Tans tore apart the Dublin tenements, 'a community already battered by poverty'.[22] In his extended essay *Sean O'Casey's Theatre of War*, Ronald Ayling makes a case for the relevance of O'Casey's plays. He highlights the fact that similar scenes from *The Shadow of a Gunman* are being enacted across the globe up to the present day.[23]

ONE-ACT INTERLUDE

The Shadow of a Gunman was a dramatic success that played to packed houses at a time when the country lived in the shadow of the Civil War. O'Casey's response was to write two one-act satires on the political situation in the Free State, *The Cooing of the Doves* and *Kathleen Listens In*. Both plays were written and submitted in the months leading up to the decisive general election on 27 August 1923 that reaffirmed support for the pro-treaty Cumann na nGaedheal party. Unlike the Dublin trilogy (1923–6), which are plays of reflection on the events of 1916 to 1923, these were hard-hitting comic and ironic commentaries on contemporary events. They also demonstrate how O'Casey's mind was focused on the political and social shortcomings of the newly emerged Free State. In a letter in 1961, O'Casey said that *Kathleen Listens In* 'was written specifically to show what fools these mortals were in the quarrelling factions soaking Ireland in anxiety and irritation after the Civil War',[24] and to counter 'the cult of the dead hero and the glorification of martyrdom'.[25] They also reveal O'Casey's tentative engagement with expressionist techniques in the way that he strips his characters of their individuality, a technique he reproduced in the second act of *The Silver Tassie* (1928) and in a more complete form in *Within the Gates* (1934). The characters are given representative names such as the Socialist Labourer, the Native Speaker in *The Cooing of the Doves*, the Farmer and the Business Man from *Kathleen Listens In*, and so forth. Gabriel Fallon, who acted in *Kathleen Listens In*, claimed that it was 'Brecht before Brecht'.[26] They are also significant in relation to the development of O'Casey's dramaturgy, in the way that he fuses politics with satire that is so evident in *Juno and the Paycock* and *The Plough and the Stars*.

The setting of *The Cooing of the Doves: A conversation in one act* is a public house, with an election meeting in progress in the vicinity of the bar.[27] All the stock characters that populate *The Plough and the Stars* are present, The Republican Labourer, The Socialist Labourer, The Native Speaker, The Forrester and The Carpenter. No one is spared in this political comedy about plunging the country into a bitter civil war that offered no vision for social advancement. The Socialist Labourer and The Carpenter reappear in the *Plough* as the Covey and Fluther Good, along with the bogus quotes from Karl Marx:

> THE SOCIALIST LABOURER: We'll see what you know about Labour: what does Karl Marx say in the 220th Chapter of *Das Kapital* on the Mechanism of Exchange?[28]

However, unlike the *Plough*, O'Casey balances these satirical outbursts by including another character, The Socialist Clerk, who is allowed a modicum of sanity and is perhaps a reflection of O'Casey's views:

> THE SOCIALIST CLERK: But the day of the common people'll come when the workers'll stand on the principles enunciated by Fintan Lalor, that the ownership of Ireland, moral and material, is vested in the people of Ireland.[29]

The Abbey rejected the play, and the script was lost. However, in 2006 the manuscript resurfaced and was sold at auction and is now in the library of Princeton University in the United States of America.

O'Casey's one-act play *Kathleen Listens In* was completed a few months after the end of the Civil War. *Kathleen Listens In* was part of a triple bill alongside Shaw's *The Man of Destiny*, which must have given O'Casey a real sense of achievement. Now he could fill the Abbey week after week, and he was up there on the billboard alongside Bernard Shaw. In March 1922, during the lead-up to the Civil War, O'Casey published a short story, 'The Seamless Coat of Cathleen', in *Poblacht na hÉireann*, a republican anti-treaty paper published by Erskine Childers.[30] The story is an allegorical account of the treaty debate which had taken place in the Mansion House in January. He utilised the Bible story of the soldiers squabbling over the robe worn by Jesus on the cross to illustrate the partition of Ireland and the debate over dominion status. His sympathies for the anti-treaty republican side are evident in this Swiftian-style phantasy. He reworked the story as a one-act play of the same name and sent it to the Abbey for consideration. The script was returned a week later with a comment from Lennox Robinson saying they had read the play and liked it a great deal, especially the 'humour and the element of phantasy in it. At the same time it is too definite a piece of propaganda for us to do it.'[31] A year later, O'Casey resurrected the script, updating and rewriting it to take account of the political situation in the months following the end of the Civil War. He submitted the revised script to the Abbey as *Kathleen Listens In*, and it premiered in October 1923.

Kathleen Listens In was a topical play in which Kathleen, the daughter of O'Houlihan, is a modern young woman who lives in a Free State house, which her father had acquired by selling the family cow; in other words, his republican principles. She is wooed politically by a Free State politician, a farmer, a republican and a socialist, each vying for her vote. *Kathleen Listens In* is a knock-about allegorical morality play that has lost its edge with the passage of time. According to O'Casey, the play was received in total silence; whether this was through a lack of understanding of the political point that O'Casey was making or just bafflement at the ironic comedy on the stage is hard to say. The theme had currency and should have been clear enough to the audience. O'Houlihan is repairing his house from the ravages of the recent turmoil and paints the door green, while his wife spends her time doing the laundry, proclaiming, 'I don't think there's a house in the whole wide world that there's so much washin' to be done as there is in this house'.[32] O'Casey was determined that the Free State's dirty linen would be washed in public, even if that meant the play was received in stony silence. What concerned O'Casey was whether the Free State would face up to the past in an honest way and, more importantly, offer some hope into the future. Jimmy, a workman who is repairing the house and a member of the Labour Party, goes on strike, demanding that they paint the house red. He announces to all and sundry that he is 'Th' hardest worked an' th' worst fed in the house – I'll emigrate to Russia, so I will'.[33]

O'Casey's image of Kathleen is radically different from the traditional romantic image of Cathleen ni Houlihan, especially as portrayed by Yeats in his 1902 play of the same name. O'Casey takes his cue from Laurence Doyle's speech in Shaw's *John Bull's Other Island*: 'If you want to interest him in Ireland you've got to call the unfortunate Island Kathleen ni Houlihan and pretend she's a little old woman'.[34] Like Shaw, O'Casey deliberately undercuts Yeats' iconic play, which personified a poetic and romantic view of Ireland that had no reality in the state that emerged at the end of the Civil War. O'Casey spurned any emotional appeal based on a heroic past and demanded that a rational and prosperous future be mapped out for the citizens of the newly independent state. Christopher Murray illustrates how these two one-act plays were an indication of how O'Casey 'would thereafter use comedy to highlight a fundamentally serious subject'.[35]

JUNO'S LAMENT

Juno and the Paycock, first produced at the Abbey in 1924, is set during the terrible events of the Civil War. Captain Boyle, a strutting self-centred 'paycock', dominates the stage with his presence, but it is Juno, a God-fearing, determined woman, who holds the family and the play together. *Juno and the Paycock* is a great tragic drama, but O'Casey tempers the tragedy with comedy to make it bearable. Captain Boyle is the focus for the comedy; the Falstaff figure from Shakespeare, who hides his failures behind a mask of comedy. A product of the slums, broken by poverty, drunkenness and chronic unemployment, a shadow of the man he might have been, Boyle finds redemption in talk and in his brutal and pathetic attempts to impose his authority on his family. O'Casey was not a habitué of public houses, but he knew from personal experience that the likes of Boyle existed in every street and tenement in Dublin. In the play, the promised legacy from a relative's will offers the possibility of a better life.[36] In the few weeks before they realise the legacy will not materialise, O'Casey provides a glimpse of the humanity and possibilities in Captain Boyle's character. In different circumstances, he might have amounted to something, which is why audiences have always had sympathy, and even a liking, for this broken brute of a man. The execution of the captain's son Johnny Boyle by his former comrades in the IRA for informing on his neighbour and comrade was based on a real event. Captain Wogan, a republican, was captured by Free State soldiers, and his mutilated body was dumped on the outskirts of Dublin.[37] His murder, among many other terrible incidents, was still of recent memory, and the audience during that first production would have contained many ex-combatants from both sides of the Civil War.

The dominant theme in *Juno and the Paycock* is one of betrayal, allied to hope. Johnny Boyle betrays his comrade Tancred, just as Jerry Devine betrays his socialist principles in the way he rejects Mary Boyle. All of these betrayals heighten the connections between the interior life of the tenement and the world outside. O'Casey always referred to it as a play about Johnny Boyle set against the background of the Civil War.[38] In painting Johnny's character, O'Casey seems to point to a misguided idealism that led him to betray the ideals of the revolution, but in making Johnny the central tragic figure of the play, O'Casey makes him less of a man. John Crowley, who directed *Juno and the Paycock* at the Donmar Warehouse in London in 1999, suggested in an interview that 'it feels as if Johnny's story is one draft short, and if we examine the first draft of the play, Johnny's story is far less significant'.[39] In writing up Johnny's character, O'Casey never filled in the background. While we know that Johnny was wounded during the War of Independence and lost his arm in an explosion in the Civil War, just a few months before the action in the play takes place, what is not clear is why he betrayed his republican comrade Tancred, who was abducted and shot by the Free State forces.

Boyle and Tancred were neighbours and friends who lived in the same tenement. They both fought on the anti-treaty side in the Civil War. There are several explanations commonly put forward for Johnny's betrayal. Firstly, that he was broken psychologically by the experience and suffering from what today would be called post-traumatic stress, and was therefore not responsible for his actions. The second and more insidious explanation is that Johnny had lost faith in his republican ideals and had become an informer for the Free State. O'Casey's pacifist supporters also like to point out that O'Casey was condemning war in all its aspects because of the suffering it unleashed on the helpless people in the tenements. None of these explanations seems adequate. O'Casey set out to rid Ireland of the 'dead weight of heroes', which he maintained had paralysed the people from taking any action that might transform their lives. O'Casey believed that the idealism of Wolfe Tone, Robert Emmet and the men and women of 1916 had been transformed into an abstraction devoid of any social content. Describing the political limitations of the Irish nationalist movement, Peadar O'Donnell reinforces O'Casey's contention:

> The economic framework and social relationships ... were declared outside the scope of the Republican struggle; even the explosive landlord-tenant relationship, the rancher-small farmer tension. The

> Republican movement was inspired by 'pure ideals'. In the grip of this philosophy the Republican struggle could present itself as a democratic movement of mass revolt without any danger to the social pattern; without any danger to the haves from the have-nots … under the shelter of pure ideals the Irish middle class held its place within a movement it feared.[40]

Years later, O'Casey expressed his dissatisfaction with the play, and we can see why. Johnny's character lacks the depth or complexity that might provide the political or psychological background for his betrayal of his friend and comrade. This weakness in characterisation and the political context of Johnny's actions has left O'Casey open to the accusation that *Juno and the Paycock* was an attack on the republican movement that offered no alternative except to condemn violence for political ends. The feminist and republican activist Rosamond Jacob was scathing in her opinion of *Juno and the Paycock*, and in particular of the character Johnny Boyle; she recorded in her diary that the best part was 'when two IRA men with revolvers came in and dragged out that intolerable Johnny to be shot'.[41]

O'Casey had little time for sentimentality about life in the tenements. Mary Boyle, with her green ribbons and silk stockings, like Nora in *The Plough and the Stars*, has ambitions for a better life, to have her own house and a future free of the degrading poverty that surrounded her. Mary enjoys the cinema and dances, but she also reads books and tries to educate herself about the finer things in life. She is a trade unionist on strike in support of a sacked fellow worker. Significantly, this is a 'sympathetic strike' reminiscent of an earlier and more militant period of working-class struggle. She is not, however, a caricature of a young socialist and liberated woman. O'Casey's description of Mary displays all the strengths and weaknesses of a woman from her situation:

> She is a well-made and good-looking girl of twenty-two. Two forces are working in her mind – one, through the circumstances of her life, pulling her back; the other, through the influence of books she has read, pushing her forward. The opposing forces are apparent in her speech and her manners, both of which are degraded by her environment, and improved by her acquaintance – slight despite it be – with literature.[42]

Mary has a core of decency that is lacking in Jerry Devine and the schoolteacher, Charlie Bentham. She stands by her fellow worker, though personally disliking her. When her mother laments the loss of money coming into the house, Mary replies: 'What's the use of belongin' to a Trades Union if you won't stand up for your principles? Why did they sack her? It was a clear case of victimisation. We couldn't let her walk the streets, could we?'[43] Walking the streets – or prostitution – was a prospect that, by the end of the play, Mary would be facing but for the humanity and solidarity of her mother.

Mary Boyle is a modern woman, or as much of one as she can be, given her background in the tenements. However, she knows that in twenty years' time her lot will be that of her mother, slaving to keep the family together unless she manages to better herself. For a young woman from Mary Boyle's background, marriage to someone as ambitious as herself or from a middle-class background was the only possibility. Jerry Devine, an aspiring trade union official, fits the bill, but her head is turned by the middle-class schoolteacher Bentham; 'with his walkin' stick and gloves' he appears to have a lot more to offer Mary than Jerry Devine. Mary is a typical woman of her class and time, conditioned to lack confidence in herself and to be dependent on men. She becomes pregnant by Bentham, who then betrays and abandons her.

Jerry Devine is a man of shallow principles, representative of the type of trade union official who has grown comfortable and forgotten about the concerns of those he purports to represent. O'Casey had little time for the careerists who had replaced the principled leadership of Larkin and Connolly in the trade union movement. He hated the way the new elite, whether government or trade union officials, adopted the dress and manner of the departed British establishment. His critique of trade union officials finds expression in the character of Jerry Devine. He is a careerist who knows just enough to impress his fellow workers and rise in the ranks of the bureaucracy, but not enough to use that power and knowledge for the benefit of those he represents. Literature and learning were an essential part of O'Casey's life. However, Jerry Devine's understanding of literature is shallow, a few phrases and lines for an emotional appeal to impress his listeners, whether it is his co-workers or Mary Boyle. On the other hand, Mary Boyle's engagement with poetry and the plays of Ibsen are an attempt to understand the world about her and to try to better herself intellectually. Jerry Devine's rejection of Mary Boyle, when he finds out that she is pregnant by the schoolteacher Bentham, is unsettling given his verbal expressions about solidarity and the 'brotherhood of man'. The portrayal of Jerry Devine is not primarily about weakness of character, but an attack on the type of people who occupied Liberty Hall and the upper echelons of the trade union movement; careerists who are terrified to take any action, political or personal, that might jeopardise their position.

MOTHER COURAGE

Juno has been described as the Mother Courage of the tenements, whose strength and humanity shines out in times of adversity.[44] Juno has courage, awareness of others, a grasp of reality, and above all an ability to learn from experience and her mistakes. Nevertheless, it is a mistake to believe that O'Casey was idealising Juno; instead, he paints her as 'a calculated rebuff to the glorified figure of Kathleen ni Houlihan as symbolic of Ireland'.[45] In the early productions of the Irish Literary Theatre, W.B. Yeats and Edward Martyn, among others, depicted Kathleen as one of the warrior-women who lead men into battle. Juno's circumstances limit her world to her family and her immediate surroundings. When she hears of the execution of a neighbour's son, her immediate reaction is one of relief that her son Johnny has not been friendly with him for some time. She rebukes Mary for wearing ribbons while on strike because she thinks this will encourage the employers to believe that they are overpaying their employees. Herbert Goldstone compared Juno to the heroine in Brecht's play *Mother Courage and Her Children*: 'Like Mother Courage, Juno simply doesn't realise that she has let the very conditions of life which have victimised her become her ultimate standard of value'.[46] Surprisingly, given the moral climate of the time, the audience made little of the fact that, at the end of the play, Juno leaves her abusive husband and goes off with her pregnant and unmarried daughter to start a new life together. She abandons Boyle because she knows 'he'll be hopeless till the end of his days'.[47] When Mary exclaims that her poor child will have no father, Juno's reply is one that any feminist would be proud of: 'It'll have what's far better – it will have two mothers'.[48]

In developing the character of Juno, O'Casey must have been aware of the prayer-like poem 'The Mother' that Patrick Pearse had written for his mother, Margaret, not long before the 1916 Rising. Pearse's poem would have been familiar to the audience in 1924; it speaks of her sorrow, tinged with the joy of knowing that her sons had died for Ireland:

> Lord, thou art hard on mothers:
> We suffer in their coming and their going;

> And tho' I grudge them not, I weary, weary
> Of the long sorrow – And yet I have my joy;
> My sons were faithful, and they fought.[49]

Margaret Pearse was promoted as an idealised mother figure for the wives and mothers of the new nation, long-suffering, and heroic in the face of adversity. The last few lines of Pearse's poem have an affinity with Juno's plea following the death of her son, except that Juno had no joy in her son's death, just the knowledge that this terrible deed was a product of the Civil War that overwhelmed her family and the country:

> What was the pain I suffered, Johnny, bringin' you into the world to carry you to your cradle to the pains I'll suffer carryin' you out o' the world to bring you to your grave! Mother o'God, Mother o'God, have pity on us all! ... Sacred Heart o' Jesus, take away our hearts o' stone, and give us hearts o' flesh! Take away this murdherin' hate, an' give us Thine own eternal love![50]

Despite the death and destruction that surrounds the Boyle family and their neighbours, the play is not without hope. Juno learns the hard way the need for understanding and solidarity with her neighbour, Mrs Tancred, who also lost her son during the Civil War. Mary and Juno start a new life together, knowing that community and solidarity are their only hope for the future. They cannot escape the tenement and the poverty that pervades their lives, but they can escape from the 'state o' chassis' that almost destroyed their future.

The closing scene in *Juno and the Paycock* is one of the most challenging parts for an actor. Juno's speech, where she regrets the lack of compassion on her behalf when Mrs Tancred's 'poor son was found as Johnny's been found now',[51] has to convey both her sorrow and compassion and, at the same time, her hope for the future, as she repeats the prayer that Mrs Tancred said for her dead son in the previous act. Then Mary and Juno slowly exit the stage, at which point any other writer would have typed 'Curtain', but O'Casey indicates a pause. The play ends with a brief drunken scene that is as forlornly comic as the closing scene in Beckett's *Waiting for Godot*. Boyle and Joxer stagger onto the stage, and Boyle concludes the play with the immortal line 'th' whole worl's ... in a terr ... ible state o' ... chassis!'[52]

While Dublin audiences, with some reservations, appreciated *Juno and the Paycock*, when it opened in Cork the following year some hint of the problems that would beset *The Plough and the Stars* became evident. There were religious objections;[53] the text was censored and bowdlerised, with every reference to religion or sex removed or sanitised. The prayer spoken by Mrs Tancred and Juno Boyle was deleted, and, to avoid the undesirable fact that Mary Boyle was seduced and became pregnant by Bentham, some dialogue was added to suggest that Bentham had married Mary before he deserted her. Whether O'Casey was troubled, or even aware, of this blatant censorship of his work is not known, but his work was never again censored or attacked without the 'green crow', as he liked to call himself, defending the literary and political integrity of his work.

Joe Dowling's production of *Juno and the Paycock* at the Gate Theatre in Dublin in 1986 was a harsh portrayal of social reality. Donal McCann, who played Captain Boyle, gave a more brutal portrayal than the classic comic Falstaffian character associated with Barry Fitzgerald in the 1924 Abbey production. In Dowling's production, the comedy was retained, but behind the comic mask was a suppressed violence threatening to erupt at any moment. McCann portrayed Boyle as the 'chap from upstairs coming in drunk and calling you every name under the sun and offering to cut your throat', and the next morning he would be all hail-fellow-well-met.[54] The way McCann fingered his belt in the scene where Boyle learns about Mary's pregnancy left the audience in no doubt about the beating Mary would receive. Dowling also injected the portrayal of the Irregulars[55] with a degree of brutality that referenced the current political climate in the North of Ireland, and according to John Crowley 'he was injecting O'Casey's anti-heroism with an edge which he was then trying to extend to a modern Irish political context'.[56] McCann's portrayal of Boyle is one of the classic performances in modern Irish theatre, but Dowling's attempt to 'nudge the audience' towards a contemporary reading of the play did not please everybody.

O'Casey was a politically committed dramatist in whose work aspirations for peace, brotherhood and happiness are subverted by war, class differences and sectarianism. In the midst of the Civil War, Captain Boyle says, 'we've nothing to do with these things one way or the other', but the unfolding tragedy that affects the Boyle family undermines that position.[57] O'Casey portrays the tension between the desires of ordinary people to live their lives in peace and the real world of war and strife intruding into their lives. The Boyles cannot hide from the chaos enveloping them, and O'Casey suggests that the audience cannot either.

CHAPTER 10

The Plough is Hitched to the Stars

The interpretation of history is a moveable feast, and it is constantly updated 'to ensure that the past it reconstructs remains up to date and in fashion'.[1] Or, as Seamus Deane has suggested: 'Historians do not write about the past; they create the past in writing about it'.[2] By the early 1920s, a process was at work that 'mythologised' the 1916 Rising, in the way that Roland Barthes uses the word, where images and words are linked by habitual association and accrue significances not necessarily inherent in them, which then take on the appearance of truth.[3] Given that proposition, it was almost inevitable that Stephen Rea's production of *The Plough and the Stars* at Dublin's Gaiety Theatre in 2000 would be judged against the backdrop of the recent peace process in Northern Ireland. The production was criticised for taking liberties with the play, not least for updating it to take account of the current circumstances. On the other hand, the *Irish Times* reporter watching it as he savoured a moment of hope in the peace process wrote that 'it was almost unbearably moving. The characters on the stage, much younger than is usual in productions of O'Casey, could have walked off the streets of Derry or Belfast.'[4]

In 1991, on the seventy-fifth anniversary of the 1916 Rising, Garry Hynes' bold and savage, expressionist production of *The Plough and the Stars* at the Abbey Theatre was not to everyone's liking; it delivered a blow by reminding us that 'this was always meant to be a shocking play'.[5] However, twenty-five years later, despite the controversy that has dogged *The Plough and the Stars*, the political content provoked almost no comment during the Abbey production on the hundredth anniversary of the rising in 2016. The contemporary setting of the play and the production values were the major concerns of the critics, even though the director Sean Holmes saw it as 'an argument with Ireland ... This play is as much about 1926 as it was about 1916. It was an argument with the new state and the betrayal of the promise, as O'Casey saw it, of what the flag represented for an alternative type of state'.[6] O'Casey's critique starts from the reality of the state that emerged after independence rather than an imagined state based on the potential outcome of the 1916 Rising. In 1926 O'Casey posed a question, 'where stands the Republic?' for which so many had sacrificed so much. Seán O'Faoláin, who took part in the War of Independence and fought on the anti-treaty side in the Civil War, was also highly critical of the conservative Free State dominated by Catholic ideology that emerged from the ruins of the Civil War. O'Faoláin wrote at the time of the Civil War: 'we are blessed by a series of writers who have the courage to face experience and record it'.[7] O'Casey was such a writer, one who was fearless in speaking out.

In *The Irish Times* in 1966, on the fiftieth anniversary of the 1916 Rising, O'Faoláin sketched out a letter he would like to send to an old comrade. In essence, he posed the same question that O'Casey had asked forty years earlier:

> So my friend, for what did you fight in 1916? Was it really for this Ireland which you have been calmly supporting ever since? ... I have no word for anybody except, in a great pity, for the dead whom we are now about to honour fifty years after we have forgotten what they meant for us to create in their names.[8]

Revolutions and wars are bloody and frightening experiences, and the participants are sometimes physically and mentally broken in the course of these events. In *The Plough and the Stars*, O'Casey undercuts the 'heroic' status accorded to the rebels in popular history. The imprint of Bernard Shaw's *Saint Joan* is noticeable in the politics of *The Plough and the Stars* in the way that Shaw demythologises Joan's religious, romantic and patriotic legend.

In a contemporary review, T.P. O'Connor described O'Casey as 'the prophet of disillusionment'.[9] However, O'Casey was reflecting a commonly held view of the new state. Geraldine Dillon said that at the time, they 'traced all our evils, big and small, to England, and thought if we were politically free we would also be free of the scroungers, bootlickers, and political prostitutes who surrounded us'.[10] However, by 1925 the 'scroungers and bootlickers' had taken over the Free State, and they set about shaping it in their own image. The Free State that emerged from the War of Independence suffered a spectacular loss of nerve. Kevin Whelan has suggested that the post-independent state faced two choices:

> One choice of the independent state was explicitly to embrace a revolutionary remodelling of Irish society and the Irish state, and to strive for an Ireland that was genuinely international, securely Irish, and non-provincial. The other option was to strangle those

> transformative energies at birth and to collapse back into a gratefully provincial, pseudo-Gaelic, Catholic backwater, mirroring similar tendencies in the statelet of Northern Ireland ... In the Civil War of 1922-23, the second option eclipsed the first.[11]

The Plough and the Stars was not a statement about the terrifying effects of war or an anti-war polemic, but an attempt to demolish the myth of 1916 as something sacred and unblemished and in the process face up to the reality of the state that emerged. O'Casey was accused of besmirching the reputations of the rebels by showing that the Irish Citizen Army rebels Langon and Clitheroe were fearful of death and by the actions of Captain Brennan, who deserts his wounded comrades. In the last act, when the battle is lost, Brennan discards his uniform to save himself from being arrested, as several rebels did in the last hours of the rebellion.[12]

O'Casey was trying to rebalance the historical record; to demythologise the 1916 Rising and present the rebels as flesh and blood characters with all the weaknesses and strengths of real people.[13] During the siege of the South Dublin Union, Captain Tommy McCarthy and his men from the 4th Battalion, who were defending an outpost in Roe's Distillery, abandoned their post on the Thursday evening without informing the battalion leadership. Their actions left the flank of the South Union garrison exposed and weakened the entire defence of the garrison. In his statement to the Bureau of Military History, McCarthy justified his actions: 'After withdrawing it was every man for himself ... after our withdrawal there was no reaction except that I was a much-maligned man, but I still say that under similar circumstances I would adopt the same attitude'.[14]

During the siege of Boland's Mill, Éamon de Valera's second-in-command left his post on the Thursday night as defeat closed in on the garrison,[15] just as Captain Brennan does in the last act of *The Plough and the Stars*. However, O'Casey was not presenting Captain Brennan as a coward. In act three, Brennan stays with a wounded comrade and only leaves his post when all is lost and continued defiance seems hopeless. In *The Plough and the Stars,* O'Casey suggests that history should be less judgemental, and he attempted to undercut the romantic interpretation of the rising as poetry and drama played out on the streets of Dublin. Revolutions are bloody and fearful events that involve real people; a minority are heroes, some are fearful, and most are a little of each.

The Plough and the Stars is a play full of ambiguity. Despite the starkness of his critique of the 1916 Rising, his admiration for the bravery of the rebels is evident in the way Fluther replies to a British army sergeant who accuses the insurgents of not fighting fair:

> FLUTHER (unable to stand the slight): Fight fair! A few hundhred scrawls o' chaps with a couple o' guns an' Rosary beads, again' a hundhred thousand thrained men with horse, fut, an' artillery ... an' he wants us to fight fair! (To Sergeant) D'ye want us to go out in our skins an' throw stones?

And when a British soldier, Corporal Stoddart, tries to justify his actions, Fluther replies:

> CORPORAL STODDART: Ow, a man's a man, an 'e 'as to foight for 'is country, 'asn't 'e?
> FLUTHER (aggressively): You're not fightin' for your country here, are you?[16]

The Spanish painter and revolutionary Francisco Goya was a particular favourite of O'Casey, and the looting scene in *The Plough and the Stars* is straight out of Goya. The scene caused offence to many in the audience as it appeared to demean the ideals of the rebels. Looting was widespread, and O'Casey was right to include that aspect of the rising. However, the scene can also be construed as an intimation of what 1916 should also have been about: the expropriation of the Irish capitalist class. This underlying, but never overt, socialist theme develops as the play progresses. The petty squabbling is cast aside. A sense of them and us develops – of community, of solidarity – and a politicisation that is unstated is, nevertheless, implicit in the play's ending. In an interesting class analysis of *The Plough and the Stars*, Bernice Schrank suggests that in the first half of the play, the 'us' are the working-class tenement dwellers, and the 'them' are the nationalists: the same people who crushed the workers of Dublin and continued to exploit them. This is the class divide that O'Casey is emphasising. However, in the last act, the political emphasis shifts when the play dramatises the British presence bringing death and destruction to the tenement dwellers. Schrank implies that, in the course of the play, O'Casey redefines the competing class forces; the 'them' is now British imperialism, and the 'us' are the nationalists who are standing against the British presence in Ireland.[17] O'Casey reflected the reality of the shift in the balance of forces – from the revolutionary syndicalist politics of 1913 to the nationalist politics of 1916 and the War of Independence.

O'Casey implies that the 1916 Rising was the wrong war for Dublin's tenement dwellers and the British soldiers on the other side of the barricades. However, O'Casey's implied suggestion that they should put aside nationalism, jingoism and religion and unite in the class war did not find favour with his audience in 1926. In *The Voice of Labour*, Tom Irwin rebuked O'Casey, suggesting that he was 'not yet so famous that you can take the liberty of insulting your [fellow] country people, whether they live in tenements or die in front of firing squads. To the actors I would say: Don't assist anyone who sets himself out to do this'.[18]

In April 1922, *Banba*, a magazine published by the Gael Co-Operative Publishing Company in Dublin, printed a story called 'A Tale of Easter Week'. It tells the story of Paddy and Mary Brady, who live in a small 'top-back' tenement in Dublin with their infant child. The Bradys were held by their neighbours to be 'stuck up' and to 'think a deal of themselves'; their situation is similar to that of the Clitheroes in *The Plough and the Stars*. Paddy is a member of the ICA and on Easter Monday reports for duty to Liberty Hall. While Paddy is with his comrades in the ICA, tragedy strikes the tenement where they live: Mary's young baby dies. Shortly after, a message arrives to say that Bill McGrath, a neighbour, has been killed in the fighting. Mary is grief-stricken at the death of her baby, and her first instinct is to send word to her husband to come home; she needs him. However, Mary hesitates, remembering the words of Mrs McGrath when she heard the news of her husband's death: ''Tis a fine thing to die for Ireland ... All those men who were fighting somewhere down in the city, were fighting for Ireland – were ready to die for Ireland – and Paddy he too was ready to die for Ireland'.[19] The note Mary sends to Paddy does not mention their dead child or her need for him to return home. Mary, like Mrs McGrath and the brave Citizen Army volunteers, was prepared to do her bit and suffer for Ireland.[20] 'A Tale of Easter Week' is, in almost all essentials, the story of Jack and Nora Clitheroe from *The Plough and the Stars*, except that in O'Casey's version there is no heroic ending or glory in dying for Ireland. Captain Brennan returns to the tenement to inform Nora that her husband Jack Clitheroe was killed in action:

> CAPTAIN BRENNAN: He took it like a man. His last whisper was to 'Tell Nora to be brave; that I'm ready to meet my God, an' that I'm proud to die for Ireland'. An' when our General heard it he said that 'Commandant Clitheroe's end was a gleam of glory'. Mrs Clitheroe's grief will be a joy when she realises that she has a hero for a husband.[21]

Brennan's speech is straight out of the story in *Banba*, but with a real twist: O'Casey strips away the romance of 'dying for Ireland' and reveals the heartbreak and tragedy that are part of any revolutionary upheaval. There are no heroics in O'Casey's work. Nora's grief for her dead husband cannot be assuaged or turned to joy by the thought of Jack as a hero of the revolution. Her grief turns to madness as she wanders around the house, her child stillborn from the trauma. She has lost everything, and at that moment O'Casey plants the question in the mind of the audience: for what purpose was all this suffering and destruction? Just as in Amos Oz's novel *Judas*, the main character, looking back on the war of 1948, which led to the foundation of the state of Israel, repeats the Israeli mantra that the deaths and destruction that took place were not in vain. Nevertheless, he cannot escape an inner voice that questions the outcome: 'I seemed to hear Shealtiel Abravanel asking me silently if I still believed that it was all worthwhile'.[22]

The similarities between the story in *Banba* and *The Plough and the Stars* are so striking that it is difficult to believe that it had not influenced O'Casey. He may have known the publishers, as he had several letters published in *The Gael*, which also published *Banba*, and in October 1921 O'Casey had placed an article for R.M. Fox with the magazine, so he may have seen that issue. Every writer takes inspiration from what they have read or experienced, or from history; what matters is what they do with the material. Have they something imaginative to say that transforms it into an original piece of work? *Banba* was just one of a host of magazines and newspapers in the post-independence period that were busy transforming the uncompromising revolutionary message of 1916 into a safe, heroic myth devoid of any social content that could challenge the political hegemony of the Free State.

THE FIGURE IN THE WINDOW

The Abbey audience had enjoyed the irony and comedic qualities of *The Shadow of a Gunman*; it suited the mood of a country grown tired of death and war. *Juno and the Paycock* had shaken their complacency about the past, but in *The Plough and the Stars* O'Casey plunged a dagger deep into the heart of the myth of heroic sacrifice. For a section of the audience, this was a step too far. While respecting O'Casey as a great dramatist, Peadar O'Donnell was just one of many republicans who were bitter about O'Casey's work: 'His *Plough and the Stars* I find nauseating. There is nothing in this play from whom any revolutionary action could proceed'.[23] A modern critic, James Moran, writing in the same vein, suggests that it was written from an ultra-left perspective 'to denigrate the Rising' and that it was 'a cynical attack on 1916'.[24]

O'Casey's treatment of Patrick Pearse in *The Plough and the Stars* was one of the issues that led to the riots by republican sympathisers on the fourth night of the production. Pearse never appears in the play, nor is he mentioned by name. A Pearse-type figure, speaking from a platform outside the window of the pub, is simply listed as 'The Figure in the Window'. O'Casey utilised three of the best-known speeches by Pearse: two excerpts from 'Peace and the Gael' (December 1915) and one each from 'The Coming Revolution' (November 1913) and the 'O'Donovan Rossa: Graveside oration' (August 1915).[25] He combined different sections of these three speeches for dramatic effect, which offended his republican critics, many of whom accused O'Casey of distorting what Pearse had actually said. His nervousness over his treatment of Pearse led to a pre-production addition to the script (which was not included in the produced or published version). He added some additional lines to the speech delivered by the Pearse character: 'In every age will be found Irishmen willing and eager to fight for the sovereign freedom of their country'.[26]

Pearse's detractors have variously described him as a crypto-fascist, repressed homosexual, autistic, and a man who celebrated a cult of violence. Pearse was a complex individual, and any number of quotations can be produced to back up these accusations.[27] At times, his recourse to the language of blood sacrifice displayed a reckless excess, even allowing for the fact that such language was common across Europe, often described as a continent besotted with militarism. *The Irish Times* greeted the First World War as a chance for nationalists and unionists to 'share the same baptism of blood'.[28] James Connolly had little time for all this talk of blood sacrifice, and neither had O'Casey. Connolly had served in the British army and knew the reality of war. O'Casey knew that war was not a 'terrible beauty' or a litany of 'heroic deeds', but a brutal affair that broke men both physically and mentally.

A month before the 1916 Rising, Pearse published *The Sovereign People*, a summary of his views on what a free Ireland might look like: 'Separation from England would be valueless unless it put the people – the actual people and not merely certain rich men – of Ireland in effectual ownership and possession of the soil of Ireland.'[29] This essay is similar to O'Casey's articles from a few years earlier in the way Pearse tried to fuse the national and social question into a coherent vision of an Irish republic. O'Casey was not demeaning or denigrating Pearse in the way he portrayed the 'Figure in the Window', or the way he presented the passages from Pearse's speeches. He held Pearse in high regard despite his mistaken view of him as a strike-breaker during the 1913 lockout. Pearse was a committed nationalist, but he was not neutral on the issue of class. In October 1913, at the height of the lockout, Pearse stated: 'My instinct is with the landless man against the lord of lands; and with the breadless man against the master of millions'.[30] In O'Casey's autobiographies, there are few criticisms of Pearse; he admired Pearse as an educationalist, a lover of literature and drama, and for his nobility of character:

> Patrick Pearse, while filled with the vision of a romantic Ireland, was also full of an Ireland sensitive, knowledgeable, and graceful; a doer of things noble, and a lover of things beautiful; and through his remarkable school St. Enda, showed he was eager to coax others out of the dim thicket of convention into a clearer light.[31]

O'Casey's tribute to Pearse, as he faced death, is a very moving passage that could only have been written by someone who admired and respected him. He writes of that moment when the executioners aimed their rifles at Pearse's heart:

> You never even paused, for that was what you guessed you'd come to; you came close to them; the stupid bullets tore a way through your quiet breast, and your fall forward to death was but a bow to your enemies. Peace be with you, and with your comrades too.[32]

O'Casey wrote these reflections on Pearse over twenty-five years after the events he describes. The passage of time had allowed O'Casey to take a more balanced and softer view of Pearse's achievements as an individual, an educator and a republican.[33]

In 1924, when he sat down to write *The Plough and the Stars* it was against the backdrop of the tumultuous events that had scarred Europe and Ireland over the previous ten years. O'Casey set out to puncture the smug complacency of the Free State establishment. In the new state, Pearse, Connolly and their comrades were stripped of their ideas and radicalism, and a mantle of Catholic iconography draped over their shoulders. In ancient Rome, as it changed from 'republic' to 'empire', it was essential for the ruling elite to pretend that nothing fundamental had changed. In

Ireland, as the country changed from 'empire' to 'republic', the Free State elite implied that everything had changed in order to copper-fasten their position in the new state.

O'Casey set out to dismantle the myths constructed about 1916 by both Free Staters and republicans to justify their positions, and in doing so he brought the ire of 'the 1916 widows' down on his head. O'Casey demanded that people look at the reality of what had been achieved for all the talk of 'blood sacrifice' and 'romantic Ireland'. Pearse or Connolly cannot be blamed for the conservatism and backwardness, economically and socially, of the Free State, as they had never envisaged such an outcome. However, O'Casey did fault those who came after them for promoting the cult of sacrifice and romantic nationalism that overwhelmed the social and economic demands of the revolution.

CULTURE AND POLITICS

O'Casey was aware of the fluid relationship between culture and politics and knew that his use of Pearse's speeches might be controversial. Nevertheless, he was caught off-guard by the objections to the sexual references in the play. He assumed the changes in the text that the Abbey board had suggested had settled that question. There had been problems and bitterness during rehearsals. F.J. McCormick objected to the term 'snotty' in the text, and Eileen Crowe refused to play the part of Mrs Gogan because of the line that any 'kid' of hers 'was got between the borders of the Ten Commandments'.[34] The upper-class lady from Rathmines who gets stranded in the city centre during the rising was written at the last moment to provide a part for Eileen Crowe. On the other hand, Ria Mooney relished the sensual role of the prostitute Rosie Redmond, even though Ethel Mannin subsequently referred to her as 'the Abbey whore'.[35] Rosie Redmond's bawdy song at the end of the second act was cut because of objections by the production manager, Michael J. Dolan, although the song is included in later editions of the play. George O'Brien, the government's appointee on the Abbey board and a fervent Catholic, only agreed to a production on condition that certain sections were amended – the love scene in act one, the introduction of the prostitute in act two – and that objectionable and lewd phrases and modes of expression were removed or rewritten.[36]

The War of Independence and the Civil War took their toll on the Abbey Theatre artistically and financially. Close to bankruptcy, the board asked the new government to take over the Abbey as a national theatre. The government refused but was willing to provide a small annual subsidy. In return, the Abbey had to agree to a government appointee on the board and accept any reasonable method of supervision by the government. This condition carried the threat of state censorship, which raised its head during the board's deliberations over the production of *The Plough and the Stars*. Having stood up to Miss Horniman[37] over the right to direct the affairs of the theatre almost twenty years earlier, Yeats and Lady Gregory were unlikely to accept any government interference for the sake of the £850-a-year grant. Lady Gregory made it clear what she expected of Yeats: 'If we have to choose between the subsidy and our freedom, it is our freedom we choose'.[38] To their credit, they stood firm and saw off O'Brien's efforts to censor the text.

Riots or protests have a long tradition in the Irish theatre, going back at least to the time of Thomas Sheridan and the Kelly riots at the Smock Alley Theatre in 1747.[39] In O'Casey's time, the 1907 protests over Synge's *The Playboy of the Western World* recurred during the Abbey Theatre's tour of the United States in 1911. The protests against W.B. Yeats' *The Countess Cathleen* in 1899 were instigated by students from the Royal University of Ireland, while conservative nationalists initiated the protests over Synge's *Playboy*. However, the attack on *The Plough and the Stars* came from educated republicans, intellectuals, academics and sections of the liberal left. They included Liam O'Flaherty, Austin Clarke, F.R. Higgins, Hanna Sheehy Skeffington and Maud Gonne MacBride. The rejection by his fellow writers of what he considered to be his best work to date hurt him deeply. O'Casey was upset that the new school of writers, those in revolt against the romanticism of the revival period, attacked the play in the pages of the *Irish Statesman*, a magazine that enjoyed the respect of progressive intellectuals.[40]

According to Arthur Griffith and the moral guardians of public opinion, at the time of the *Playboy* riots in 1907 there were no prostitutes or sensual women in Ireland.[41] This delusion was one of the reasons why a section of the audience objected to Pegeen Mike in *The Playboy of the Western World* and Rosie Redmond in *The Plough and the Stars*. The Abbey Theatre backed onto the area in Dublin known as Monto, one of the largest red-light districts in Europe. The Abbey patrons could hardly have been unaware of its existence as Monto was headline news for a number of reasons. On 12 March 1925, ten months before *The Plough* opened, a force of gardaí, backed up by the Legion of Mary, raided Monto and threw the women working there out onto the street or into the notorious Magdalene institutions. Shortly afterwards, the newspapers were full of the murder of the prostitute Honor Bright, and the arrest of a doctor and a garda superintendent suspected of her murder. Honor Bright, born Lizzie O'Neill, was from the Liberties. She was sacked from her job for having a baby out of wedlock and turned to prostitution to survive. When Rosie Redmond appeared on the stage of the Abbey, members of the audience shouted 'Honor Bright' to show their disapproval.

The essential difference between the riots that greeted the *Playboy* and the *Plough* was that in 1907 there was hope that Ireland had a promising future; by 1926, that hope had dissipated. After the defeat of the republicans in the Civil War, all they had left was the recollection of the possibilities lost in a failed revolution and the memory of the martyred 1916 leaders to hold firm to. The setting of the *Plough* during the 1916 Rising was central to the protest that ensued. It was one thing to show Christy Mahon from *The Playboy of the Western World* as a bit of a scoundrel, but to even suggest that some of the ICA volunteers behaved like cowards was an affront to their memory; especially on the stage of the 'national theatre'. Writing about the political situation in Northern Ireland in 1970, Brian Friel felt that an interval of ten or fifteen years would need to pass before a play on the theme of the Northern 'Troubles' might be written.[42] O'Casey's Dublin dramas were written and produced long before the scars of the Civil War had healed.

The play opened on 8 February 1926, and the reviews were positive. Scant attention was paid to the prostitute Rosie Redmond, and there was no comment on the Irish flag in the pub or any suggestion that the play impugned the memory of those who had fought in 1916:

> The first curtain went up with the packed theatre in a state of tense expectation, after each of the four acts there was a demonstration of approval, and when the end came the author received an ovation … The introduction of Rosie Redmond, a street girl, was a risky thing on the part of the author, but with Miss Mooney portraying her we felt again that Mr O'Casey was giving us Dublin life as it was lived.[43]

The second night sold out, with people clamouring for a ticket, but this time there was a warning of the protests to come: 'some four or five in the pit objected to the Volunteers bringing the flag into a pub in act two'.[44] Joseph Holloway records that several notables in the audience did not like the play, including Lord Chief Justice Kennedy, who declared 'that he thought it abominable'. Oliver Gogarty was, however, very supportive: 'It'll give the smug minded something to think about'.[45] On the fourth night, the audience began to heckle and whistle during the second act, drowning out much of the dialogue with shouts of 'O'Casey out' and 'Honor Bright'.[46] By act three, chaos reigned. Shoes were thrown at the actors, and about twenty women rushed the stage, including Sighle Humphreys[47] and the writer Dorothy Macardle.[48] A young man clambered up on the stage, struck Maureen Delaney in the face, and then aimed a blow at May Craig. However, Barry Fitzgerald, a boxer in his younger days, hit him with a blow that sent him sprawling across the stage. Somehow, they cleared the stage, and the curtain was lowered. W.B. Yeats stepped forward to address the audience amid shouts of 'Up the Republic' and hisses and boos. His speech was inaudible to most of the audience, but there is a record of what he said as he had the foresight to furnish a copy of his speech to *The Irish Times* just before the trouble started:

> I thought you had got tired of this. It commenced fifteen years ago. You have disgraced yourselves again. Is this to be an ever-recurring celebration of the arrival of Irish genius? Once more you have rocked the cradle of genius. The news of this will go from country to country. You have once more rocked the cradle of a reputation. The fame of O'Casey is born tonight. This is his apotheosis.[49]

As O'Casey recounted to Barry Fitzgerald many years later, he had to look up apotheosis in the dictionary when he got home before he realised that Yeats had elevated him to the status of a god, at least in literary terms.

When the police arrived, they escorted the protestors from the theatre. The production then proceeded, despite a few minor interjections from sections of the audience. Before the curtain went up again, the actors, headed by F.J. McCormick, lined up on the stage. McCormick distanced himself, and by implication the rest of the cast, from O'Casey by saying that 'he wished the actors should be treated distinct from the play'.[50] Shelah Richards, who played the part of Nora Clitheroe, writing in her unpublished memoir, 'felt this was a betrayal: we were involved, the play was a masterpiece, O'Casey our hero and we were prepared to fight, literally, for him and his play. The pro-O'Caseyites summarily manned the curtain and brought it swinging down on that actor [McCormick].'[51] In the heated debate that followed over the following weeks, Gabriel Fallon defended O'Casey's play and made it clear that McCormick was not speaking for all the actors on that occasion. Yeats' decision to call in the police was also controversial; it smacked of censorship and ran counter to Yeats' concept of the theatre as a forum of debate. The arrival of the police was also a reminder of the uproar over their role during the *Playboy* riots in 1907. O'Casey was not responsible for calling the police, as some of his detractors later claimed; that was Yeats' decision alone.

During the interval, Joseph Holloway became aware that a storm was brewing when he heard Dan Breen, a legendary IRA man who had fought in the Civil War on the republican side, say that 'Mrs. Pearse, Mrs. Tom Clarke, Mrs. Sheehy Skeffington, and others were in the theatre to vindicate the manhood of 1916'.[52] These women were the 'widows of 1916' who, in the post-Civil War period, had constituted themselves as 'the guardians of memory'. The protests were organised by Frank Ryan of the University College Dublin Republican Club, Cumann na mBan and the 'widows of 1916', but other elements objected on moral grounds. The *Catholic Bulletin* denounced the play in an eight-page rant against O'Casey, Yeats and the ascendancy clique who controlled the Abbey, the supporters of divorce who wrote for *The Irish Times*, and the government subsidy to the Abbey; the reviewer only relented when he appeared to run out of invective.[53]

The play continued its run with the help of a large police presence during each performance. On the Friday night, in an attempt to kidnap Barry Fitzgerald, a contingent of armed men called to his house demanding to see him. Luckily, Fitzgerald had stayed away from home that night, having been informed of the threat. On Saturday, the players remained in the theatre between the matinée and the evening performance to avoid any possible trouble. Riots and kidnappings were not the only danger the Abbey Theatre had to fear during those turbulent years, but Yeats and Lady Gregory refused to buckle in the face of threats or intimidation. *The Plough and the Stars* ended its sell-out run as scheduled without any further interference. On the last night, an enthusiastic audience called for the author, and O'Casey reluctantly came forward to say a few words of thanks.

A WAR OF WORDS

By the end of the week's run, the disagreements had spilt over into the newspapers. There were the usual right-wing comments that appear on such occasions. The *Evening Herald* ran an unsigned piece by 'an onlooker' that was typical of several contributions over the following weeks: 'It is repulsive for several reasons, and such a play would not be permitted by the Government of any other country – certainly not in America, France, Germany, or under Mussolini at the present time … There is an effort abroad to destroy nationalism and supplant it by internationalism'.[54] O'Casey lost no sleep over the *Evening Herald* and the rest of the moralists; he would bide his time until the moment was ripe to deal with them. What bothered him was the opposition from people he admired and respected. Frank Ryan was a republican and a fellow socialist. Hanna Sheehy Skeffington was a socialist and fighter for women's rights and the widow of Frank Sheehy Skeffington, whose political apotheosis had literally and figuratively taken place during Easter week 1916. Liam O'Flaherty was one of a new generation of writers who had thrown off the shackles of the revival and reached out to the broader European modernist tradition, having published his first significant work, *The Informer*, a few months earlier.[55]

Round two kicked off with a letter in the *Irish Independent* the following Monday. Hanna Sheehy Skeffington responded to an editorial in the paper regarding the protest:

> The demonstration was not directed against the individual actor, nor was it directed to the moral aspect of the play. It was on national grounds solely, voicing a passionate indignation against the outrage of a drama staged in a supposedly national theatre, which held up to derision and obloquy the men and women of Easter week … the only censorship that is justified is the free censorship of public opinion.[56]

Sheehy Skeffington was also attacking Yeats for calling in the police. The question of free speech and the right to criticise a play was also an issue. Sheehy Skeffington's disagreement with O'Casey's position on republicanism and socialism predated the Civil War, as she had made plain in a review of O'Casey's pamphlet on the Irish Citizen Army some years earlier.[57] O'Casey hit back at his critics in a long letter defending the historical accuracy of the play regarding both the heroism and the cowardice displayed during Easter week. He also alluded to the issue of uniforms and whether the Tricolour was ever seen inside a public house.[58]

Liam O'Flaherty's letter in the *Irish Statesman* was a long, rambling and mostly incoherent attack on *The Plough and the Stars* and W.B. Yeats' attempt to stifle the protests. O'Flaherty declared that he was not a nationalist, but that he was 'an admirer of any man who has the courage to die for an ideal', and he went on to say that 'the most glorious gesture in the history of our country was the gesture of those who died in 1916'.[59]

O'Flaherty's defence of the ideals of 1916 was at odds with his anti-heroic portrayal of his protagonists in *The Informer* (1925) and *The Assassin* (1928). A few months before the production of *The Plough and the Stars*, O'Flaherty had visited O'Casey in the company of Edward Garnett, his London publisher. They discussed his work, and according to O'Casey, both expressed support for the play. That was one of the reasons why he was shocked by O'Flaherty's letter. The other was the realisation that O'Flaherty was using him, and the occasion of the controversy, to attack Yeats and the old guard of the literary revival. O'Casey had withdrawn from the Radical Club a year earlier because he believed it was just a front for an attack on W.B. Yeats. O'Flaherty and his friends had formed the club as a forum for intellectual workers, artists and writers to prepare Irish audiences for the arrival of the avant-garde.[60] O'Flaherty and the artist Patrick Tuohy took opposite sides in the controversy over O'Casey's *The Plough and the Stars* during a debate in the Radical Club:

> O'Flaherty led the charge ... against his playwright friend, while Tuohy, an Easter Rising veteran and Citizen Army comrade of O'Casey's, defended the play's anti-heroic view of the Rising. Rosamond Jacob notes that O'Flaherty spoke in the debate 'with much more decent feeling than I'd expect – but didn't give Tuohy a fair chance'.[61]

Tom Irwin, writing in the trade union journal the *Voice of Labour*, castigated O'Casey for his attack on nationalism and the legacy of James Connolly: 'Mr. O'Casey's purpose I can understand, but cannot accept the consequences.' Irwin was disturbed by the play; it seemed to impugn the memory of Pearse and Connolly from a working-class perspective. Yet, of all the reviews of the play, Irwin appears to have captured O'Casey's point of view in a way that no one else had:

> Mr. O'Casey indicts war because it is only the poor who give all and receive nothing. Death, insanity, child-murder, are the inevitable consequences. Who gains by it all we do not know, nor do we want to. We only know that poverty pays the full price. In *The Plough and the Stars* humanity's cry against that price is a lyrical one.[62]

Irwin had seen the play on the Monday before the disturbances on the following Thursday night and suggested in his review that because of O'Casey's attack on Pearse, 'An Irish audience may one day turn away from this play'; it only took another three days for that to happen.

The debate continued in the press in the following weeks, becoming more entrenched and vitriolic. In the *Irish Statesman*, both Liam O'Flaherty and the poets Austin Clarke and F.R. Higgins questioned the artistic merit of the play in order to undermine the political content.[63] The *Voice of Labour* added another piece of invective to the clamour by attacking O'Casey for his association with James Larkin and rehashed the arguments concerning O'Casey's resignation from the ICA in 1914. However, O'Casey did have his supporters; the writer Lyle Donaghy and the Abbey actor Gabriel Fallon spoke out in defence of O'Casey and the play.[64] The upshot of all this public exchange of letters was that Sheehy Skeffington challenged O'Casey to a public debate, a challenge he willingly accepted. O'Casey had used this tactic on several occasions in the past and was confident enough in his ability as a speaker to accept the challenge. The debate took place on 1 March 1926 in the Mills Hall on Merrion Row under the auspices of the UCD Republican Club. Arthur Cleary, a university lecturer and a noted republican, was in the chair. The republicans had ensured a good turnout of their supporters. Most of the Abbey actors turned up, but interestingly none of the directors saw fit to stand with O'Casey on this occasion. The literary and political glitterati were also present: T.C. Murray, Maud Gonne MacBride, Mary Kettle, Charlotte Despard, Tom Nally, Lyle Donaghy and Joseph Holloway.

O'Casey had prepared well, making extensive notes on the political differences between Connolly and Pearse, the right to protest, and the fact that the plays were written for an Irish audience, not for a London one as his detractors claimed. Sheehy Skeffington was a formidable speaker, and this time she did not hold back from attacking him artistically and politically. She claimed that *The Plough and the Stars* 'was a travesty of Easter week, and that it concentrated on pettiness and squalor, unrelieved by a gleam of heroism'.[65] She accepted that O'Casey's work had 'the mark of genius'; but her praise was just the prelude to a critical dagger in the heart:

> He has rather the art of the photographer rather than the art of the dramatist. These scenes are all put together, and the natural conclusion is that this is a typical picture of the men of 1916. There is not a single gleam of heroism throughout *The Plough and the Stars*. The theme of the play right through is the folly of it. That is why it cut to the bone.[66]

As was the custom, O'Casey then rose to propose a vote of thanks to Sheehy Skeffington before making his own contribution. However, he took ill after a few sentences and had to sit down. The poet and Trinity College student

Lyle Donaghy stepped in and spoke until O'Casey had recovered. O'Casey then replied in detail to the specific criticisms surrounding the play, the issue of the flag in the public house, the prostitute Rosie Redmond, and the reality of life in the tenements. The furore in the newspapers and at the meeting over the flag in the public house was just sheer hypocrisy. Máire Comerford, in her memoirs, related that during the War of Independence, she was shocked to find that the attorney general carried out his business in a public house,[67] as did many other functionaries of the revolutionary government. O'Casey went on to say that 'he was not trying, and never would try, to write about heroes; he could only write about the life he knew and the people he knew'.[68] Referring to the criticism that he wrote his plays for an English audience, who would enjoy him denigrating his fellow countrymen, he replied to applause that 'all my plays were written for Dublin'.[69]

O'Casey had opened his speech by declaring that Sheehy Skeffington 'saw everything through the eyes of a politician, and he through the eyes of a dramatist'. That statement immediately put O'Casey on the back foot. He was correct to defend his right as an artist to express himself on the stage without reference to any group of people. However, he might have been more effective if he had fought on both fronts. He should have defended his critique of the 1916 Rising and that of the Free State implied in the play. Instead, he allowed others to set the agenda and was left chasing after petty details about whether a Tricolour had ever seen the inside of a public house.[70] Joseph Holloway reported that the debate had been 'conducted in the most peaceful way and in the best of good humour, each taking and receiving hard hits in their turn'.[71] Nevertheless, O'Casey had come off second best, partly because of his failure to defend himself politically and the overwhelming republican presence on the night that supported the very able Hanna Sheehy Skeffington.

O'Casey was never a man to forgive easily. But, to his credit, he forgave Hanna Sheehy Skeffington and the young Frank Ryan. In time, they became both friends and political allies. Hanna's son, Owen Sheehy Skeffington, defended O'Casey when the *Standard*, a right-wing Catholic newspaper, ran a series of articles attacking him shortly before the premiere of *The Bishop's Bonfire* in 1955. The articles referred to the debate over *The Plough and the Stars* in 1926. Owen Sheehy Skeffington replied in defence of O'Casey:

> In all the years since that debate Sean O'Casey has never spoken or written of my mother save in the highest terms of appreciation and

> admiration. Moreover, I would affirm that were my mother alive today she would feel nothing but disgust for the current STANDARD hate-campaigns conducted by anonymous character-assassins.[72]

The play was revived at the beginning of May 1926 and sold out for the entire run. Sheehy Skeffington and her friends stood outside with their placards denouncing the play. A more sinister protest was the threat by republicans to blow up the theatre. A significant police presence ensured that the run came to a successful conclusion with only the occasional minor incident. The lash of the mob became an all too frequent experience. In 1930, when Hitchcock's film *Juno and the Paycock* was shown in Limerick, two reels of the film were stolen from the cinema and burnt by a crowd in the street. The trouble in Limerick led to the cancellation of subsequent showings in Waterford and Derry. When the film was released in the United States, it was retitled *The Shame of Mary Boyle*, which changed the tone of the film entirely.[73] In 1966, *The Plough and the Stars* was considered too controversial for the Irish national television station to broadcast during the fiftieth commemoration of the 1916 Rising. However, Lelia Doolan's production was broadcast later in the year to much acclaim.

Despite these constant criticisms and attacks, a minority spoke out in favour of artistic integrity. In 1947, the Abbey production of *The Plough and the Stars* was interrupted by the dramatist Roger McHugh and the poet Valentin Iremonger, who stood up and denounced what the Abbey Theatre had done 'to O'Casey's masterpiece'. They were protesting at a production that was unadventurous and lazy, and that had transformed O'Casey's work into a piece of nostalgia devoid of any life or character.[74] Like the earlier controversy, this also spilt over into the newspapers. Both Bernard Shaw and Paul Vincent Carroll denounced the production and demanded the resignation of the managing director Ernest Blythe.

The Plough and the Stars went on to be the most successful play in the Abbey's repertoire, both at home and abroad. It has been translated into over sixteen languages and admired around the world. Unfortunately, Yeats was a bit premature in announcing O'Casey's apotheosis. By 1926, O'Casey had reached the zenith of his popularity; from then on, he would have to fight a rear-guard action to find a stage for his work. Paradoxically, Yeats was the first to pull the rug out from under his feet. In 1928, just two years after pronouncing O'Casey one of the immortals of Irish theatre, Yeats rejected his next play, *The Silver Tassie*, thereby ensuring an irrevocable artistic breach between the Abbey Theatre and its most successful playwright.

O'Casey asked a question in the Dublin plays: Was it for this wretched Free State that Jack Clitheroe and Johnny Boyle lost their lives? He never manages to answer that question adequately, yet behind the bluster and the comedy, O'Casey implies, perhaps in a negative way, a synthesis that could break the political logjam. In *The Plough and the Stars*, republicans accept the illusory solutions offered by nationalist politics, while the socialists accept a notion of solidarity based on class alone. The Easter Rising tested these positions; O'Casey's strategy was to demythologise the rising and the dominant nationalist discourse that created it. He was striving to present the national question in terms of class rather than some idealised throwback to a Gaelic past. However, he never successfully resolved the contradiction between the green and the red, either in his politics or in his drama. Moreover, this contradiction has bedevilled his critics ever since. Seán O'Faoláin is one of the few critics who understood with the utmost precision what O'Casey was suggesting in the Dublin plays: 'Sean O'Casey's plays are thus an exactly true statement of the Irish Revolution whose flag should be, not the tricolour, but the plough and the stars of the labouring classes'.[75]

PART 4

CHAPTER 11

The Temptations of Fame: 1926–36

Whatever O'Casey felt about the outcome and the ruckus over *The Plough and the Stars*, he had little time to reflect on it. He was invited to attend the London production of *Juno and the Paycock*. On 4 March 1926, like thousands before him, he took the boat from Dún Laoghaire – but with the firm intention of returning to Dublin. Kilburn, in London, is about as far from Euston Station as you can carry a heavy suitcase. However, O'Casey did not need to hump his case up the Kilburn High Road to find digs like generations of Irish men and women who went before him. When he stepped off the train on 5 March 1926 the theatre impresario J.B. Fagan was waiting in a taxi to whisk him off to the Kenilworth Hotel in Bloomsbury. That evening Fagan and O'Casey attended a performance of Chekhov's *Uncle Vanya* at the Duke of York's Theatre. Within days, Fagan had established O'Casey as a minor celebrity around London. He arranged newspaper and radio interviews to publicise the opening of *Juno and the Paycock* on 8 March. Lady Gregory, who was in London at the time, introduced O'Casey to her circle of friends, including the Labour Party leader and former prime minister Ramsay MacDonald. For good measure, O'Casey also became acquainted with Herbert Asquith, the leader of the Liberal Party. Asquith subsequently wrote to O'Casey complimenting him on *The Plough and the Stars* and suggested that they should meet to discuss matters of interest.[1]

Lady Gregory also introduced him to the painter Augustus John and suggested he paint O'Casey's portrait. Invitations followed, introducing him to London's artistic and literary set, including Sir John and Lady Hazel Lavery, Bernard Shaw, his wife Charlotte, and Lady Londonderry. On 23 March, O'Casey was awarded the Hawthornden Prize for work of literary value, which included a very welcome £100 to go with the literary accolade. The *Daily Express* reported that London's leading hostess, Lady Londonderry, had taken O'Casey under her wing, invited him to dinner, and was generous enough to allow him to dispense with the formality of evening dress. However, the same report said that on another occasion, O'Casey was turned away from 'the home of a prominent millionaire' by the butler because he was not properly attired.[2] Shortly afterwards, O'Casey was offered honorary membership of the Garrick Club in London,[3] but the atmosphere in the club was not to his liking, and he graced the premises on only one occasion. He received an invitation to speak at the Critics' Circle, but his provocative views were unwelcome, and a return invitation was not forthcoming. One accolade that he was delighted to accept was an honorary membership of the Thames Lightermen, an ancient guild that organised the men who worked the boats in the London docks.[4] No doubt, J.B. Fagan had a hand in publicising the fact that O'Casey had accepted an invitation to a gala dinner hosted by the Irish Club in London. Among those attending, as reported by *The Irish Times*, were the prince of Wales, the earl of Derby, Sir John and Lady Lavery and various ambassadors, generals, lords and princes of the British empire. However, O'Casey made it clear in a letter to *An Phoblacht*, which also carried the story, that he would not have accepted the invitation under any circumstances and that 'I expect you to publish my contradiction of your correspondent's lousy lie'.[5]

Near the end of March 1926, not long after he arrived in London, O'Casey told a reporter that he could not live there and 'was going back to Dublin soon to work'.[6] Within three months, he had changed his mind. In July 1926, the *Irish Independent* reported that O'Casey had departed from Dublin 'more in sorrow than in anger' and taken a flat in London on a three-year lease. 'I like London ... and London likes me ... it may mean three years penal servitude for me, but, begorra, it cannot be worse than Dublin'.[7] He also liked the twenty-six-year-old Eileen Carey, a beautiful young actor who was the understudy for the role of Nora in *The Plough and the Stars*, which opened at the Fortune Theatre that May. While Eileen was a significant reason why O'Casey remained in London, there were other factors as well. When the *Plough* was revived at the Abbey in early May, there were protests by republicans, and the police were called upon once again to restore order. It must have seemed to O'Casey that if Dublin did not appreciate him, at least London did.

THE GENERAL STRIKE

O'Casey may have been overwhelmed by the attention of the press and the literary lion-hunters in London, but he was aware of the great struggles that galvanised the British working class in a fight for decent wages and conditions. In an interview with a British newspaper, he posed a question:

'What's the use of singing *The Red Flag* when men will accept 30s for a week's hard labour'.[8] A few weeks later, the British working class answered O'Casey's rhetorical question. In the first week of May, the Trades Union Congress (TUC) called for a general strike to defend the wages and conditions of over a million coal miners. The parallels with the dispute in Dublin in 1913 were obvious, but this was on a scale that threatened the survival of the British state. Workers set up councils of action, often under communist leadership, to organise picketing, food distribution and information. Just as the TUC leadership had sold out the locked-out workers in Dublin in 1913, they abandoned the miners for the fig-leaf of a non-binding agreement, which included wage cuts and longer working hours. The miners were left to fight on alone; eventually, poverty and starvation took their toll, and as winter set in they were forced to return on any terms they could get. Thousands were victimised or sacked, and those who returned to work had to accept lower pay and longer hours.[9]

O'Casey had a personal as well as a political interest in the general strike. All the theatres were closed, including the Fortune Theatre, where *Juno* was playing.[10] O'Casey immediately sent a cheque, a message of support to the Miners' Federation, and four signed copies of his books which were sold for 25/- each. Jack Jones, on behalf of the miners, replied, thanking him for his donation and his public support for the strike and inviting him to address meetings of the federation. Jones went on to express his appreciation of O'Casey's work, which he had seen and read.[11] O'Casey had also arranged for a special matinée performance of the *Plough* for the benefit of the miners' strike fund. Despite the agreement of the actors and management, the plan collapsed when permission was refused for A.J. Cook, the secretary of the Miners' Federation, to speak during the interval. O'Casey was furious with the support committee who had cancelled the performance because of the perceived slight to A.J. Cook:

> Was the primary need that of hearing Mr Cook speak, or that of getting the funds for the women & the children of the Miners? ... It was, in my opinion, a stupid thing to do – as stupid for your Committee to cancel the Matinee because Mr Cook wouldn't be permitted to speak, as it was for the TUC to refuse help because it came from Russia.[12]

From that time on, he refused to let anyone, from either the left or the right, make a speech during the interval in any play of his and offered to personally pay for any expenses incurred by the committee due to the cancellation of the performance. The *Liverpool Post and Mercury* printed a letter of support for the miners that he sent to the Women's Committee for the Relief of Miners' Wives and Children.[13] The following year he sent a donation and a message of support to Robert Wilson, the Labour Party candidate in the by-election in Leith, who had supported the miners. As a result, O'Casey received a rebuke from William Blackwood, who worked for the *Daily Mail*, reminding O'Casey that his 'literary and artistic admirers' would be appalled at seeing his name on a 'virulent Red pamphlet' published by the 'Anti-Christs and the Bolsheviks of Britain'. O'Casey replied in his usual fashion, suggesting that his literary admirers 'can go to hell' and that he would continue to jolt them and that he had every intention of supporting the 'Bolshies', even if they were, as Blackwood suggested, 'shaking the devil's paw'.[14]

O'Casey was totally supportive of the strike, as evidenced by contemporary letters and reports. However, the strike also revealed the personal and political contradictions thrown up during his London apprenticeship and the social circles that he now moved in. Billy McElroy, part wide-boy, part businessman and racehorse owner, had put up money to support the London productions of *Juno* and *The Plough and the Stars* and had replaced Fagan as O'Casey's minder and publicist. McElroy was from a Belfast and Scottish background and, according to O'Casey, was a 'roguish, bombastic, laughable' man with a 'wonderful personality'.[15] Despite their political differences, they became good friends, and McElroy was the best man at O'Casey's wedding to Eileen Carey in 1927.

The miners' strike continued for another six months after the collapse of the general strike. Coal was in short supply throughout the country. A colleague of McElroy's had access to a coal slagheap in the north of England and approached McElroy about setting up a joint venture to exploit this asset. McElroy asked O'Casey to place all he had financially at his disposal and to go guarantor for a bank loan to exploit the find. O'Casey later recalled that the coal was 'terrible stuff', but it gave out heat and 'business firms would take anything ... It was bought cheap and sold dear'.[16] A few months later O'Casey was repaid his loan by McElroy and released from his obligations. Many years later, O'Casey dismissed the incident by claiming that McElroy 'made more out of me than I made out of him' from the venture.[17] That O'Casey agreed to this business deal is baffling. During the lockout in Dublin in 1913, O'Casey had castigated Patrick Pearse in the harshest of terms for using the trams during the lockout.[18] Now he was financing a businessman to help break the miners' strike. A year later, when the defeated miners returned to work on the employers' terms, O'Casey wrote to Lady Londonderry to thank her husband, who was a leading member of the Coal Employers' Federation, for keeping 'an unprofitable mine open to save the miners from hardship and unemployment'.[19] It is hard to imagine that O'Casey would have written to William Martin Murphy to thank him for taking back the tram workers who were locked out in Dublin fourteen years earlier.

LONDONDERRY SET

O'Casey's association with the literary and social set that he encountered during his first few years in London – and particularly the right-wing and reactionary set that hovered around Lord and Lady Londonderry – is perplexing. According to his daughter, O'Casey liked Lady Londonderry, and as Eileen loved the social aspect of the group, he went mainly to please her.[20] However, he did meet several interesting writers, artists and filmmakers who populated the salons of the Ladies Londonderry and Astor, which helped advance his career. As O'Casey remembered it, 'the plays proved to be a passport for Sean into the big, big houses'.[21] At a gathering in a 'great Conservative Mansion … where the wines were rare and the fitting gorgeous', he described how the British prime minister, Stanley Baldwin, took him aside to ask about the character of Éamon de Valera. O'Casey was of the opinion that Baldwin had little interest in what he had to say and that he was being patronised as an amusing new writer 'invited to an assembly in a grand salon'. Later that evening, Edward Carson, the former leader of the Ulster unionists, came over to enquire in a most condescending manner if O'Casey was providing sound advice to the prime minister, while Winston Churchill, 'the aging D'Artagnan of the Conservative Party', strutted around the room.[22]

At one of Lady Londonderry's soirées, he met and became friends with Ramsay MacDonald, one of the most right-wing leaders of the Labour Party. He was briefly prime minister in 1924 and again during the national government of 1931–5, dominated by the Conservative Party and supported by a minority of Labour members of parliament, which introduced dramatic spending cuts to prevent a run on the pound. MacDonald was subsequently expelled for his actions in splitting the Labour Party, but all of this seemed to pass O'Casey by. During MacDonald's second spell as prime minister, they exchanged letters on the state of the coal industry. MacDonald invited him to Chequers, the prime minister's country estate, to discuss matters of interest: 'You understand so many things which the ordinary person does not. I would like very much if you would come and see me here one weekend when I am down, and I shall write to you when I get back from holiday'.[23] In 1934, O'Casey invited MacDonald to the opening of *Within the Gates*, however MacDonald was unable to attend for reasons of state.

Patronage is always a two-way process; those in positions of power, financially and socially, can advance the career and prospects of those they choose to sponsor, but there is a price to pay for such patronage. Despite O'Casey's understanding of the way he was patronised and, at times, paraded to amuse the Londonderry set and Lady Astor's circle, he continued to associate with them for several years. O'Casey's social and publicity whirl in London did not go unnoticed in Dublin. Brinsley MacNamara felt that he was playing the stage Irishman in London and, whereas in Dublin he avoided all photos or interviews, now he 'courted publicity at every turn'. Holloway, who always had his ear to the ground for Dublin gossip, noted that 'last year it was all O'Casey; now it was all shun O'Casey'.[24]

Charles Stewart Henry Vane-Tempest-Stewart, seventh marquess of Londonderry, was a direct descendant of Lord Castlereagh, the executioner of the United Irishmen in 1798, and a member of one of the wealthiest aristocratic families in Ireland or Britain. The family seat was Mount Stewart in County Down, and he owned vast estates throughout the United Kingdom. He was a unionist and a minister in the Northern Ireland government from 1921 to 1926. He was part of the die-hard faction of the Conservative Party, and his 'political outlook remained in essence that of a nineteenth-century nobleman'.[25] He was a Nazi sympathiser and an acquaintance of Hitler, Göring, and especially Ribbentrop, Hitler's envoy in London.[26] His wife, and O'Casey's friend, Lady Edith Londonderry, had established her own political and artistic circle, an exclusive dining club for the rich and the powerful that helped to enhance her husband's political ambitions. It was known as the Ark Club, and members were given names from myth or fable: Winston Churchill was 'Winston the Warlock', Ramsay MacDonald was 'Hamish the Hart', Lady Londonderry was 'Circe the Sorceress', and O'Casey was 'The Spider'. The Ark Club was the British establishment at play, but it also served a political purpose: here, connections were made, and plots hatched.[27] For the writers and artists who provided the glamour and the glitz, this was the price they paid to obtain introductions and commissions for their work.

Another socialite of O'Casey's acquaintance was Lady Astor. Bernard Shaw, a frequent visitor to Cliveden, Lady Astor's country house, introduced

O'Casey to the Astors. The 'Cliveden set', like many of the British upper classes, were pro-German and favoured appeasement with the Nazi regime. Lady Astor was anti-Catholic, anti-communist and anti-Semitic. 'In a letter to US Ambassador to Britain Joseph P. Kennedy Sr., Nancy speculated that Hitler could be the solution to the "world problem" of Jews. In 1939, the MP Stafford Cripps referred to her in Parliament as "The Member for Berlin"'.[28]

What attraction O'Casey held for these upper-class women is difficult to ascertain. He had a succession of friendships with the leading lights of British society – Lady Londonderry, Lady Astor, Lady Lavery and Lady Rhondda. While he did dine with Lady Ottoline Morrell on one occasion, he had little time for her left-wing and more liberal Bloomsbury set of writers and artists. He disliked their writing because he believed they had sucked all the life-force and vitality from literature.

In September 1934, O'Casey accepted an invitation to spend a week at the home of Lady Londonderry at Mount Stewart in Northern Ireland. He was on his way to New York to oversee the rehearsals for *Within the Gates*. Lady Londonderry had also arranged to stand guarantor for £200 at O'Casey's bank to finance the trip. On several occasions during this period, O'Casey and his family also availed of the hospitality of Lady Astor when they needed to stay over in central London. His letters to Lady Londonderry, Lady Astor or his friend and publisher Harold Macmillan, the future Conservative prime minister, reveal his warm friendship and respect for them and his ability to excuse the worst excesses of their politics. London had softened O'Casey's pride, in many ways for the better. In 1913, he had refused the offer of a pair of old boots from James Larkin, even though his own were beyond repair. His pride would not allow him to accept a helping hand during those terrible days. Now, he was staying in the homes of the aristocracy and accepting their largesse. Despite all this frivolity, he had not reneged on his political beliefs. The outbreak of the Spanish Civil War in 1936 reignited his active support for the socialist movement, and in particular for the USSR. In 1938 he had no problem remonstrating with Lady Astor for her comments to his wife Eileen on the situation in Russia following the Moscow trials of the old 1917 revolutionary leaders: 'I understand you fired a shot at me saying that "Russia was killing all her intelligent people" ... An intelligent traitor's more dangerous than a stupid one. The Red army's none the worse for the loss of a few of Hitler's friends ... Everything isn't perfect there; but nothing is perfect here'.[29] Lady Astor was right about the Moscow trials, but for her, this was just a stick to beat the left with rather than a defence of the gains made by the 1917 revolution. O'Casey was no less severe when, in 1943, Lady Astor supported the release of the fascist leader Oswald Mosley, who had been interned in Britain at the outbreak of the war:

> Your kind card has prompted me to beseech you to take thought before you wave your fists in defence of Mosley ... I was shocked when I read your defence of him ... If you still want to oppose Communism, oppose it by defending finer things than that peacock-feathered jay.[30]

After that exchange, their friendship faded, as it did with Lady Londonderry, but contact was maintained. In 1962, David Astor (son of Lady Astor) made a discreet offer to fund a private pension for O'Casey to ease his financial worries. O'Casey replied, refusing the offer: 'But even in the lean years, I should not have taken an offer of this kind, for, David, I am a proud man, sometimes fiercely so, and it is almost impossible for me to be beholden to anyone'.[31] His connections with these people undoubtedly influenced O'Casey, but none of his critics has suggested that he was ever corrupted by them. The fifth volume of his autobiography is a distressing account of a writer trying to support his family and not willing 'to give up any of his principles for Big House patronage'.[32] I doubt if O'Casey had any regrets about his friendships with his upper-class friends, but they faded into the background after the O'Casey family moved to Totnes in Devon in 1938.

THE SILVER TASSIE

Despite the temptations that London provided, O'Casey, in 1927, was hard at work on a new play. He heard his friend Billy McElroy sing Robbie Burns' song 'The Silver Tassie', which provided not only the title of the play but also the core idea:

> Go fetch to me a pint o' wine,
> An' fill it in a silver tassie;
> That I may drink before I go,
> A service to my bonnie lassie.[33]

The setting is the First World War, and the first act takes place in familiar O'Casey territory, the tenement of the Heegan family. Harry Heegan returns home with the silver cup or 'tassie' after scoring the winning goal in the final of a soccer competition. But Harry, on leave from the army, has to return to France. The second act is set in the trenches of France in a highly stylised and expressionist manner. The third and fourth acts are set in a hospital ward and the dance hall of his local football club in Dublin.[34] Harry has been severely wounded and is confined to a wheelchair and can only look on in anger and despair at the sound-limbed bodies of his friends as they dance the evening away.

The inspiration for *The Silver Tassie* can also be traced to Wilfred Owen's poem 'Disabled', which Owen wrote during the time he spent convalescing in an army hospital in Scotland during the First World War. In Owen's poem, a footballer, like Harry in act one of *The Silver Tassie*, is carried shoulder-high following a sporting victory and, drunk with adulation, decides to enlist. 'Disabled' expressed the tormented thoughts and recollections of the young soldier and athlete confined to a wheelchair due to the war. All he can do is look on longingly as the 'women's eyes / Passed from him to the strong men that were whole'.[35] In the closing scene of *The Silver Tassie*, the two disabled soldiers, Harry and Teddy, take leave of the revelry and the dancing and depart into the world of the living dead. The last words are spoken by Susie Monican, whose life has been transformed by her experience as a nurse in the war, in her case from a sexually repressed woman dominated by religion into a sensual woman who wants to live life to the full:

> SUSIE: It is the misfortune of war. As long as wars are waged, we shall be vexed by woe; strong legs will be made useless and bright eyes made dark. But we, who have come through the fire unharmed, must go on living.[36]

Logically, *The Silver Tassie* completes the sequence of the Dublin plays, a quartet recording the social and political upheavals that affected Ireland in the first decades of the twentieth century. The play is about transformation, at both a personal and a dramatic level, written and conceived after O'Casey left Ireland. The *Tassie* was his first attempt to break free from both the Irish historical context and the realist elements that dominate his earlier work. He was determined to write it in a new way; 'he wanted a change from what the Irish critics called burlesque, photographic realism, or slices of life'.[37] He wrote about war as a universal condition rather than in the context of individual characters rooted in a specific historical era. Even though three of the four acts take place in a Dublin tenement, this is not an Irish play. There are no references to the politics of the time or characters that represent the political aspirations of Irish nationalism or the working class. Neither are there any establishment figures, such as a John Redmond figure, to justify politically or morally Ireland's participation in the war or as a counterpoint to the play's central message.

The Canadian actor Raymond Massey directed the London production of *The Silver Tassie*, and the sets were designed by the artist Augustus John, both of whom went beyond what O'Casey had envisaged for the non-realist presentation of the second act. These changes are evident in the subsequent 'staged version' editions of the play.[38] Massey used music and experimental lighting to heighten the expressionist style of the second act. The audience was confronted with Augustus John's juggernaut of a set containing a montage of images from the First World War: the remains of a bombed-out monastery with its jagged walls and broken stained glass windows, a large howitzer gun in the ruins of the church, with a soldier lashed to the gunwheel, is facing out towards the audience; a life-sized crucifix hangs precariously from the wall, and the hands of dead soldiers protrude from the ground where they were hastily buried. O'Casey was present at the rehearsals and was willing to try out on stage, and in the text, any suggestions by the director that he felt improved the overall cohesiveness of the play.[39] The war scene in act two is written in a stylised and symbolic way that leans heavily on the expressionist methods of German theatre. The battle of the Somme in 1916 may have been in O'Casey's mind as the setting for the second act, as he may have seen the film documentary *The Battle of the Somme* at the Theatre Royal Dublin in September 1916,[40] but the play is not about historical representation. O'Casey mentions no specific battle, and the expressionist presentation of the war scene is deliberately distorted to represent the dissonance of war. O'Casey sets out in great detail how the set should look: 'In the war zone: a scene of jagged and lacerated ruins of what was once a monastery ... Every feature of the scene seems a little distorted from its original appearance'.[41] This experimental production was part of a process that transformed his concept of drama, as evident in his next play, *Within the Gates* (1934).

O'CASEY AND EXPRESSIONISM

Expressionism in drama usually involves a subjective and emotional representation of reality through symbolism, abstraction and experimentation. Expressionism does not involve reproduction of superficial detail, but an exposé of its essence and the reality behind outward appearance.

Expressionism was not a style that the Abbey was comfortable with, or to Yeats' taste. However, Yeats did support Lennox Robinson when he founded the Dublin Drama League in 1918, which presented several plays in the expressionist style by dramatists such as August Strindberg, Ernst Toller, Georg Kaiser and Eugene O'Neill. After his return to Ireland in 1925, the playwright Denis Johnston helped to make the expressionist method more accessible there through his involvement in the Dublin Drama League and the New Players. Johnston produced plays by the German expressionists Kaiser and Toller for the Drama League. Gabriel Fallon estimates that O'Casey attended about 60 per cent of the league's performances.[42] After O'Casey moved to London, he attended performances at Peter Godfrey's Gate Theatre Studio, usually in the company of Johnston or the painter Augustus John. The Gate was the only London playhouse that offered an expressionist repertoire as it was a private theatre club and, therefore, exempt from the ban on German political theatre. Denis Johnston suggested that, as early as 1926, O'Casey's 'dialogue is becoming a series of word-poems in dialect; his plots are disappearing and giving place to a form of undisguised expressionism under the stress of a genius that is much too insistent and far too pregnant with meaning to be bound by the four dismal walls of orthodox realism'.[43] His new drama was not consciously part of a movement. Like Ernst Toller and Eugene O'Neill, he spoke with his own voice; he was an innovator who constantly experimented with structure and plot. He attempted to fuse realism, expressionism and poetic fantasy in a personal and distinctive way rather than being influenced by any particular movement. Following *Within the Gates*, his work was, for the most part, realist, perhaps in an attempt to make the poetical fantasy and expressionist techniques more acceptable. Despite this, O'Casey's drama from the 1930s onwards can stand alongside that of Federico Lorca, Bertolt Brecht, T.S. Eliot or Antonin Artaud as part of a general movement away from realism on the stage.

O'Casey's rejection of realism was both a revolutionary and an evolutionary process. In an essay from 1937, 'Green Goddess of Realism', he argues against his former 'realist style' and in favour of a more modern expressionist or symbolist style.[44] The essay also illustrates the way class politics informed and shaped his aesthetic in the aftermath of his departure from Ireland in 1926. O'Casey was never comfortable with the agitprop style of the 1930s that was popular with left-wing theatre groups. In *The Star Turns Red* and *Red Roses for Me*, he attempted to capture 'for a revolutionary agenda the richness of an aesthetic that had become the property of bourgeois high culture'.[45] And this literary strategy is what elevates his drama from that period above and beyond that of agitprop. Ronald Ayling points to the connections with Brecht's 'epic drama' in *The Silver Tassie* and the later plays, such as *Figaro in the Night*, in the way that O'Casey uses Brecht's technique of 'distancing' or 'alienation' to jolt the audience's perception of the play. In the realist theatre, each scene exists for another, as plot and character evolve over the course of the play; the epic form progresses by sudden leaps. Each scene exists for itself, approximating the form and structures that O'Casey was striving to achieve.[46] Art and literature sometimes develop in a disjointed way; at certain times in the history of culture, particular ideas or movements develop and become dominant, and a group of writers or artists moves forward in parallel. However, expressionism was not a tightly bound movement; rather, it was the 'interaction of independently creative individuals',[47] several of whom influenced O'Casey's work, especially after he left Ireland.

He was well informed about dramatic developments. His engagement with the expressionist drama of Toller, Kaiser and O'Neill predates *The Silver Tassie*. As early as 1925, he was in contact with Raissa Lomonovska, an emissary of the Soviet Union who brought new works by Soviet and communist writers to the attention of Western readers and publishers. He was up to date on developments in Soviet and German film and theatre and had read Huntley Carter's books on modern continental cinema and theatre.[48] He was familiar with the expressionist films of Fritz Lang and Sergei Eisenstein (whom he met in London at a party after the showing of *Battleship Potemkin* in 1929).[49] According to Shivaun O'Casey, he saw the Habima Players, a Jewish theatre group that had its origins in the Moscow Arts Theatre. They were at the forefront in their use of expressionist techniques, masks and stylised design, all of which influenced O'Casey's thinking when writing *Within the Gates*.[50]

Much ink has been spilt trying to explain O'Casey's debt to the playwright Ernst Toller and the German expressionists. The opening scene of Toller's *Transfiguration*, in which the skeletons of soldiers spring from the grave and perform a dance of death, and also the hospital scene in the third act, find an echo in *The Silver Tassie*. O'Casey's second act – in terms of structure and style, in the way he strips the characters of their individuality by calling them 'first soldier', 'second soldier', and so on – is similar to the structure and style of *Transfiguration*. Also apparent is the way O'Casey incorporates Toller's ability to juxtapose expressionism and realism within the one play.[51] Toller explained how he tried to:

> break away from the photographic reproduction of external reality and in dramatic terms to reshape the world about him in the light of a single essential idea ... Conventional notions of structure, language and character were radically altered. Plot came to combine internal and external action; language was terse and penetrated to the essence of things; character became representative of type.[52]

In an interview with a British journalist, Toller 'indicated that Sean O'Casey's *Juno and the Paycock* made a strong impression on him'.[53] But to what extent O'Casey owed a debt to Toller and expressionism is a matter of debate. Toller was one of many politically committed artists and writers in Weimar Germany allied with the left. He was a member of the Independent Social Democratic Party. Unfortunately, during the terrible sectarian period of the Communist Party in the 1930s, Toller was attacked by the communists because of his political affiliation, which then spilt over into an attack on his literary endeavours. That may be one of the reasons for O'Casey's frequent denial of Toller's influence on his work. Regardless of O'Casey's denials, Toller's influence is visible in his drama from that era. Like Piscator, Brecht, Kaiser, and the generation of artists and writers radicalised by the horrors of the First World War and the rise of fascism in post-war Germany, Toller was conscious of the connection between his work and the process of social revolution.[54] In a letter from jail in 1923, Toller summed up their desire to dramatise the collective struggle of the working class to create a new and fairer society: 'The ancient theatre had its Prometheus, the man who believed he could overcome fate and make an end of all suffering; in our day a whole class has taken the place of a single hero'.[55] While O'Casey was aware of German political theatre, individual protest rather than collective struggle dominates his work. O'Casey was certainly aware of Toller's work. His copy of Toller's *Masses and Man* is inscribed with his name and is dated 1924. He recognised the power of Toller's writing: 'it seems to me that this Expressionism is an important element in the present and coming Drama'.[56] In a review of Toller's *Seven Plays* in the *New Statesman* in 1935, he wrote: 'Here are the plays for the modern theatre whether one likes them or not ... Each play is a serious reflection from a worthy and intelligent dramatist on the impact with which life has shaken him'.[57]

Unlike writers in Germany, O'Casey's drama after he left Ireland was never linked directly to a mass working-class movement where art, literature and drama were important features.[58] German expressionist and epic theatre was always more than a matter of form or technique.

Expressionist institutions, theatres, reading rooms, periodicals, printing presses and cafés existed in almost every major town. The border between the drama on the stage and reality on the streets was porous and blurred: 'The theatre had become reality for them [the audience] and soon it was no longer the stage versus the auditorium but a single great meeting-hall, a single great battle-field, a single great demonstration'.[59] Richard Allen Cave has described how German expressionism owed a great deal to the directors and actors, the collaborative ethos and the makeshift theatre groups 'whose limited resources compelled them to be inventive with coloured lighting and shadows, with make-up and stylized arrangements of simple stage-units, groups of rostra and dark curtains, to achieve the aesthetic effects demanded by the dramatist'.[60] It may well be that expressionism's most significant achievement was the work of directors such as Piscator and the practical side of production rather than the work of its playwrights. O'Casey was aware of German expressionism and the constructivist and futurist movements inspired by the Russian Revolution. In Russia, Mayakovsky put his artistic endeavours at the disposal of the Bolshevik government in his capacity as a poet and playwright. Toller saw himself as part of a generation of socially committed artists who attempted to shape political events. During the Nazi era, his books were banned, and he was forced to flee abroad. In 1935, Toller was invited to speak at a left-wing meeting in Rathmines Town Hall in Dublin. At the request of the Nazi government, he was banned from Ireland by de Valera's government, and armed police surrounded the venue.[61] On the eve of the Second World War, in a last desperate gesture against the Nazi regime, Toller took his own life.

The influence of expressionism on O'Casey is a contentious issue among his critics. Heinz Kosok, who has written extensively on O'Casey's experimental drama and its reception in Germany, believed that German expressionism had a negative effect on O'Casey's drama. Ronald Ayling and Carol Kleiman maintain that any attempt to place *The Silver Tassie* or *Within the Gates* exclusively within the context of Toller's work, or classical German expressionism, is not a helpful way to approach O'Casey's plays. Kleiman also contends that there are substantial differences between the expressionism of Strindberg and Toller and what she terms O'Casey's 'homemade expressionism'.[62] She illustrates how O'Casey was critically linked to the 'theatre of the absurd' and later to Beckett's work, but with a more optimistic view of human values in the way that O'Casey's characters affirm life in whatever way they can. O'Casey's expressionism was not always a matter of form but of feeling – its ability to shock us into discerning the world in a different way. O'Casey's engagement with expressionism came some time after the movement had reached its peak. Nevertheless, he incorporated elements into his drama in the form of a 'simplified expressionism' that is evident in the 1942 production of *Red Roses for Me.*

REJECTION

O'Casey had great hopes for *The Silver Tassie*. In a letter to Lady Gregory, he wrote, 'I have certainly put my best into it, and have written the work solely because of love and a deep feeling that what I have written should have been written'.[63] So confident was O'Casey that the Abbey would produce the play that he sent Lennox Robinson a 'list of those whom I imagine would fill the principal parts'.[64] He was devastated by the Abbey's rejection and Yeats' dismissive critique. Terry Phillips' interesting analysis of the rejection of *The Silver Tassie* because of the climate of deliberate amnesia about the First World War at the end of the 1920s adds to our understanding as to why Yeats and the Abbey board rejected the play and the initial hesitancy of the London theatres to produce it.[65]

Bernard Shaw's support for the play hardened O'Casey's determination to defend the integrity of his work: 'what a hell of a play! I wonder how it will hit the public. Of course, the Abbey should have produced it.'[66] Yeats and the Abbey board of directors treated O'Casey dreadfully. Whatever their personal views of the play, they owed O'Casey a production. Whether the Abbey could handle a play of this complexity was another matter. Their carelessness in the way they conveyed the decision to reject the play added to the disappointment felt by O'Casey. The result was an exchange of letters between O'Casey and Yeats that included threatened lawsuits and literary insults on both sides and illustrates the damage it did to the career of O'Casey and the future of the Abbey. This extract from the exchange of letters reflects the bitterness of the situation:

> YEATS: I am sad and discouraged; you have no subject. You were interested in the Irish Civil War ... But you are not interested in the Great War ... You never stood on its battlefields or walked its hospitals, and so write out of your opinions ... Dramatic action is a fire that must burn up everything but itself.
>
> O'CASEY: Now how do you know I am not interested in the Great War? Perhaps, because I never mentioned it to you. Your statement

> is to me an impudently ignorant one to make, for it happens that I was and am passionately interested in the Great War ... Do you really mean that no one should or could write about or speak about a war because one has not stood on the battlefield? ... It is all very well and very easy to say that 'the dramatic action must burn up the author's opinions'. The best way, and the only way, to do that is to burn up the author himself.[67]

And that is precisely what the Abbey did; they burnt their connection with one of the finest playwrights of the twentieth century. Yeats suggested that to save face, O'Casey should announce to the press that he had withdrawn the play for further revision. However, O'Casey refused to go along with the charade of withdrawing the play and forced the Abbey to reject it. He sent the entire correspondence to the newspapers in England and Ireland, where the controversy raged over the following six months. There was no winner in this dispute. O'Casey never wrote another play for the Abbey, and the Abbey lost its finest playwright. Nevertheless, the Abbey must ultimately accept the blame for their disastrous handling of the affair, as both Yeats and Lady Gregory realised when it was too late to repair the damage.

Another casualty of the *Tassie* fiasco was the Irish Academy of Letters. The academy was set up in 1932 to promote creative literature in Ireland and to honour those writers whose work was deemed praiseworthy in both an Irish and international context. Both W.B. Yeats and Bernard Shaw signed the invitation to O'Casey to be one of the elite twenty-five academicians. O'Casey was one of seven who refused the invitation, as did James Joyce and Douglas Hyde. Undoubtedly, the row with the Abbey still rankled, and in a very public manner, O'Casey published his refusal to accept the nomination in a letter to *The Irish Times*.[68]

The Silver Tassie was eventually produced in London in October 1929. Barry Fitzgerald, whom O'Casey had suggested for the Abbey production, played Sylvester Heegan, and Charles Laughton, who subsequently had a successful career in films, played Harry Heegan. Lady Gregory, who was in London during the run, admitted that she had been wrong about the artistic merits of the play and that the Abbey should have produced it. The relative success of the London production opened up a wider debate about the decline of the Abbey and its increasingly conservative artistic policy. The London run of *The Silver Tassie* received mixed reviews. Seán O'Faoláin felt that O'Casey had over-reached himself and should return to the characters and techniques of his earlier plays, saying that 'before he exhausted the possibilities of the techniques he knew, Sean O'Casey turned to a technique that proved beyond his powers'.[69] In the early Dublin plays, O'Casey wrote out of a poetic affiliation with the time, place and characters of his drama. However, no gifted writer wants to remain the voice of the street if it is the entire world that he wants to address. The American playwright Clifford Odets suggested that by 1934 O'Casey was no longer speaking for the parish, but rather 'testing his voice on the stages of the world', though understanding that 'few poets have left home and lived to tell the tale'.[70]

Following the reconciliation between O'Casey and Yeats, the Abbey agreed to produce *The Silver Tassie* in 1935. Seán and Eileen O'Casey travelled over to Dublin for the opening on what was to be his last visit to Ireland. There were objections to the religious imagery in the play and the perceived attack on religious beliefs. Brinsley MacNamara, the author of the controversial *The Valley of the Squinting Windows* and a director of the Abbey, threatened to resign when 'his suggestions for amending the play were not accepted. In his view, certain portions of the play were offensive.'[71] Father Gaffney in the *Standard*, a Catholic weekly, denounced the play 'as an outrage to the faith' and campaigned to have it banned.[72] O'Casey, in a letter to the *Irish Press*, defended his play against accusations of blasphemy: 'I have tried to answer some of the objections raised, not by a dramatic critic, but by a theologian, and with all respect, I hold that he has something to learn about theology, as I am certain that he has a lot to learn about dramatic criticism'.[73] The 1951 revival by the Abbey at the Queen's Theatre in Dublin saw further objections and protests, notably from Brian O'Nolan, who wrote under the pen-name of Myles na gCopaleen in *The Irish Times*: 'In the Queen's Theatre, the Abbey makes its debut with as loathsome and offensive a "play" that has ever disgraced the Dublin boards. The second act is a perfectly plain, straightforward travesty of Catholic Church ritual. The rest is bunkum and drool'.[74]

NEW YORK

Seán O'Casey set sail for New York in September 1934 to attend the rehearsals of *Within the Gates*, hoping for critical and financial success. The play was scheduled to open in New York in October, followed by a tour of thirteen North American cities. *Within the Gates* was his first full-length play written in a poetic expressionist style, without an Abbey production in mind. Primarily, *Within the Gates* is an attack on the Church of England's failure to respond to the social crisis of the 1930s and, at the same time, a twentieth-century morality play.[75] The play is set in Hyde Park in London, the haunt of down-and-outs, where a poet, an evangelist and a bishop fight to save the soul and life of a young woman who has turned to prostitution out of desperation. She approaches the well-meaning bishop for help during a personal and spiritual crisis. The bishop, unknown to her, is also her father from an illicit relationship twenty years earlier. Unable or unwilling to offer any real help for fear of discovery, his proposal to hand her over to a convent in an attempt to save her soul has a particular poignancy in light of the subsequent scandals in Ireland surrounding the Goldenbridge and Magdalene homes for unmarried mothers and their children. O'Casey structured the play as four seasons: a spring morning, a summer noon, an autumn evening and a winter's night. The shifts in seasons, days and time are symbols of the ages and development of human life. The play is in some ways a development of *The Silver Tassie*. But here, poverty and unemployment, rather than war, destroy the soul and spirit of O'Casey's characters. Despite their destitute condition, O'Casey maintained the play was essentially a 'cry for vigorous and effective life',[76] a theme he developed in nearly all his subsequent plays.

Within the Gates was a significant play in O'Casey's development and, according to Robert Hogan, 'a kind of personal catharsis, a full and complete statement of his world view'.[77] Walter Kerr of the *New York Times* was one of many critics who admired O'Casey but believed that 'when asked to make the crucial decision of his creative life, chose courageously, and chose wrongly'.[78] Robert Hogan considered that his excursion into expressionism led him into a literary impasse. In a conversation with George Jean Nathan in 1934, O'Casey declared:

> I was advised then – and since – by shortsighted critics and other busybodies to return to my early style and write only of the Dublin slums and their people. But I'd done that and wanted to develop. Why should the door be slammed on an author? ... Has he no right to grow, to experiment with fresh methods, even if he falters at them when he begins?[79]

Although Brooks Atkinson and George Nathan were enthusiastic in their support for the play, the reviews were mixed. George Nathan in *The American Spectator* was ecstatic: '*Within the Gates* is not only one of the finest plays of our time; it is one of the most successful amalgams of true literature and true drama that the modern stage has ever known'.[80] While this was to be expected, given that Nathan, with the support of Eugene O'Neill, had left 'no stone unturned to get it the best possible production',[81] other critics were more cold and caustic. The *New York American* reported that while the play reads well, 'the stage betrays all that is worst and weakest about it. The stage reduces it to a sullen charade.'[82] Even the theatre critic of the *Daily Worker*, the paper of the Communist Party of America, which was usually supportive of left-wing writers, thought it 'one of the dullest, emptiest, crudest, most pretentious evenings I have spent in the theatre'.[83] The London production fared no better with the critics; the *Daily Express* dismissed it as 'ranting socialistic nonsense'.[84] The enthusiasm for the play displayed by George Nathan, Eugene O'Neill and Brooks Atkinson made rejection all the more bitter. O'Neill said that *Within the Gates* was a 'rare and sensitive poetical beauty. I wish I could write like that.'[85] For Atkinson and Nathan, *Within the Gates* provided a modern poetical alternative to the 'sterile frivolities of Broadway comedy and the ideological simplicities of agitprop drama'.[86]

When Boston banned *Within the Gates* and Toronto followed suit, the rest of the American tour was cancelled. The ban dealt a financial blow to O'Casey, now married with a young family, but the artistic effect this had on his work was more significant. Despite the distillation of scholarship relating to O'Casey, it is difficult to comprehend the rejection of him by the age in which he lived. His standing in the literary canon is not too far behind the dramatic giants of his day, Ibsen, Chekhov, Shaw and O'Neill. Yet in the United States, after 1935, he found it almost impossible to obtain a production in any of the major playhouses. The small art-houses such as the Gate in Dublin or similar venues abroad could have provided an arena for his work. However, O'Casey had no intention of writing for the avant-garde theatre. He was aiming at a revolution in public taste, no less, even though the public usually resent having their literary habits changed. The Edwards/MacLiammóir Company (Gate Theatre) in Dublin offered to produce *The Silver Tassie* in 1930. But, as so often happened with O'Casey, he misinterpreted their motives, believing that they only wished to cash in on the notoriety attached to the play, and rejected their offer with such venom that the Gate Theatre did not produce an O'Casey play until 1986, long after the death of all concerned. Christopher Murray has suggested that the work of Clifford Odets and the production methods and values of the Group Theatre in America could have provided a model for O'Casey.[87] The Group Theatre, dedicated to the principles of the Moscow Arts Theatre, challenged the conventions of Broadway by the sheer spectacle of their productions. The radical left-wing ethos of the Group Theatre, their collective approach emphasising the coherence of the group over the individual, could have provided a literary home for O'Casey. However, by the end of the 1930s, secluded in Devon, he was cut off from the living theatre. He was, in one sense, a displaced intellectual, cut off from the Irish theatre and isolated from the modern drama that London or New York could have offered.

The rejection of *The Silver Tassie* by the Abbey Theatre and the critical failure of *Within the Gates* were devastating blows to O'Casey. Despite this setback, he continued, sometimes successfully and to varying degrees, using expressionist techniques in *The Star Turns Red*, *Purple Dust*, *Oak Leaves and Lavender*, *Red Roses for Me* and *Figaro in the Night*.

CHAPTER 12

Rise o' the Red Star

In the late 1930s, O'Casey described Moscow as 'a flame to light the way of all men towards the people's ownership of the world'.[1] Moscow was just the final stop on an intellectual journey that had commenced long before the Abbey accepted his first play. In his public pronouncements, he appears to have had little interest in Marxist theory. Except for his discovery of *The Communist Manifesto* in 1915,[2] Marx is referenced on only four other occasions in the autobiographies and then only in passing. In the first volume of the *Letters*, which covers the period 1910–41, there are only five references to Marx, and in the subsequent three volumes, nothing of any theoretical substance appears. The theoretical issues that filled the pages of publications associated with the Communist Party such as *Left Review* or the *Marxist Quarterly* did not seem to interest O'Casey. It was the living tradition of Marxism that exited him: workers discovering their collective identity as a class, fighting to abolish poverty and wage slavery.

O'Casey was aware of the revolutionary developments in Russia in 1917 and beyond. He was a member of the Socialist Party of Ireland and took an active part in the agitation in support of the Russian Revolution. He recalled how he raised 'his voice at the Dublin meetings, held to protest against the interference waged by the powers in order to down the struggling Revolution'.[3] As early as 1925, he was in contact with Raissa Lomonovska, an emissary of the Soviet Union in literary and artistic matters.[4] In the 1920s he also refers to the magazine *International Theatre*, which dealt with theatre developments in the USSR. He had direct access to the political situation in the USSR through his friend and mentor James Larkin, who led an Irish delegation to Moscow in 1924 and was subsequently elected to the governing body of the Communist International. When Macmillan first published his plays in 1925, he parcelled them up, with a great sense of pride, and posted them off to the USSR, 'filling the first leaf of the book with fervent good wishes for the future of the great Socialist Federation of States'.[5] In one of the dozens of letters and polemical essays that O'Casey wrote for the Soviet press, he recalls the impact of Lenin in Dublin in the aftermath of the Russian Revolution:

> Then the name LENIN came suddenly into the papers, saying he was leading a Revolutionary Party which had overthrown the bourgeois Provisional Government and had declared a soldiers, workers, and peasants Socialist Republic! ... But who was Lenin? Whoever he was, the Capitalist Press in their references to him showed him to be a dangerous man; and, so, to Sean O'Casey he was surely a real friend of the workers ... Lenin's name is still a power within us, still a torch, still a star to show the light, to lead the way.[6]

O'Casey's commitment to the communist cause is frequently downplayed or ignored by a section of his literary admirers. His American friend and biographer David Krause believed that it was the 'Red Star of Bethlehem' that influenced his politics as much as, if not more than, Karl Marx: 'Sean actually preached his own unorthodox gospel of evangelical communism; and his curious faith owes more to the Holy Ghost than the Communist Manifesto'.[7] Saros Cowasjee, an early biographer, also suggested that O'Casey's communism was a substitute for religion and 'reduced to its barest is nothing more than a deep concern for the poor and the neglected'.[8]

The reality of O'Casey's enduring relationship with the communist movement is evident. In 1938 he began a long association with the *Daily Worker*, the paper of the Communist Party of Great Britain. He served on the committee of the Society for Cultural Relations between the Peoples of the British Commonwealth and the USSR and supported several Communist Party political and cultural organisations. At the suggestion of Jack Lindsay, a member of the Communist Party and a writer and critic, O'Casey began corresponding with Timofei Rokotov, the editor of *International Literature*, in Moscow and with Mikhail Apletin, secretary of the Foreign Commission of the Soviet Writers' Union, in London. From 1938 onwards, O'Casey was a prolific contributor to the *Daily Worker* in Britain and America, and the foreign-language press of the USSR.

SPANISH CIVIL WAR

In February 1936, after years of instability, a Popular Front government, with the participation of the Communist Party, was elected in Spain. In July, army officers led by General Franco staged a military coup against the republican government. The coup was a pivotal moment in the politics of the 1930s. What Franco had not anticipated was a spontaneous anti-fascist uprising. Workers formed anti-fascist committees and organised militias. They managed to repel Franco's army and, in the process, took control of several major cities.[9]

The rise of fascism in the 1930s and especially the Spanish Civil War had a profound effect on O'Casey. In a letter to Harold Macmillan in November 1936, he wrote, 'I am praying to God that the Spanish Communists may win'.[10] Six months later, he wrote to George Jean Nathan in America, 'I'm still doing all I can to speed on the good work in Spain where the workers & thinkers & poets are alive in the flames of the barricades'.[11] In an unpublished article, 'The Black Flag of Fascism', he set out his position in uncompromising terms: 'There is no room for peace in the Fascist policy ... We must strike it down by every means in our power; with ball and bomb; by a shrewdness of union with all decent people; with the bitter and scathing use of the spoken and written word'.[12]

Volunteers came from all over the world to join the International Brigade in the fight against fascism in Spain. The first volunteers arrived in October 1936. Over 40,000 people from nearly forty countries volunteered to defend the Spanish republic, including 2,500 from Britain. About 240 volunteers came from Ireland, mainly from the ranks of the Communist Party, the Northern Ireland Labour Party, the IRA and the Republican Congress. Initially, Frank Ryan and Peadar O'Donnell, leading members of the Republican Congress, had been reluctant to commit their limited forces to the war in Spain. Ryan believed that socialists should stand their ground in Ireland and that 'the front-line trenches of Spain are right here'.[13] What changed his mind was the intervention of Cardinal MacRory, who publicly denounced the Republican Congress for their support of the Spanish republic. The decision of General O'Duffy, the leader of the fascist movement, the Blueshirts, to form an Irish Brigade to fight for Franco was another factor that led to the formation of an Irish unit of the International Brigades. Frank Ryan's statement as the first group left for Spain emphasised this point:

> It is also a reply to the intervention of Irish Fascism in the war against the Spanish Republic, which if unchallenged, would remain a disgrace on our own people. We want to show that there is a close bond between the democracies of Ireland and Spain. Our fight is the fight of the Spanish people, as it is of all peoples who are victims of tyranny.[14]

Peadar O'Donnell's book on Spain, *Salud!* (1937), was written to influence public opinion in Britain and Ireland. O'Donnell went to great lengths to dispel the image of the war as a contest between Christianity and a godless communism, a point that O'Casey made in one of his letters on the Spanish war: 'It looks as if Ireland would be split in two very viciously indeed, over the Spanish War. We have a "Christian Front" here (in Ireland) which worships Franco and lives to exterminate Communism'.[15]

Frank Ryan fought in the last few months of the War of Independence, and in the Civil War that followed on the republican side. He was a journalist and edited several newspapers for the IRA. Ryan split from the IRA, along with George Gilmore and Peadar O'Donnell, to form the left-wing Republican Congress in 1934. Ryan was the most senior officer in the Irish unit in Spain. He was wounded in March 1937 and returned to Ireland to receive treatment. He travelled via London and met with O'Casey. Despite what had happened in the past, O'Casey had the highest regard for Ryan. In 1939, in a letter to F.R. Higgins at the Abbey Theatre, he recalled the row over the *Plough* and Ryan's part in it. O'Casey went on to say that Ryan 'has become one of my friends – I was never an enemy of his; and we often played hurly together, more than twenty golden years ago'.[16] He arranged for Ryan to call to his house, and Eileen O'Casey remembers a 'handsome, idealistic young Irishman' who spent two days with the O'Caseys discussing the events in Spain.[17] O'Casey refers to the visit by Ryan and two of his comrades: 'Frank Ryan, who leads the Communist Irish in Spain, is coming up to see me – he has been wounded – and it was he who led the attack on "The Plough" long ago – and I expect to have a fine evening with him and two others who have gone thru hell'.[18] O'Casey could see that Ryan's health was broken and tried to persuade him not to return to Spain. He suggested that it would be far better for Ryan to return home and continue the fight for his ideals in Ireland. However, nothing he said could persuade Ryan to change his mind. Ryan felt that his duty was to his men in Spain and that 'he couldn't think of leaving the boys by themselves'.[19]

In 1937, Nancy Cunard and the poets W.H. Auden and Stephen Spender published a pamphlet, *Authors Take Sides on the Spanish Civil War*, and sent out a questionnaire on the war to virtually every leading British and Irish writer. O'Casey replied with these stirring words: 'I am with the determined faces firing at the steel-clad slug of Fascism, from the smoke and flames of the barricades.' Joyce simply acknowledged receipt of Auden's letter, while Beckett famously replied 'uptherepublic!'[20]

In October 1938, in an attempt to appease international opinion, the republican government in Spain disbanded the International Brigades and requested that all foreign volunteers return home. However, it was too late for Frank Ryan; Franco's forces had captured him in March 1938. At the end of the war, they handed him over to the Nazi government in Germany, where he remained until his death in 1944.[21] After Ryan's capture and imprisonment in Spain, O'Casey joined in the campaign to have him released. In 1939, he spoke to the *Sunday Referee* newspaper regarding an article on Ryan demanding his release. He also wrote several letters to *The Irish Times* in 1952 defending Ryan from an attack on his character and his Catholicism by Hamish Fraser, a former member of the International Brigade who became a convert to Catholicism.[22] O'Casey defended and supported all those who had fought or contributed to the fight against fascism in Spain. The political position in Ireland and the fate of the Irish Battalion in Spain seem to have motivated O'Casey as much as the anti-fascist element of the war. In 1938, O'Casey wrote a letter of support to the socialist newspaper *Forward* for the duchess of Atholl in the West Perthshire by-election.[23] She had resigned the Conservative whip because of the government's domestic policy. In 1937 she went to Spain to witness for herself the reality of the Civil War. Her book, *Searchlight on Spain*, published by Penguin in 1938, and her new-found support for the republican side in the conflict, had an immense effect on British public opinion. She was known as the 'Red Duchess', which was at least progress compared to the views of some of O'Casey's other aristocratic friends. But all was in vain; the war ended with victory for the fascists in 1939.

George Orwell went to Spain in 1936 to join the fight against the fascists. He saw first-hand the counter-revolutionary character of Stalinism and the Communist Party's betrayal of their socialist and left-wing allies.[24] Orwell and his comrades on the revolutionary left were hunted down on the streets of Barcelona by their supposed allies in the Communist Party. He returned to England, still a convinced socialist, but with a greater sense that Stalinism was an enemy within the movement. Out of this experience, Orwell wrote *Homage to Catalonia*, a wonderful description of the revolutionary process and an exposé of Stalin's betrayal of the revolution in Spain. He went on to write two biting satires on Stalinism, *Animal Farm* and *Nineteen Eighty-Four*.

Orwell became a hate figure for the Communist Party after his return from Spain and the publication of *Homage to Catalonia*. Harry Pollitt, a leading member of the Communist Party, described Orwell as 'a disillusioned middle-class boy'.[25] O'Casey, like many influenced by the Communist Party, believed that Orwell was a traitor to the movement and his *Letters* and *Autobiography* contain several disparaging remarks about Orwell. He justified this invective on the basis that 'the worst things said about Orwell were said by his friends; quoted by me in the book'.[26] His dislike of Orwell stemmed from literary as well as political differences. In the *Observer* newspaper in October 1945, Orwell's review of *Drums under the Windows* set off a literary spat that reflected little credit on either of them. Even though Orwell never set foot in Ireland, he had strong opinions on Irish politics and culture. He objected to the sympathetic treatment English reviewers generally gave Irish writers, where 'literary judgement is perverted by political sympathy'. Orwell ridiculed O'Casey's portrayal of himself in the third person, 'which gives an unbearable sense of narcissism'.[27] In a previous review, he had characterised O'Casey as a 'knee-jerk nationalist'.[28] In a total misreading of O'Casey, Orwell accused him of abusing England while 'preferring to live in the country, which is the object of [his] hatred'. In turn, O'Casey misunderstood Orwell's point about the 'special status of Irish writers in England', believing this referred to financial matters rather than political issues, as Orwell had intended. O'Casey sent a long rambling reply to the *Observer* in which he accused Orwell of contradicting himself and making misstatements about Ireland, which was not published. This literary dispute masked a deep political divide, particularly regarding their respective attitudes to Stalin and the Soviet Union. In 1954, four years after Orwell's death, O'Casey took the opportunity to make a public reply to Orwell. In the last volume of his autobiography, *Sunset and Evening Star*, he accused him of being a renegade socialist and questioned whether he ever did 'a hand's turn' to improve the condition of society, and suggested that 'he yearned to drag all life down with himself into his own stony despair'.[29]

REVOLUTIONARY PLAYS

O'Casey responded to the political and economic crisis of the 1930s and '40s by writing a series of plays that Jack Mitchell has termed his 'revolution plays': *The Star Turns Red*, *Purple Dust* and *Red Roses for Me*.[30] With the exception of *Red Roses for Me*, they have received little attention from anglophone critics and are rarely performed. In March 1937, he said he was 'thinking about a play called *The Star Turns Red – Star of Bethlehem*'.[31]

However, the origin of *The Star Turns Red* goes back to 1925 and a letter to Lady Gregory where he stated that:

> I happened to mention to a German Labour comrade, whom I met at the Abbey, that I was thinking of writing in the future a Labour play to be called *The Red Star*. Since then I have received appeals from Leningrad and Moscow to let them know when the play is to be commenced and when finished ... Well, comrades and all as they are, they will have to wait till the proper time may come for the new birth.[32]

O'Casey dedicated *The Star Turns Red* to 'the men and women who fought through the great Dublin lockout in nineteen hundred and thirteen' but significantly, he states that the setting is 'tomorrow or the next day'.[33] *The Star Turns Red* was his literary contribution to the fight against fascism in Spain and Germany and significantly in Ireland as well. In a letter, he spelt out his purpose: '*Star Turns Red* was, of course, a curse on the Nazi-Fascist powers; plus, the attempt to form the "Blueshirts" in Ireland'.[34] The play depicts the world of the 1930s, where the centre had politically dissolved, and the options facing humanity were either socialism or barbarism.

Although the concept for *The Star Turns Red* had been in his mind for over a decade, O'Casey found it difficult to write about Jim Larkin and the events of 1913 in a way that did them justice.[35] Spain provided a focus for the play, but when he sat down to write it in 1938, the republican government was facing defeat, and the controversy about the show trials in the USSR was at its height. The play reflects this in the way that loyalty to the working class and the USSR overcomes personal doubts about the revolution. Echoes of the great historical events of the twentieth century are everywhere: the Dublin lockout of 1913, the dominant figure of James Larkin, the Russian Revolution of 1917 and the Spanish workers' uprising in 1936. The drama unfolds against the background of the Nazi takeover in Germany and the Catholic Church's flirtation with the corporate state. *The Star Turns Red* was O'Casey's most trenchant literary statement on communism, fascism and the Catholic Church's support for Franco, with walk-on parts for Paddy Belton's Christian Front and the Blueshirts in Ireland.[36]

The way O'Casey inverted the traditional colours to signify the political allegiance of the two priests in *The Star Turns Red* is of interest. The Red Priest is the reactionary fascist, and the Brown Priest is the lover of the poor and supporter of the workers' uprising. Red is the traditional symbol of the left, but in the Catholic Church, red is the symbol of power. In a programme note for the 1946 production by Unity Theatre, O'Casey explained that:

> The Red Priest is at first confusing to working-class audiences who, from his title, expect him to be the representative of a revolutionary point of view. It should be explained that the Cardinal Secretary of State at the Vatican is the powerful one there politically. He is clad in Scarlet and is called the 'Red Pope' ... and on this ... is built the character of the Red Priest: the implacable enemy of the workers.[37]

However, in all subsequent editions of the play, the fascist 'Red Priest' is denoted as the 'Purple Priest', which helped clear up any confusion this caused in the minds of English left-wing audiences.[38] He also took the opportunity to settle a few old scores. A thinly disguised Jim Larkin takes his revenge on the conservative trade union bureaucrats who hounded him out of the ITGWU. In this rerun of the 1913 lockout, Larkin triumphs over his old adversaries. Here a committee member informs Red Jim:

> BRALLAIN: You may as well know, first as last, that we have deposed you! The Red Priest's our President and our Patron. We've too much love for the men to let you wreck the Unions by your savage and ceaseless opposition to the Church and the Christian Front.[39]

One of the accusations made against Larkin by the leadership of the ITGWU after his return from America was that he had spent union funds without authorisation.[40] In act two, Red Jim demands the keys to the safe so he can give money to the family of a union member killed by the fascists. The union secretary replies:

> SECRETARY: It's the Committee's orders – no money to be given without written permission.
>
> RED JIM: No money without written permission, eh? Whose permission? The Saffron Shirts' or Sir Jake Jester? This is one of your new rules?
>
> BRALLAIN: Ay, one of them. It was time to nick the hand that tries to thin out the assets of the Union to nothing. Last Christmas, when the reserve was good, you poured away half on hams and geese for needy members. It's the Committee's order, and you'd better obey it.[41]

In contrast to *The Plough and the Stars*, which lends itself to the pacifist reading of the Dublin plays favoured by many American academics, O'Casey defends and justifies revolutionary violence in *The Star Turns Red*. There is no questioning whether the killing and destruction is justified. In the final scene, Jack is killed defending the revolution, but when all seems lost, the soldiers desert and join the workers. 'The Internationale' is heard in the distance as Red Jim tells Julia, a communist and Jack's sweetheart:

> RED JIM: He's not too far away to hear what's happening. You'll nurse, now, a far greater thing than a darling dead man. Up, young woman, and join in the glowing hour your lover died to fashion. He fought for life, and life is all; and death is nothing!

The play ends with a tableau where:

> Julia stands up with her right fist clenched. The playing and singing of 'The Internationale' grow louder. Soldiers and sailors appear at the windows, and all join in the singing. The Red Star glows, and seems to grow bigger as the curtain falls.[42]

O'Casey described *The Star Turns Red* as 'a confession of faith', and 'the best [play] of its kind that has been written', although he did add, 'which isn't saying a lot'.[43] There is no ambiguity in the clash of ideologies; he is clear about which side he supports. In *The Star Turns Red*, O'Casey moved beyond Ireland by incorporating the 1913 lockout into the international fight against fascism and for workers' rights across the world.[44]

Technically, the play is traditional in form; it uses a box set and depends for its emotional stimulus on characterisation. The play has an epic theme, but the classic method of production has limited its potential to emerge as epic theatre. *The Star Turns Red* is the closest to an agitprop style of drama that O'Casey ever wrote. David Krause called it a 'bald political tract', while Roland G. Rollins said it was a 'turgid, political drama, which indicts Fascist tyranny, religious complacency, and capitalist inequality'.[45] This response was not unexpected from his American critics, who were writing in the 1960s at the height of the Cold War; but O'Casey fared no better at the hands of his communist critics. The initial review by the *Daily Worker* theatre critic on 13 March 1940 was favourable: '*The Star Turns Red* is the best thing Unity has done. If you miss it, you will miss a great theatrical event.' However, the following week one of the Communist Party's intellectual heavyweights gave a political assessment of the play, which was far from favourable. Randall Swingler felt that O'Casey's communism 'is not that of Karl Marx or Lenin ... his workers are a little wooden ... O'Casey gives a very distorted picture of trade union practice'.[46] O'Casey defended his play in a letter to the editor of the Moscow journal *International Literature* and showed far better political and aesthetic judgement than his socialist critics:

> Were Red Jim to speak as a Marxist, the audience here or in America ... would take no notice; only the converted, those already Marxists, would listen. Now I don't want to talk to those who are already [in] our way of thinking – they are already on the march; but I do want to get in touch with those who are lagging behind.[47]

So far, no theatre company has managed to successfully fuse the propaganda and the dramatic aspects of the play. Ironically, the support for republican Spain and its anti-fascist politics gave it currency when O'Casey wrote the play. However, when it came to staging the play in 1940, the political atmosphere in Britain had changed. The Hitler/Stalin pact and the outbreak of the war in 1939 made it almost impossible for a commercial theatre to accept a play advocating socialist revolution.

UNITY THEATRE

In 1939 O'Casey sent the first draft of *The Star Turns Red* to the Abbey Theatre, but nothing came of this, and the play was not produced in Ireland until 1978. *The Star Turns Red* was produced in London in 1940 by the left-wing Unity Theatre Club, and it is impossible to do justice to the play without considering the context of the time and his relationship with Unity Theatre.[48] The Lord Chamberlain's Office had judged the play 'subversive' and banned any public performance. Unity was a private members' theatre club, and therefore the ban did not apply. This was an uncomfortable time to be a supporter of the Communist Party. The USSR's insistence that the European conflict was an imperialist war and the real enemy in Britain was their own ruling class lost the party many friends and supporters. This led to tensions within the Unity Theatre membership. O'Casey supported the Soviet Union's position,[49] and his views on the war led to a clash with the Labour MP George Strauss, a member of Unity's general council, who took the opposite view. Strauss wrote in *Tribune* that O'Casey and the Communist Party's policy of opposition to the war was 'in its results treachery to the working class and aid to Hitler'.[50]

In 1934, *Left Review* had asked why there were so few plays that deal with the working class, noting that *Stevedore* in America and *Six Men of Dorset* in Britain were honourable exceptions.[51] Unity Theatre accepted the challenge. *The Star Turns Red* fitted both the political and artistic mission of the group. The play suited Unity's concept of committed theatre in that the audience was left in no doubt about the outcome of the struggle between the workers and the fascists. O'Casey had an uneasy relationship with the Unity Theatre Club. On the one hand, he was supportive of their political objectives. A club circular in 1937 stated that they intended to create 'a workers' cultural centre, art classes, theatre, cinema, lectures, and a library'.[52] Unity projected itself as the National Theatre of the Working Class. While supportive of Unity Theatre, O'Casey was conscious of their limitations in artistic matters and the way Communist Party control tended to stifle the aesthetic ambitions of the group.[53]

Unity Theatre developed from the Left Book Club and the small working-class theatre and literary groups that existed across Britain in the 1930s. An early manifesto of Unity Theatre stated, 'Unity is a peoples' theatre, built to serve as a means of dramatizing their life and struggles and as an aid in making them conscious of their strength'.[54] In their first few years, Unity rejected conventional realism as bourgeois, and even left-wing dramatists such as Shaw, O'Neill or O'Casey found little favour because of their association with mainstream theatre. The workers' theatre movement rejected realism for the same reasons as O'Casey; it merely reflected surface reality without being able to analyse material relations or the deeper connections and contradictions in class society. They embraced a new form of drama, agitprop, which was a 'juxtaposition of slogans, chants, stereotypes, dialogue, mime, satire, and songs' with their own style of 'mass speaking and expressive gesture'.[55] The intellectual establishment tended to look down on working-class drama, which was perceived to be less literary, and a debased form of drama infected with propaganda, even though Toller, Piscator and Brecht all came from that tradition.

In the mid-thirties, the political shift by the Communist Party from class confrontation to Popular Front politics[56] resulted in a reconciliation between agitprop and conventional theatre forms. The politics and the production values of theatre were transformed, resulting in some of the most interesting drama of the period, particularly by the Group Theatre in America and Unity in London. In 1937 Unity acquired new theatre premises seating 250 in the St Pancras area of London. Appropriately, they staged *Waiting for Lefty* by Clifford Odets on the opening night. Shortly afterwards, Unity launched *New Theatre* as the official publication of the club, with a message of support from O'Casey on the front page:

> I hope the Unity Theatre Club will grow into a great power ... will smash the myth that culture and the enjoyment of art is confined to what is sometimes called the 'better classes' ... the beginning of the Theatre of the workers can hardly be great, but even the beginning can easily be as good as the garbage that is heaped on the golden shrine of the present day theatre.[57]

In the next issue, in a lengthy interview, O'Casey called on the trade unions to support Unity: 'Until the Trade Unions take this lead from the workers and build Unity Theatres in every town in England, Scotland, and Wales our work is not half done'.[58] By the end of the 1930s, Unity Theatre groups existed in a number of the major cities in Britain. Their example inspired the formation of the New Theatre Group in Dublin and the Left Book Club Dramatic Group in Belfast in 1937 along similar lines.[59]

In 1938 O'Casey was elected to the general council of Unity Theatre, and in 1939 they published some extracts from his book of essays, *The Flying Wasp*, in the members' bulletin. James Bridie, one of the founders of the Glasgow Unity Theatre, which produced several of O'Casey's plays, said that 'If Unity had a guiding star it was O'Casey'.[60] The Unity group of theatres provided an outlet for O'Casey's later work at a time when the commercial theatre in Britain showed little interest.[61] In addition to *The Star Turns Red* in London, *Purple Dust* in 1943 and *Cock-a-Doodle Dandy* in 1949 had their world premieres in the People's Theatre in Newcastle upon Tyne.[62]

O'Casey was grateful for the support of Unity during those difficult years, but whether he would have taken the opportunity to forge a long-term working relationship with Unity or adapt his work to suit their political and aesthetic ambitions is another matter. Ewan MacColl, in Manchester, wanted their group to 'become a weapon for the people who wanted to tear down the capitalist system' and 'make something better for themselves'.[63] Unity's style of theatre did not suit O'Casey's more lyrical and experimental form. Unity was aware of the problem and accepted that amateur actors were more suited to a declamatory style of acting rather than the poetical and imaginative theatre of O'Casey. In different circumstances, given his political support for the Unity project, he could have found an outlet for his one-act agitational plays that were within the competence of the company's amateur players and popular with the Unity audience.

An alliance with Unity need not have impinged on his more formal and imaginative drama for the commercial and experimental theatre. He never wrote explicitly for Unity, but his one-act plays were always popular with the group and were performed on numerous occasions.

Scripts at Unity were read for political as well as artistic merit, and changes were suggested on both counts. Even a playwright of O'Casey's stature was offered the benefit of the Play Department's advice.[64] To what extent O'Casey was aware of the tensions inside Unity over whether to produce *The Star Turns Red* is not known. Frank Lesser, the political commissar for the Communist Party in Unity, remembers a meeting that continued for over a day and a half where the political and artistic merits of the play were discussed and dissected. Some Unity members were delegated to meet with O'Casey to discuss their reservations about the play. At that time, the Communist Party was trying to construct a political alliance with democrats and progressives to fight against fascism. Working-class revolution, as depicted in *The Star Turns Red*, was not on their agenda. They also had reservations about the way O'Casey portrayed the trade unions and the anti-clerical nature of the play, which they believed might alienate those organisations from the Popular Front movement they were trying to construct. There was also a moralistic element to their objections: the heroine, Julia, was seen 'as been rather free in her attitude to sex'.[65] O'Casey took his time to decide whether to go ahead with the Unity production, but the difficulties were overcome, and the play went into rehearsal in January 1940. O'Casey did not attend the rehearsals or even see the production. He delegated Peter Newmark, a former Cambridge University student with whom he had corresponded, to oversee the rehearsals and report back on the production. Newmark was a member of the Communist Party, but O'Casey seemed to trust his judgement in artistic matters while accepting his inexperience:

> I'm glad you are going to rehearsals, it will do you good: give you experience & show you what a terrible place the theatre is ... Don't be too anxious. John Allen [the director] can only do his best; and that he'll do, I know. We must be satisfied with what Unity can give.[66]

The 1940 production of *The Star Turns Red* ran for over eighty performances and was an important play for Unity. The production was the first time they had attempted a work of this magnitude and complexity. Unity, a voluntary and amateur group, was well aware of its limitations: 'We are under no illusion that we amateurs can do full justice to the quality of this magnificent play, but we have done everything that hard work, enthusiasm, and sincerity can do'.[67] Even James Agate in the *Sunday Times*, who had little sympathy for O'Casey's politics, was moved to proclaim it 'a masterpiece' that built on the promise of *The Silver Tassie*.[68]

In January 1946, O'Casey travelled up to London to discuss the forthcoming revival of *The Star Turns Red* at the Unity Theatre. He used his time in London to catch up with some 'friends of the *Daily Worker*' and officials at the Soviet embassy.[69] The Unity revival, directed by Ted Willis in 1946, ended badly. O'Casey was not impressed by reports of the production and even less impressed that he had no communication regarding royalties or payment for the six-week run. He took his work and his politics seriously, and even the Communist Party felt the lash of his pen if they attempted to interfere with his work or his integrity as a writer. In a strongly worded private letter to William Rust, the editor of the *Daily Worker*, O'Casey spelt out his annoyance:

> Since it seems your journal is connected with the activities of Unity Theatre, since Mr Ted Willis, Unity Theatre's producer is evidently one of your staff, and since the aims of the Theatre seem to be identical with your own; it is [right] that I should put the following matter before you.[70]

After explaining his problems with the production, both artistically and financially, he went on to say, 'I am handing over the matter to the League of Dramatists, for it is necessary that other dramatists should be cautious about giving their work to Unity Theatre. I am also writing to the group demanding that my name be removed from the list of members of the Council'.[71] Despite this disagreement, relations with the group were maintained. Glasgow Unity Theatre produced *Purple Dust* in 1946; although O'Casey did not see the production, he seemed pleased with the reports that it was 'a gay & rousing production',[72] even though a Communist Party member in Glasgow wrote to O'Casey objecting to the political line of the play. O'Casey replied, 'there may be messages in the play, if you look for them. But I never have, and never will, just put plain slabs of propaganda in a play. This can be done better in an article'.[73]

There were also productions of his plays in theatres associated with Unity in Newcastle, Liverpool and Leeds. In 1949, O'Casey felt confident enough in the integrity of Unity to recommend both the London and

Glasgow groups to Roger McHugh, a young Irish playwright who asked his advice regarding a production in Britain of *Rossa* originally produced at the Abbey Theatre in Dublin a few years earlier. O'Casey also suggested that if McHugh agreed, he would send a copy to the Union of Soviet Writers for translation. In May 1953, Unity Theatre in London produced a programme of three of O'Casey's one-act plays under the title *Three in a Row*, which consisted of *Time to Go*, *End of the Beginning* and *Hall of Healing*. However, when Unity in London requested permission to produce *Cock-a-Doodle Dandy* in 1957, O'Casey refused, saying that he had no quarrel with Unity, but that he believed the play was beyond their ability to perform it in the way that O'Casey envisaged. He was also wary of the political constraints that hampered their artistic ambitions: 'They run around seeking what they'll never find. They, & all they say about the drama, worry me. They don't read enough. They hear little men in little groups speaking, & are deaf to what the world says'.[74]

THE *DAILY WORKER*

O'Casey was a regular reader of *The Irish Times*, the *Daily Worker* and the Irish-language paper *Inniú*. The Communist Party launched the *Daily Worker* in 1930, and from about 1938 onwards O'Casey was a regular contributor of articles and letters to the paper. The outbreak of the Second World War in late 1939 brought problems for the *Daily Worker*. After a series of political twists and turns, the paper came out against the war on the basis that it was an imperialist war between the two big powers in Europe. In June 1940, the editorial board was dissolved amid fears that the members would be individually held responsible if the state took any action against the paper. As a precaution, they appointed a new advisory editorial board, which included a number of prominent public figures: the scientist J.B.S. Haldane, the dean of Canterbury, and Seán O'Casey. In January 1941, police officers raided the offices of the *Daily Worker*, and the paper was suppressed by order of the Home Office. In the months before, as the cry went up to ban the *Daily Worker*, O'Casey contributed an article to a pamphlet, *Hands off the Daily Worker*, in which he defended the paper against the accusations that they were hindering the war effort. He concluded by saying that 'tens of thousands of workers, whose skills the country needs to prosecute the war ... will feel that an attack has been made upon them' if the paper is banned.[75] Following the suppression of the paper, the editorial board, including O'Casey, issued a pamphlet, *The Case for the Daily Worker*, to be circulated in 'every factory, warehouse and farm in the land', calling for the ban to be rescinded.[76] After the German invasion of Russia in 1941, O'Casey wrote to Winston Churchill, reminding him they had once met at one of Lady Londonderry's soirées. He went on to say that now, as the Soviet Union 'is a welcome friend' in the war against fascism, the government should lift the ban on the *Daily Worker*. He enclosed a page taken from the Soviet *Daily War News* to illustrate how the *Daily Worker* could be of use to sustain morale and war production in the factories.[77] Following the military alliance with the USSR, agitation to lift the ban succeeded, and the *Daily Worker* resumed publication in August 1942. When the paper was re-launched at the end of the war, O'Casey was listed as an editorial board member and remained so until the board was dissolved in 1950.[78] In response to a query from a scholar in 1957 regarding his relationship with the *Daily Worker*, he replied, 'I never resigned the position of membership of the board, nor had I ever any intention to do so. I am a subscriber to the Funds, and a Shareholder in the Company. Each day, I read the *Daily Worker*'.[79] O'Casey also contributed a series of articles to Russian-based journals such as *International Literature*, *Literaturnaya Gazeta* and *Novy Mir* and continued to write for the socialist and Soviet press until his death in 1964.[80]

CHAPTER 13

The Literary Popular Front: 1936–56

After the economic crash of 1929, it seemed apparent to several writers and artists that capitalism might not survive in its current form for any significant length of time. The Bloomsbury set of English writers, intellectuals and artists who came together in the first decades of the twentieth century espoused a harmless liberalism and a hedonism that made little impact on wider society. The horrors unleashed by the First World War radicalised an entire generation, and the Bloomsbury set gave way to the Auden group of writers and poets who burst through the 1920s to announce the 'pink decade'.[1] Many on the left in the 1930s were writing with the certainty that the future would be socialist. Political pilgrimages to the USSR in that decade by the likes of Bernard Shaw, Sidney and Beatrice Webb, André Gide, Harry Kernoff and Leslie Daiken reinforced the widespread belief in the communist future among the artistic and literary community.[2] E.P. Thompson recalled that 'visitors returned from the Soviet Union with stories of the poet's dream already fulfilled'.[3]

Inspired by the war in Spain and the fight against fascism, the Workers' Theatre Movement set out to transform the cultural radicalism of the period into a political force. Unlike his Irish contemporaries in the London communist milieu who became part of the 'interconnecting British Left intellectual circles', O'Casey never saw himself as part of this new literary popular front.[4] Nevertheless, both of his plays from the 1930s, *Within the Gates* and *The Star Turns Red*, were inspired by the political and social upheavals of the decade. In the case of *The Star Turns Red*, its association with the radical Unity Theatre Club placed it firmly within that milieu.

Victor Gollancz launched the Left Book Club in Britain in 1936; by the end of the year, the club had over 40,000 members. It quickly became an umbrella group for left-wing activists, writers and artists.[5] Publications such as *New Writing* or *Poetry and the People* attempted to combine aesthetic feeling with social attitudes. *New Writing*, edited by John Lehmann, introduced European writers to British and Irish audiences. *Left Review* became the vehicle for many of the young writers involved in socialist politics, not all of whom were members of the Communist Party. *Left*

Review was a genuine attempt to create a British Marxist cultural tradition. O'Casey's only contribution was to the May 1938 issue that printed May Day greetings from several prominent left-wing individuals:

> Labour is battling in Spain, Labour is battling in China, and we have before us and behind us, on our right hand and on our left hand, the massed and mighty forces of the U.S.S.R. The Red Flag is flying where it never flew before. It is the flag that carries life.[6]

Apart from the Unity Theatre Club, he rarely engaged with the left-wing journals or the working-class literary and artistic movements that mushroomed across Britain in the 1930s. After his move to Devon in 1938, O'Casey was part of a Marxist discussion group, along with several local communists and left-wingers, who occasionally met in his house. However, he had little time for their rigid and doctrinaire approach to politics and literature, especially when he discovered that only 'one had ever read Dickens, and he was accused of being a Bourgeois'.[7]

The prevailing sense of impending disaster was made real following the outbreak of the Spanish Civil War in 1936, and the most important writing of the period was an effort to respond to that crisis. The young revolutionaries attempted to fuse politics and aesthetics into a movement whose triumph seemed historically inevitable. However, there was an unresolved tension at the heart of the dream that art could be political, appreciated by the masses, and yet produced to the highest aesthetic standards. Unfortunately, this debate happened at a time when the Communist Party was squeezing the life out of cultural production. Socialist realism – a combination of elements from the proletarian cultural movement in the 1920s allied to traditional realism – became the theoretical basis for Soviet culture in 1934. Experimentation was discouraged; movements in art and literature were denounced as counter-revolutionary if they did not conform to the schema demanded by the party. Their dogmatic pronouncements about literature were perhaps the principal reason why O'Casey never joined the Communist Party at that time.[8] In a letter in 1955 to Jack Lindsay, a leading member of the cultural section of the British Communist Party, he explained that in the past, he had written some sharp things to his friend Mikhail Apletin in Moscow complaining that Zhdanov[9] 'was bullying writers with his narrow shell of literature'.[10] The Zhdanov Doctrine laid down a very narrow realist basis for Soviet literature, and writers were expected to conform to these guidelines.

Stephen Spender wrote of the dangers faced by writers in the 1930s when belonging to the left had become a career choice. He suggested that within the ranks of the Communist Party, writers had a tendency to commit literary suicide.[11] In those circumstances, it was not surprising that many of the Auden generation either drifted away from left-wing politics or, in some cases, became hostile to the socialist project. O'Casey never abandoned his support for communism. He remained a committed supporter of the Communist Party until his death in 1964, but he never allowed the party to dictate what he could or could not write. What concerned him most was not artistic intervention in politics, but political intervention in art. In a letter to the *Literary Gazette* in Moscow, he protested against the ostracising of Nobel prize-winner Boris Pasternak and his expulsion in 1958 from the Union of Soviet Writers. Writing to Jack Lindsay, he complained about the excesses of socialist realism and the quality of the reviews in the *Daily Worker*: 'try to get your workers to accept the fact that a play must be regarded, must be criticized as a play, and not as a piece of propaganda'.[12] However, at times his support for the USSR could be dogmatic and unthinking. In an article on censorship in *The Bell* in 1945, he naively expressed the view that, in contrast with the West, books were not censored in the USSR.[13]

THE REVOLUTION LOST

As the Russian Revolution degenerated in the 1920s, Stalin and his supporters waged a relentless internal war against those who showed the slightest opposition. By the time of Stalin's death in 1953, the Soviet secret police had sentenced over four million people for political crimes against the state. Over 800,000 prisoners were executed, and an unknown number died in the labour camps of the Gulag system.[14] Since the collapse of the Soviet Union in 1989, historians have been able to reconstruct from the Soviet archives the life stories of many of those who perished. In *Left to the Wolves*, Barry McLoughlin has provided a micro-history of the critical events in Soviet and Irish history, which illustrate, at a personal level, the extent of the terror. He describes the lives of three Irish socialists, Pat Breslin, Seán McAteer and Brian Goold-Verschoyle,[15] who arrived in Moscow in the 1930s and disappeared during the purges.[16] Breslin, who worked for the *Moscow Daily News*, which catered mainly for foreign residents in the Soviet Union, died in captivity in Moscow, and McAteer was shot as a spy in 1937. The Soviet Red Cross, in a blatant lie, later informed Jim Larkin's son that McAteer had disappeared during the Nazi occupation of Odessa. Brian Goold-Verschoyle was kidnapped in Spain by the NKVD (Soviet secret police) and transported to Russia, where he died in prison in 1942.[17] O'Casey may have known Breslin and possibly McAteer from his time in the Irish Citizen Army, although he could hardly have been aware of what happened to them. O'Casey probably had no conception of the scale and extent of the purges, and like Bernard Shaw, he believed they were justified to safeguard the revolution. However, both O'Casey and Shaw closed their eyes to the overwhelming evidence of the revolution's degeneration and the counter-revolutionary nature of Stalinism. The alternative, fascism and the horrors it unleashed on the world, was such that the vast majority of left-wing writers and intellectuals either refused to believe what was happening in Russia or were prepared to overlook these events.

The Moscow trials of the old party leaders and top officials occurred between 1936 and 1938. They were charged with conspiracy to assassinate Stalin and other Soviet leaders and plotting to restore capitalism in Russia. One of the British Communist Party's leading intellectuals, T.A. Jackson, wrote an article in *Left Review* on the Moscow trials, which helps explain why O'Casey, like so many writers and artists, accepted the outcome and the truth of the trials. Jackson suggested that the defendants 'lacked faith in the capacity of the Soviet system – which produced first their fear of fascism, then made them try to do a deal with fascism, and finally led them to helping fascism'.[18] That argument had a logic that O'Casey, like many others, accepted as an explanation for the executions and imprisonments that followed. The *Daily Worker* reported extensively on the trials, highlighting the alleged confessions of twenty-one leading party members who were accused in the case of the 'Anti-Soviet Bloc of Rights and Trotskyites'.[19] This report in the *Daily Worker* gives a flavour of the political atmosphere in the Communist Party in Britain at the time of the trials:

> Every weak, corrupt or ambitious enemy of socialism within the Soviet Union has been hired to do dirty, evil work. In the forefront of all the wrecking, sabotage and assassination is Fascist agent Trotsky. But the defences of the Soviet Union are strong. The nest of wreckers and spies has been exposed before the world and brought before the judgement of the Soviet Court.[20]

Eighteen of the twenty-one people on trial were sentenced to death, and the other three were sentenced to twenty-five years in jail. O'Casey followed the trials in great detail. In a series of letters in the *Daily Telegraph*, *Time and Tide*, *Forward* and the *Daily Worker*, he defended the treason trials and the attacks by the regime on the political and personal characters of the accused. He participated in a lively and vexatious dispute in the press over Malcolm Muggeridge's reports of the Moscow trials in the *Daily Telegraph*. The *Telegraph* refused to print his letter defending the USSR and the legitimacy of the trials, or his subsequent letter, where he accused Muggeridge of being a coward and 'a cock who won't fight'.[21] The dispute spilt over into the pages of the *Daily Worker* and *Forward*, a socialist newspaper published in Glasgow, where O'Casey claimed that: 'There was no evidence of torture. There was not even a black eye among the lot of them. The OGPU evidently couldn't hold a candle to the Black and Tans'.[22] Muggeridge sent an extensive reply to the *Daily Worker* pointing out the absurdities of the confessions made by the accused to the charges laid against them and expressed surprise that 'such a fine dramatist, an Irishman, with a vigorous and independent mind' insisted on the truth of charges so fantastic 'that if they were made in a British or German, still more an Irish court, he would be the first to laugh them to scorn'.[23] The *Daily Worker* refused to publish Muggeridge's letter. At Muggeridge's request, *Forward* published the letter with a note challenging O'Casey to a public debate on the issue, an offer he did not accept. O'Casey also took time out from this dispute to respond to an editorial in *Time and Tide*: 'Will TIME AND TIDE tell us how and where and when the journal became privileged to know the facts proving the trial to be fraudulent and a horrible farce? For a start, the statement that "Stalin has exterminated all those who were of importance in the revolution" isn't true'.[24] He remained resolute on this matter despite the grave misgivings of many socialists and intellectuals over the legitimacy of the trials.[25] He defended his position and that of the Soviet invasion of Finland in 1941:

> When the execution of the Trotsky group of traitors had taken place ... I stood by what had been done, and publicly too, as you can see by looking up the files of the *Daily Worker* and the Glasgow *Forward*. Again, when the Soviets set out to make their Finnish border more secure, again when the howl went up, I defended the USSR as you can see by looking up the files of the *Tribune*.[26]

Many writers and artists disappeared or died in the camps during the Stalinist era. Victor Serge outlined the problem posed by the 'universal cowardice' of the many Western writers and intellectuals who remained silent throughout an entire decade during which 'their Russian colleagues, writers like Mandelstam, Pilnyak, and Babel, personally known to them and translated into every language, were massacred'.[27] O'Casey was no different from the legion of writers and fellow travellers who continued to give public support to the USSR during the 1930s and '40s. He downplayed the extent of the terror and the executions or excused them as an aberration.

In act two of *Oak Leaves and Lavender* (1946), O'Casey introduces a scene for no apparent dramatic reason other than to rehash the argument over the recent treason trials in the USSR. The scene arose from O'Casey's discussion with a local woman from Devon.[28] In the play, Deeda Tutting and her husband worked in the USSR in the 1930s. He worked in the offices of the Comintern but disappeared during the purges. Deeda challenges Drishogue, a young Irish communist and RAF pilot, about what happened to her husband:

> DEEDA: My husband worked beside me. He, too, found his dream was false. (*With a shrill and positive whine.*) He suddenly disappeared like thousands of others – perhaps millions – into a concentration camp. If it weren't for you and other Liberals here, Stalin daren't have done it.
> DRISHOGUE (*mockingly*): You'll be telling me in a minute that Stalin himself is the one man left outside a concentration camp.
> DEEDA (*tearfully*): Arrested without a word, without a sign, my poor husband's dead by now for certain.
> DRISHOGUE (*calmly*): Well, if the behaviour you're showing now is usual with you, I don't wonder he disappeared.[29]

In his autobiography, O'Casey recounts this incident and how he ended the conversation with the woman: 'the more you shout, Lady, the less I hear'.[30] And that was the problem. O'Casey and thousands of others did not want to hear what committed socialists and revolutionaries had to say about what was happening in the USSR.[31] It is easy to set up a straw woman such as Deeda Tutting in order to knock her down, but O'Casey would have benefited by engaging with the questions regarding the rise of Stalinism and the destruction of the revolutionary ideals of 1917 that George Orwell, Leon Trotsky, Victor Serge, E.P. Thompson or James T. Farrell raised if he wanted answers to the political questions that concerned him.

What was understandable and even excusable in the 1930s, given the rise of fascism, could only be intellectually or politically sustained with great difficulty after the workers' uprising in opposition to the regime in

East Germany in 1953, Khrushchev's denunciation of Stalin's crimes at the Twentieth Party Congress in Moscow in 1956, and the suppression by Russian tanks of the Hungarian Revolution a few months later.[32] Long after the demise of the Soviet Union, the historian Eric Hobsbawm described the impact of that momentous year on the supporters of the Communist Party: 'I cannot think of any comparable event in the history of any major ideological or political movement. To put it in its simplest terms, the October Revolution created a world communist movement, the Twentieth Congress destroyed it'.[33]

HUNGARIAN REVOLUTION

In 1956, O'Casey's political beliefs were tested to the limit when Russian tanks crushed the Hungarian uprising.[34] That year was a low point in his life, compounded by the death of his son Niall, with whom he had fierce arguments over the events in Hungary in the weeks before Niall died. The Berg Collection, in the New York Public Library, contains a twelve-page manuscript, *Words*, where O'Casey pours out his anger and hate at the Catholic Church, the media and the West for their support of the Hungarian Revolution: 'Mindszenty? A Cardinal, Prince-Prelate of the church comes on the stage Vatican-wise. Who's he? Dressed like a radiant turkeycock what symbol does he bring with him?'[35] No extract can express the anger and depth of feeling in this disconnected stream of consciousness, which he brought to dramatic fruition in a more subdued manner many years later in one of his last plays, *Behind the Green Curtains*.[36]

His youngest son Niall followed in his father's footsteps regarding politics. However, like many young socialists, he was deeply troubled by the revelations about Stalin's crimes and the Suez Canal crisis in October 1956. The nationalist government of Gamal Abdel Nasser nationalised the Suez Canal in July 1956, which took the world and especially the British and French stockholders by surprise. British and French forces attacked Egypt in the Canal Zone in response, while Israel, with their support, occupied the Gaza Strip and key points on the Sinai Peninsula. Niall, along with his sister Shivaun, marched in the demonstrations in London against this imperialist adventure. O'Casey opposed Western intervention in Egypt. However, like many older socialists who had experienced the war and the Holocaust, he was ambivalent about the Israeli invasion of Egypt and at the time expressed a 'deep and wide sympathy with the sturdy Israeli. I think it is time that the Jews should have a national place on which to rest the soles of their feet ... they were justified, or, at least, had a good reason for pushing their dangers a little further from their border.'[37]

When the USSR suppressed the Hungarian Revolution later that year, O'Casey and many of the old guard who had lived through the Second World War stood by the Soviet Union. For O'Casey, the Cold War was just another attempt to 'stamp out the power of socialism, fully grown in the USSR.'[38] Niall, however, was one of the many thousands of supporters of the Soviet Union who were deeply troubled by the events in Hungary. On several occasions, he drove down to Devon from his college in London to spend the evening arguing with his father over the Soviet intervention. He wrote a letter to his father outlining his distress about these developments:

> I hope you will find the enclosed press cuttings of interest from today's *Daily Worker*. The Old Guard is having quite a tough time at present. Resignations on the staff include Malcolm MacEwan, 'Gabriel', Philip Bolsover; on the verge are many others, including Sheila Lynd. The attitude of the executive over Hungary on many matters has been quite untenable. One can imagine the mistakes that have been made in Eastern Europe as being the same here, as if the Soviet Union had liberated us from Hitler, and had set up J.R. Campbell and his gang as Government. This isn't Communism at all.[39]

In Ireland, as in the O'Casey household, the Hungarian Revolution and the release by the Nagy regime in 1956 of Cardinal Mindszenty, who had been under house arrest since 1948, topped the news agenda. Cardinal Mindszenty was an outspoken opponent of the government, and the campaign for his release became a cause célèbre in the West. Eileen O'Casey remembers the family sitting quietly at the table over dinner, Seán silently fuming and 'strangely stubborn and hard'. He maintained that anybody who was against the leadership in Hungary should be shot. Eileen found it hard to believe that 'hating cruelty and oppression as he did, he seemed completely to accept the need for those harsh measures in Hungary'.[40] A short time later, on 29 December, Niall died after a brief illness of acute lymphoblastic leukaemia. He was just a few weeks short of his twenty-second birthday.

In his introduction to the 1956 section of O'Casey's *Letters*, David Krause misrepresents the differences regarding the Hungarian uprising between Michael O'Riordan, the general secretary of the Communist

Party in Ireland, and his wife Kay, who was also a member of the party. Krause portrayed the differences as those between a communist husband and a Catholic wife.[41] This was, in fact, a dispute between two committed communists, as documented in detail by their son Manus O'Riordan.[42] Michael, like O'Casey, supported the Russian intervention as necessary to save the Hungarian communist government. Kay defended the Hungarian students and workers in their demands for civil rights and political reform and supported the moderate and reforming Imre Nagy, who had been installed as prime minister a short time before. The Nagy government declared an end to the single-party system and released Cardinal Mindszenty from house arrest. Hungary also withdrew from the Warsaw Pact group of countries and declared neutrality.

Seán O'Casey was always incredibly supportive of Michael and Kay O'Riordan's efforts to sustain the Communist Party in Ireland, particularly during the Catholic Church's onslaught against the party in the 1940s and '50s. The differences of opinion in the O'Riordan family regarding the events in Hungary mirrored those in the O'Casey family. Accounts of the uprising in Budapest were confusing. Was this a genuine workers' uprising to throw off the tyranny of Stalinism and a fight for a more democratic and socially inclusive society, or a reactionary revolt to restore capitalism with the support of the Western imperialist countries? On 4 November 1956, Soviet troops were ordered into Budapest to put down the rising of students and workers who had come out in support of the new regime. Nagy was captured and executed after a show trial in 1958. He was replaced as prime minister by Janos Kadar, who was, in effect, a puppet of the Soviet regime.

In an editorial, the *Daily Worker* suggested that the workers had rallied around the party and government in Budapest to smash the reactionary and fascist elements. In a blatant attempt to discredit the revolution, it cited Nagy as declaring that counter-revolutionaries and anarchists were responsible for the revolt.[43] These political slanders and untruths caused a crisis both in the Communist Party and on the staff of the *Daily Worker*. A number of the staff resigned, including Peter Fryer, whose reports from the front line in Hungary were suppressed. Fryer reported that '[I] saw for myself that the uprising was neither organised nor controlled by fascists or reactionaries' and that the Soviet troops thrown into battle 'fought against the common people of Hungary, workers, peasants, students and soldiers'.[44] O'Casey was unmoved by either Niall's arguments or the reports coming out of Hungary. In a long letter to Kay O'Riordan, he set out his position:

> I'm afraid that I agree with Michael. To me, there isn't a shadow of a doubt that those who hate, and always hated, Communism (Socialism, if you like) tried to seize hold of the popular discontent in Hungary, and use it to overthrow all signs of Socialism there, and set up the old regime of landlord, clerical and lay, and fascist boss, so that in the future Hungary might be changed from a socialist country into an armed camp and arsenal for a possible attack on the USSR, if ever the glorious chance came. If you read all of the accounts, written by biased reporters, you can see that it tried to go too far; that bitter revenge was meted out to any communist captured – no holy protests against this! ... a strong party government, headed by Kardar [Jan Kadar], did what was terribly necessary to save Socialism for the Hungarian People, with the aid of the Red Army.

However, he ended the letter on a conciliatory note: 'Well, my dear, you must use your own judgment to form your own opinions, about all the things that happen, and far from me to try to change them'.[45]

The fact that in Britain, thousands of members and supporters abandoned the Communist Party after the events in Hungary only strengthened O'Casey's determination to defend the USSR. He also refused to accept the accounts of Stalin's crimes that emerged at the Twentieth Party Congress in Moscow in 1956. In a letter to his friend Brooks Atkinson in America, he wrote:

> As for Stalin, I don't accept the reported versions of the speeches said to have been made by Bulganin and Khrushchev. The denunciations made of the man's mistakes are, to me, but an implied idea that he should have been infallible ... As for the 'cult of personality' ... no more than Parnell was Stalin responsible for having a picture of himself on every banner, in every home.[46]

Many years later, the historian Eric Hobsbawm reflected on his decision to remain in the Communist Party after the events of 1956. His thinking in many ways mirrored O'Casey's position:

> I was strongly repelled by the idea of being in the company of those ex-communists who turned into fanatical anti-communists, because they could free themselves from the service of 'The God that Failed' only by turning him into Satan. There were plenty of them about in the Cold War Era.[47]

O'Casey understood the limitations of the USSR, but in a world threatened by nuclear destruction, he maintained that it was the only hope for humankind. He opposed capitalist exploitation, still believing in a socialist ideology in which people put the interests of the community before their own. O'Casey was just one of the many socialists who, like Jean-Paul Sartre, believed that Hungary was an aberration and that we should 'judge communism by its intentions not by its actions'.[48] Following the revelations at the Twentieth Party Congress and the events in Hungary, the historian E.P. Thompson and a number of former members of the CPGB launched a dissident publication, the *New Reasoner*, which in time led to the development of new left-wing organisations untainted by Stalinism. Unfortunately, O'Casey was hostile to these new developments and denounced those who had 'deserted' the Communist Party as traitors, just as in the past he had denounced J.B. Priestley and the fellow travellers, who in his eyes had deserted the working class and gone over to the side of reaction.[49]

Despite all the evidence to the contrary, for O'Casey, Brecht and many others, communism, as represented by its living form in the USSR and Eastern Europe, was an ideology of cooperation, pacifism and human friendliness. When confronted with the dangers of fascism in the 1930s, O'Casey, like many others, was prepared to overlook the sins of the USSR. In the post-war era, the Cold War and the development of atomic weapons that could annihilate all humankind was another reason why so many were prepared to support the regimes in the Eastern bloc. The USSR was perceived as a counterweight to the aggressive and imperialist adventures of the United States and its allies.

O'CASEY AND SOVIET CULTURAL POLICY

O'Casey was one of the most trenchant critics of Soviet cultural policy and was never afraid to speak out on behalf of artists and writers who were demonised for failing to adhere to the party line. He defended Bernard Shaw from 'the little-boy communists, Laski and Palme Dutt casting their own little vicious stones' at Shaw.[50] He took the Soviet literary establishment to task for attacking the poet T.S. Eliot. While accepting that Eliot was 'an old Tory and a churchman', O'Casey went on to say, 'No one should mind an honest enemy. What you have to be afraid of is a dishonest friend'.[51] He always defended his independence as a writer. In an interview in 1955, O'Casey insisted he was a communist; 'but I'm not a Communist pamphlet. There are a whole lot running around who are no more than Communist pamphlets.' He denounced Soviet art, claiming that it was 'dry as dust, out of date ... You honour Tolstoy and Chekhov, but you'll never have another if you don't be brave'. He recalled how, when Stalin died, a drawing by Picasso for a French communist paper was rejected by a party bureaucrat; 'if I'd been editor of that paper, I'd have written to that Soviet official and said, Go to HELL!'[52]

O'Casey always had a realistic view of Soviet art and literature and despised the 'boy meets tractor' style of literature promoted by the literary Stalinists of the Socialist Realist period. In reply to a young artist who wrote to O'Casey asking his advice on how to get a sense of class consciousness into his painting, O'Casey insisted that an artist's work must be controlled by a proficiency in technique, rather than ideology. He hated the way communist critics denounced modernism in art or literature as decadent or betraying the worst aspects of formalism. Writing to a young coal miner who aspired to be a writer, O'Casey mocked the anti-formalistic slogans of socialist realism:

> The worst formalism I know is the formalism of the chattering phrases uttered and muttered by the Communists themselves ... Harry Pollitt hasn't the faintest about literature in general. James Joyce would but irritate him; and the same can be said of 90% of the Communists in England.[53]

Writing to a Bulgarian comrade, he regretted the lack of artistic freedom in the communist bloc: 'Communists should not be so dogmatic about Literature and Art, about which most of them know little or nothing'.[54] Despite this trenchant criticism, O'Casey's work was respected in the USSR. According to Shivaun O'Casey, she discovered that his plays were performed all over Russia in working-men's clubs when she visited Moscow in 1989. As no royalties were ever paid, the family had been unaware of these performances.[55] In 1964, the Soviet Union published an extensive reference guide and bibliography of his work, and in 1980 academics in the USSR organised a conference in Moscow to celebrate Seán O'Casey's centenary.[56]

In the *Anglo-Soviet Journal* in 1946, O'Casey reviewed a new edition of the poems of Vladimir Mayakovsky, a poet and writer whom he liked and admired.[57] Mayakovsky was one of the best-known poets from the 1917 revolutionary period, but he was denounced at the end of the 1920s by the new literary regime that controlled cultural production in the USSR. He was smeared in the Soviet press and shouted down as being 'too obscure' at a public reading of his latest work. The Association of Proletarian Writers denounced Mayakovsky on the grounds of 'insufficient closeness to, and concern for, the people'. Shortly afterwards, in April 1930, in an act of desperation and despair, Mayakovsky took his own life.[58] In his review, O'Casey attempted to square the circle by saying that, on the one hand, Mayakovsky was the authentic voice of the revolution and that the battle 'to defend, step by step, and line by line, his way of singing his own song of the Soviet' took 'a heavy toll from the energy and passion of the poet', and 'it was a shame' the way it ended. On the other hand, there is only a veiled criticism of the USSR for the way it treated Mayakovsky. O'Casey, repeating the slanders in *Left Review*, went on to say that the people responsible were 'later revealed as Trotzkyites'.[59]

O'Casey's attention was not entirely focused on Ireland or the USSR. He was disturbed by the backlash against socialists in America, particularly those active in the artistic and literary arena. The House Un-American Activities Committee (HUAC) was a congressional group charged with investigating allegations of communist influence and subversion during the early years of the Cold War. In October 1947, during its probe of alleged communist influence in Hollywood, ten members of the American film industry were cited for contempt by HUAC for refusing to answer the question, 'Are you now, or have you ever been, a member of the Communist Party?' The Hollywood Ten, as they became known, received jail sentences and were banned from working in the film industry.[60] O'Casey wrote a letter of support to *The Author*, the official journal of the Society of Authors: 'The fact is that in the case of the Hollywood Ten, it wasn't the Ten who acted illegally, but those who condemned them'.[61]

There are numerous letters in the O'Casey archive in the National Library of Ireland to and from American socialists and liberals who were summoned to appear before the HUAC hearings. They include Elizabeth Gurley Flynn, the American union leader and communist convicted in 1953 under the Smith Act of conspiring to teach and advocate the forcible overthrow of the United States government. O'Casey wrote an open letter denouncing her arrest and imprisonment.[62] In 1953, he wrote to the president of Temple University, Philadelphia, in support of Barrows Dunham, who had been dismissed by the university from his teaching post. During HUAC's investigation of alleged communist influence in American colleges, Dunham was charged with contempt when he pleaded the Fifth Amendment and refused to answer questions about his background.[63]

Counter-Attack, a red-baiting organisation founded by two former Federal Bureau of Investigation agents, denounced both O'Casey and Dunham as 'dangerous characters'.[64] O'Casey was also friendly with and supportive of the Hollywood scriptwriter Donald Ogden Stuart and his wife, the writer and political activist Ella Winters. They were blacklisted during the Red Scare in 1950 and emigrated to England to avoid further prosecution. All of which brought O'Casey to the attention of the FBI. An extract from the files in 1942 notes that 'O'Casey is an Irish writer' and is 'apparently quite radical'. Another memorandum sent to J. Edgar Hoover, the director of the FBI, in 1959 refers to an article 'The Day the Worker Blows a Bugle' that O'Casey had published in *Masses & Mainstream*, an American Marxist publication, and states, among other allegations, that 'Sean O'Casey resides in England, and is openly a believer in Socialism and Communism'.[65]

THE POLITICAL RESPONSE

The critical response to O'Casey's support for communism ranged from Mitchell, Lowery, Greaves and Newsinger on the left to the more politically neutral Krause, Hogan and Murray, who were more concerned with O'Casey as a dramatist. They viewed his support for the USSR as a distraction that hampered his potential as a dramatist. On the other hand, Herbert Goldstone suggested that the problem with *The Star Turns Red* was not that it is 'too Communistic' but that 'it isn't Communistic enough', and O'Casey's problem with this play and others from the period may have been that 'he no longer believed as fervently in Communism as he did earlier in his life'.[66] Any assessment of the views of Goldstone or the other critics from that generation has to take into account the fact that the collected letters were not available until volume one was published in 1975. In his biography of O'Casey (1960), David Krause displayed little interest in O'Casey's politics. Krause was writing at the height of the McCarthyite witch-hunt against left-wingers in America. For a young academic, it may have been safer to concentrate on O'Casey the dramatist rather than the politician. His dismissal of the political differences portrayed in *The Star Turns Red*, on the basis that the communists are as bad as the fascists, showed little understanding of the period: 'One of the main troubles is that there is little to choose between the ruthless fanaticism of the two slogan-shouting groups. The Communist fist is as ominous as the Fascist salute, and the snarling epithets of both sides are practically interchangeable'.[67]

Seán O'Casey, like John Hewitt, Peadar O'Donnell and Louis MacNeice, understood that the crucial political issues of the 1930s went beyond whether or not to join the Communist Party and that a writer could be more useful to the movement outside of the Communist Party as they would be free from the pull of propaganda and could tell the truth as they saw it. The dogmatism of socialist realism alienated many writers and artists who could not conceive of artistic production and life as a political activist in the political and cultural milieu controlled by the Communist Party. A generation of writers, many of them committed socialists, were lost to the movement and, in some cases, became hostile to the project itself. O'Casey saw it differently: 'One thing I am certain of; Communism need not injure a playwright. Almost everything I've written (except juvenile stuff) was written as a Communist'.[68] Any sustained reading of his letters and journalism makes clear his total commitment to the socialist cause. The O'Casey archive in the National Library of Ireland contains dozens of letters and articles by O'Casey and from correspondents in the USSR, Britain, America and Ireland, covering the whole span of O'Casey's political life regarding his support for the USSR and the communist movement across the world.[69] In 1942, O'Casey's reply to John Irwin, a British army officer, concerning the rise of communism in Europe contained both his hopes for the future and his understanding that the path forward may be rocky and uncertain and that there might be abuses along the way:

> Communism, so far from being the end, is but the beginning. I look for it, not that we may rest from our labours, but that we may begin them. They have begun in the USSR; we haven't been able to start yet. No-one can determine how we can prevent things from being mismanaged or abused under Socialism; that must be evolved during the transition period, out of actual experience.[70]

The Cold War atmosphere also meant that O'Casey received several abusive letters concerning his support for the USSR. A letter from an American resident in 1949 was typical; it starts by criticising his work and continues: 'If you think Communism so wonderful, why don't you go to Russia and take George Bernard Shaw with you'.[71] Given the anti-communist hysteria of the period, it is not surprising that the FBI in America kept tabs on him and that he also featured on the infamous list of communist supporters that George Orwell, to his shame, supplied to the British Home Office in 1949.[72]

The events in the Eastern bloc in the 1950s affected O'Casey personally and politically, but his faith in the long-term future of the Soviet Union endured. He knew there were economic and political problems in the USSR, although publicly he always defended the regime. In one interview, O'Casey admitted that if he had lived in Russia, he would most likely be 'put up against the wall and shot'.[73] He believed that, given time, the USSR could overcome these problems and evolve towards a genuinely communist state that guaranteed rights and prosperity for everyone. He told a future biographer that 'Russia is not Communist. It will take another sixty years before it goes Communist. Your India may take as long as one hundred and fifty years.'[74] O'Casey contributed dozens of articles to Russian literary magazines and messages of support to peace initiatives by the Eastern bloc countries.[75] Nevertheless, as the 1950s progressed, he lost patience with the Communist Party in Britain over their sectarianism. He found the style of the *Daily Worker* annoying and said it was 'like a Labor edition of the R[oman] Catholic *Universe*'.[76] Replying to his friend from Unity Theatre, Peter Newmark, who had left the Communist Party in 1954, he wrote:

> I don't wonder you left the Communist Party. God almighty how stupid a lot of them can be! I gave up writing for the *Daily Worker* when I found conceited clowns taking chunks out of what I had written with great care & trouble; & altering the titles I had taken so much trouble to think out.[77]

Despite his annoyance with the paper, the turbulent events in the Eastern bloc after 1956 refocused his attention and support for the *Daily Worker*. But the gravity of discontent on the other side of the 'Iron Curtain' and the emergence of new movements beyond the control of the Communist Party seem to have made little impact on him.

Given that O'Casey's socialism was imbued with a sense of decency, compassion and humanity, his unbridled support for the USSR and the Stalinist regimes can be difficult to comprehend. There is no easy answer to the question as to why so many closed their eyes to what was happening in the USSR and the Eastern bloc countries. The reasons were complex, and varied from individual to individual. There is no straightforward way to look back and make judgements about what E.P. Thompson described as 'the enormous condescension of posterity'.[78] An American socialist active in the 1930s described the contradictions between the problems and accomplishments of that generation:

> In it, one joined Spanish antifascism and the Congress of Industrial Organizations and the black struggles and the New Deal and the

> Warsaw Ghetto and the Soviet Union, in a gigantic confraternity of the overwhelming majority of mankind, which, if only given its head, if only freed from the plutocrats and fascists and colonialists, would rapidly and instinctively inaugurate a reign of human niceness. There were many, many things wrong with that vision, and it was sometimes manipulated to rationalise cruelty rather than promote kindness. And yet, for all of its confusions and evasions and contradictions, if it was a corruption, it was the corruption of something good that always remained in it ... I knew the crimes committed by the GPU [USSR secret police] in the name of antifascism in Spain; and yet, I never cease to thrill at the songs of the International Brigades.[79]

How O'Casey would have reacted to the collapse of the Soviet Union is impossible to gauge. Reflecting on the regime, Leopold Trepper, a former Soviet official, wrote: 'I do not regret the commitment of my youth. I do not regret the paths I have taken ... I know that youth will succeed where we have failed, that socialism will triumph, and that it will not have the colour of the Russian tanks that crushed Prague'.[80] Perhaps that is how O'Casey would have seen it as well and continued to send his 'blasts and benedictions' across the world in his lifelong fight to ensure that workers would have a bunch of flowers, as well as a loaf of bread, on their table. Little remains of the radical literary and artistic movement from the 1930s, and it is mostly forgotten today. But it had an extraordinary impact on Western cultural life out of proportion to the Communist Party's political influence. Not all of it was praiseworthy, nevertheless, much of it was sincere, and some of it deserves to be remembered.[81]

CHAPTER 14

War and Imperialism

By the end of the twentieth century radical theatre had been in decline for several years, and even writers of the stature of Brecht, Shaw or O'Casey were considered outdated and were now 'nothing more than an object for nostalgia'.[1] However, war and revolution and the economic meltdown in the first decades of the twenty-first century revitalised the political play. The revival in Dublin, Broadway and the West End of plays from the period just before and after the First World War, including O'Casey's *The Silver Tassie*, was no accident and reminded us that the 'old wars are our wars, the old issues are our issues',[2] even if decked out in Edwardian skirts and old uniforms. In his life and writing, O'Casey was concerned as much as any writer, and considerably more than most, with the effect of war, particularly the impact of urban warfare, on civilian populations. Like his friend Bernard Shaw, he probed humanity's ambivalence about war even as he satirised this destructive relationship.

David Krause's biography, *Sean O'Casey: The man and his work* (1960), was the first comprehensive assessment of O'Casey's life and work.[3] This beautifully written study is a literary work in its own right. However, Krause misrepresents or softens O'Casey's political and religious beliefs. O'Casey's support for communism and the Soviet Union is reduced to an apolitical humanism. His professed atheism is discarded in favour of a belief in a loving God allied to a hatred of the power of organised religion. In the post-war period, Krause was instrumental in portraying the Dublin plays as anti-war dramas.[4] O'Casey's questioning of the 1916 Rising was not about the morality of war but because he believed it was the wrong war for the working class – one of the many underlying, though complex points he makes in *The Plough and the Stars*. The issue for him was never a choice between moral or military force; it was always a tactical question as to what was most effective at a given time in history.

O'Casey was a politically committed dramatist in whose work deeply held human aspirations for peace, brotherhood and happiness are subverted by war, class and sectarianism. Gabriel Fallon, along with David Krause, and many of his modern critics, present the three Dublin plays as anti-heroic pacifist plays where the humanity of the tenement dwellers stands in contrast to the militarism of the rebels.[5] In a similar vein, Jules Koslow paints O'Casey as a pacifist who questions 'whether even one life is worth sacrificing for the cause, or whether the resultant misery to a mother, for instance, does not make the cause, even the victory of the cause, seem hollow and horrible'.[6] These pacifist readings are contradicted by any extensive interrogation of his work, his political beliefs, or his political activity over the entire period of his adult life. O'Casey joined the Irish Republican Brotherhood sometime around 1905. The IRB believed that armed insurrection was the only way to end the British connection in Ireland. His differences with the IRB related to their attitude to class politics and, in particular, their failure to give wholehearted support to the Dublin workers in 1913. He was a member of the Irish Citizen Army and the acting secretary until his resignation in August 1914. His resignation was over political and tactical questions rather than the use of violence for political ends.

In the introduction to the Hungarian edition (1957) of *Juno and the Paycock*, in his last reflections on the play O'Casey summed up his views about the Civil War and about the issue of violence for political ends:

> A Civil War should be waged only for a deep and great cause, like the overthrow of the tax paid without representation that evoked the American War of Independence, the overthrow of feudalism as in the French Revolution, and the establishment of political and economic rule and ownership by the people as in the October Revolution of the Soviets.[7]

O'Casey's point would not have been lost on an audience who had witnessed the crushing of the Hungarian workers' uprising by Soviet troops just a year earlier. O'Casey had no moral qualms about supporting the Soviet invasion of Hungary in 1956 to put down what he believed to be a counter-revolution. In the 1930s and '40s, his support for the war against fascism in Spain and support for the Soviet Union after the Nazi invasion in 1941 was unqualified. However, a number of his nationalist and post-colonial critics have suggested that there is a problem with O'Casey's expressed position on violence for political aims. They imply that in his drama, O'Casey glosses over or never adequately refers to the 'right of nations to self-determination', or the fight against imperialism, in the way Connolly and Lenin explained it, or whether it was legitimate to use violence in those circumstances.[8]

The horrors of the First World War psychologically and politically scarred the German dramatists Bertolt Brecht and Erwin Piscator, and their experiences shaped their approach to theatre in later life. Their literary and political calendar was reset on the first day of the war. From that date onwards, their literary endeavours became purposeful. They were revolutionaries whose political platform was the theatre. The first chapter of Piscator's book on theatre, which recounts his experience of the war, was headed 'From Art to Politics'. For Piscator, as for Brecht, the war politicised and transformed his drama in both content and form.[9] O'Casey, in contrast, went from politics to drama as a means of political expression. O'Casey came of age in a period of social disorder, civil war and military oppression. What makes O'Casey so interesting is how he reacted to that experience. He was an active participant in the events leading up to the 1916 Rising and the War of Independence. His 1919 pamphlet *The Story of the Irish Citizen Army* and his heartfelt broadsheets on the death of his friend Thomas Ashe were not only concerned with the politics and direction of the Irish revolution but were also critical of the conduct of the Allied forces in the war in Europe. Out of this experience came the Dublin trilogy, in which he wrote of war and its horrors, but also of poverty and inequality that deforms human life and can be as destructive as war itself. O'Casey was primarily opposed to the violence of poverty, disease and social repression, and if armed struggle was needed to achieve his objectives, then so be it. Nevertheless, O'Casey also recognised that there is an ugly side to revolution that idealists rarely acknowledge.

Much abuse has been heaped on the tenement dwellers of Dublin who took the opportunity during the 1916 Rising to take their revenge on the rich. In the heat of the revolution, the poor and the dispossessed enjoyed a festival of revolt for a few days as they looted and appropriated what they had only seen through shop windows. O'Casey was one of the few writers and commentators who understood and approved of their actions. O'Casey rendered with brutal precision the savagery of war, particularly as it affected the civilian population, and in the process made an original contribution to the presentation of war in art and literature. Bernice Schrank and Ronald Ayling are two of the few academics who have a broad understanding of O'Casey's outlook on war.[10] Schrank considers that O'Casey's attitude towards violence and war was always pragmatic: 'When O'Casey judges that a particular act of violence or war undermines the class interests of his characters, he opposes it; when he regards it as advancing their interests he supports it'.[11] Unlike Yeats, who wondered, 'Did that play of mine send out / Certain men the English shot?'[12] O'Casey never had any such doubts, but he forces us to look at the question of war from the point of view of those who do the dying and the suffering and who get scant reward for their efforts. He followed in the footsteps of V.I. Lenin, who wrote about the 1905 Russian Revolution: 'while the proletariat is doing the fighting the bourgeoisie is stealing towards power'.[13]

Oak Leaves and Lavender, which O'Casey wrote in 1944, gave critical support to the British war effort during the Second World War, presenting a democratic celebration of the ordinary people's support for and their suffering during the war, as well as exploring the international nature of the Allied war effort. Ronald Ayling points out that O'Casey's support for the war was not a purely personal ideological stance, but one fully justified by the nature of the conflict.[14] However, there is a contradiction at the heart of this play that Ayling glosses over. Like many Communist Party members and fellow-travellers, O'Casey did not support the war in 1939. He felt immense sympathy for the people of Britain during the air-raids in the first years of the war, but this only hardened into a pro-war position with the Nazi invasion of the Soviet Union in 1941. O'Casey's support for the Second World War was not pro-British, but pro-Soviet.

Several critics have presented *Oak Leaves and Lavender* as a corrective to Noël Coward's *In Which We Serve*. O'Casey's play is a more down-to-earth portrayal of the British people's support for the war and the cost in suffering and loss than the frivolous upper-class representations of Coward and his friends. In contrast to the Dublin plays, the emphasis here is less on the suffering of the ordinary man and woman than on their contribution to the war effort. In *The Silver Tassie*, O'Casey condemns the futility of the First World War. The pointlessness of the sacrifice of Harry Heegan in *The Silver Tassie* stands in stark contrast to the heroic death of Drishogue in *Oak Leaves and Lavender*.

John Jordan described *The Silver Tassie* as a portrayal of 'war without any anaesthetic ... no heroics, no fine sentiments, no ennoblements through suffering'.[15] The first act is a representation of human frailty, pettiness and meanness in the shadow of a war they do not understand. None of the characters have any concept of the barbarity of the war that Harry and his two friends have signed up for. T.A. Jackson, in *Workers' Weekly*, in a review of the published version of *The Silver Tassie*, was not well disposed towards what he called 'all the old Caseyite pessimism', but he went on to say that, 'By hook or by crook, somehow, some time, and somewhere it must simply be produced. Its theme is the war and the destruction it works on men's souls even more so than upon their bodies'.[16] However, as Christopher Murray has pointed out, 'The text sidesteps the casualties of war and endorses the dance of life. This leaves unresolved the question of responsibility for war and its destructiveness'.[17]

Hugh Hunt directed *The Silver Tassie* at the Abbey in 1972, when the Troubles in the North of Ireland provided a new context for the play. The Garry Hynes production for Druid Theatre Company in 2010, following the Iraq War and the rise of the new imperialism across the Middle East, provided a modern framework for the play; a political context that allowed the First World War to return as a focus for debate about the meaning of imperialism. *The Silver Tassie* is a play of reflection on the First World War. In contrast, *Oak Leaves* was written at the height of the Second World War, when the Allies were on the threshold of victory and when the post-war period seemed to hold out the hope of a socialist Europe. O'Casey was following in the steps of Brecht and his cohorts, who were confident that a new world order would emerge from the destruction of the war. In *Oak Leaves and Lavender*, Monica, who is in love with Drishogue, a young Irishman and former volunteer in the International Brigade, who enlisted in the Royal Air Force, expresses her fears for his safety:

> MONICA: I sometimes wish you hadn't ventured into danger for the love of England!
> DRISHOGUE: Love of England! Good God, Woman, I have no love for England!
> MONICA: But aren't you fighting for her?
> DRISHOGUE: No, I'm not! I'm fighting for the people. I'm fighting against the stormy pillagers who blackened the time-old walls of old Guernica, and tore them down; who loaded their cannon in th' name of Christ to kill the best men Spain could boast of.[18]

Pobjoy, the conscientious objector in *Oak Leaves and Lavender*, is painted in a disdainful and mocking manner, and his hatred of violence and anti-war sentiments are portrayed as the stance of a coward. When Pobjoy exclaims, 'I don't believe in violence', Feelim remonstrates in a manner that is reminiscent of Frederick Douglass' famous reply to those who opposed violence in order to end slavery:

> FEELIM: Life is full of violence, and we're in the middle of life ... There's violence in fire, wind, and water; in th' blast that brings a well to being; in the plough that cleaves th' ground; there is violence even in th' push that sends the leaves fluttering to the ground in the autumn.[19]

O'Casey stated his position very clearly in this play. The war was in defence of the Soviet Union and violence is justified to defend it: 'Woe unto any nation making war on the Soviet Union! She will slash open the snout, and tear out the guts of any power crossing her borders!'[20] *Oak Leaves* was not just a depiction of the misery and suffering caused by war but an examination of war as a precursor to radical social change. However, I do not believe that at any stage in the post-war period O'Casey revisited his view of the war in the aftermath of the Nazi invasion of the USSR as anti-fascist or pro-Soviet in order to take account of the suffering inflicted by the Allies on the civilian populations of Dresden or Hiroshima.

A FIGHTER ALL HIS LIFE

O'Casey was not a pacifist, nor was he against war. In 1942, in a letter to a conscientious objector in America, he stated his position: 'With conscientious objection I have naught to do, for I have been a fighter all my life, finding some wars to be just ones, and especially this present fight to the death to destroy the spiritual and temporal horror of Fascism'.[21]

The imperialist nature of the First World War is now generally accepted, and the analysis put forward by the minority in the socialist movement has been vindicated both in theory and in practice. In 1917, the Bolsheviks took power in Russia, advancing the slogan of 'Peace, Bread, and Land'. But the class nature of the Second World War is more difficult to categorise because of the fascist and barbaric elements of Hitler's war machine. Liberal and left-wing opinion has often portrayed it as a war between fascism and democracy, or as Eric Hobsbawm described it, between 'progress and reaction'.[22] What complicated the matter for socialists such as O'Casey were the political twists and turns by the Communist Party in the years leading up to the war. Having denounced the West for its failure to conclude an alliance with the Soviet Union against the fascist aggression of Germany, communist parties around the world were astonished when a non-aggression pact between Stalin and Hitler was announced on 23 August 1939. The treaty opened the way for Germany to invade Poland on 1 September without fear of Russian interference. Moscow had reversed the line that all European communist parties had advocated since 1935. According to Moscow, this was no longer a war of fascist aggression. The allies in the Western Alliance were now engaged in an imperialist dispute and, if anything, were more interested in defeating communism than in fighting Hitler.[23] At the outbreak of the war in 1939, O'Casey, along with writers such as Walter Greenwood, Rosamond

Lehmann and Sylvia Townsend Warner, was a signatory to the Communist Party-inspired People's Convention, which opposed the war.[24]

This was not the war that O'Casey or the comrades in the CPGB had expected or for which the party had prepared them. For a young recruit to the party such as Eric Hobsbawm:

> The line that the war had ceased to be anti-fascist in any sense, and that Britain and France were as bad as Nazi Germany, made neither emotional nor intellectual sense. We accepted the new line, of course. Was it not the essence of 'democratic centralism' to stop arguing once a decision had been reached, whether or not you were personally in agreement?[25]

The CP's new position caused deep splits among the leadership in the British party, but most party members seemed to accept the decision handed down by Moscow, although Hobsbawm reported that a number of comrades drifted away from the CP over the following two years. O'Casey was not a party member; however, he accepted the new position as a necessary expedient, given that the west European countries had refused to support the USSR when it was threatened by Hitler. O'Casey took time out to reply to Peter Newmark, a young CP member from Cambridge, who had expressed his reservations about the pact between Hitler and Stalin: 'I think you're wrong about Russia. What was done was, in my opinion, the best that could be done under the circumstances'.[26] After the outbreak of the war, he wrote an article, 'What Are Our War Aims?', for the *Picture Post* on 11 November 1939, the anniversary of the armistice that ended the First World War. In a provocative polemic, given Britain's perilous position, O'Casey spelt out the CP's position on the war:

> Peace at once, and then war. War to throw down the barriers to keep us from the practical things being done in the USSR and to force us into the madness of the impracticable things they want us to do here; peace communism, instead of war communism; war on the sham hypocrisies, and stupidities in high places: war to drive the rottenness out of our children's blood and bones; war for citizenship for our young men who are good enough to die, but not good enough to vote ... peace abroad, and war at home against these things, here and now.[27]

The German invasion of the Soviet Union in June 1941 led to another U-turn by the Communist Party. They redefined the conflict as a war against fascism. Party members and supporters in Britain, including O'Casey, were initially disorientated by this turn of events. O'Casey, writing to a member of the CPGB, said that 'Hitler's attack on the USSR has somewhat bewildered me too. I thought Hitler would go Left. Well, there they are now, locked in a fight that, however it goes, will destroy a lot of fine work done by the Soviets'.[28] Contemporary reports suggest that party members and supporters were pleased that they did not have to swim against the tide of mainstream British public opinion. The members, who previously had denounced Britain's participation in an 'imperialist war', were now devoted to promoting friendship with the USSR in an all-out anti-fascist crusade.

In light of this new-found friendship between the USSR and Britain, O'Casey lobbied British publishers to send copies of any work they published that had an anti-fascist or left-wing theme to the Soviet Union. He wore his hammer and sickle badge around Totnes in Devon and, along with Eileen, was active in the Totnes Council for British/Soviet Unity. Eileen served in a charity shop to raise funds for the Soviet Union. They held all the usual raffles, flag days and sales of work, which raised over £400 for a bed in a Soviet hospital. Eileen did not share O'Casey's commitment to the communist cause, but such was her devotion to Seán that 'if he asked her to walk along with a red flag, she would do it'.[29] O'Casey helped in any way he could, writing articles and letters supporting the war effort in the USSR. He sent a telegram to the office of *International Literature* in Moscow, linking himself 'up in spirit with the Soviet people'. He contributed a series of articles of a literary and propagandist nature to Soviet journals using the pen-name The Green Searchlight: 'We have not yet got the burning will of the united Soviet peoples shown by their gigantic and amazing resolution to utterly destroy that strange savage phenomenon called Nazism which is hiding the blue of the sky from our eyes'.[30]

His letters to and from his left-wing friends, who, like the rest of the country, now considered themselves to be military experts, make interesting reading. In the course of his correspondence with his friend Jack Carney they discussed the progress of the war and, in particular, whether the Soviet Union could hold out: 'Stalingrad, & round about it, is great news. I must admit that I never expected a push here; & being human, & liable to err, expected the call often that the "Red Army had evacuated Stalingrad"'.[31] A few months later, he writes to Carney regarding the progress of his campaign to have books from the West sent to the USSR and on the progress of the war: 'I have written to twenty USA publishers asking them to send books to Moscow. Moscow is bobbing about everywhere'.[32]

IRISH NEUTRALITY

Ireland's neutrality during the war was always a contentious issue, both in Ireland and Britain. There were accusations by the British establishment of betrayal, that Ireland was hiding behind the shield provided by the Allied armies while making no contribution to their collective defence. That was an unfair accusation as Ireland, while formally neutral, assisted the Allies in many ways. Tens of thousands of Irish men and women served in the British armed forces or worked in British factories supplying war materials, and Irish agricultural and industrial exports to Britain continued throughout the war. Ireland did far more than any other neutral European country to assist the Allies' war effort. At an official level, Ireland may have been 'neutral in favour of the Allies', but the problem that faced the Irish government was not whether to be neutral, but how to be neutral.[33] Many well-informed observers considered that a section of Irish society was hoping the German Axis would emerge victorious. This view was not an acknowledgement of support for the fascist ideology of the Nazi Party, but a legacy of the 'unfinished' War of Independence and the partition of Ireland in 1922. The Irish government feared an attack by Germany, but given the political situation, they felt that they were unable to formally support the British war effort until such an attack took place. In addition, the IRA's bombing campaign in England in early 1939 lost Ireland many friends and supporters and created difficulties for Irish workers in Britain, who were now viewed with suspicion by the public.

To his immense credit, O'Casey defended Ireland's right to decide whether to remain neutral or not, with the same conviction that led him to defend the USSR. This was not an easy time to speak out on Ireland's behalf, especially if you were living in Britain. In January 1940, he wrote a piece for *Irish Freedom*, a left-wing paper for Irish socialists and republicans in Britain, headed 'Ireland Should Be Against the War':

> I think it would be wise for Ireland to go out definitely against it [the war]. For the many, it is a stupid war; for the few it is a profitable war ... So, with Mitchel, to hell with all this hypocrisy and sham; and on with the fight for Ireland's freedom, for India's freedom, for freedom of all men till the earth and the fullness thereof is wholly ours.[34]

As the demand by the Allies for the use of the Irish seaports on the Atlantic seaboard increased,[35] O'Casey spoke out in support of the Irish government's refusal to surrender the ports to Britain, and for perhaps the only time in his life, disagreed with his friend Bernard Shaw: 'Under the present circumstances, then, what is the better thing to do … surrender the ports to England, as Shaw proposed, or hold tight to them against all comers?'[36] His position on Irish neutrality did not change in line with the position taken by the CPGB after the invasion of Russia in 1941. In August 1943, he wrote an article for the *Daily Worker* outlining Ireland's contribution to the war effort in an attempt to deflect criticism in Britain. The editor, William Rust, who was a good friend of O'Casey's, refused to publish it. Even though the *Daily Worker* rejected the article, O'Casey continued to agitate in support of Ireland's position. He wrote to the Committee of Foreign Writers in the USSR asking for their support in the event of Britain taking any action against Ireland at the end of the war. He requested the Irish writer Leslie Daiken to supply him with information regarding Irish support for the war:

> By all means let me have any instances of Irish activity in this war. I have a hunch they may be needed when it ends. Fools – as far as Ireland is concerned – like Herbert Morrison will probably try to injure her when the time comes to count the cost. I've sent a much longer article on the same lines to the USSR Committee of Foreign Writers as a preliminary for possible help when the cannons go silent.[37]

In 1944, O'Casey contributed a 7,000-word essay to a book edited by his friend Leslie Daiken and published in Britain as *They Go, the Irish: A miscellany of war-time writing*. The purpose of the book was to illustrate Ireland's support for the war effort and deflect the mounting criticism in the British press of Ireland's neutrality and her refusal to make the 'treaty ports' available to the Allies. O'Casey's essay looks back on the history of Ireland's involvement with and support for England, from the time of the Norman invasion right up to the present:

> And so it has gone on for hundreds of years, Ireland never failing, willy nilly, to be at England's side whenever England was beset by a foe; and so it goes on now, for to mention but three out of hundreds of heroes, Finnegan-Fogerty, Esmonde and Finucane have been but for a few moments dead, and dying, they died for England.[38]

He went on to say that not alone had Ireland sent out thousands to fight and die in the war against fascism and to defend England, but Irish labourers have also 'dug the coal from the English pits; they have loaded and unloaded her cargoes from her ships in every dock; they have reaped her corn and lifted her spuds from almost every field and got small gains from it all'. He pulled no punches in this polemic and suggested that the blame for Ireland's neutrality was a legacy of British misrule in Ireland and the ongoing partition of the country: 'for the Ireland of today has been largely moulded by an English lord of misrule for the past thousand years; and this boyo is more responsible for her present-day neutrality than Ireland herself can ever be'.[39] At the end of the war in 1945, he wrote an article for the *Irish Democrat*, a socialist paper produced in Britain for Irish workers and exiles, defending Ireland's reputation: 'In Thousands they Rallied for the Allies but not one Fired a Shot for the Nazis'.[40] Despite his unstinting criticism of the conservative and reactionary nature of Irish society in the post-war period, O'Casey always stood up for Ireland's reputation if he felt the country was being unfairly maligned.

THE COLD WAR

At what exact point in history the wartime cooperation between the Allies morphed into the Cold War is difficult to determine. A convenient date was the announcement in March 1947 of the Truman Doctrine in America, which was introduced to contain Soviet expansion.[41] East and West settled into an era of mutual distrust, in which each side explained its actions as a defensive response to the other's aggression. In February 1948, the Communist Party, supported by the USSR, seized control of the government in Czechoslovakia. The USA responded with the Marshall Plan to help rebuild Europe's shattered economies and, with the military backing of the North Atlantic Treaty Organisation, contain the possibility of communist-backed governments taking power in Western Europe. The situation was further complicated by the USSR's acquisition of the atomic bomb in 1949. Both superpowers were now constrained from using all-out war as an instrument of policy against each other as it was the equivalent of a mutual suicide pact. Both sides used the threat of nuclear war for purposes of negotiation or for domestic purposes, confident that the other side did not want war either. This posturing led to tensions that almost plunged the world into a nuclear holocaust during the Cuban missile crisis of 1962.[42]

The most significant mobilisation of radical forces in the 1950s in Britain was around the issue of nuclear disarmament. The peace movement succeeded in bringing together a diverse coalition in opposition to the testing and possession of nuclear weapons. Throughout the 1950s, O'Casey lent his name to a series of letters by writers and artists demanding an end to war and for the destruction of nuclear weapons by all sides in the Cold War conflict. Writing to the *Daily Worker* in June 1950, he said, 'To do things, we must be sure of life. To be sure of life, we must first ban the atom bomb. Let it rust away, let it rot away where it lies on its stockpile'.[43] He set out his position very clearly: 'There is no such thing as a conservative or Communistic atom bomb. The bomb is no respecter of persons'.[44] He kept to his own position on the issue of war. When, in 1952, the British Peace Council asked him to condemn the use of germ warfare by the United States in the Korean War, he refused, as they had provided no evidence to back up their claim concerning 'the alleged use of [such weapons] in Korea'.[45] O'Casey's opposition to all nuclear weapons diverged from the position of the Communist Party in Britain. The CPGB was slow to support the Campaign for Nuclear Disarmament, preferring instead to promote the idea of the 'People's Bomb' in the USSR, which was categorised as a deterrent and not as a threat to the West. Despite this, the party did gain a measure of credit as the *Daily Worker* was the only national newspaper to report the activities of the peace movement.[46]

In the *Irish Democrat* in 1952, eighteen Irish writers, including O'Casey, Austin Clarke, C. Day-Lewis and Mary Lavin, signed a letter calling for peace: 'As writers we want peace, and through our work will try and get it; we pledge ourselves to encourage an international settlement through peaceful negotiation'.[47] O'Casey and other leading figures published signed letters and peace manifestoes in several newspapers, including the *Manchester Guardian*, *The Irish Times*, *Daily Worker* and *Pravda* (Moscow). He received numerous invitations to support or attend meetings to protest against war and the nuclear threat, including an invitation from the president of the World Peace Council to attend a meeting of the council in Berlin. In 1958, he was delighted to accept a request to sponsor the Northern Ireland Committee of the World Youth Peace Festival that was taking place in Moscow. 'If you imagine me to be a suitable Sponsor, go ahead and make me one. Of course, my hope and pride are in the young who carry the torch of life, in full flame ... If – as Shaw's last words said – "If they are not wasted by another war" ... I enclose a sub of £3-3-0 to help'.[48]

His children, Breon, Niall and Shivaun, were active in the peace movement, which was a source of immense pride to him. In a letter in 1955 he describes working for the peace movement and his membership of the British Peace Committee.[49] He was also a member of the Atomic Scientists' Association in Britain and the USA, and it seems that he was well versed both in the science and politics of nuclear physics: 'I have been an associate member of Atomic Scientists' Association for years & if only more of us were, in the USA & here, we shouldn't be so damned ignorant of what the Russians can do without us'.[50] In 1957, along with three other prominent public figures from non-nuclear countries, he co-authored an appeal to the Disarmament Subcommittee of the United Nations in support of a test ban treaty, which they published in the *Manchester Guardian*:

> May we, speaking for countries unarmed with nuclear weapons, but subject to the same fears, appeal to the five Powers represented on the subcommittee not to allow differences of opinion on other issues to prevent agreement on the suspension of the tests? Russia has proposed a two-to-three-year ban with the requisite controls. The Western Powers have proposed a shorter period. This is a question, surely, for negotiation, not a matter of principle.
> Sean O'Casey (Ireland), H.K. Handoo (India), David Pitt (West Indies), Tefkros Anthias (Cyprus).[51]

O'Casey continued to support initiatives, many of them originating in the Eastern bloc countries, for peace and nuclear disarmament up to the time of his death in 1964.

Despite Seamus Heaney's warning that 'no lyric ever stopped a tank',[52] O'Casey's drama is radical in that it forces us to confront and examine our relationship with war and violence. He denounced the futility of war unless accompanied by radical social change. More than most writers, his work brought theatre and politics into a conscious connection. His drama has a particular resonance in Irish politics because it avoids the idea of Ireland as a special case whose fate is rooted in historical or political inevitability or in violence and irrationality.

CHAPTER 15

Religion, Gender and Identity

Seán O'Casey was one of the great iconoclasts of the twentieth century, an old-fashioned slayer of venerated institutions and cherished beliefs. Many of his friends and critics believed that his attacks on the church coarsened his work. Despite this view, O'Casey was a profoundly spiritual writer, not unlike his contemporary Bertolt Brecht, an atheist who considered himself to be the last great Christian writer.[1] O'Casey, who was born and raised a Protestant in a predominantly Catholic Ireland, had none of the uncertainty or ambiguity that haunted the hyphenated identity of the Protestant ascendancy. The poverty of his Protestant characters Bessie Burgess or Mrs Breydon, who, like his mother, lived and died in a tenement, personified the distance between O'Casey and the prosperous Anglo-Irish ascendancy. He was not only a Protestant but a 'poor Protestant', with the same connotations in Dublin's elite circles that 'poor white' would have in the American South.[2] *The Harvest Festival* (1919) and *Red Roses for Me* (1942) are probably the plays most influenced by O'Casey's East Wall working-class Protestant background, which gives his views on class a distinctive edge that is missing elsewhere in Irish literature. The three Dublin plays, written between 1921 and 1926, are in one sense his most Catholic plays and represent life in the Georgian slum tenements rather than the East Wall area, even allowing for the incursion of some Protestant characters like Bessie Burgess and the Grigsons.[3] O'Casey was one of the few Irish writers who had a profound and personal understanding of working-class life in both the Protestant and Catholic communities.

As he approached his twentieth birthday, a world of opinions and political alternatives was opening up for O'Casey. The centenary celebrations for the 1798 United Irishmen rebellion, the controversy over the Boer War, the first stirrings of the literary revival, and a resurgent Irish nationalism both confused and excited him. Nevertheless, religion still played an important part in his life. The arrival of the Reverend Harry Fletcher as curate in St Barnabas Church in 1897 gave a renewed impetus to O'Casey's waning interest in his religious practice. Harry Fletcher was a young, enthusiastic, open-minded man, a lover of art and literature and especially the novels of Dickens. O'Casey believed that Fletcher was driven out of St Barnabas by the Orange Order clique, who controlled the select vestry and objected to his High Church tendencies. He was mistaken in this, as Fletcher left because he wished to move to London. In the following year, 1899, the Reverend Edward Griffin was appointed rector. Griffin had a profound effect on O'Casey; he was learned and compassionate and became a real friend. While paying tribute to O'Casey in a sermon following his death in 1964, the dean of Christ Church recalled his 'immense and affectionate regard for the Reverend E.M. Griffin' and referred to the fact that O'Casey had to deal with a 'colony of Ulster Railway workers, who were members of the Orange Order'. He went on to speak of him as one who had 'immortalized the hopes and fears, the loves and hates of the plain people of Dublin'.[4]

Under Griffin's tutelage, O'Casey became much more involved in the religious and social activities of the parish. He was an active participant in church services, teaching Sunday school and Bible classes, and was secretary of the Foreign Missions Committee. Despite his growing involvement in the Gaelic League and the Irish Republican Brotherhood, he remained active in the church until 1909, when he took offence at the purchase of the church organ in England. In religious practice, O'Casey was High Church, in politics decidedly nationalist, which put him at odds with the Orangemen who foiled his attempt to be elected to the select vestry. Eventually, O'Casey succeeded in driving out the Orangemen by organising a campaign against them, with the result that they lost their seats at the subsequent vestry election. While he may have been wrong about the Orange Order's conspiracy to get rid of Harry Fletcher, he was right about their campaign to drive out any 'Romanish' influences from St Barnabas.[5] Windows were broken, clergymen intimidated, and services interrupted to such an extent that questions concerning the disturbances were asked in the House of Commons in London in 1904:

> I beg to ask the Chief Secretary to the Lord-Lieutenant of Ireland whether he is aware that the Rev. R.D. Patterson, of St Barnabas Church, Dublin, has on several occasions complained to the police authorities that divine service in his church has been disturbed by the throwing of stones upon the roof, and that the notice board in front of the church has been damaged.[6]

Edward Griffin's daughter described how, when his turn came to read during the service, O'Casey made up the prayers 'using some biblical passages but mostly his own words about the glory of God' and that 'he would have made a great preacher'.[7] His familiarity with the King James Bible and the Book of Common Prayer is given full range in the character of the evangelical Protestant Susie Monican in *The Silver Tassie*. She quotes from the Bible to criticise the sinful actions of Sylvester Heegan and Simon Norton, who reply with suitable quotes to defend their actions. Old Testament idioms and metaphors energise much of his writing, where the voices of Elijah and Job are mixed with the perspectives of socialist ideology, leaving some of his supporters intimidated by the combination of biblical rhetoric and revolutionary zeal. O'Casey infused this legacy with the tolerant Protestant tradition of Milton, Shakespeare and Shaw. At times he can appear to accept a far-off God while hating the church's leaders as men who despise reason, whether Catholic or Protestant.

AN GALL FADA

O'Casey was twenty-seven years old when his first article, 'Sound the Loud Trumpet', appeared in 1907. This was an ironic satire on British rule in Ireland:

> While causing all our misery, it only sought our happiness; while destroying our industries, it only wished to strengthen our humility; while banning our education and history, it only endeavoured to educate us. Thank heaven we had sufficient gratitude to send over a hundred of our leaders to venerate the god of British Rule in the Temple of Westminster.[8]

He used the pseudonym An Gall Fada, which translates as 'The Tall Protestant' or perhaps 'The Tall Foreigner'. He sent a copy to his local Protestant minister, expecting words of encouragement, but was shocked by the reply: 'The man who wrote that article, John, is a traitor, and ought to be in jail'.[9] Therefore, we can assume that he had begun to form his 'traitorous' views by his mid-twenties and was in the process of rejecting the East Wall legacy of British civilisation for the native legacy of Gaelic Ireland. He joined the Gaelic League and, as an expression of his support, changed his name to Sean O Cathasaigh. Intellectually, he had broken from his Protestant East Wall background long before he moved out in 1920. *The Harvest Festival* (1919) is a sharp attack on the narrow-minded religious and political prejudices of the local Protestant clergy and parishioners, who stand rebuked over their failure to support the militant struggle of working people to improve their living conditions.

His attacks on the Catholic Church in *The Bishop's Bonfire* and *The Drums of Father Ned* were not aimed at the Catholic majority but at a hierarchy that tolerated poverty and injustice. He had every reason to attack the Catholic Church, which denounced and censored his books and plays. In the aftermath of the *Plough* riots in 1926, the *Catholic Bulletin* devoted eight pages to excoriating O'Casey, the 'Subsidised New Ascendancy and their hangers on' in the Abbey Theatre.[10] In 1935, the Christian Young Men's Society denounced *The Silver Tassie* as infringing the 'canons of Christian reverence'.[11] In the same year, the Reverend Terence Connolly, a faculty member and librarian of Boston College, bitterly opposed his play *Within the Gates* and led the way in having it banned in Boston.

In his later work, O'Casey always left open the possibility that religion could play a progressive role in the battle between 'life forces' and 'death forces'. The Marxist critic Jack Mitchell suggests that in *The Star Turns Red*, O'Casey 'shows the workers in the process of realizing themselves as the true heirs of Christ, as the second, better coming of the Prince of Peace'.[12] O'Casey was often accused of bigotry because of the way he attacked the Catholic Church. Undoubtedly, his Protestant background hampered his critique of the role of the Catholic Church in Ireland. Maud Gonne, who converted to Catholicism shortly before her marriage to Major John MacBride in 1903, and who found herself in a similar position, said that she 'had often longed to denounce the priests and could not because I was a Protestant, but now I can'.[13] Despite his atheism and hatred of church authority of whatever faith, O'Casey had several lasting friendships with a series of clerics, priests and nuns. In 1917 he sent personal hand-painted Christmas cards to Father Brady of the St Laurence O'Toole parish, Reverend E.M. Griffin of St Barnabas Church and Sister Gonzaga in St Vincent's Hospital. In 1926, he donated one of his royalty cheques to Sister Carew of the Sisters of Charity.[14]

His friendships, as well as his disagreements, with priests and clerics all over the English-speaking world are a testament to his respect for those who lived the true message of the Bible.[15] In later life, O'Casey was heartened by the reforming pontificate of Pope John XXIII, whom he believed to be 'a sensible man'.[16] The American Jesuit Father Michael Gallagher was just one of the many priests who appreciated and corresponded with O'Casey: 'I don't think you could make out a grocery list that wouldn't be worth reading aloud'.[17] It is a simple matter for O'Casey's detractors to allege that he was prejudiced against the Catholic Church and contrast this with his apparent reluctance to criticise the Protestant faith. He had a visceral hatred for the Catholic archbishop of Dublin, Dr McQuaid, whom he described as the 'arch-druid o' Drumcondra'. The Reverend Clinton, the Protestant rector of St Burnupus in *Red Roses for Me*, was undoubtedly one of O'Casey's favourite characters. O'Casey portrays him as a champion of the poor who warns his friend, Ayamonn Breydon, that the authorities intend to use violence against the striking workers. On the other hand, his portrayal in the play of the bigoted vestryman Dowzard, who was based on a real-life character and the subject of an article by O'Casey in the *Irish Worker*,[18] is proof that in O'Casey's work 'Catholics held no monopoly on narrow-mindedness and hypocrisy'.[19]

Cyril Cusack was not the only person to write about O'Casey as a religious dramatist, suggesting that in O'Casey's world, particularly in the later plays, there is both loss and redemption. Desmond MacCarthy also believed that O'Casey's 'imagination and moral judgements, too, are saturated with Catholicism'.[20] Despite this, Ireland found it difficult to accept or forgive O'Casey. His protest against poverty and inequality was perceived as an attack on religion that bordered on blasphemy. Julia in *The Star Turns Red* speaks out against the abusive priests and ministers:

> JULIA: Against you, dear one, we have no grudge; but those of your ministers who sit like gobbling cormorants in the market-place shall fall and shall be dust and shall be priests no longer.

O'Casey believed that if the church were to have a future, it needed to choose between the 'Purple Priest of the politicians and the Fascists' and the 'Brown Priest of the poor':

> JULIA: The Purple Priest of the politicians is patrolling the streets, cursing with book and bell and candle any who have cried or murmured a welcome to Communism.
>
> JACK: Ah, if the Brown Priest would only step to the fore and cry out with a loud voice, a host would follow him![21]

O'Casey had no time for the Catholic Church's pronouncements on social issues. He believed the church failed to stand up for the poor or recognise the gross inequalities that were a product of the capitalist system. Both in the plays and in the autobiographies, he rails against the papal encyclical *Rerum Novarum* because he believed it hoodwinked the workers into believing that workers and bosses could work together for the betterment of society.[22] He was never afraid to pit Karl Marx against the latest papal pronouncement: 'The Roman Church builds her social contract on the Rearum Noharmum Harum Scarum Rerum Novarum, but we build ours on the Communist Manifesto: this time it is our philosophy that is built on a rock, theirs on a hill of sand'.[23] Many socialists, including O'Casey, believed the papal encyclicals were simply an attempt to defuse any revolutionary determination to establish socialism. O'Casey contributed an article, 'Study Course for a Vatican Recruit', for a pamphlet published by the Communist Party in Britain, *The Pope, the People, and Politics* (1948). In it, he suggested a course of study for the ex-communist Douglas Hyde, who had converted to Catholicism, about the chaos and war associated with the Christian religion and 'the murder, rape, beatings, and robbery that were everyday events' during the Christian era.[24]

After independence, O'Casey was fearful for an Ireland that was drifting towards theocracy. The constitution of 1937 formalised the alliance between church and state by inserting a clause that recognised the 'special position of the Catholic Church' in Irish society.[25] Over the following decade, the church's influence grew enormously, particularly in health and education. O'Casey challenged the traditional components of post-independence Ireland shared by church and state alike. He used the humanity of religion to appeal for a more humane society. He understood and articulated in an artistic way what Karl Marx meant when he wrote, 'Religious suffering is, at one and the same time, the expression of real suffering and a protest against real suffering. Religion is the sigh of the oppressed creature, the heart of a heartless world, and the soul of soulless conditions'.[26] O'Casey never belittles the religious beliefs of his characters but aims his attack at religious institutions that leave the mass of people in poverty and ignorance. In *Juno and the Paycock*, he lashes out at the clergy:

> CAPTAIN BOYLE: The clergy always had too much power over the people in this unfortunate country ... Didn't they prevent the people in '47 from seizin' the corn, an' they starvin'; didn't they down Parnell; didn't they say that hell wasn't hot enough nor eternity long enough to punish the Fenians?[27]

Given the religious climate of the time, perhaps he felt constrained in making a full-frontal attack on the clergy and cloaked his criticism in the comic figure of Captain Boyle to make it more acceptable. After he left Ireland, he felt no such constraints and the religious hierarchy of all persuasions felt the lash of his pen.

Catholic iconography is evident in much of his work. O'Casey was influenced by the biblical imagery that formed such a central part of the English socialist William Morris' style of writing.[28] However, James Larkin, who spoke with all the passion and power of a Redemptorist preacher, combining religious imagery with fiery socialist rhetoric, was the inspiration for much of the religious symbolism in O'Casey's work. He described how the flag of the ICA fired in his mind the idea for the title of *The Plough and the Stars*: 'I had been one, with Jim Larkin, to welcome the flag ... to unfold it, to fix it to the staff; to expose it, like a sacrament to the Citizen Army members'.[29] Here is Larkin writing about the 'judicial murder' of the trade union leader Joe Hillström (Joe Hill) in America in 1916: 'Joseph Hillstrom, one of the Ishmaelites of the industrial world ... they crucified him on their cross of gold, spilled his blood on the altar of their God – Profit'.[30]

Despite his devotion to Larkin, O'Casey was not uncritical of Larkin's relationship with the church. He recounted a visit by Jim Larkin to his home in Devon in 1942, where they talked about a Catholic mass for trade union leaders. Larkin had insisted his son, young Jim, attend as a representative of the Workers' Union, even though young Jim was not religious. It confirmed for O'Casey just how dominant the church was in Irish society:

> When Big Jim had become timid of the Church, there would be little hope for Irish Labour for some time to come. Some time ago, George Gilmore sent me a picture of a Demonstration of Protest about Cardinal Mindszenty's jailing, showing the Workers' Union marching with banners and band in the heart of the demonstration. This Demonstration is a theme in *Behind the Green Curtains*, but there I deal, not with the Union, but with the intelligentsia.[31]

Several of his American allies sought to deny the socialist aspect of O'Casey's politics, stressing the humanitarian and the religious undertones in much of his work instead and substituting the 'Star of Bethlehem' for the 'Red Star of Socialism'.[32] O'Casey's attitude to religion was complex and, at times, contradictory. Because he lived and worked among the workers in Dublin, he understood the difference between religious beliefs that were a comfort in a heartless world and the power and destructive authority of the church hierarchy that he despised.

CENSORSHIP AND REJECTION

Seán O'Casey was one of the most sensual writers of his era. In all of his work, he presents sexual love as positive, joyful and life-affirming. But the deadening forces were everywhere – a touch of sex and 'the Jesuitical nose begins to sniff'.[33] In 1935, the Catholic Church in Boston, with the support of the Unitarian and Methodist Churches, instigated the campaign to ban *Within the Gates*. They said the play 'scoffed at religion' and portrayed a 'sympathetic regard for immorality'. The mayor of Boston described it as 'nothing but a dirty book, and in my opinion full of commonplace smut'.[34] The authorities needed to obtain a copy of any book they proposed to ban to prove it was 'depraved'. In an imaginative attempt to prevent this, several Harvard students tried to buy up every copy of the play from the local bookstores, but the police commissioner had already obtained a copy, and the ban went ahead. The students circulated a petition against the ban around the Boston colleges and collected over 400 signatures. Harvard University faculty members expressed their disapproval of the ban, and several declared that 'Boston had been deprived of a great artistic experience'.[35] Professor Dana, formally of the drama department, announced that as a protest, he would hold a public reading of the play in the college hall, but the police department refused a permit, and the college authorities cancelled the reading. However, all was not lost. Later that evening, a group of over fifty people gathered at the home of the secretary of the Community Church, where Professor Dana read extracts from the play. Given the role played by the various Boston churches in the crusade to ban the play, it is worth noting that the Community Church and the Church of the Redemption lent their names and resources to the campaign against the ban. Emerson Schwenk, a preacher, read extracts from the play at the Sunday night services in the Church of the Redemption despite the presence of a police detective and stenographer. In the wake of the publicity, the proposed tour of North America was cancelled. The production returned to New York, where it played for a further six weeks. The Boston students organised a special 'freedom train' to attend the rescheduled performance in New York. According to Robert Lowery, the actress Lillian Gish, who played the Young Whore in the play, met the train at Grand Central Station and served refreshments to the Boston theatre-goers.[36]

The bans and proscriptions on his work diverted O'Casey's gaze from the world of literature back to the more mundane world of the parish. He became preoccupied with censorship and church control in Ireland. This was a necessary fight even if, artistically and financially, there was a price to pay. For the last twenty-five years of his life, O'Casey fought a long-range battle with Irish society. In a letter to *The Irish Times* in December 1949,[37] he refers to the thirty pages of typescript where he had recorded instances of clerical interference in civil matters. In the Berg Collection in the New York Public Library, there are a series of articles, mostly unpublished, that deal with the hypocrisy of the Irish state in sexual, political and religious matters. He lashes out against corporal punishment, quoting an article in *The Statesman* of 20 September 1958 reporting the most brutal cases of punishment against boys and girls by the Sisters of Mercy and the Christian Brothers.

O'Casey was never afraid of the moral naysayers or the unofficial censors. When W.B. Yeats rushed to his defence during the riots over *The Plough and the Stars* and proclaimed that 'the fame of O'Casey is born here tonight',[38] he appeared safe from the unofficial censors and free to write as he pleased. Despite Yeats' declaration, the mood in Ireland was changing. The economic crash of 1929 and the political and moral lurch to the right left O'Casey isolated and with few friends to sustain him. In time, even his close friend for over thirty years from their Abbey Theatre days, Gabriel Fallon, turned against him. In truth, little had changed since Yeats' defence of John Millington Synge over twenty years earlier: 'The quarrel of our Theatre today is the quarrel of the Theatre in many lands; for the old Puritanism, the old bourgeois dislike of power and reality have not changed'.[39] The new Puritans were to have their day. Alfred Hitchcock's film *Juno and the Paycock* was banned in Boston in 1931 because it glorified drunkenness. The Abbey Theatre tour of the United States in late 1934 provoked a rebuke from the Fianna Fáil government. Éamon de Valera wrote to Lennox Robinson objecting to the choice of O'Casey's Dublin plays because they would 'certainly arouse shame and resentment among Irish exiles'.[40] The letter also requested that all theatre programmes published in America clearly state that the Irish government was not sponsoring the tour. In England, the printers of the magazine *Time and Tide* refused to print the issue that contained O'Casey's 'I Wanna Woman', a story of sexual desire and frustration, on the grounds that it was immoral. Political objections to the content of his plays in Germany, Austria, Switzerland and France added to his problems.

In December 1934, the Censorship Board in Ireland ruled that O'Casey's book of essays, *Windfalls*, was 'in its general tendency indecent' and recommended a ban on all editions. The ban was O'Casey's first experience of official censorship, as opposed to the ranting of political and religious extremists. The prohibition on *Windfalls* and *Within the Gates* and the negative response to the production of *The Silver Tassie* in 1935 at the Abbey Theatre intensified his difficulties. In 1939, the Irish censor banned the first volume of his autobiography, *I Knock at the Door*, and Macmillan, his publisher in New York, refused to publish an American edition of *The Star Turns Red*. The fight against the moral censors had an effect on O'Casey, as it did on many writers. Jack Mitchell has suggested that O'Casey's experience of censorship and rejection in the 1930s, while threatening his work, did not lead to a lessening of his vision in the long term. In his later work, Mitchell believes that O'Casey left behind the uncertainty of the thirties and that his output in the post-war era presents an optimistic vision of the future, with images of heroes and leaders of a new type drawn from the rank-and-file of working people. Nevertheless, he concedes that there was a return to the parish.[41]

WOMEN

In any discussion on the position of women in Irish society, the role of religion and sexual morality is usually paramount, and O'Casey's letters to women all over the world reflect this fact. When Henrik Ibsen wrote *A Doll's House* in 1879, it was as a direct result of his concern for the position of women in society. When Ibsen's heroine, Nora, slams the door behind her as she walks out to an uncertain future, we can hear the call to freedom. Unfortunately, O'Casey's work is seldom viewed in the same way.

Julia in *The Star Turns Red*, Nora in *The Plough and the Stars* and Mary Boyle in *Juno and the Paycock* are all portrayed as women who like their hats, bows and revealing dresses. They are sensual women who enjoy life, music and dancing. Nevertheless, they are trapped by the material conditions of their life, and unlike Ibsen's middle-class women, they are rarely in a position to 'slam the door behind them'. Mary Boyle is presented in the play as having high ideals. She reads books to better herself, notably Ibsen's *A Doll's House*, 'the theme of which reflects her life of enclosure and subjection'.[42] In *The Plough and the Stars*, O'Casey portrays Jack Clitheroe in a traditional role in his marriage to Nora. Despite the contention of Hanna Sheehy Skeffington and her feminist friends that Nora Clitheroe 'did not represent the feeling of Ireland's women',[43] O'Casey portrays Nora as a woman who understands the contradictions that women from her class had to face: 'your little, little red-lipped Nora's a sweet little girl when th' fit seizes you; but your little, little red-lipped Nora has to clean your boots every mornin', all the same'.[44] But Nora, trapped by poverty and the oppression of women in society, is not in a position to do anything about it.

Despite these subtle observations in the way O'Casey portrays women in the Dublin plays, David Krause and Ronald Ayling are just two of the many critics who have described Juno as a classic symbol of womanhood; a feminine paragon who accepts her role as mother and nurturer, in contrast to the violent nature of men.[45] However, a close reading of the text reveals Juno as a woman almost broken by the material conditions she has to endure, but with the strength and independence of character to walk out on her abusive husband, together with her pregnant daughter, to start a new and uncertain life together. Given their economic circumstances, this was a 'call to freedom' as vocal as anything Ibsen ever wrote. Yet, this aspect of O'Casey's work is rarely interrogated or even acknowledged by critics. Given the creeping moral rectitude in Ireland in the early 1920s, this was a brave statement to make. The fact that this was shown at the Abbey Theatre, with all its connotations as 'the national theatre', was an important challenge to the conventional perception of a woman's place in Irish society.

O'Casey's work is constantly critiqued in terms of the differences between men and women in their attitude to violence while emphasising the role of women as nurturers and homemakers. Given the development of feminist theory, what is surprising is how few critics have moved beyond this analysis, or indeed moved beyond the three 'Dublin plays' and explored the role of women in his later plays, where a far more developed dynamic exists. Here, women are stronger, bolder, more sensual, and have a determined independence. In *The Bishop's Bonfire*, Keelin is not afraid to reject the older farmer her father and the local priest have chosen for her.[46] As long ago as 1999, Elizabeth Hazlehurst took issue with feminist critics who ignored the work of O'Casey.[47] She pointed out that he supported the autonomy of women and that he approved of women in public life, as he made clear in a letter in 1960:

> Women are holding a big meeting & march in London on Saturday the 6th, against all thermo-nuclear armament; it is organised by the National Assembly of Women, of which I am an ardent supporter. I look forward to the day when Women shall be members of all Summit Conferences – They should have been there long ago.[48]

Hazlehurst quotes O'Casey regarding his impatience with the slow progress of women towards equality: 'We are all fine fellows, while still keeping women in their place, leaving windows open for them but keeping women in their place'.[49] As early as 1914, he championed equality in the pages of the *Irish Worker*: 'The Irish Citizen Army recognises that the woman is as much a citizen as a man'.[50]

Since then, little has changed; in a review of the New York production of *Juno and the Paycock* in 2013, all the old and tired clichés were repeated: 'His great dramas are, in the words of Frank O'Connor, "hymns of praise to women". As such, *Juno and the Paycock* is also a scathing rebuke to the fecklessness of men'.[51] In 2016, the *Irish Examiner*'s review of *The Plough and the Stars* picked up on Frank O'Connor's theme: 'The struggle for the birth of a child is the work of love while the armed struggle for the birth of a nation state is the work of hate'.[52] These interpretations overlook the possibility of interrogating the Dublin plays in a way that explores the intersection of class and gender. A welcome development is an analysis by the feminist critic Susan Cannon Harris who, in her book on sexual politics and the international left, devotes a substantial section to a critical but interesting analysis of O'Casey's work in a way that reimagines 'a left politics in which anti-capitalist politics and identity politics are no longer perceived to be in competition with each other'.[53] In her essay 'Writing Working-Class Irish Women', Heather Laird draws attention to the way O'Casey in *Juno and the Paycock* uses the trope of 'the struggling working-class mother … to underpin a critique of "abstract" politics' that have nothing to say about their situation in life.[54] This critique can also be extended to the character of Mrs Foran in *The Silver Tassie*, who is portrayed as a 'slave' to her husband, whose subjugation increases as the play develops. Also of interest is an essay on O'Casey by Michael Pierse, which highlights the way the 'suppression of women's sexuality is of acute concern in his work' and the fact that 'it is not their inherent superiority to men that O'Casey seeks to highlight. Rather, he foregrounds their social subjugation in a rotten society'.[55]

However, there are problems with how O'Casey portrays women in the three Dublin plays. Where are the heroic working-class women from 1913, such as Rosie Hackett,[56] or the women who fought in the 1916 Rising and played a prominent role during the War of Independence? Would the plays have benefited from a more nuanced development of the women characters along these lines, or at least a suggestion somewhere in the background that such women existed? Politically, that is undoubtedly the case. Whether the enduring quality of the plays would have benefited from this is open to question. Another way of looking at O'Casey's portrayal of women in the Dublin plays is to suggest that O'Casey was trying to shift the mood of the audience, to mould it in a different direction. He implied that, in their own way and their own circumstances, women from the tenements were just as heroic as Constance Markievicz, Maud Gonne, Kathleen Lynn, or the host of middle-class women who populate the pages of Irish history.

O'Casey was a man of his time, and occasionally he was susceptible to repeating the platitudes about women that some of his critics voice about his work. In an interview in 1958, when asked about the courage of women in the Dublin plays, he said that it came from 'fortitude – and patience – and understanding ... Men are more idealistic, stupidly idealistic. They are not as realistic as women.'[57] Despite this, the later plays written after he left Ireland are an attack on what he called the 'ferocious chastity' of the Irish, where sensuous young women throw off the strictures of family and church and escape into exile and sexual freedom.[58]

WOMEN IN THE NEW STATE

Anniversaries sometimes allow us to re-examine the past in a new light. During the 1916 centenary, a number of publications highlighted women's contribution to Irish history. Sinéad McCoole, Margaret Ward and Roy Foster, among others, capture the enthusiasm, radicalism and determination of that revolutionary generation of women who were resolute about reconstructing the world around them. They were a unique generation of women – educated, politically active, and in many cases sexually liberated while uncompromising in their support for the republic. Their letters and diaries make clear they were prepared to challenge, publicly and in their personal lives, the sexual mores of the time. They were also part of a conscious challenge to the patriarchal domination of the Catholic Church.[59]

Their memoirs capture the disappointment felt by these women when the Free State proved to be such a conservative and reactionary place that had little in common with the radicalism and idealism of 1916. As in everything else, the new government used the idealism of 1916 as a cover for its conservatism regarding the position of women in the new state. Dorothy Macardle's book *The Irish Republic* (1937)[60] was described as 'A hymn to de Valera'. However, she was so disillusioned by the attack on women's rights and the socially conservative nature of de Valera's 1937 constitution that she described the time she took to write it as 'seven wasted years'.[61] In an article on Dorothy Macardle in 1958, the *Irish Press* remarked on the contribution of women to Irish politics: 'The Irish independence movement owes much to the brave women who took a full share in it'.[62] However, as Leeann Lane, in her book on Dorothy Macardle, suggests, women, when applying for their military service pension, stated that they 'felt let down economically by a state they helped to create'.[63] Alice Milligan, a playwright and lecturer for the Gaelic League, was just one of the many women who were totally 'disillusioned by the clericalism and narrow-mindedness of the post-revolutionary dispensation'.[64] Their dreams of a new and equal Ireland were shattered. They had to endure censorship, social repression, intellectual degradation, prison and financial loss. They had, however, one advantage over O'Casey's tenement dwellers: they continued to live in the genteel suburbs of Rathmines or Rathgar.[65] Many of these women should have been O'Casey's natural allies. In the aftermath of the Civil War and de Valera's break with Sinn Féin in 1926, a number became active in left-wing circles. Whether it was O'Casey's political disagreement with Constance Markievicz in 1914, the row over *The Plough and the Stars* in 1926 with Hanna Sheehy Skeffington and the widows of 1916, or his innate dislike of their middle- and upper-class backgrounds that alienated him from this milieu is difficult to ascertain. Whatever the reason, O'Casey, was derisive of their contribution to Irish political life, with the exception of Hanna Sheehy Skeffington.

Friedrich Engels wrote that in the ancient world, the overthrow of mother-right and the rise of class society 'was the world historic defeat of the female sex. The man took command in the home also; the woman was degraded and reduced to servitude.'[66] He could have been writing about Ireland in the 1920s. The veteran Sinn Féiner P.S. O'Hegarty led the assault on that generation of women, devoting a chapter in his book *The Victory of Sinn Féin* (1924) to the role of women in the Civil War.[67] The chapter was headed 'The Furies', where O'Hegarty set about these women, portraying them as warmongering harpies:

> The gunwoman lived on war, on excitement, on stunts, and nothing save war, and gradually shut out everything but those. She saw nobody, talked to nobody, save other gunwomen, lived for nothing save war ... They became practically unsexed, their mother's milk blackened to make gunpowder.[68]

O'Hegarty and his friends spelt out the future for women in the Free State: they would be reduced to servitude. This outcome stands in sharp contrast to the hopes of women like Máire Comerford, who wrote, 'In our lovely new world of revolt, were many who had no more personal grievance against life than I had. We were from various strata of society, but we were rank and file republicans in love with the new freedom we hoped to make secure'.[69] The Dublin plays, and in particular *Juno and the Paycock*, are about the shattering of those dreams and hopes, highlighting the lives of the poor who live and die according to their economic circumstances rather than for patriotism or because they were 'in love with the new freedom'. Another way of looking at *Juno and the Paycock* is that O'Casey was using the ideology of motherhood to illustrate the failure of the revolution to do anything for women.

O'Casey was secretary of the Women and Children's Relief Fund during the lockout in 1913. He shared the poverty and hunger these women had to endure. They were not in a position to leave letters, journals or diaries that future historians could utilise to uncover their past. James Connolly, writing about women's position in society, said, 'The worker is the slave of capitalist society, the female worker is the slave of that slave ... in spite of this they have ever proven valuable assets in every progressive movement in Ireland'.[70] They are the women that O'Casey gave a voice to, those who lived on the margins of society in the slums of Dublin. They were more than just passive victims of history who held the family together in times of great stress and violence. Such a woman is Minnie Powell in *The Shadow of a Gunman*, a courageous young woman who, in different circumstances, might have played a part in the revolutionary movement. Or Mary Boyle in *Juno*, a trade unionist out on strike to defend a fellow worker, or Julia in *The Star Turns Red*, who, despite all her uncertainties, joins with her fellow workers in a revolutionary struggle for a better society. O'Casey gave dignity to the likes of Rosie Redmond in *The Plough and the Stars*, who is reduced to selling her body for a living. They are the women who were the heart and soul of the great struggles during the 1913 lockout. O'Casey understood that one day their awakening would come, and they too would rise up to take their rightful place in the world.

O'CASEY SPEAKS OUT

Decades before the Murphy and the Ryan reports into the abuse of women and children in church-run institutions in Ireland were published in 2009, O'Casey was one of the few public figures prepared to speak out on these issues.[71] His daughter Shivaun revealed how, in his letters, he provided solace and advice to a host of Irish women. For three years, O'Casey corresponded with an unmarried Irish woman who was distraught when her child was taken from her by the church: 'This woman, whose child was taken away, became a journalist when she was older and she was aware of him as a writer and as a progressive thinker … He told her about other women he knew of who had been forced to give up their children'.[72] He also carried on an extensive correspondence with a young Catholic girl who was the daughter of an Irish major in the British army. The character of Foorawn in *The Bishop's Bonfire* was based on her. She had taken a vow of chastity on the advice of her local priest in order to remain pure of heart and thought and had sought O'Casey's advice on the matter. Their letters reflect an extended friendship over a ten-year period, where he constantly advised her to put her foolish thoughts aside and live her life to the full: 'These things in Pagan times, instead of being impure, obscene – as we blather about them now – were held much more honourably and sacredly than we hold them now … So don't bother, or try not to bother, your head about sex so much'.[73] His attempt to open her mind to the reality of Catholicism and communism provoked the ire of a Jesuit member of her family who was trying to rescue her from the triple damnation of sexual impurity, O'Casey and communism.[74]

O'Casey's anger and compassion regarding the treatment of women are evident in the letters written to newspapers, to clerics of all descriptions, and to strangers who asked for his help and advice. Shivaun O'Casey recalls that 'He was aware of the crippling dominance of the Catholic Church and the dreadful amount of young girls who had to come to England for abortions. He thought abortion should be the woman's decision and health and schools should be free'.[75] O'Casey believed that women had the right to choose in matters that affect their lives, such as contraception and abortion. Not long after he was married, he had to face up to such a situation in his own life. Eileen O'Casey continued to work in the theatre after they were married. She became pregnant during a brief affair with Lee Ephraim, a married friend and former lover.[76] Her attempt to induce an abortion was unsuccessful, leaving her ill and depressed. She told Seán what had happened, and despite the hurt arising from the affair, he arranged for her to see a specialist in Harley Street, where she had an abortion. Writing about this in later years, Eileen said that 'the whole incident seemed to fortify our marriage; I recognised Sean's full qualities, and he appeared to love me more than ever'.[77] Eileen wrote about her abortion in 1973; even now, it is difficult to envisage what a brave decision that was. Eileen spoke out on behalf of the many women who had written to Seán over the years when they faced the problem of an unwanted pregnancy or had their child placed in an orphanage against their will. They were not in a position to speak out on their own behalf, but Seán always replied, offering comfort and advice. Eileen wrote about her abortion in a low-key way and on her own terms. What matters is that Eileen had the courage to speak out when few other women could.

In 1961 O'Casey published two short stories in the American men's magazines *Scene* and *Cavalcade*. In reality, they were the *Playboy* equivalent of their time, where large sums were paid to established writers to give the soft-porn section of the magazine an element of respectability. O'Casey resurrected the short story 'I Wanna Woman' for publication in *Cavalcade*.[78] The story concerns Jack, a young London man who picks up a prostitute. He pays a large sum of money for sex and loses his expensive watch during the encounter. This is a story with a moral, where Jack is portrayed as a shallow figure, while the prostitute emerges as a lively, sensual woman in control of her own destiny. O'Casey builds on the Rosie Redmond character from *The Plough and the Stars*, whose humanity remained intact despite the demeaning work she is engaged in, and created a character free from the stereotypes sometimes associated with women in the sex trade.

Of far more interest was his story 'The Job', which appeared in the magazine *Scene* in the same year. 'The Job' is the story of a young woman actor auditioning for a part in a new play. The story has currency given the revelations about sexual harassment in Hollywood and elsewhere in the entertainment world. The opening lines would have been familiar to many young women actors: 'She felt the producer's avid eyes watching her. Don't let anxiety show, she told herself. He mustn't know how desperate I am, how badly I need the job'.[79] O'Casey must have been aware of such instances of sexual harassment in the theatre world, or it may be the case that he was writing from his future wife's experience as an aspiring actor in the 1920s.

Despite O'Casey's liberal attitude to sex and sensuality, reading his views on homosexuality is unsettling. Even allowing for the fact that homosexuality was illegal, and O'Casey was reflecting a common prejudice shared by many on the left, this cannot excuse some of his comments. He had no scruple about using terms of abuse such as 'queer' or 'cissy' when referring to a number of well-known homosexuals in the literary and artistic world, whom he referred to collectively as the 'Primaqueeri'. His dislike of homosexuality coloured his approach to Micheál MacLiammóir and Hilton Edwards of the Gate Theatre in Dublin and appears to be one of the reasons why what could have been a fruitful artistic collaboration never came to anything. The Oxbridge background and the homosexual culture of writers such as Auden, Spender, Isherwood and John Lehmann created a distance and mistrust regarding O'Casey's attitude towards them. His view of Joe Orton's play *Entertaining Mr Sloane* was tainted by the bisexual nature of one of the characters. In his last essay, 'The Bald Primaqueera', published after his death in 1964, he writes about Orton's play: 'So, while remaining a man, he can, at a drop of the trousers, become a perfect woman-imposter'.[80] O'Casey's pronouncements on homosexuality were made against a background of widespread paranoia on both sides of the Atlantic that associated homosexuality with espionage and where the 'anti-Communist purges in the United States coincided with the purging of known homosexuals in the federal government, and the entertainment industry'.[81] This was an instance where O'Casey was on the wrong side of history. Nevertheless, at great personal cost, he was one of the few voices prepared to speak out against the destructive theocracy that damaged so many lives in Ireland and elsewhere, and for that, we should be thankful.

PART 5

CHAPTER 16

The Shadow of the Vatican: 1950–64

In 1950, approaching his seventieth birthday, O'Casey was as busy as ever. Over the following fourteen years, until his death in 1964, he published two further volumes of autobiography, nine plays, and a series of essays collected in two volumes, in addition to his political activities and voluminous output of letters to friends and enemies across the world. In May 1951, the Irish Workers' League asked him for an endorsement for Michael O'Riordan in the forthcoming general election. O'Casey replied, 'A message from me! D'ye want to destroy the man? A message from me would be as good as a message from Mars ... In lieu of a message, I enclose a subscription to the funds'.[1] Despite O'Casey's objections, the Irish Workers' League cobbled together a number of quotes from the rest of the letter where O'Casey had praised O'Riordan's qualities as a socialist and a trade unionist and issued an election handbill headed 'Sean O'Casey and the Elections'. O'Riordan was denounced from the pulpit in his local church as 'Red O'Riordan'. He received only a handful of votes, but a message of support from O'Casey would have meant something to that minority willing to put their mark beside the name of 'Red O'Riordan'. Unfortunately, there is no record of a reply to Dr Noël Browne and the National Progressive Democrats, who wrote to O'Casey asking for his support for the party in the 1961 general election. Browne's letter ends on an optimistic note: 'We hope we win because I feel the whole fabric here is crumbling rapidly'.[2] Nevertheless, O'Casey did suggest to a young Irish woman who was feeling depressed that she should go and help 'Dr Noel Browne and his friend Jack McQuillan. Look at Kitty Brady and the great fight she made for the Progressive Democratic Party down in County Carlow! She is a brave young woman'.[3]

Despite O'Casey's attachment to the socialist project, the absence of working-class characters of any substance in his post-war drama is striking, a point that several of his socialist critics have made. In 1953, the young Irish writer and socialist Patrick Galvin sent an open letter to O'Casey and attempted to have it printed in *Tribune* and the *Irish Democrat* in London. The letter complained about O'Casey's one-act play *Hall of Healing*, which the Unity Theatre Club in London had produced: 'Socialism, you will surely agree, is concerned with the dignity of man and of labour. I find almost all the characters in the *Hall of Healing* not merely lacking in dignity but obsessed with a vulgarly ostentatious parade of their incurable Joxerishness'.[4] This led to an exchange of letters concerning O'Casey's attitude to the working class, socialism and young writers. Galvin said that the trio of plays at Unity 'served to confirm in me once and for all that you are not a socialist' and accused him of being out of touch with Ireland and displaying:

> a total lack of confidence in the working class ... The hopelessness which you portray in the *Hall of Healing* is out of date ... it seems to me particularly obnoxious in 1953, when the Dublin unemployed are showing themselves decidedly un-lumpen in their capacity to organise ... One could no more imagine any of these draught-bemused cretins of yours marching behind the Plough and the Stars and facing police batons, as the Dublin unemployed did a week or two ago, than expect them to take wing into the stratosphere.[5]

Subsequently, O'Casey published sections of the correspondence without Galvin's permission. The young firebrand demanded an apology from O'Casey and threatened him and his publishing company Macmillan with a libel action if an apology was not forthcoming. The following year Galvin suggested that they publish the open letter and the subsequent correspondence in pamphlet form. This was the last straw as far as O'Casey was concerned; he replied, 'If there be an apology flying about at all like a saucer, it should land on my doorstep rather than yours. Indeed, I owe a deep one to myself for, in the first instance, being so damnably stupid in taking any notice of your first OPEN LETTER TO ME'.[6]

Seven years later, a more mature Galvin wrote to O'Casey to apologise for his youthful indiscretion: 'To say I blushed again on reading those letters is to put it very mildly indeed'.[7] Despite this admission, Galvin had raised a significant point in his criticism of O'Casey's work and, in particular, his drama from the post-war period. O'Casey was by then a socialist of some standing who was reasonably well versed in Marxist theory and practice, though it was grounded in the 1930s Stalinist tradition. Where working-class or socialist forces make an appearance, they are too small or weak to make a difference. In plays such as *The Drums of Father Ned* or *Behind the Green Curtains*, the workers are invariably trapped between the fight for better pay and conditions and their subservience to the church and the gombeen businessmen, who between them kill off any prospect of economic or social advancement.

O'Casey did not seem to be aware of the changes in consciousness and militancy taking place in Ireland. A new generation was emerging who would make an impact in the trade union movement, the housing action committees, women's equality, and the civil rights movement in the North of Ireland. Many of these young activists, like Patrick Galvin, instinctively looked to the likes of Seán O'Casey, Peadar O'Donnell, George Gilmore, John de Courcy Ireland or Owen Sheehy Skeffington for leadership and support. In the 1950s, these struggles were but straws in a very cold wind, but they were real and a herald of change to come.

In 1969 Patrick Galvin wrote to David Krause concerning the 'open letter' from 1953, stating that 'he now saw the whole controversy about Socialism and art and O'Casey in a different light' and acknowledged the debt owed to O'Casey:

> Writers of my generation (and background) have always demanded too much of O'Casey. We seemed to believe that in some mysterious way he owed us something; when in fact it had always been the other way round ... Needless to say, O'Casey had betrayed no one. If betrayal there was, we had betrayed ourselves. You took O'Casey as he was, warts and all, or you left him alone. The wonder of it is that he managed superbly well to survive the attentions of his friends and the wishes of his enemies. No Irish writer of my generation can repay the debt we owe to O'Casey. He kept the flag flying against Church and State for longer than most of us can remember. And though he was certainly not always right, by intention he was never wrong. May he rest well.[8]

AT HOME IN THE VILLAGE

In the post-war period, O'Casey turned his attention towards what he perceived to be an oppressive Catholic theocracy that was stifling Irish society. Surprisingly, the plays from this period are set in a small town or rural village rather than an urban or working-class setting. In 1954, the Rev. Dr John O'Brien of Notre Dame University in the USA published *The Vanishing Irish*, a book of essays dealing with the drastic decline in the Irish population and, in particular, the reason for the exceptionally low marriage rates.[9] Taking up the issues highlighted in the book, O'Casey blamed the morbid obsession of the church with sex as the reason for this decline.

This was a theme that O'Casey explored in his major plays, from *Cock-a-Doodle Dandy* in 1949 to *The Drums of Father Ned* in 1958. Unfortunately, audiences did not want to believe or even hear what he had to say about the reactionary role of the church in Ireland. His portrayal of the church's role in Irish society also meant that his work had little appeal for an international audience. Irish social commentators maintained that O'Casey was out of touch with the state of the country and that his work presented a false and unreliable impression of the situation in Ireland. In 1949 Seamus Kelly in *The Irish Times* described *Cock-a-Doodle Dandy* as:

> A blindly and bitterly destructive blast against an ... authoritarian clerical tyranny that never could or would be endured in this Ireland ... that never existed outside the imagination of a lonely and homesick man in Devonshire ... and is full to the brim with misanthropic misinterpretations of Ireland that have cancerously grown in our best playwright since he shook the bog from his boots.[10]

As it turned out, given the shocking revelations about clerical physical and sexual abuse, the situation in Ireland was even worse than that portrayed by O'Casey.

From the 1940s onwards, O'Casey assembled a dossier of cuttings, newspaper notes and letters about the church's actions in Ireland. He used these notes in his next three plays to develop the background details and the characters of the various priests and reactionaries that populate his work. They were also used to rebut accusations that he was out of touch about the church's role in Ireland. In a letter to *The Irish Times*, he defended the historical integrity of his work:

> All in '*Cockadoodle Dandy*' happened in Ireland; the priest ordering a farmer to dismiss a worker who was 'living with a woman', the farmer refusing; the priest striking so that the man died; a very quiet inquiry after. A woman dragged by her hair before another priest for 'going with a married man'; the priest making her go down on her knees and swear she'd leave the district? Or he'd cause God 'to coffin her' ... I have the records of them all here.[11]

The political fallout from the 'Mother and Child scheme' in 1951 strained relations between church and state in Ireland. Dr Noël Browne, a member of Clann na Poblachta and minister for health in the Fine Gael-led coalition government, put forward a bill to provide free health care for mothers, and children under sixteen. The hierarchy condemned the bill on the grounds that it contradicted Catholic social teaching. The bishops set out their objections in a letter to the taoiseach:

> The scheme contained provision for the physical education of children and for the education of mothers. These are matters in which the State had no competence. Furthermore, they could cover topics, such as birth control and abortion, on which, the Catholic Church has definite teaching.[12]

The Irish Medical Association was not far behind in letting the government know of their objection to any 'free scheme' that might impinge on their lucrative practices. Dr Browne published a series of letters in *The Irish Times* detailing how the church had worked behind the scenes to defeat the bill. The government caved in due to the bishops' pressure and paid the price at the subsequent general election.[13]

Archbishop McQuaid of the Dublin diocese was the spokesperson for the Irish hierarchy in the controversy over the 'Mother and Child scheme'. McQuaid was the dominant figure in relations between church and state in the 1950s, to whom government ministers were expected to defer. On most occasions, a private exchange of letters with those in authority was enough to convey the church's position. At other times, a public pronouncement was felt necessary. In January 1955, Archbishop McQuaid, with the aid of the *Standard* newspaper, vilified a delegation of Dublin journalists and trade unionists who had accepted an invitation by the Soviet Cultural Society to visit Moscow. As a result of this rebuke, James Kelly (also known as the writer James Plunkett), a trade union official and friend of O'Casey's, felt it necessary to resign his position as an official in the Workers' Union of Ireland.[14]

O'Casey, to his credit, was never afraid to call out the malevolent influence of 'the arch-druid o' Drumcondra' on social and moral affairs and was one of the few people of his era to stand up to the archbishop's theocratic control. His reply to a request by the Irish Labour Party to tone down an article on 'Labour and Religion' for the *Irish People* so that its publication would not be 'harmful to the Labour Party' is illustrative of his courage, and the cowardly acquiescence of the liberal class in Ireland to church control:

> I am amused to read that the article 'would be harmful to the Labour Party'. Since the Labour Party are evidently afraid to say anything against the biggest enemies of their Movement, then there is no Labour Party ... And, though not actually living in Ireland, I know

> something about it. If you mean that I would take no risk, were I living there, you are woefully mistaken.[15]

In 1949 O'Casey wrote a one-act play, *Hall of Healing*, about the Dublin Poor-Law dispensary system. Although O'Casey wrote the play just before the Mother and Child scandal, it was not published until 1951, at the height of the debate over the health service in Ireland. No Irish theatre company staged the play while it had currency and something to say about the failure of the health service to provide for the low-paid or poorer sections of Irish society. In fact, the play was not produced in Ireland until 1966 at the Abbey Theatre, where with one exception, the reviews were less than flattering.

Shortly after the publication of *Hall of Healing*, O'Casey wrote a letter of support to Mary Keating, who had reported on the dispensary system for *The Irish Times* in 1951 and who lost her position as a result of the article. O'Casey described his own experience of spending:

> years of my life in cold, drab waiting-rooms on visits to the doctors to get rid of pain for an hour or two, induced by what is called 'Malnutrition', but whose true and unholy name is 'Starvation'. I have pasted your report into the typescript copy of my one-act play, *Hall of Healing*.[16]

O'Casey denounced the 'Red Ticket' system where the old, the poor and the sick huddle together in cold and dilapidated dispensaries hoping to see a doctor. He went on to denounce de Valera and the politicians who let this happen and suggested that instead of visiting the monasteries and convents in Rome, if de Valera 'visited the dispensaries of Ireland, he'd be doing better work for God, for Ireland, and for his people'.[17] *Hall of Healing* had a London premiere in 1953 at the Unity Theatre Club. The reviews were generally favourable, especially about how O'Casey exposed the lack of medical facilities for the poor in Ireland. However, the *Daily Worker* saw it differently; they characterised it as an attack on 'the cowardice of the people when they fail to combine against the power that humiliates and destroys them'.[18] This insensitive review may have been another reason why O'Casey stopped contributing to the paper at that time.

A CYCLE OF PLAYS

Cock-a-Doodle Dandy (1949) belongs to a cycle of plays, including *The Bishop's Bonfire* (1955) and *The Drums of Father Ned* (1958), that are situated in Ireland at a time which James Moran has very perceptively described as in need of 'a second period of decolonization' to counter the censorship, church control and misogyny of the Irish state.[19] They are an attack on tradition, where the spirited young men and women of the village throw over the pretensions of the buffoons, clerics and petit-bourgeoisie who control society. O'Casey portrays in a ruthless way the small rural businessmen and the shopkeepers who, at the first sign of progress, run in fear into their shops to 'fumble for their last halfpence in the greasy tills'.[20] *Cock-a-Doodle Dandy* is set in the village of Nyadnanave, loosely translated as the 'nest of the knaves'. The three major plays from this period have a rural setting, which seems to fly in the face of the modernist project, where the urban and metropolitan are privileged over the rural and the traditional. On the one hand, he appears to be satirising the peasant play so beloved by the Abbey Theatre while exposing the hypocrisy of the rural ideal of 'athletic youths and the laughter of happy maidens' promoted by Éamon de Valera and successive Irish governments.[21] Most colonised countries have a strong sense of the past and are nostalgic for an idealised world that existed before the colonial power arrived. In Ireland, this nostalgia found expression during the literary revival, where the imagery of the west of Ireland became a rallying cry for the project. While the nostalgia was genuine, the reality of the state that emerged failed to live up to their expectations. O'Casey, in this cycle of plays, set about dismantling that illusion.

In December 1949, the People's Theatre in Newcastle-upon-Tyne premiered *Cock-a-Doodle Dandy*, a morality play that dealt with Ireland's preoccupation with sex and puritanism.[22] *Cock-a-Doodle Dandy* is a mixture of realism, magic, fantasy and superstition, particularly in the incarnations of the Cock, where the differences between the natural and the supernatural are dissolved. The play has some affinity with a style of writing known as magical realism that emerged in the 1960s.[23] O'Casey dedicated the play to James Stephens, whose book *The Crock of Gold* may have inspired some of the more fantastical elements in the play.[24]

The young woman, Loreleen, represents progress and the joy of life, at various intervals in the play she is magically transformed into a cock. The rooster, or the Cock, with human attributes, is in the tradition of Shakespeare's ghosts, who appear at times of crisis and is the harbinger of revolt. The Cock is the alternative within us, the symbol of burgeoning life denied by the priest and the politician. Under the spell of the Cock, women emerge from their houses dressed in vibrant clothes and enchant men into a festival of dancing, merriment and drinking where all the old hatreds and restrictions are put aside. The arrival of Father Domineer ends the merriment, and all the villagers, except Loreleen, bend the knee in obedience to the priest. Father Domineer, whose very name resonates with clerical authority, is depicted as a killjoy who wields a mailed fist in an attempt to stifle sexual desires and civil liberties in the name of religious orthodoxy. The play portrays the conflict between the joy of life and the forces of reaction as represented by the Cock on the one hand and on the other by the church and the small businessmen of the village. O'Casey also hits out at the cult of miracles claimed by pilgrims visiting the religious shrines at Lourdes and Fatima; a dying girl returns from Lourdes without being cured and announces that she rejects outright the church's teaching on miracles.[25]

The Cock represents a state of mind – O'Casey himself perhaps – an avenging jester who inspires the young people of the village, but he alone cannot defeat the unholy alliance of the priest and the gombeen businessmen when their power 'is sanctioned by the stupidity of the mob'.[26] There are no collective victories for the young people of the village or for the workers who go on strike for better pay; just individual acts of defiance. In the end, just as in *Juno*, Loreleen and her stepmother Lorna leave the village 'to a place where life resembles life more than it does here'.[27] The play was received in Ireland with both anger at O'Casey and pity for how low he had fallen. *The Irish Times* accused O'Casey of viewing Ireland 'through the wrong end of a telescope with a flawed and twisted lens'.[28] *Cock-a-Doodle Dandy* was O'Casey's favourite play, and he believed that 'although the action manifests itself in Ireland, the spirit it describes is to be found anywhere in the world'.[29]

In 1955, Cyril Cusack agreed to produce *The Bishop's Bonfire* at the Gaiety Theatre in Dublin. This was an important play for O'Casey, as it was the first time that a new play of his had opened in Dublin for almost thirty years. Cyril Cusack was president of the Catholic Stage Guild, and he showed immense independence of spirit, knowing that a play about the role of religion in Ireland would possibly meet the same kind of protests that greeted *The Plough and the Stars* thirty years earlier.[30] Despite this, Cusack, whom O'Casey regarded as a 'very good self-respecting Catholic',[31] felt it necessary to send a copy of *The Bishop's Bonfire* to a priest in London for guidance on the matter. Father Hilary was not impressed and pressured Cusack to drop the play. However, Cusack stood his ground, and the production went ahead.

In the weeks leading up to the opening, the *Standard*, a conservative Catholic newspaper, whipped up opposition to the production: 'O'Casey flays all manner of Catholic Ecclesiastics, Irish religious organisations, and Catholic writers … O'Casey has prostituted his undoubted ability in the cause of anti-God and anti-Clericalism'.[32] The following week the *Standard* urged its readers to make a stand in relation to O'Casey's politics and his blasphemous play: 'It is the boasted aim of Communism to "tear God from his Heaven". Where do you stand?'[33] However, the threatened demonstration by the right-wing and anti-Semitic group Maria Duce never materialised. There were, however, protests outside the Gaiety Theatre on the opening night and booing during the performance. Students from University College Dublin protested about the anti-Catholic nature of the play. However, the students from Trinity College Dublin and the People's College, who opposed any attempt to disrupt the performance, supported O'Casey. Ina Connolly Heron, the daughter of James Connolly, gave an account of the demonstration:

> When asked by the reporters what brought us down so early the students replied they came from the law courts when they heard that the opposition had been reinforced by the University College Dublin [students]. We want to show O'Casey that Dublin belongs to him. There were cheers and waving of hands, every-one felt they wanted to express their joy at O'Casey's latest production.[34]

She also reported that the supporters of O'Casey were 'singing Solidarity and The Red Flag' as they arrived. The newsboys (street newspaper sellers) turned up to support Larkin's old friend and lit 'a bonfire with the *Standard*', the Catholic newspaper that had denounced O'Casey and his play. When the gardaí tried to extinguish it, 'the cry of the Gestapo and the RUC are here went up'.[35] Despite the controversy, the production was booked out for an extended five-week run.

The Bishop's Bonfire is about fear and the sham piety that intimidated anyone who dared raise a voice against tradition and clerical authority. The play has several themes that were of concern to O'Casey, including a monster bonfire of 'immoral' books to welcome the bishop to the village, a not-too-subtle metaphor for the debilitating censorship crippling Irish minds. In a scene that has no relevance to the drama, except to make an ironic comment on the anti-Russian Cold War propaganda that had taken hold, O'Casey introduces a lieutenant from the Irish army to warn the citizens of an imminent Russian invasion, saying that Ireland should arm itself with American jeeps and walkie-talkies in order to defend itself.[36]

The Bishop's Bonfire is much more pessimistic in its outcome than the plays that went before it, as the priests and the property owners come together to stamp out any possibility of happiness and freedom. The local curate, Father Boheroe, is a progressive, but he is too timid a reformer to have any hope of success. He suggests to the young lovers, Keelin and Daniel, that having escaped 'the dominion of the big house with its lion and unicorn on the front; don't let yourselves sink beneath the meaner dominion of the big shop with cross and shamrock on its gable'.[37] Daniel, an unskilled labourer, is another of O'Casey's fearful workers who envisages emigration to England with his lover, Keelin, in order to overcome the objections of her father, the priest and the town. But neither have the strength of character to seize their opportunity and escape to a better life. The play ends with a bonfire that is, in reality, the funeral pyre of all their hopes for the future.

The reviews were mixed; Edna O'Brien, in her review of the 1961 production at the Mermaid in London, put her finger on the problem with the play. Her main objection 'was its evasion' and she suggested that while 'Ireland is riddled with guilt and failure and a beautiful dream gone wrong', surely 'Irish [people] and outsiders may ask for something more';[38] in other words, some form of hope that life might change for the better in Ireland. The review by Gabriel Fallon of *The Bishop's Bonfire* led to the final sundering of a friendship that had lasted over thirty years. O'Casey and Fallon became friends through the Abbey Theatre, where Fallon was one of the few Abbey personnel to publicly support O'Casey during the row over *The Plough and the Stars* in 1926. After O'Casey left for England, they exchanged letters that were always affectionate and supportive. Fallon's doctrinaire Catholicism and O'Casey's communism were matters they mostly tried to avoid lest it disturb their friendship. Fallon was a member of An Ríoghacht (League of the Kingship of Christ), a conservative Catholic group founded in 1926 to ensure that Catholic social teaching and doctrine was embedded in the legal structure of the Irish Free State. In the 1930s, it was the basis of Father Denis Fahey's semi-fascist organisation, Maria Duce. Fallon, to his credit, had fought against this extreme development and campaigned to have it suppressed by the church authorities. In 1936, Fallon joined the staff of the *Irish Monthly* (published by the Jesuits) and two years later became the drama critic of the Catholic newspaper the *Standard*, a paper that O'Casey held in contempt. O'Casey believed that these Catholic connections were affecting Fallon and told him so in a letter in 1943: 'Honestly? I'm a little tired of these "offences to Catholics". Who are they above anyone else to him who doesn't believe in the Catholic Faith? I have hardly written a line that hasn't been offensive to someone or other, then why should I single out the Catholics for special consideration?'[39] Over the following decade, their friendship came under severe strain and almost fractured over a vicious review of *Red Roses for Me* in the *Standard* in 1946. Fallon wrote that he was both angry and sorry to 'witness the incandescence of genius doused in an overflow of its own wilfulness'. He accused O'Casey of portraying a 'Protestant hero', denigrating his Catholic neighbours by portraying their devotion to the statue of 'Our Lady of Eblana' as 'hocus-pocus'. He went on to say that this portrayal was 'a piece of cold-calculated bigotry'.[40] The final break came over his review of *The Bishop's Bonfire*. Fallon disliked both the play and the perceived attack on religion: 'however much the *Bishop's Bonfire* blazed in the imagination of Mr O'Casey, the dramatic fire that turned *Juno* and *The Plough* into an incandescence of greatness is now a handful of grey ash'.[41] Fallon, like many of O'Casey's critics, both religious and political, came to the conclusion that it was 'an unresolved personal problem' and a 'guilt complex' that led him to repudiate 'his people, his country, and their most cherished beliefs, even while he protested that he did nothing of the kind'.[42]

AN TÓSTAL

The Dublin International Theatre Festival was launched in May 1957 on the initiative of the Dublin Tóstal Council.[43] The inaugural programme was outstanding. The highlights were *The Importance of Being Earnest* by Oscar Wilde at the Olympia, Denis Johnston's *The Old Lady Says No!* at the Gate, and *The Playboy of the Western World* and *Juno and the Paycock* at the Abbey. Seven plays by Yeats were on the programme, in addition to plays by Balzac and Molière. However, the Pike Theatre production of *The Rose Tattoo* by Tennessee Williams, directed by Alan Simpson, which opened the festival in May 1957, ended in disaster and a warning of what O'Casey would face the following year. The play contains a stage direction where a contraceptive is thrown on the ground, but in the Pike Theatre production this action was mimed because it was impossible to obtain one in Ireland! When the production had completed its run, Alan Simpson was arrested and charged with having 'produced for gain an indecent and profane performance'. The case dragged on for over a year before Simpson was acquitted, but the cost financially and to his reputation had taken a heavy toll on Simpson and the

Pike Theatre.[44] O'Casey, along with John Osborne, John Gielgud and Peter Hall, in an open letter to the *New Statesman*, launched a fighting fund in Britain to assist Simpson in meeting the costs of his defence.[45] As a result of the court case, membership of the Pike fell from 2,000 to 300. The financial situation became untenable, and the company folded in 1961.

The programme for the 1958 festival was in preparation while the *Rose Tattoo* case was still before the courts. One of the highlights was a new play by Seán O'Casey, *The Drums of Father Ned*, which was always going to be contentious given the controversy over the perceived anti-clericalism of *The Bishop's Bonfire* at the Gaiety three years earlier. Allan McClelland had created *Bloomsday*, adapted from Joyce's novel *Ulysses*,[46] and Samuel Beckett had submitted three mime plays for production, together with a staged reading of *All That Fall*.

The English director George Devine wrote: 'when a playwright brings a new play into the theatre, he is carrying a bucket of blood, and he must expect some of it to be spilt!'[47] This was the case when the programme for the 1958 festival was announced. The previous July, Brendan Smith, the theatre festival director, had written to O'Casey, 'Presuming we could agree on producer, cast and business details, would you consider giving the Festival the world premiere of your new play?'[48] O'Casey was supportive of the festival and believed it might stir up the country out of the torpor that affected it. O'Casey sent a copy of *The Drums of Father Ned* for consideration, and in the letter to Brendan Smith, he made clear that 'the sending of the MS by me to you doesn't in any way commit me to finally deciding that the Festival can have it'.[49] Despite O'Casey's hesitancy, and given what had gone before, the directors of the Globe Theatre took it upon themselves to write to O'Casey indicating that they were unhappy with the structure of the play and requested permission for the director 'to make such alterations as he requires'.[50] O'Casey had no agreement with Norman Rodway and Godfrey Quigley to produce the play, nor was he comfortable with Jim Fitzgerald as director: 'their letter demanding the right to alter the play as they all thought fit came as a complete shock to Sean'.[51]

Meanwhile, the Dublin Congress of Trade Unions communicated to the archbishop of Dublin their dissatisfaction regarding the staging of 'plays of an objectionable nature' during the festival. The controversy erupted when Archbishop McQuaid's letter informing the trade unions that he had refused permission for a Votive Mass to inaugurate the festival was made public. In an extraordinary display of arrogance, the Irish hierarchy also called on the American bishops to lobby 'Irish representatives in the United

States in relation to two plays in the programme of the 1958 Dublin Theatre Festival, which the Archbishop of Dublin regarded as objectionable'.[52] The exact sequence of events that led to the cancellation of the festival is still unclear. In early February 1958, a spokesman for the Dublin Tóstal Council reported that the director rejected the play because O'Casey had refused permission for them to make 'structural alterations to make it suitable for the Dublin public'. O'Casey simultaneously announced that he was withdrawing the play: 'It is plain to me now that there is no theatre into which O'Casey can be allowed to fit ... So I have fashioned the decision to withdraw the play from production in the Republic of Ireland during the Tóstal, or after the Tóstal is done'.[53]

Three days later, the council decided to drop the dramatisation of *Ulysses*. Samuel Beckett then withdrew his plays in protest, and the festival collapsed in a blaze of allegations as the dirty linen of Irish literary and artistic life was once again washed in public. O'Casey put his side of the story in an extensive letter to *The Irish Times* defending the integrity of his play and suggesting that the accusation of 'structural' faults 'was but an untidy way of getting rid of him', by those who feared a belt of the archbishop's crozier 'dinging in their ears'.[54] Archbishop McQuaid's letter to Father Patrick Tuohy, who had read over the plays on behalf of the Tóstal committee, made it plain where the actual decisions on these matters were made: 'I would like you to take means to remove any such misunderstanding, for I shall be obliged to take very definite action if either *Ulysses* or O'Casey's play be chosen by the Tóstal. *The Rose Tattoo* ought to have been a lesson to the Tóstal'.[55]

The cancellation of the theatre festival was one of the bleakest days in modern Irish cultural and social history. It seemed to validate every criticism O'Casey had made of the theocratic Irish state over the previous thirty years. Following this unseemly row, O'Casey banned professional productions of all of his plays in the Republic of Ireland:

> I must stand by the memory of Joyce and by Samuel Beckett who very manfully withdrew his plays as a protest. I can't allow my play to be done there in S[outhern] Ireland, till these other plays find a footing there too. In all honesty to my brother writers, Joyce and Beckett, I can't do anything else.[56]

A few brave people wrote letters of support to O'Casey, including the writer and former trade union official James Plunkett, the Irish Association of Civil Liberties, and Sybil le Brocquy, who wrote to say that the people of Ireland 'owe you a national apology'.[57] Thanks to the efforts of Brendan Smith and a handful of others, the theatre festival, independent of the Tóstal committee, was reborn in 1959 as the Dublin International Theatre Festival, which continues with great success to this day.

The Drums of Father Ned is set in the period leading up to the village celebrations of the An Tóstal festival. The young people of the village are in awe of Father Ned and his message of joy and sensuality that breathes new life into the community. Although Father Ned never appears on stage, he is the antithesis of Father Domineer and the other clerical killjoys from the earlier plays. He is portrayed as a progressive and a humanitarian who encourages the young people of Doonavale to sing, dance and follow the beat of his drum towards a political future that, in 1958, few could imagine was possible in Ireland. Unlike O'Casey's previous two plays, the main protagonists are allowed small victories: steps along the way to a better world. Michael and Nora marry despite the opposition of their parents and priest. They stand for election to the local council, determined to throw over the old Civil War divisions that paralysed life in the town. O'Casey's friend and first biographer David Krause believed that the play was a joyous response to the book-burners and those who tried to suppress or censor his work. Krause very eloquently makes the case that *The Drums of Father Ned* was a statement of O'Casey's hope for the future and perhaps a partial reconciliation with Ireland in the last decade of his life.[58] The play eventually received a European premiere at the Queen's Theatre in east London in 1960. Although O'Casey was not pleased about some of the cuts made by the director, it received favourable reviews.

Unfortunately, few of these post-war plays are performed today. There are problems in presenting them because their historical and geographical context limits their relevance for a contemporary audience. The Arches Theatre in Glasgow produced *Purple Dust* in 1994 and *Cock-a-Doodle Dandy* in 1996, in what the director described as 'a rough theatre that is very much in the spirit of those later plays',[59] where the inner realism was more important than the images portrayed on the stage. Politically, these plays are challenging and at times contradictory. O'Casey was attempting to deconstruct the old social values and substitute a positive plea for imagination, vitality and change, but they sometimes lack the intellectual rigour necessary to clarify his intentions.

ALL CHANGED

The Second World War changed everything, and theatre was no exception. In 1948, Samuel Beckett began writing *Waiting for Godot* as a response to and an escape from the experience of 'humanity living on the edge of extinction'.[60] In the process, he transformed theatre, even if audiences, and O'Casey, struggled to understand the play's symbolism or the way it would change the future of drama. In Beckett's drama, form tends to overtake content; and in the process, Beckett transformed what can be expressed on the stage. Drama is never separate from the social conditions from which it emerges, and what it depicts always reveals something about the beliefs of its creator. Beckett and his contemporaries conceived a new beginning in theatre where 'everything becomes theatre'. The ability of Harold Pinter or Samuel Beckett to use silence or minimalist responses as a means of illuminating the inner reality of the modern world was a development that O'Casey and many of his contemporaries could not relate to, or perhaps even understand, as he made clear in an article in *Encore* in 1956:

> Beckett? I have nothing to do with Beckett. He isn't in me; nor am I in him. I am not waiting for Godot to bring me life; I am out after life myself, even at the age I've reached. What have any of you to do with Godot? There is more life than Godot can give in the life of the least of us. That Beckett is a clever writer, and that he has written a rotting and remarkable play there is no doubt; but his philosophy isn't my philosophy for within him there is no hazard of hope; no desire for it; nothing in it but a lust for despair, and a crying of woe.[61]

Despite his rejection of Beckett's dramatic philosophy, his daughter Shivaun O'Casey believed that the Howard Davies production of *Juno* (2011), at both the National in London and the Abbey Theatre, was devoid of 'sentimentality' and that there was 'an honesty that was true to the text ... The bridge into Sam Beckett's work could not be clearer in this version, particularly in the final scene'.[62]

Whatever his thoughts on Beckett and the 'theatre of despair', O'Casey was equally dismissive of the efforts of Joan Littlewood, Ewan MacColl and the Theatre Workshop in Manchester to create an urban working-class theatre using drama as a political weapon. Despite the urging of his friend Hugh MacDiarmid to allow Littlewood and MacColl to produce *Cock-a-Doodle Dandy* in Manchester, he refused permission, pleading contractual agreements with American producers. O'Casey had little time for the cabaret-style productions of Joan Littlewood after her move to the Theatre Workshop in east London and believed that her production of Brendan Behan's *The Hostage* in 1958 had done a disservice to the author in the way that 'she tampered with his work'.[63]

The Angry Young Men of the 1950s, John Osborne, Arnold Wesker, and the Royal Court Theatre, under the direction of George Devine, shocked the sensibilities of middle England with their 'kitchen-sink' drama of disillusionment. Their impatience with the status quo contrasted with the genteel drawing-room dramas in the West End plays of Noël Coward or Terence Rattigan that were well past their sell-by date. This interlude was, however, but a brief blossoming; many of these young writers not only failed to develop artistically, but in time they also jettisoned their radical pretensions. O'Casey's response to these developments, whether it was the theatre of Beckett and his contemporaries, that of Osborne and Orton, or Littlewood and Arnold Wesker, shows how out of touch he was with developments in modern theatre in the last decades of his life.

In 1946 O'Casey published an article, 'The People and the Theatre', in the first issue of *Theatre Today*, a magazine published by Fore Publications, which was associated with the Communist Party in Britain. In this polemical piece, he put forward the proposition that 'the people are the theatre ... every art is rooted in the life of the people ... The question for all artists is this: Is the colour and form of what has been taken from their life done well, or done badly?'[64] In the unpublished draft version of this article, O'Casey included a section defending left-wing drama:

> Then there is what is called the Left-Wing manifestation of art and of the theatre, at which there has been a quick and constant lifting of noses, and loud sniffs of contempt. The little art that may be hiding in it is (it is said) smothered in propaganda ... I submit that because we are often displeased - often rightly so - with 'proletarian' art, we have no authority to declare that it is invariably hollow, tiresome, and worthless.[65]

Despite this, O'Casey had lost patience with the new generation of writers of agitational plays, whom he believed were mere 'hangers-out of opinions, voiced by puppets dressed up for the occasion in the garments of men and women'.[66] However, he did make an exception for John Arden, the author of the anti-war play *Serjeant Musgrave's Dance*. O'Casey was suspicious of the new wave of radical theatre that tried to introduce drama to working-class communities beyond the confines of London. In 1961, he dismissed Arnold Wesker and Shelagh Delaney's attempt to launch a new theatre company, Centre 42.[67] Their project set out to develop a drama that combined work of the highest literary standards with a left-wing ethos. In an article that seemed out of character with his professed views, O'Casey poured cold water on the prospects for Centre 42 and the ambitions of Wesker and company, suggesting instead that they should forget about 'bringing culture to the masses' and concentrate on bringing 'something fresh' to the London theatre.[68] O'Casey was not the only sceptic regarding Centre 42; the hangover from the political pressure that artists and writers were subjected to in the 1930s and '40s by the Communist Party meant that many on the left were suspicious of such projects. Wesker was to complain: 'The other and fairly upsetting thing is that the response of the left in this country to the idea of Centre 42 has been so poor. Socialists in this country are so battered and bruised that they don't believe in themselves let alone anybody else'.[69] Due to a shortage of funding, Centre 42 folded in 1970. Despite his dismissal of the new wave of working-class drama, in one of his last letters in 1964 O'Casey congratulated the People's Theatre in Newcastle, who had moved into a new building. He hoped they would outshine the established theatres such as Chichester and the Old Vic in Bristol: 'I send you all an old Irish playwright's thanks for what you have done for the theatre'.[70]

CHAPTER 17

Knocking on the Door

The critical neglect of O'Casey's autobiographies, essays and especially his letters undervalues both his ability as a prose writer and the remarkable account that the letters contain of the literary and political history of the twentieth century. Between 1939 and 1954, O'Casey published six volumes of autobiography. After his death in 1964, four volumes of his letters were collected and edited by his friend and biographer David Krause. Some of his admirers have suggested that 'O'Casey might be remembered more for his prose than for his drama' and in time the autobiographies would be seen as 'one of the most enduring works of this century'.[1]

However, this was an assessment that few other critics shared; time has not been kind, and the autobiographies have few friends today. Since the publication of the first volume in 1939, critical reaction has been fiercely divided. Irish literary critics were mostly hostile; Seán O'Faoláin found them 'wearisome belly-aching, a corrosion of self-pity'. Oliver St John Gogarty wrote that O'Casey had a 'grudge against life'. Padraic Colum questioned O'Casey's originality, suggesting that the autobiographies had come from the pen of a writer 'who had read his James Joyce'. George Orwell dismissed them as 'basic Joyce'.[2] In 1966, Sean McCann edited a series of essays collected in *The World of Sean O'Casey* in which he posed a question, 'was O'Casey in exile a man without that vital spark of genius? Were his autobiographies wayward and uneven? Were the letters he wrote the mirror of a grouser, a bitter man?'[3] Over the following 250 pages, McCann and his cohorts answered in the affirmative. In his assessment of the autobiographies, Ulick O'Connor was typical: 'what he has given us is on the whole second-rate. The style frequently verges on the ludicrous ... At times it becomes like the whining of a spoilt child'.[4] This view was balanced by several scholarly interpretations by American critics in the 1980s, which refocused attention on the literary value of the autobiographies. However, the letters, which account for nearly a third of his output, have received relatively little attention.[5]

Such diverse reactions are not unusual in the case of such a controversial writer as O'Casey. Books and writers have their seasons, and his literary reputation has both suffered and prospered over the last eighty years, according to fashion. The attack on the historical accuracy of the autobiographies and his integrity by Tony Butler, Desmond Greaves and Gabriel Fallon damaged O'Casey's reputation.[6] They cast doubt on O'Casey's interpretation of Irish history and politics. For political or personal reasons, his detractors have shaped the apparent historical inconsistencies into a weapon to belittle him. At the same time, his critics used the fragmentary expressionist style of the autobiographies to question their accuracy. The political attacks on O'Casey's views were sometimes disguised by a bogus literary critique of the free-flowing third-person form utilised by O'Casey. In a review of *Drums under the Window*, the Ulster unionist writer St John Ervine fired the first salvo in the right-wing journal *The Spectator* in November 1945. He questioned the historical accuracy of O'Casey's autobiography and suggested that neither O'Casey nor anyone else 'could remember conversations that took place thirty years ago'.[7] St John Ervine set the tone for subsequent critics. Republicans, socialists and right-wing Catholics hostile to O'Casey's interpretation of history followed on from Ervine's broadside. Tony Butler, in the Dublin *Evening Herald* in 1980, on the centenary of O'Casey's birth, claimed that O'Casey 'cheated in a literary competition; stole everything that was not nailed down while working in a city company and was a downright fraud when it came to his much proclaimed socialism'.[8] Butler stated that O'Casey was not a product of the slums, that his father was a pillar of the Protestant middle classes, and claimed that the autobiographies were not based on fact. These latter-day critics accused him, in effect, of being a liar and a cheat.

O'Casey's actions hardly warranted such condemnation. At the age of twelve, he filched a lump of bacon from a shop when there was nothing at home for the family to eat. He recalled one occasion when facing hardship, his saintly mother put aside her religious scruples and sewed pockets into his jacket so that he could appropriate household goods from his workplace. O'Casey was not a lesser man for what he did; instead, these were understandable acts of survival. He never tried to conceal his past, and he justified those actions that troubled the religious scruples of his mother by telling her that 'it is not a sin for a needy person to steal from a company. After all a company has no soul. Such a theft may be against the law, but I do not look at the law as a binding force.'[9] In his play *The Bishop's Bonfire*, in a different context, he put forward a rationale for such behaviour in a literary reformulation of Karl Marx's theory of surplus value: 'I'm stealing a little from a lot stolen from many'.[10]

O'Casey never described the books as autobiography; on the few occasions he alluded to them, he placed the term in inverted commas. In a letter in 1931, the first reference to the work, he refers to a 'semi-biography' he is contemplating.[11] The issue of historical accuracy has bedevilled critical assessments of the autobiographies. Christopher Murray's detailed biography has finally put these diversionary arguments behind us and opened up O'Casey studies to a new generation of scholars and theatregoers who are not wedded to the concept of the autobiographies as the primary source material for O'Casey's life. They are a recreation of his early life in epic form; a modern artistic interpretation in the mould of H.G. Wells' *Experiments in Autobiography*, James Joyce's *Portrait of the Artist as a Young Man*, or even William Thackeray's experimental fictional autobiography from 1852, *The History of Henry Esmond*, where the narrator used the third person to refer to himself in the past. However, a purely literary or artistic approach to the autobiographies raises several problems that limit an appreciation of the synthesis between literature, politics and social history that O'Casey was trying to achieve. There is not enough detail to anchor the events he describes, in terms of time and place, to the outside world. A more holistic approach is necessary, which goes beyond history or literature, to fully appreciate the value of the autobiographies.

At its simplest, autobiography is 'an individual's written account of chosen experiences from his life'.[12] This implies a process of selecting representative events in a subjective and sometimes even a contradictory way. Such choices are informed and shaped by contemporary culture and society and in many cases are ideologically driven.[13] In almost every chapter, O'Casey deals with the essential truth regarding the righteousness of the cause of labour and 'the great achievements of the Soviet Union', truths forged by the circumstances of personal history.[14] Despite what Padraic Colum described as O'Casey's propensity to insert 'political pamphlets' into the narrative,[15] his social, political and artistic vision is linked to his past experiences.

Autobiography, like fiction, is the art of 'supreme fabrication'; therefore, it is as a creator of himself and of his world that O'Casey, as represented in the autobiographies, should be considered. In structure and style, they challenge stock interpretations of history. He goes beyond realism to paint a picture that provides a deeper understanding of the motives or driving force of the people behind the events that conventional history merely records. 'Comrades', the chapter concerning the period of the Civil War, recounts the extra-judicial execution of a republican volunteer, Kevin Lanehin, by a

Free State colonel and former comrade, Mick Clonervy.[16] The incident he describes is factual, but O'Casey fabricates the details of the chase, capture and horrific execution of Lanehin. O'Casey records the incident with an ironic detachment that reveals the senselessness and utter brutality of the Civil War in a way that a factual recording of the event would find hard to convey. This chapter is the least autobiographical of the first four volumes. O'Casey hardly features except as an observer speaking directly to the reader about the viciousness of a senseless civil war. In the chapter 'The Raid', O'Casey describes an incident which also formed the basis for *The Shadow of a Gunman*. The tenement in Mountjoy Square where O'Casey was living in 1920 was raided by the British. His first thought on hearing the door smashed in was whether they were 'the Tommies or the Tans'.[17] In this concise sentence, O'Casey conveys the fear the Black and Tans engendered and the brutality of their methods.

The issue of trust is crucial for the historian, but O'Casey's autobiographies are not seductive fictions that blur the line between the real and the imagined. He was not alone in letting 'art vie with history' in his memoirs. As Michael Kenneally has pointed out, both W.B. Yeats and George Moore have combined artistic and historical interpretations in their autobiographies that have raised questions about their historical accuracy.[18]

However, meaning can become blurred in the outpouring of words that tumble from his pen. He seemed incapable of utilising the controlled language or the sparse intensity of a Beckett or Pinter. In 1945 Beckett switched to writing in French in order to 'escape from mother Anglo-Irish exuberance ... From excess to lack of colour'.[19] Beckett knew the power of brevity, whereas O'Casey sporadically lost control, and on those occasions his style would have benefited from a more controlled flamboyance. He is at his best in the direct passages that express the joy and pleasure of life rather than the expressionist passages, which can be excessively effusive. Granville Hicks felt that the autobiographies were ill-tempered, sentimental and long-winded, 'yet the reader puts up with all this, not only because the best is so good but also the force of the man comes through bad and good alike'.[20] At times his style borders on pastiche, but his use of the third-person narrative format allowed him to stand back from the events described and keep one foot firmly on the ground. His use of this format is sometimes problematic, at times, we are unsure who is narrating the story and whose life is being described. But somehow, he managed to avoid the miserabilism that plagues so much of the modern Irish memoir.

HISTORICAL GUIDE

It is legitimate to ask questions of a work of non-fiction that we would never ask of a work of art. Martin Margulies' book *The Early Life of Sean O'Casey*, written in 1970, managed to recover the testimony of many of the surviving family and political acquaintances that filled some of the gaps that were missing in O'Casey's account of his early life. However, as David Krause has pointed out, Margulies' account needs to be taken with a pinch of salt as it provided an opportunity for those slighted by O'Casey to settle old scores.[21] Unquestionably, the issues raised by the likes of Margulies, Butler, Fallon, McCann and Greaves needed to be addressed. The problem is not the background information they had uncovered. O'Casey, among other things, exaggerated his lack of schooling and misrepresented his support for the Boers during the South African war in 1899 and his ability to speak Irish in 1900.[22] How much of this was a conscious rewriting of the past and how much a flawed memory conflating time and events over forty years later is impossible to know, and therefore must remain conjecture. O'Casey was disliked and critically abused because he refused to accept the inward-looking conservative consensus that emerged in the early years of the Irish Free State.

With some exceptions, these arguments do not need to be rehearsed again at any great length. The intellectual wheat has been separated from the chaff, and the straw men who were left to advance these untruths, distorted charges and malicious gossip were killed off over forty years ago by Krause, Lowery, Ayling and others in the pages of the *Seán O'Casey Review* and the *O'Casey Annual*. Despite this, unease or uncertainty continues to afflict critical interpretations of the autobiographies. In his introduction to the extract from O'Casey's autobiographies in *The Field Day Anthology of Irish Writing*, Seamus Deane quotes or cites only the negative reviews the autobiographies received. Deane goes on to say that 'O'Casey's style was, and remains, distasteful to many ... his histrionic method is often embarrassingly unsuccessful', while conceding that 'there are times when it achieves unexpectedly moving effects'.[23] In *The Politics of Irish Drama* (1999), Nicholas Grene, coming from a literary perspective, writing on 'class constructions' in O'Casey's drama, suggests that:

> [In] the six volumes of *Autobiographies* ... the past was reconceived throughout to correspond to the needs of the then present: the need to settle old grudges, to justify opinions, to dramatise the story of the

> poor boy from the slums struggling towards creative fulfilment. As such retrospective re-creations, they cannot be trusted as providing the raw material for the 1920s plays.[24]

The difficulty with Grene's interpretation, as with so many others, is that it privileges O'Casey's dramatic work at the expense of the autobiographies. The autobiographies are not accepted or interrogated as a literary creation in their own right or a historical record of the period. They exist primarily as a background or resource for interpreting O'Casey's plays.

A more interesting question is whether O'Casey, in the first four volumes of the autobiographies, expressed the reality of life as experienced by the slum-dwellers of Dublin. O'Casey never objected to the term 'slum dramatist' being applied to his work. He embraced the term and wore it as a badge of honour in the way that later generations of black consciousness or gay activists appropriated terms that had in the past demeaned them, such as 'black' and 'queer', and redefined them as an expression of their pride and confidence in themselves as black or gay men and women:

> It had often been recorded in the Press, by those who could guess shrewdly, that Sean was a slum dramatist, a gutter-snipe who could jingle a few words together out of what he had seen and heard. The terms were suitable and accurate, for he was both, and, all his life, he would hold the wisdom and courage that those conditions had given him.[25]

O'Casey was never afraid to parade his background in the face of those who tried to patronise his work or the working-class characters that populate his drama. We know that he did not grow up in a slum, though in later life he did live in a slum area. According to the census of 1911, three members of the Casey family living in two rooms and five members of the Duffy family living in two rooms occupied the small two-storey house on Abercorn Road. Gabriel Fallon recalls visiting O'Casey in his room on the North Circular Road in 1924; he noted that the house 'was a *respectable* tenement, its hall door closed'.[26] By the standards of the Dublin slums at the beginning of the twentieth century, the Casey family were near the top end of the hierarchy of poverty.

After he lost his job on the railway in 1911 because of his support for the Irish Transport and General Workers' Union, O'Casey experienced poverty, hunger and suffering. Following the death of his mother in 1918, he moved into a tenement in Mountjoy Square, where he shared one room with Micheál Ó Maoláin, and in 1922 he moved into a room on the North Circular Road. There is no special pleading or false representation of his circumstances in the autobiographies. However, he enjoyed one privilege over his Catholic neighbours: his Protestant connections provided the opportunity for regular employment and social advancement. He obtained jobs at Hampton and Leedom, Eason & Son, and the Great Northern Railway through his church connections. If he wished, he could have used these connections to obtain a manual job or a clerical position in a secure lower-middle-class establishment. Instead, he made a conscious choice to share the poverty of his fellow workers in the tenements and work as a labourer on the railways. He knew real poverty, rather than the bohemian poverty of the public school-educated George Orwell, as recorded in *Down and Out in Paris and London* or *The Road to Wigan Pier*. O'Casey was not an outsider or social scientist documenting the lives of the downtrodden. He had little time for the middle-class socialist do-gooders who attached themselves to the working-class movement. He always believed that Orwell was a bit of a fraud because he had the option of returning to the comfort of his upper-middle-class existence if life in the slums became unbearable.

O'Casey may have shaken the dust of time from the shoulders of history, but he has left us with six volumes that deal in a fictionalised truth rather than basic facts as he recounts the troubled years of his life. If challenged, O'Casey always defended the historical accuracy of the books and backed it up with chapter and verse. In a letter to a friend in 1952, he comments on the alleged inaccuracies: 'Bar the obvious fantasy, they are an accurate portrayal of men and things, there with you and here with me'.[27] The critics may not have been receptive to O'Casey's style, but Ireland paid him the supreme compliment of banning the first two volumes of his autobiography. There is nothing fake in the modernist style of O'Casey. The biblical tradition of parable and metaphor, either stated or implied, is also utilised to gain access to the truth in a way that a realistic statement is incapable of doing. There are no dates in the autobiographies; sometimes, the events he describes are transposed in time and place. He moved beyond the limits of the confessional autobiography and strayed into the arena of memoir and the autobiographical novel that we take for granted today. The autobiographies are part of his literary output rather than a simple retelling of his past life. In the Irish autobiographical canon, the twentieth century is framed by James Joyce's *Portrait of the Artist as a Young Man* (1916), Tomás Ó Criomhthain's *An tOileánach* (1929) and John McGahern's *Memoir* (2005). Within this continuum, few writers have equalled O'Casey's achievement, yet the autobiographies remain a relatively unexplored resource languishing on the fringes of the academic world. In the last volume, *Sunset and Evening Star*, published in 1954, O'Casey, isolated in Devon, had little left to say. It is a commentary on the world rather than a recollection by someone who was part of the significant events he describes. Even if the quality of the writing falls away in the last two volumes, all six volumes deserve consideration and a distinguished place in the annals of Irish literature.

THE *LETTERS*

O'Casey was a prolific letter writer and spent a good portion of his week replying to his correspondence. Some were of a business nature, but mostly it was letters to friends and strangers across the world. David Krause, the editor of O'Casey's *Collected Letters*, amassed almost 2,500 letters in the four volumes published between 1975 and 1992. There must be hundreds more, especially from his early life, which have not survived. Many of the letters are to prominent literary and political figures such as W.B. Yeats, G.B. Shaw, Lady Gregory and Jack Carney. Most of the letters are to ordinary people who wrote to him, sometimes in anger but mostly in admiration; people who became both his private and a necessary audience during the years when his plays were seldom performed: 'He revealed a remarkable self-portrait in his letters, in which his life emerges as a work of art'.[28]

There are very few letters up to the time he left Dublin in 1926. Almost all the letters from that period were to newspapers or magazines concerning the various political campaigns that concerned him. There are only thirteen letters from November 1921 to July 1924, one of the most intense periods in modern Irish history. These few letters are interesting from a literary point of view as they deal with his relations with the Abbey Theatre. However, there are few references to the momentous political events that were taking place around him. Regardless of this gap, his letters are important, mainly because his private correspondence has a freshness and immediacy that is generally lacking in books and articles that are by their nature more reflective and structured. At times, the 'public' O'Casey displayed a monumental lack of fear, never rushing into an argument until he was sure it was to his detriment. Hardly a year passed in which he was not involved in one acerbic controversy or another. Nevertheless, the 'private' O'Casey, 'more gentle, more compassionate, more tolerant and more generous', is also revealed in these letters.[29] They provide a self-portrait of O'Casey that is informal and unguarded but also, at times, quite vitriolic. They reveal O'Casey himself as the most striking and eloquent character he ever created. In the latter part of his life, he must have been aware that his letters would be open to public scrutiny, but there is no sense in the letters that O'Casey had one eye on the future or any element of self-consciousness that the world might be reading over his shoulder. When asked by an American teacher who wished to publish a selection of his letters if he wanted to censor or modify any of his private views, O'Casey replied with characteristic candour: 'I don't fear anything I've written, though I might laugh ruefully at a lot of it ... However the foolish things I've done, said, or written, are part of the living man, and should not be concealed so as to suggest infallibility'.[30]

Even in his last years, he replied at great length to a number of American postgraduate students and future biographers such as Ronald Ayling and David Krause, answering their 'flock of questions' regarding his early life and work. Those letters also contain, sometimes at great length, his reflections on politics, the church, Ireland, communism, and the latest books and plays that had come his way. In an extensive letter to Ronald Ayling in 1960, he outlined how he saw the world after his return from the United States and his visit to Ireland in 1935:

> Then my thoughts were far away, for I had been in close touch with Moscow and new hopes were centered on what would eventually happen in China – the Red Flag was flying high, if not in Ireland, in many, many other parts of the world. The fight in Ireland was now entirely different; it was to be against the reactionary Labour Leaders, the clergy, Prot[estant] and Cath[olic], the bigger business men – the last by no means the worst now. The comrades didn't understand this; they did criticise the Lab[our] Leaders and Business men, but left the Clergy alone.[31]

The four volumes of letters are also a valuable resource in tracing O'Casey's development as a dramatist and his conception of the theatre as an art form.[32]

O'Casey's letters to journals and newspapers in Ireland, England, America and the Eastern bloc countries are an invaluable source for historians of the twentieth century. His letters exposing the reactionary role of the Catholic Church in Ireland were written over forty years before the revelations concerning the abuse of women in the Magdalene laundries and the scandals of sexual abuse by the clergy came into the public domain:

> I have many friends in Ireland, but they live in unsettling conditions, in which it is hard to speak one's mind in the nature of thought beyond the accepted rule and order of the Roman Catholic Church. Most of the Bishops there are of the Mindszenty type, arrogant, dominating, expecting instant obedience to every little thing they may say, even to the choosing of a site for a school.[33]

His letters to the *Irish Worker* in 1913 and to Jack Carney, an official in the Workers' Union of Ireland and a close friend of Jim Larkin, provide a real insight into Irish labour history. A typical gossipy letter to Jack Carney in 1943 talks about the war, the USSR, the Vatican's attitude to Charles de Gaulle and the situation in Ireland:

> Have you heard from Jim [Larkin] since he became a T.D.? Is the new Lord Mayor any good? And Mick Colgan seeking a seat in the Senate. How he used to mock me when I wheeled from the O'Tooles towards Liberty Hall! And Sean O'Faolain studying Marx – so Mr Daiken says. I'd like to think it was all due to a love of Labour; but I doubt it. Colgan's probably looking for a nice comfortable seat; & O'Faolain is feeling the pressure of canons minor & major, shoving him out of the busy Catholic hive.[34]

Unfortunately, his friendship with Jack Carney ended in 1949 in a row over the role of Michael Quill, the president of the Transport Workers' Union in New York. Carney had asked O'Casey to sign a copy of his autobiography and dedicate it to Quill. O'Casey refused:

> Afraid I can't sign one for Michael J. Quill who very recently sold out according to reports from America the Busmen's demand for a bigger wage. He has been accused by the men of doing what he shouldn't have done, suddenly agreeing with the employers' proposals, so that the men had no alternative but to go back, without their demands being satisfied.[35]

Quill was a member of the Communist Party in the 1930s but had turned 'Cold War warrior' during the red-baiting McCarthyite period. In 1948 he banned communists or their supporters from holding office in the Transport Union, which was also a factor in O'Casey's decision. Carney felt let down by his refusal, and their correspondence ended shortly afterwards.

O'Casey never hesitated about firing off a letter to a newspaper or magazine if he felt his work had been slighted or misrepresented. The tragedy of his break with the Abbey Theatre over their rejection of *The Silver Tassie* was played out in the British and Irish newspapers at O'Casey's insistence. His letters to Yeats and especially Lady Gregory in the years that followed make painful reading, especially given his admiration and love for Lady Gregory. On the other hand, the letters O'Casey sent to strangers across the world – to students, priests, housewives, young women, struggling writers, and a host of unknown correspondents – reveal his generosity of spirit. His letters are also a running commentary on the most traumatic fifty years of the twentieth century. His *Letters* and *Autobiography* deserve a place on the bookshelf of every scholar of Irish literature and history, yet today they languish in the academic broom cupboard, neglected and unloved.

CHAPTER 18

Politics, Art and Literature

All great works of art or literature must be assessed primarily on their artistic merit; that is the function of aesthetics. However, any discussion of Seán O'Casey's drama inevitably breaks out of the realm of aesthetics and into the realm of politics. Henri Matisse remarked that 'all art bears the imprint of its historical epoch, but that great art is that in which this imprint is most deeply marked'.[1] Seán O'Casey wrote for a purpose, and his work bears the imprint of its time and place; therefore, it is legitimate to ask political questions about his work. He wrote of the tensions and contradictions between public and private emotions in times of war and civil strife and the use of violence for political means and its tragic consequences.

Modern revisionism starts from the concept that we have arrived at the end of history, and history is revised to justify the status quo. O'Casey saw it differently – he questioned Irish history because he believed the outcome was still uncertain. The seventy-fifth and the hundredth anniversaries of the 1916 Rising gave rise to a debate among historians and politicians about the legacy or legitimacy of the event.[2] Roy Foster, the most coherent and eloquent of the revisionists, has suggested in his book *Modern Ireland: 1600–1972* that the Easter Rising was an exercise in irrationality and that the legacy of 1916 was the sectarian violence in Northern Ireland that reignited in 1968.[3] On the other hand, the historian John A. Murphy has consistently rejected the idea that defending the ideals of the 1916 generation and the legitimacy of the rebellion either inspired the violence in the North of Ireland or legitimised the modern IRA. Since the ending of the Troubles in Northern Ireland, much of the heat has gone out of the revisionist debate. However, the extended debate on revisionism damaged O'Casey's reputation. He was caught up in the crossfire of this exchange and not just by the conservative element in this debate. More than any other writer, O'Casey has been subject to an insidious political axe-grinding by sections of the left and the republican movement to justify their own entrenched positions. Rather than take on his political critique of nationalism, his dramatic vision has been subject to a sustained intellectual attack. The

Dublin plays were faulted for their lack of balance, formalism, photographic realism, reductionism, and an artistic acceptance of outmoded forms. The core argument by the nationalists was that 'the theatrical paradigms established by O'Casey were not ones equipped to meet the demands of the contemporary situation in the North'.[4] Many of his post-colonial critics insist that 'O'Casey never sees or at least never presents in his plays any understanding of the important role played by nationalist ideology' in Irish politics.[5] But that is precisely what O'Casey was warning about – how nationalism had dominated Irish politics to the exclusion of class politics.

Joe Cleary is one of the many writers who suggested that during the period of the Troubles, given O'Casey's status and engagement with nationalist politics, many dramatists would have looked to O'Casey as a model. Cleary argued, however, that it was 'a mode that would prove disabling'.[6] Seamus Deane also considered that O'Casey's drama did not fit the political demands of the Northern Ireland situation after the outbreak of the Troubles in 1969: 'if we are to conceive our present political situation in terms suitable for the theatre, we must do so by submitting to the demands of the situation, rather than envisaging it in the light of O'Casey'. Deane, as with so many other critics, criticised the outdated portrayal in O'Casey's work of the contrast between the sentimental humanity of women and the militarism of men.[7] However, this negative critique was answered by both Rónán McDonald and Nicholas Grene, who suggested that '*The Plough* represents a reaction to revolution which is not counter-revolutionary in political intention'. Grene went on to say that it counters the unifying and idealising 'thrust of the narrative of the Rising as a national icon'.[8]

In a Field Day publication during the discussion on revisionism in the early 1990s, Declan Kiberd, one of Ireland's few public intellectuals, was exceptionally critical of O'Casey.[9] He claimed that O'Casey's 'self-justification' marred the artistic balance of *The Plough and the Stars*, and as a former member of the ICA, 'He may have felt the usual survivor guilt of one who took no part in the war. He recoiled, for honourable reasons, from the carnage, but the natural aggression that remained unpurged in his personality was finally vented on the rebels in his play'.[10] Kiberd's statement was a rehash of a similar accusation made earlier by C. Desmond Greaves.[11] O'Casey may have had mixed feelings or been uncertain about whether or not he should have joined his former comrades on the barricades. However, Greaves and Kiberd are mistaken about survivor guilt, which implies a psychological anguish that impaired his ability to make an assessment of the rising. In the letters O'Casey sent to comrades interned in Britain in the immediate aftermath of the rising, there is no sense of guilt or regret about not participating in the rebellion or any condemnation of the rebels' actions. Instead, he speaks admiringly of his friends and they, in turn, appreciated the letters and the support that he expressed.[12] Kiberd is also mistaken in his claim that O'Casey resigned from the ICA over the issue of uniforms. The way O'Casey ridicules the Foresters' uniform[13] worn by Uncle Peter in *The Plough and the Stars* as something 'gone asthray out of a toyshop' is a statement that related to an important debate that had taken place prior to the 1916 Rising.[14] O'Casey was among a number of activists at the time who mocked the Foresters' uniform as pretentious fancy dress, suggesting that uniforms marked out the members of the ICA as enemy targets.

Kiberd accused O'Casey of distorting the evidence and suggested that the popularity of *The Plough and the Stars* in the 1970s and '80s was not just because of the 'brilliant productions by Joe Dowling and Garry Hynes, but mainly because it was touted by the designer-Stalinists who have so successfully impoverished the contemporary debate about the past'.[15] The designer-Stalinists of the Workers' Party may have latched on to O'Casey as a stick with which to beat the Provisional IRA; however, O'Casey's work has not only survived the demise of the Workers' Party as a significant force on the left but has subsequently enjoyed a minor renaissance. It is perfectly valid to question O'Casey's politics and the representation of republican values in *The Plough and the Stars*, but to suggest that because of this representation the play is artistically unbalanced is both unfair and mistaken.

Declan Kiberd took a second look at O'Casey in his essay 'After the Revolution: O'Casey and O'Flaherty'. Kiberd wrote this in the aftermath of the Good Friday agreement, which ended the latest phase of the Troubles in Northern Ireland. He deals with *Juno and the Paycock*, both in terms of its reception by the Free State audience in 1924 and its contemporary relevance. This is an insightful essay that is still critical of aspects of the play but recognises its strengths as well. Kiberd's ability to be both profound and accessible to readers beyond academia is to be admired. His essay is an assessment of the post-revolutionary disillusionment at the heart of O'Casey's *Juno and the Paycock* and Liam O'Flaherty's novel *The Informer*. Kiberd defends the republican tradition by suggesting that O'Casey's point was that 'nationalism rather than real republicanism has triumphed, and with it the self-interest of the propertied class'.[16] Kiberd's insights into the political and dramatic impact of the play seem to vindicate O'Casey's ambition: 'The family as metaphor for the state is clearly implied, but in terms that mock the Free State ... An audience might laugh at Boyle's swagger only to realize that it was chortling at the fundamental contradiction that disfigured its own state'.[17] The fact that O'Casey had taken an axe to the smug complacency of the Free State would have been evident to the ministers, officials and their hangers-on who attended the first night of *Juno* or *The Plough and the Stars* in the 1920s. Kiberd suggested that *Juno* is 'O'Casey's darkest play', one that lays bare all that is wrong with the world, but that O'Casey is less clear in implying what he stands for. O'Casey exposes the irrelevance of the nationalists and the impotency of the workers, but he never takes it one step further to 'raise questions about the entire social system which gives rise to such blindness'. Kiberd pays tribute to the energy of the language and the style that 'carries hope of a redeeming perspective on things'.[18] Undoubtedly, there are problems with the political aspects of the Dublin plays; O'Casey was not rigorous enough in measuring up to the exacting questions raised in the plays about the outcome of that exciting decade.

Joe Cleary, in *Outrageous Fortune*, reiterates many of the criticisms of O'Casey put forward by post-colonial theorists such as Seamus Deane and Declan Kiberd. However, Cleary's book has the advantage of being written after the ending of the Troubles and is, therefore, able to take a more global and considered view of O'Casey's drama. Secondly, he locates it at the centre of the grittier naturalist response to the romantic revivalism of the previous period. Cleary contends, with justification, that O'Casey's political position in the Dublin plays is not intellectually robust. He goes on to say: 'there are no characters from one end of the cycle to the other who are allowed the mental capacity to wrestle with such issues'.[19] O'Casey took Lady Gregory's advice about concentrating on character too literally. He was determined to avoid the mistakes that mar *The Harvest Festival*, which is little more than a Shavian-style debate on stage. However, his emphasis on characterisation leaves the Dublin plays open to the criticism that they lack intellectual robustness or political resolution.

The starting point for any political critique of the Dublin plays is to accept that O'Casey was presenting the 1916 Rising and the subsequent War of Independence as the historical progression of the 1913 lockout. O'Casey was attempting to reflect the reality of the newly independent Free State. Nationalism had failed to deliver for the masses on the potential for radical social advancement that the working-class struggle of 1913, the socially progressive content of the 1916 Proclamation, and the Democratic Programme of 1919 envisaged. However, a new generation of scholars, freed from the shackles of the revisionist debate, working on the borders between literature and history, such as Susan Cannon Harris, Victor Merriman, Paul Murphy, James Moran and Michael Pierse, who are not wedded to a nationalist interpretation of O'Casey's work, have highlighted the role of class politics in O'Casey's drama, which has opened up new and interesting avenues of debate.[20]

POLITICS AND DRAMA

C. Desmond Greaves' book *Sean O'Casey: Politics and art* (1979) was the first full-length and extensive analysis of the relationship between O'Casey's politics and his work.[21] The fact that it was published by Lawrence & Wishart, the British Communist Party publishers, added to its political significance. However, Greaves' critique of O'Casey displays little understanding of his politics and even less of his art. Greaves presents O'Casey as an ultra-leftist in politics, an 'artistic type' who 'could hold no more than one idea in his head at a time'.[22] According to Greaves, O'Casey's politics consisted of a linear development starting with his militant Protestantism, then the Gaelic League, the Irish Republican Brotherhood, Larkinism, a long period of disillusionment with republicanism, and finally, his support for the Communist Party. Each shift necessitated the negation of the one that preceded it, which proved that O'Casey was a classic 'ultra-leftist unconcerned with the actual wrongs that people are trying to right' and that he had an 'exaggerated concern with objectives that cannot immediately be attained'.[23] Greaves believed that the wellspring of O'Casey's drama and autobiographical writings was his attempt to rearrange history and his personal life to retrospectively justify his decision not to participate in the 1916 Rising. However, Jack Mitchell and Robert Lowery demolished Greaves' crude reductionist interpretation of O'Casey over many issues in the pages of the *Seán O'Casey Review* and the *O'Casey Annual*.[24] They believed that a work of art should not be judged by political imperatives alone. They maintained that artists and writers must be free to explore their unique perspective on life and suggested that a more lenient set of guidelines should be used to judge their work.

Elsewhere, the political and critical response to O'Casey's drama has always been provisional and uncertain. Internationally, his reputation has both suffered and prospered, according to circumstances. In Britain in the 1950s and '60s, despite O'Casey's association with the radical Unity

Theatre group, the heavyweights of the intellectual left were dismissive of his work. Raymond Williams, a father figure of British critical theory, took exception to the way O'Casey used song, alliteration, colour and sentimental melodrama to invoke emotional involvement by the audience. Williams went on to say that the misplaced comedy in O'Casey's drama was nothing more than a degenerate artistic form of naturalistic caricature, though he did acknowledge that the second act of *The Silver Tassie* is 'one of the most remarkable written in English' in the twentieth century.[25] A fellow socialist and critic, Francis Mulhern, implied that *The Plough and the Stars* was just a demoralised interpretation of the 1916 Rising that O'Casey could not artistically define.[26] However, Williams wrote a more favourable and balanced assessment of O'Casey's drama in his 1968 essay 'O'Casey: The rhetoric and the reality'.[27]

French audiences rejected *The Plough and the Stars* in the late 1940s because they considered it mocked the integrity of the resistance fighters during the Second World War. On the other hand, in the late 1950s, during the Algerian War of Independence, O'Casey's work gained acceptance by that section of French society opposed to the occupation. In the 1960s, O'Casey's work was popular in French regional theatres during the period of cultural renewal, instigated by the socialist minister for culture, André Malraux.[28] In Korea in the 1930s, despite the censorship during the Japanese occupation, O'Casey was regarded 'as a subversive and innovative playwright on the colonial scene by virtue of being appropriated by Yu Chi-jin, who used O'Casey's plays as models when creating his own works'.[29] The radical Spanish playwright Alfonso Sastre, working within the constraints imposed by the Franco dictatorship, created Spanish versions of O'Casey's *Red Roses for Me* (1969) and *The Shadow of a Gunman* (1973) as a way of evading censorship and calling for political change in Spain.[30] In the 1970s, the Iranian director Kazem Shahryari's production of *The Shadow of a Gunman* landed him in jail as the Shah's secret police detected parallels with the political situation in Iran.[31] And a Finnish production of *The Plough and the Stars* in 1972 rewrote the ending to indicate the continuity of the nationalist struggle in light of the IRA campaign in Northern Ireland.[32]

As early as 1931, the *Irish Worker* reported that 'the plays of Sean O'Casey are having a wonderful success in Germany'.[33] In the 1950s and '60s, as the English-speaking world turned away from O'Casey, German productions added to his reputation and consolidated his position as an innovative writer of international standing.[34] However, given the Cold War climate, it was not surprising that there were two fundamentally different approaches to O'Casey's work. East Berlin, and in particular Brecht's theatre, welcomed him because of their shared political philosophy. In West Germany, even though the acclaimed director Peter Zadek championed his drama, his work was not without controversy.[35] The Schiller Theatre's production of *The Silver Tassie* caused an uproar in June 1953 when it opened in West Berlin, just three days after the workers' uprising against the Stalinist regime in East Berlin. The innovative and unconventional staging provoked protests and controversy among an audience still scarred by the atrocities of the war. The disturbances were among the worst episodes in modern German theatre as an anti-Semitic and Nazi element in the audience shouted down the performance.[36] Ten years later, another production of the same play in West Berlin encountered hostility, which was not surprising given the anti-war theme of the play during the heightened Cold War atmosphere over the construction of the Berlin Wall. In 1968, a production of *The Star Turns Red* in the Wuppertal Opera House in West Germany resulted in walkouts and noisy interruptions by the audience. The local mayor demanded that the production should be halted, and denounced O'Casey as a supporter of communism.[37] Despite these problems, German productions explored how his plays, particularly his post-Dublin drama, could be staged. Given the tradition of Brecht and the Berliner Ensemble, and the technical abilities of German theatre, they were able to highlight the way O'Casey integrated the tragic and the comic in order to explore human relations on a more personal level. *Purple Dust*, which was staged by the Berliner Ensemble in 1966 and ran in repertory for twelve years, showed O'Casey's stagecraft at its best. Hans-Georg Simmgen wrote about how these productions, though perhaps overstating the case, were a development of the 'creative and critical element of Brecht's theatre work', and how O'Casey's plays would remain a measuring rod for the development of the modern theatre.[38] For about thirty years from the 1950s, theatres in East and West Germany fostered an interest in O'Casey's drama. Over 100 productions of his work, mainly in East Germany, were staged during that time, including most of the post-Dublin plays.[39] Sadly, this was not the case in the city of his birth. Dublin had turned its back on one of the finest playwrights it ever produced.

Seán O'Casey was one of the most innovative and thoughtful dramatists of the twentieth century, and it is interesting to reflect on his struggle to develop a synthesis between politics, form and content that paralleled European developments in drama. Like Brecht, O'Casey set himself against 'Tragic Theatre' because he believed that 'nothing human can possibly be outside the powers of humanity'.[40] Perhaps 'optimistic tragedy' is a better description of his work; inherent in the death or defeat of his working-class heroes and anti-heroes is the possibility of progress.

Modernism was the artistic response to the political and cultural crisis that overwhelmed the first decades of the century, and for a time, political and artistic expression seemed to fit together. Modernism was a reaction to the old Victorian order and a rebellion against the idea of art as a commodity. Unfortunately, in the last years of his life, O'Casey recoiled from any form of theatre that disengaged entirely from economic or utilitarian issues. His final essay is a polemic against the 'theatre of decay and despair', in which he fulminates against Antonin Artaud's Theatre of Cruelty, Eugène Ionesco, Harold Pinter and Joe Orton, whom he felt, in Lukács' memorable phrase, had taken up residence in the 'Grand Hotel Abyss':[41]

> Artaud! Artaud!
> Pounding a play to a wordless thesis
> Beating up life into bloody pieces.[42]

He had no time for what he called 'This Filthy Theatre argument' or 'The Theatre of Pessimism as they call it'. He likened their world to 'an oyster with nothing in it',[43] although he excused Beckett and Brecht, as they had an element of life in them and were poets as well as playwrights. His isolation in Devon meant that O'Casey encountered the plays of Beckett, Artaud or Ionesco as literature rather than experiencing them as living theatre. This may be one of the reasons why he was so dismissive of some of the most influential writers who transformed drama in the latter half of the twentieth century. The minimalist theatre of Beckett, or what has been termed 'Anti-Theatre', espoused a drama without sympathetic characters in a specific situation. O'Casey was a weaver of words, a storyteller rather than a minimalist in the modern style. Even though O'Casey professed an inability to understand or relate to the new departures in drama, there are a number of minor influences in his later plays, for example the language, structure and technique of Antonin Artaud and the dramatic practice of Eugène Ionesco.[44]

The Marxist philosopher Georg Lukács' attack on modernism found a resonance among many of the writers and artists who were influenced by Soviet cultural theorists.[45] O'Casey stood apart from this trend and understood, more than most, how art could be part of the attempt to change the course of history without descending into determinism or abstract propaganda. Other artists and writers, influenced by the Communist

Party, simply desired to dramatise the struggles of the labour movement. Their concepts were practical rather than aesthetic, showing little formal interest in literature and art. Instead of truth and beauty, they concentrated on class struggle. In this, they were influenced by the work of the early Russian agitprop groups such as the Blue Blouses, who coined the phrase 'A propertyless theatre for the propertyless class'.[46] In the 1930s, the left enjoyed a level of influence over the production of mainstream literature and drama. By the end of the decade, that influence was mainly at an end as many artists and writers refused to accept the political and artistic twists and turns demanded by the Communist Party.[47] O'Casey, to his credit, never allowed the CPGB any influence over his work and was, therefore, little affected by the cleavage between literature and politics that continued up to the 1960s as the threads that bound artistic production and left-wing politics began to unravel. He continued his search for a form and technique that could express his socialist politics without compromising the aesthetic value of the work. Human failure is a theme that runs throughout much of his plays. However, his writing also suggests the need for mechanisms for social change, though we should be careful and avoid the temptation of just seeing his work as an extension of his politics. He constantly, though not always successfully, tried to avoid what Walter Benjamin called 'having a message in readiness'.[48] We get a sense of a writer who rose above the loyalties of the battered and discredited politics of Stalinism and its aftermath and created a literature of lasting value.

The emergence of the New Left in the 1960s, untainted by the legacy of Stalinism, forced politics back into the literary and artistic arena. The revolutionary upheavals subsequent to the events of May 1968 saw an explosion of writing, publishing and drama, which blurred the distinction between politics and aesthetics.[49] Groups such as the Project Arts Centre in Dublin, 7:84 and Kartoon Klowns in Britain, feminist theatre and black theatre looked back to the tradition of the 1930s using techniques such as agitprop to reach out to an audience in factories and communities, which traditionally did not frequent the conventional theatre. This form of political theatre was responding to a historical moment, making few demands on writers to work or write in a particular way. However, given the distrust from the past, the issue of the relationship between politics and aesthetics could not be ignored. Alongside these developments, writers such as Harold Pinter and Seamus Heaney defended the independence of art and claimed that their work had no obligation other than to itself. The outbreak of the Troubles in Ireland in the late 1960s tested Heaney's resolve in this matter. For Heaney, the challenge was not just to write a satisfactory verse but to find images and symbols that represented and responded to a community under siege.[50] These pressures led to the founding of the Field Day theatre and publishing company in 1980 as a cultural and intellectual response to the political crisis in Northern Ireland.

O'Casey was always clear about the difference between his contributions to political newspapers or magazines and his dramatic work. Theoretically, his contribution to the debate on the relationship between literature and politics was slight, but a selection of his essays on the theatre, collected in two books published after his death, are still of interest.[51] They reflect his attempt to develop both a form and a technique that was in step with the changing historical context and the range of content matter he dealt with during his career. O'Casey understood more than most of his generation that 'art never follows a flag'.[52] Ireland was for him an endless conflict of love and hate and of fulfilment and failure, and that conflict is what makes his work so interesting and at times so contradictory. Unlike his friend the Scottish poet Hugh MacDiarmid, O'Casey could never be accused of painting nationalism red. To avoid the sentimental image of Ireland peddled by the remnants of the Irish literary revival, he tried to infuse his later work with a modernist awareness.

CULTURE AND SOCIETY

The debates over the relationship between literature and politics, the role played by culture within a capitalist society, and the moral duty of a writer in an epoch of extreme crisis were issues that exercised the progressive movement during the 1930s. Unfortunately, the debate became polarised between those who supported the cultural policy of the Soviet Union under Stalin and those who believed that while art should and must respond to the historical and social context of its time, artistic production must also be allowed a high degree of autonomy. Alick West, a former student of Trinity College Dublin, wrote of the tension between culture and propaganda that dominated much of the debate in the 1930s. In his autobiography, commenting on this relationship, West wrote what is perhaps the best summary of that debate:

> In this sense it was true that culture is a weapon in the fight for socialism. But the truth depended on recognition of the greater truth that socialism is a weapon in the fight for culture. For our final aim

> was not the establishment of a political and economic structure, but the heightening of human life. Without this recognition, the slogan becomes a perversion of the truth, since it degraded culture into a means to a political end.[53]

George Orwell was one of the few left-wing writers of the period who understood that the relationship between art and politics was a historical question that could not be defined dogmatically but changed according to the circumstances of the time. In the 1930s, Orwell put the case for political commitment: 'if Fascism triumphs, I am finished as a writer'.[54] Writing within that tradition and in those specific circumstances, O'Casey produced his most openly political and agitational work, *The Star Turns Red* (1939) and *Oak Leaves and Lavender* (written in 1944 and published in 1946). They were a direct response to the political imperatives of the time; whether they can survive cut free from their historical context is another matter.

O'Casey, to his credit, stood with dramatists such as Ernst Toller, who declared that 'as a writer I speak to all who are prepared to listen, regardless of what party or group they belong to. The idea is more important to me than the slogan.'[55] Despite the best efforts of a section of the Workers' Theatre Movement to present itself as part of the modernist movement, many of the plays written and produced in the 1930s lacked dramatic content. That is not to say, as some right-wing commentators assert, that art and literature are one thing and propaganda another. Over the last hundred years or so, the relationship between politics and art has been a contentious and challenging issue for political activists considering a critical response to a work of art. Where does the balance lie between a political assessment of a work of art and an aesthetic one? The difficulty with the critical response in matters of art and literature, favoured by the Communist Party from the 1930s onwards, is that several of the most influential writers of the twentieth century, such as Yeats, Eliot and Pound, were politically on the right and in some cases supporters of fascism. A more nuanced view understood that their political opinions may have diminished the individual, but not the work. Secondly, a great deal of modernist writing does not lend itself to a political reading because of the way it rejects historicism or causality, emphasising instead essence and feeling and the distorted reality behind outward appearance.

A chasm in politics and social values separated the modernist movement from the realist literature of the nineteenth century.[56] Several Marxist literary theorists, influenced by Stalinist conceptions, were unable to deal with these innovations in style and form by writers such as James Joyce or T.S. Eliot. Karl Radek's denunciation of Joyce's *Ulysses* at the Soviet Writers' Congress in 1934 as an example of the 'decay of world capitalist literature' set the tone for what was to come:

> His basic feature is the conviction that there is nothing big in life – no big events, no big people, no big ideas; and the writer can give a picture of life by just taking 'any given hero on any given day,' and reproducing him with exactitude. A heap of dung, crawling with worms, photographed by a cinema apparatus through a microscope such is Joyce's work ... I wish to say to Soviet and foreign writers: 'Our way does not lie through Joyce, but along the high-road of socialist realism'.[57]

Radek and the ultra-realists presented Joyce as the whipping boy of modernism without understanding that the challenge of Joyce's work is to appreciate how so much seems exclusively aesthetic while at the same time it is also profoundly historical. Or that Joyce's work emerged from the historical context of the colonial relationship between Britain and Ireland while simultaneously managing to achieve a cosmopolitan outlook.[58] How all of this stood with O'Casey is difficult to judge, nor do we know whether he was even aware of the Soviets' denunciation of Joyce's work. Nevertheless, he never wavered in his admiration for Joyce, either publicly or privately:

> The glimpses of influence given in the biography were more of a desire to show my admiration for this great writer; as a symbol of standing by one who was being attacked on all sides; banned by the nation and publisher, yet unshaken and supreme in his glorious and God-given integrity.[59]

Any attempt to silence his fellow writers and artists, whether the attack came from the right or the left, was fiercely resisted by O'Casey. His condemnation of the 'concrete shelter' style of Soviet literature in 1946 was as forceful as anything published at the time: 'There isn't any doubt in my mind that the concrete shelter is as bad as the ivory tower; worse, in fact, for the ivory tower keeps in faint touch with present life, but the walls of a concrete shelter are too thick to hear even a whisper of it'.[60] O'Casey always understood that his political involvement was a civic or moral duty and the writing of drama was his vocation. His concept was not art as propaganda, but politics as a vision of a new way of life. In all his work, after he left Ireland, he attempted to defend the values of spontaneity, experimentation, artistic quality, and the writer's independence from dogma. In other words, his work was in no sense an instrument of propaganda for this or that political ideology or party but was something that had an innate connection to the fate of humanity and an active and committed attachment to its place and time.

Alan Simpson has suggested that O'Casey's plays, as social documents, with some exceptions, are still relevant if they are staged to highlight 'for contemporary audiences the universal truths contained in the plays'.[61] However, Garry Hynes' production of *The Plough and the Stars* in 1991 found little favour with the critics. She broke with the traditional Abbey production by paring down the stage to the bare minimum and using black curtains as a backdrop. Most of the actors had shaved heads, and the pale white make-up exaggerated their features.[62] Hynes' attempt to restore the politics, poverty and violence to the play did not please the critics: 'The *Irish Times* wrote of a "palpable sense of disappointment" and the *Sunday Independent* was more excoriating about "Brechtian" techniques.'[63] However, the production was a sell-out, and the public, or at least the more progressive elements, responded positively to it.

In the *New York Times*, Walter Kerr, writing about the later plays, said that many of his supporters believe 'that they were just waiting for a production or interpretation that will reveal them as masterpieces'.[64] He was, however, doubtful if that was the case. Paul Kerryson, who directed the Dublin trilogy in 1992 at the Leicester Haymarket in England, expressed similar doubts: 'His later plays showed him to be ahead of his time, but I don't think they have anything in particular to say today'.[65] Other dramatists who looked at the totality of his work saw it differently, including Arnold Wesker, Shelagh Delaney and John Livings in Britain; Arthur Miller and Lorraine Hansberry in America; Augusto Boal in Brazil; Brendan Behan, John Arden, Roddy Doyle and the Sheridan brothers at the Project Theatre in Dublin. Brian Friel spoke for a generation when writing about O'Casey: 'We all came out from under his overcoat'.[66] More than any other theatre, the Abbey owes O'Casey, and the world, the chance to find out. In *Six Characters in Search of an Author*, Luigi Pirandello dramatises the efforts of six characters in search of an author to finish their story. O'Casey is the author of at least six plays in search of an audience.

O'CASEY IN THE COMMUNITY

In 1981 Robert Lowery, reflecting on the controversies, bans and censorship that dogged O'Casey's drama, said that these incidents now overshadow the plays and that they could never again 'be performed without the controversies being reviewed and contemplated'.[67] The Dublin plays continue to be performed, although few theatre companies attempt to stage his more experimental drama. However, production techniques have caught up with O'Casey's imagination, and a new generation of directors and actors are exploring the underlying potential of his work, freed from the burden of history that has dominated, and in some cases overwhelmed, productions in the recent past. Directors are taking a fresh look at O'Casey, reinterpreting the plays rather than presenting them as traditional classics of the stage. The Druid Theatre Company's touring versions of three one-act plays by O'Casey at the end of 2021, *A Pound on Demand*, *Bedtime Story*, and *End of the Beginning*, while being innovative, managed to retain the social content contained in these comic dramas. In his programme notes, Thomas Conway suggested that these plays, in the way Druid projects them, may 'prove controversial once again' in the ongoing debate about 'the situation of women in post-"Repeal the Eighth" Ireland'.[68]

The ANU Theatre Group's production of *The Lost O'Casey* in 2018 reframed O'Casey's one-act play from 1924, *Nannie's Night Out*, as an unflinching examination of motherhood, addiction and Dublin's chronic housing crisis in a contemporary setting that points to a possible way forward for future productions or adaptions of these neglected plays.[69] In *The Lost O'Casey*, ANU channelled their rage against poverty and injustice in the spirit of O'Casey, but with a decidedly twenty-first-century edge. Both O'Casey's 1924 production of *Nannie's Night Out* and ANU's 2018 *The Lost O'Casey* 'forced audience members out of their comfort zone by confronting them with what they would prefer not to see: the unsettling reality of lives lived on the streets and behind the doors of tenement rooms or council flats'.[70]

Christina Reid's *Joyriders*, a tragicomedy about working-class life in west Belfast during the Troubles, was inspired by her visit to the Divis Community Centre and by the reaction of a group of teenagers on a youth training scheme who attended a production of *The Shadow of a Gunman*.[71] These teenagers had no preconceived ideas about the play but were amazed to see a marginalised and impoverished community under siege, not unlike their own, portrayed on the stage. Similarly, RTÉ's two-part documentary

O'Casey in the Estate portrays a group of striving actors from the East Wall area of Dublin as they rehearse for a once-off performance of *The Plough and the Stars* at the Abbey Theatre.[72] This was more than an amateur production. Through a process of rehearsal and discovery involving the wider community, the production became an exploration of their own situation and place in society. Hopefully, these productions herald an interest in O'Casey's work that goes beyond the academy or the conventional theatre. The work of critics like Victor Merriman or José Lanters offers new perspectives on how O'Casey's work can relate to the modern world and the institutional inequality that has ravaged marginalised communities and how they might utilise his work to channel their rage against a state that 'values economic over humanistic principles'.[73] Merriman suggests that: 'The contested reputation of the plays exposes critical prejudice entrenched around class, history, politics and the subordination of performance events to normative qualities owned and canonized by an elite social group'.[74] In these tentative twenty-first-century productions and explorations, local communities have looked to O'Casey to probe the issues that affect them. O'Casey was proud of the people he wrote about, and in these productions, few as they are, he has come home to the communities that nurtured him.

Epilogue

Disappointments and slights were a cross that O'Casey, like most writers, had to bear all his life, and his eightieth birthday was not without controversy. *The Ed Sullivan Show* on American TV intended to show a short film of a discussion between O'Casey and Barry Fitzgerald on St Patrick's Day. However, the film was cancelled when some 'Protestant and Catholic Irish groups' objected because they believed O'Casey was a 'rather shabby expression of Ireland'.[1] Despite this, he was not without friends. Letters poured in from all over the world, full of affection and admiration for his work. O'Casey would have gained comfort from the news that he was one of three nominees for the 1960 Nobel Prize for literature. Several universities, including Trinity College Dublin, offered to confer honorary doctorate degrees, all of which O'Casey politely refused.[2] Eighteen Irish writers, artists and actors, including Cyril and Maureen Cusack, James Plunkett, Francis MacManus and Milo O'Shea, offered to subscribe for a bed in the Children's Hospital in Dublin in O'Casey's name. O'Casey refused the offer because he believed that was the role of the state and 'a bed should be there for a need, not as a gift'.[3] Instead, they sent him a silver tankard or 'tassie' inscribed with their names, a gift he graciously accepted. Perhaps the finest tribute paid to O'Casey came from his fellow writer and exile, Samuel Beckett: 'To my great compatriot Sean O'Casey, from France where he is honoured, I send my enduring gratitude and homage'.[4] In the British New Year's honours list for 1963, the offer of a CBE (Commander of the Order of the British Empire) was understandably turned down as it was not to 'his nature or feeling'.[5] After his death in September 1964, he was finally honoured in his own land; a plaque was erected on the site in Dorset Street where he was born.[6] On the centenary of his birth in 1980, an Irish stamp was issued in his honour. In the United States, Congress issued a proclamation to honour 'Sean O'Casey: Visionary Playwright and Irish Patriot'.[7] More importantly, a number of trade unions and friends of O'Casey in the USA organised a 'Labor Salute to Sean O'Casey', all of which affirmed the affection that people had for him.

In 1964, the last year of his life, O'Casey lifted the ban on productions in Ireland to allow a trial run of the *Plough* and *Juno* by the Abbey Theatre in Dublin before transferring to London for a Festival of World Theatre honouring the 400th anniversary of Shakespeare's birth. Letters from Michael O'Riordan of the Communist Party in Ireland asking him to lift the ban and from his niece, Lorraine Beaver, undoubtedly softened his resolve.[8] In a letter written just days before he died, O'Casey gave permission for the Abbey Theatre company to perform *Juno and the Paycock* in Derry. The Catholic priest Father Edward Daly, who asked the Abbey to perform the play, was the same priest who, in a rare instance of ecumenism in Northern Ireland, had succeeded in persuading the Protestant bishop of Derry to attend a play by Brian Friel in a Catholic hall the previous year.[9] Towards the end of his life, O'Casey could see that changes were happening, and his deep-felt hopes for the future of Ireland shine through in his letter to Father Daly:

> Glad to hear the Protestant Bishop came to see a play in a Catholic Hall. Is this the beginning of the end of the stupid religious Apartheid in Ireland? I hope so, for Derry is as Irish as Cork or Cahirciveen. Let the Orange and Green flags fly over the Hall while the play is on.[10]

Despite lifting the ban just before he died, O'Casey did not enjoy a happy and carefree reunion with Ireland. Shortly after O'Casey's death in 1964, Tomás Mac Anna sent the script of *The Drums of Father Ned* to Ernest Blythe at the Abbey Theatre, suggesting that they should produce it. A few days later, the text was returned with the word 'Truflais!' scribbled on the front, or in English, 'Rubbish'.[11] Fortunately, Phyllis Ryan and Gemini Productions had no such reservations. They staged the play in 1966 in the Olympia Theatre to an appreciative audience, who were glad to see a new O'Casey play on the Dublin stage. In 1966 the Abbey Theatre invited President de Valera to open the new theatre building. In 1951, on the night the old Abbey Theatre building burned down, *The Plough and the Stars* was playing, and the directors proposed that the rebuilt Abbey should open with the same play to indicate the continuity between the old and the new building. However, the ever-cautious Ernest Blythe bowed to pressure and postponed the proposed production lest it offend de Valera and the other survivors of the 1916 Rising who would be in attendance. Instead, de Valera was treated to a harmless tableau, *Recall the Years*, by Walter Macken.[12]

EVENT-FILLED DAYS

O'Casey was uniquely placed to write about the working class because, almost alone of his literary generation, his background in the north Dublin tenements gave him access to that world. He created working-class characters that we now take for granted. O'Casey cut across the concept of the 'great men of history', who shape the world around them by their actions. In a piece in the *New York Times* in 1950, he reflected on *The Plough and the Stars*:

> If it has any 'significance' it is that a small number – or even one fine mind – may initiate a movement, but cannot bring it to success without the cooperation of what is called 'the common people'. The gallant men who rose in 1916 to strike for Ireland's independence were defeated, and what they stood for only succeeded when, years later, the people as a whole swung around from opposition to support.[13]

Dublin, like Berlin in the 1920s, represented the failure of nationalism to deliver on its promises. However, the political circumstances and potential of these two cities were quite different. If Brecht and his contemporaries articulated the capacity of modern urban men and women to throw off the concept of bourgeois individualism in favour of the technical achievements of egalitarianism, O'Casey articulated the position of the Irish working class left behind by history. Bernard Benstock, on the fiftieth anniversary of the staging of *The Plough and the Stars*, summed up the positive and the political possibilities inherent in O'Casey's dramatic vision:

> The limited and mean spirited, like Mrs Grigson and Jerry Devine and Uncle Peter, were left to flounder or atrophy or be washed away by the flood. Those with the sparks of courage shown by Minnie and Juno and Fluther Good shake off the dust of decay, rebel against parents and priests. Leave the dying towns, take over the reins of government, and if doomed to die prematurely, do so dancing.[14]

O'Casey believed that the fight against poverty was every bit as noble as the fight against the British. Writing to his old friend Jim Kavanagh in 1951, looking back on the times and the events they had shared, O'Casey said he was not ashamed or indeed unwilling to live them over again: 'It wasn't our fault that our work helped pave a smoother way for others to run to jobs, snobbery and all the opposite of what a Gaelic nation should be'.[15] There is no hint of bitterness, just an acknowledgement that, even though they failed, O'Casey and his comrades did what they could to bring about a better Ireland that cherished 'all of the children of the nation equally'.[16] He was one of the first writers to confront the fact that they had failed in that project. O'Casey's Dublin trilogy, written in the post-revolutionary period, explores the same dynamic as Toller's *Masses and Man* or Kaiser's *Gas II*, which registered the disillusionment they felt following the failure of the German Revolution at the end of the First World War and the collapse of their expectations and hopes.[17] The German revolutionary Karl Liebknecht defended the failed socialist revolution in 1919 by suggesting that 'there were defeats that were victories'; he could have been writing about the 1916 Rising. Liebknecht went on to say that there were also 'victories that were more fatal than defeats'.[18] For Seán O'Casey, the narrow-minded conservative state that emerged following the War of Independence and the Civil War was a 'victory' that felt like a defeat. In a letter written two years before his death to his old friend and comrade Barney Conway from the ITGWU, he reflected on those wonderful event-filled days:

> Each of us all the same, has had a full life, and passed through the glorious times when the workers of Ireland first declared themselves, struck out, and shook out and shook the bosses. Just think for a minute, Barney, on how we workers were then, living in squalid places, wretchedly paid, hard worked, not daring to say a word of protest against any of these evils. Then Jim Larkin came among us, and all became changed: the workers were on their feet, they had much to say for themselves, and they stood out to do battle. And right well and right long they fought; and you and I were among them, Barney. We, the workers, were on the march! The eloquent roaring voice of the great Jim Larkin became the trumpet of the Irish workers, ay, and of the English workers too, in his glorious Fiery Cross campaign. Just compare the weakness of the workers before Jim came with the strength of the workers today! We were the Pioneers of a resurgent Labour Movement, and, now, the workers are a power in every country under the warm or the cold sun. We helped to fashion this great power and position in life that the workers now have; we got scarred by how we had to live then, and by what we did, and so did our great and beloved Leader, Jim, but he was proud of all he did, and so are we, Barney; so are we.[19]

A fitting eulogy for a great writer, humanitarian and steadfast socialist.

Notes

(All online links were active at time of publication)

INTRODUCTION

1 Richard Watts Jr, *New York Post*, 7 August 1960.
2 Desmond Rushe, *The New York Times*, 13 July 1970.
3 Christopher Murray, *Seán O'Casey: Writer at work* (Dublin: Gill & Macmillan, 2004).
4 Quoted by Gerard Fay, *Guardian* (London), 21 September 1964.
5 Rónán McDonald, 'Sean O'Casey's Dublin Trilogy: Disillusionment to delusion', in Shaun Richards (ed.), *The Cambridge Companion to Twentieth-Century Irish Drama* (Cambridge: Cambridge University Press, 2006), pp. 136–49.
6 Bernice Schrank, *Sean O'Casey: A research and production handbook* (Westport, CT: Greenwood Press, 1996), p. 11. Maureen Malone, *The Plays of Sean O'Casey* (Carbondale: Southern Illinois University Press, 1969). See also Susan Cannon Harris, 'Red Star versus Green Goddess: Sean O'Casey's *The Star Turns Red* and the politics of form', *The Princeton University Library Chronicle*, vol. 68, nos 1–2, 2007, pp. 357–98. Modern criticism, with its emphasis on the meaning of texts, tends to dissolve the sense of history as a presence in literature and drama, and as a result lose contact with the historical and political context of the work.
7 Walter Benjamin, in Hannah Arendt (ed.), *Illuminations* (New York: Harcourt, Brace & World, 1968), pp. 47–8.
8 Pádraig Yeates, *The Irish Times*, 25 August 2003.
9 John Newsinger, 'Seán O'Casey, Larkinism and Literature', *Irish Studies Review*, vol. 12, no. 3, 2004, pp. 283–92. Mary E. Papke, 'Sean O'Casey's Early Plays as Larkinite Parables', *The Seán O'Casey Review*, vol. 3, no. 2, Spring 1977, pp. 105–11.
10 Paul Murphy, 'O'Casey and Class', in James Moran, *The Theatre of Seán O'Casey* (London: Bloomsbury Methuen Drama, 2013), pp. 227–38.
11 Shivaun O'Casey, Documentary, *Sean O'Casey: Under a coloured cap* (London: Green Crow Productions, 2004).
12 Heinrich August Winkler. *The Age of Catastrophe* (New Haven: Yale University Press, 2015).
13 Fredric Jameson, 'Reflections in Conclusion', in Theodor W. Adorno (ed.), *Aesthetics and Politics* (London: Verso, 1977), pp. 196–219.

CHAPTER 1: THE SHAKE OF THE BAG

1 O'Casey, *Autobiographies*, 1, p. 12. According to Shivaun O'Casey, 'Sean always said it was thirteen births' (interview with author, 2 June 2010).
2 He was christened John Casey. After he joined the Gaelic League, he changed his name to Sean O Cathasaigh, and subsequently to the more manageable Sean O'Casey.
3 O'Casey, *Autobiographies*, 1, p. 33.
4 Máirín Johnston, 'Priests and Proselytism in 19th Century Dublin', *Féile Zozimus*, vol. 1, 1992, pp. 61–6.
5 Christopher Murray, *Seán O'Casey: A writer at work* (Dublin: Gill & Macmillan, 2004), p. 13. The term 'souper' refers to the soup served up at bible classes by the Protestant evangelical societies.
6 *Irish Press*, 9 October 1936.

7 See Jacinta Prunty, *Managing the Dublin Slums 1850–1922* (Dublin: Dublin City Public Libraries, 2004). 'No matter how the figures are reworked and what excuses are made, the conclusion is unavoidable, Dublin city had the worst health record in the British Isles for the century before independence', p. 6.

8 Mollser is the tubercular (TB) young girl who dies of her illness near the end of the play and is representative of the horrific toll that TB took on the citizens of Dublin. Little Nell is a character from Charles Dickens, *The Old Curiosity Shop*.

9 *Report of the Departmental Committee into Housing Conditions of the Working Classes in the City of Dublin* (CD 7273), Parliamentary Papers, vol. 19, 1914.

10 Circular issued by British army and reprinted in *Workers' Republic*, 27 November 1915.

11 See Maria Luddy, *Prostitution and Irish Society 1880–1914* (Cambridge: Cambridge University Press, 2008).

12 George Bernard Shaw, *Plays: Pleasant and unpleasant* (London: Constable, 1924), vol. 1, p. xxv.

13 O'Casey, *Autobiographies*, 4, pp. 161–2.

14 James Connolly, in Donal Nevin (ed.), *Between Comrades: Letters and correspondence 1889–1916* (Dublin: Gill & Macmillan, 2008), p. 469. The Bolsheviks in Russia also disliked the effect of drink on the working class: '"Soberness" was written on the banner of the revolution', Leon Trotsky, *Literature and Revolution* (London: Redwords, 1991), p. 153.

15 Sean O'Casey, *The Star Turns Red* (London: Macmillan, 1940), p. 102. These two characters were based on his good friends and comrades, Barney Conway (Brannigan) and Jim Larkin (Red Jim).

16 Donal Nevin (ed.), *Trade Union Century* (Cork: Mercier Press, 1994), p. 226.

17 Mary Morrissey, *The Rising of Bella Casey* (Dingle: Brandon, 2013). A fictive biography of Isabella Casey.

18 O'Casey, *Autobiographies*, 1, p. 65.

19 Ibid., p. 18.

20 Sean O'Casey, Autobiographical Notes (1962) published in the programme for the Royal Shakespeare Company production of *The Silver Tassie* at the Aldwych Theatre, London, August 1969.

21 O'Casey, *Autobiographies*, 1, p. 32.

22 Irish Church Mission, minutes, box no. 7,254. See also Murray, *Seán O'Casey*, p. 26.

23 Quoted by Murray, *Seán O'Casey*, p. 35. Draft manuscript of *I Knock at the Door*, Holograph Notebook, vol. 9, Berg Collection, New York Public Library.

24 Kevin C. Kearns, *Dublin's Lost Heroines* (Dublin: Gill & Macmillan, 2004), p. 108.

25 O'Casey, *Autobiographies*, 1, p. 71.

26 Alan Simpson, 'O'Casey and the East Wall Area in Dublin', *Irish University Review*, vol. 10, no. 1, Spring 1980, pp. 41–61.

27 Reverend Edward Morgan Griffin, 'The bulk of our church population is composed of quay labourers, railway porters, ticket collectors, stokers ... carpenters, plumbers', *Analysis of Church Population of St. Barnabas' Church: Report 24 November 1900* (Dublin: Church of Ireland Representative Church Body Library, 1900).

28 William Halpin, http://eastwallforall.ie/?p=972 (accessed 20 November 2014)

29 Desmond Ryan, *Remembering Sion* (Dublin: Arthur Barker, 1934), pp. 81–4.

30 O'Casey, *Letters*, 4, p. 336.

31 Ibid.

32 The East Wall History Group covers the East Wall area and the entire North Dock (including North Wall, Dublin Port and North Strand) taking in all aspects of local life, from the earliest days to the end of the twentieth century. Much of their research is available

online, including a short documentary on O'Casey's association with the East and North Wall area. In addition, they organise O'Casey seminars, a summer school, local productions, and historical tours of the locations associated with O'Casey, including St Barnabas Church, and of his homes and neighbours in Hawthorn Terrace and Abercorn Road. In the first four chapters, I availed of their knowledge of the 1913 lockout, his neighbours, including the Halpin family, Patrick Lennon, the Carpenter family, and the local man on which Fluther Good in *The Plough and the Stars* was based. Joe Mooney of the East Wall History Group sent me this reminiscence by Lucy Brennan: 'Fluther Good was a small man. I remember my brother telling me that he never saw so many scars on a man's head, acquired under the heavy billy clubs of the police ... No womaniser, my grandmother wanted him to sue O'Casey for that misrepresentation, but wiser heads prevailed. His wife Lizzie stood by him come hell or high water.' See East Wall History Group at http://eastwallforall.ie/?tag=east-wall-history-group (accessed 2 March 2019).

33 Martin Margulies, *The Early Life of Sean O'Casey* (Dublin: Dolmen Press, 1970), p. 27.

34 O'Casey, *Autobiographies*, 1, p. 155.

35 Sean O'Casey, 'Sound the Loud Trumpet', *The Peasant and Irish Ireland*, 25 May 1907. The paper's politics represented an all-class alliance comprising Sinn Féin, the Gaelic League, Irish manufacturing and Irish workers.

36 O'Casey, *Letters*, 2, p. 166.

37 O'Casey, *Autobiographies*, 1, p. 35.

38 John Jordan, 'A World in Chassis', *University Review* (Dublin), vol. 1, no. 4, Spring 1955, pp. 21–8.

39 O'Casey, *Autobiographies*, 1, p. 191.

CHAPTER 2: TWENTY YEARS A-GROWING

1 Sean O'Casey, *Irish Review*, no. 44, January 1949.

2 O'Casey, *Autobiographies*, 3, p. 32.

3 Quoted in Hugh MacDiarmid, 'Sláinte Chúramach, Seán', in Ronald Ayling (ed.), *Sean O'Casey* (Nashville: Aurora, 1970), p. 254.

4 See James R. Scrimgeour, *Sean O'Casey* (Boston: Twayne Publishers, 1978), p. 21.

5 O'Casey, *Autobiographies*, 4, p. 176

6 Robert Kee, *The Laurel and the Ivy* (London: Hamish Hamilton, 1994), p. 473.

7 F.S.L. Lyons, *Charles Stewart Parnell* (Oxford: Oxford University Press, 1977).

8 Paul Bew, *Enigma: A new life of Charles Stewart Parnell* (Dublin: Gill & Macmillan, 2012), p. 165.

9 Patrick Pearse, 'The Sovereign People', in *Collected Works of Pádraic H. Pearse: Political writings and speeches* (Dublin: Phoenix, 1924), pp. 335–72.

10 James Connolly, 'Editorial', *Workers' Republic*, 8 October 1898.

11 See James Joyce, 'Ivy Day in the Committee Room', *Dubliners* (Harmondsworth: Penguin, 1965), pp. 116–33.

12 F.S.L. Lyons, 'The Parnell Theme in Literature', in Andrew Carpenter (ed.), *Place, Personality and the Irish Writer* (Gerrards Cross: Colin Smythe, 1971), p. 88. See also Andrew E. Malone, *The Irish Drama* (London: Constable, 1929), p. 22 for details of plays about Parnell. MGM in America produced a film, *Parnell*, in 1937 staring Clark Gable and Myrna Loy.

13 Lyons, 'The Parnell Theme in Literature', in Carpenter (ed.), *Place, Personality and the Irish Writer* p. 88.

14 O'Casey, *Autobiographies*, 1, pp. 58–9. O'Casey is mistaken about the dates of this conversation. His father's funeral took place in 1886 and Parnell lost his position as head of the party in 1890.

15 O'Casey, *Autobiographies*, 1, p. 87.
16 Ibid., p. 175.
17 Ibid., p. 185.
18 O'Casey, *Autobiographies*, 2, pp. 17–18.
19 The 1782 agreement was a liberal ascendancy settlement resulting in a series of changes which freed the parliament of Ireland from the restrictions on legal, trade and religious matters imposed by successive Norman and English governments on its legislative powers. This period came to be known as Grattan's Parliament after Henry Grattan, member of the Irish parliament, a campaigner for reform and leader of the Patriot Party.
20 The Whiteboys were a secret agrarian organisation that posted warnings in the name of 'Captain Moonlight' aimed at landlords who increased rents or tried to evict peasant smallholders.
21 W.B. Yeats, 'Come Gather Round Me, Parnellites', in *Collected Poems* (London: Macmillan, 1950), p. 356.
22 See David Krause, *Sean O'Casey: The man and his work* (London: MacGibbon & Kee, 1960), p. 18.
23 Carla King, *Michael Davitt: After the Land League 1882–1906* (Dublin: UCD Press, 2016).
24 Jim Kavanagh, a carpenter, was a friend and neighbour in the house at 422 North Circular Road.
25 O'Casey, *Letters*, 3, p. 212.
26 O'Casey, *Letters*, 2, p. 592.
27 O'Casey, *Irish Democrat*, April 1946.
28 Ernie O'Malley, *Rising Out: Seán Connolly of Longford* (Dublin: UCD Press, 2007), p. 15.
29 King, *Michael Davitt*, p. 82.
30 Quoted in John Leslie, *The Irish Question 1894*, first published in *Justice*, the paper of the Social Democratic Federation in Britain, in serial form, between 24 March and 5 May 1894.
31 Tom Paine, one of the great radical writers involved in both the American Revolution of 1776 and the French Revolution of 1789. See Isaac Kramnick and Michael Foot (eds), *The Tom Paine Reader* (London: Penguin Classics, 1987).
32 David Buckley, *James Fintan Lalor: Radical* (Cork: Cork University Press, 1990), p. 86.
33 James Fintan Lalor, *The Rights of Ireland* and *The Faith of a Felon*, edited and introduced by James Connolly (Dublin, 1896), p. ii. *The Rights of Ireland* may have been written by his friend and comrade Thomas Devin Reilly and published in 1848 under Lalor's name.
34 James Fintan Lalor, *Irish Worker*, 17 June 1911 to 12 August 1911.
35 Christopher Murray, 'Sean O'Casey's *The Cooing of the Doves*: A one-act play rediscovered', *The Princeton University Library Chronicle*, vol. 68, nos 1–2, 2007, pp. 327–56.
36 For an assessment of Lalor's style see L. Fogarty, *James Fintan Lalor* (Dublin: Talbot Press, 1918), p. xxxvii.
37 Ibid., p. 59.
38 O'Casey, *Letters*, 1, p. 71.
39 James Connolly, *Labour in Irish History* (Dublin: Maunsel, 1922), p. 177.
40 John Mitchel's support for slavery has tarnished his reputation. After Mitchel escaped from Van Diemen's Land in 1853, he eventually settled in the American state of Tennessee. He supported the slave-owning Confederacy in the American Civil War (1861–5), during which his two sons died fighting with the Confederate army.
41 Sean O'Casey, *Irish Freedom*, March 1913.
42 Sean O'Casey, *Irish Worker*, February 1914.
43 O'Casey, *Irish Freedom*, March 1914.
44 Shivaun O'Casey (interview with author, 2 June 2010).

45 Reprinted in Sean O'Casey, *Blasts and Benedictions* (London: Macmillan, 1967), pp. 174–5.
46 Quoted in Sean O'Casey, *The Green Crow* (London: W.H. Allen, 1957), p. x.
47 O'Casey, *Letters*, 2, p. 931. For original quote see Fogarty, *James Fintan Lalor*, p. 13.
48 O'Casey, *Autobiographies*, 2, p. 159.
49 The annual commemoration at the grave of Wolfe Tone in Bodenstown, County Kildare, to celebrate the 1798 rebellion.
50 O'Casey, *Autobiographies*, 2, p. 196.
51 Ibid.
52 O'Casey, *Autobiographies*, 3, pp. 4, 66, 222.
53 O'Casey, *Autobiographies*, 2, p. 179.
54 Ibid.
55 The Irish Volunteers and the Irish Citizen Army smuggled arms and ammunition from Germany into Howth Harbour, Dublin.
56 O'Casey, *Letters*, 2, p. 47.
57 See Brian McCabe, 'Sean Connolly: First "rebel" casualty of the 1916 Rising', *Co. Kildare Online Electronic History Journal*, http://www.kildare.ie/ehistory/2006/05/naas_sinn_fein_sean_connolly_br.asp (accessed 20 August 2020).
58 There is no record of an Ayamonn or an Eamon O'Farrel in the 1901 or 1911 census. O'Casey consistently transformed names in an alliterative way for dramatic and literary effect and used different spellings in the autobiographies.
59 O'Casey's brother, Isaac Casey (1873–1931), was known as Archie.
60 Seán and his brother Archie had formed the Townsend Dramatic Society and converted an old stable in Hill Street into a little theatre. See O'Casey, *Autobiographies*, 2, p. 131.
61 O'Casey, *Autobiographies*, 2, p. 24.
62 Dion Boucicault, *Selected Plays of Dion Boucicault* (Gerrards Cross: Colin Smythe, 1987).
63 Christopher Morash, *A History of Irish Theatre* (Cambridge: Cambridge University Press, 2002), p. 91.
64 Bernard Shaw, *John Bull's Other Island and Major Barbara* (London: Constable, 1907).
65 Ben Levitas, *The Theatre of Nation* (Oxford: Oxford University Press, 2002), pp. 18–19.
66 W.B. Yeats, 'Cathleen ni Houlihan', in *The Collected Plays* (London: Macmillan, 1966), p. 88.
67 Christopher Fitz-Simon, 'The Sir John T. Gilbert Commemorative Lecture. 2011', in *Mr J. Kennedy Miller's Very Capable Company of Irish Players* (Dublin: Dublin City Public Libraries, 2011).
68 Séamus de Búrca in Desmond Slowey, *The Radicalization of Irish Drama 1600–1900* (Dublin: Irish Academic Press, 2008), p. 236.
69 See O'Casey, *Letters*, 4, p. 467, where O'Casey describes seeing a number of Shakespeare's plays by the Frank Benson Company at the Theatre Royal, Dublin, sometime in 1888 or 1890 (most likely in 1893/4).
70 O'Casey said that it 'wasn't Boucicault so much, but rather Shakespeare, Shaw, Strindberg, Ibsen, and then O'Neill who influenced him most'. Shivaun O'Casey (letter to author).
71 James Joyce, *Selected Letters of James Joyce*, Richard Ellman (ed.) (New York: Viking, 1975), p. 83.
72 Roy Foster, *Modern Ireland 1600–1972* (London: Allen Lane, 1988), p. 433.
73 O'Casey, *Autobiographies*, 2, p. 197.
74 Ibid., p. 200.
75 Ibid., p. 179.

CHAPTER 3: THE GAELIC LEAGUE AND OTHER MATTERS

1 See Joep Leerssen, 'The Idea of Nationality', *Mere Irish and Fíor Ghael* (Cork: Cork University Press in association with Field Day, 1996), pp. 15–31 for discussion on the terminology and historical background of the nation state. See also Joe Cleary, *Literature, Partition and the Nation State* (Cambridge: Cambridge University Press, 2002), chapter 1.

2 See Anthony D. Smith, *National Identity* (London: Penguin, 1991), chapter 5.

3 Caoimhín De Barra, *Gaeilge: A radical revolution* (Dublin: Currach Books, 2019), p. 52.

4 Romanticism was an artistic, literary and intellectual movement that originated in Europe towards the end of the eighteenth century. It was characterised by its emphasis on emotion and individualism as well as a reverence for the past and nature.

5 See 'Language, History, and Myth', in Tim Benning, *The Romantic Revolution* (London: Weidenfeld & Nicolson, 2010), chapter 3.

6 Thomas Davis, quoted in Aidan Doyle, *A History of the Irish Language* (Oxford: Oxford University Press, 2015), p. 116.

7 Ernest Blythe, *The State and the Nation* (Dublin: Comhdháil Náisiúnta na Gaeilge, 1919), p. 9.

8 Tomás Mac Síomóin, 'The Colonised Mind: Irish language and society', in Daltún Ó Ceallaigh (ed.), *Reconsiderations of Irish History and Culture* (Dublin: Léirmheas, 1994), pp. 42–71.

9 Albert Memmi, quoted in Ó Ceallaigh (ed.), *Reconsiderations of Irish History and Culture*, p. 50.

10 Timothy G. McMahon, *Grand Opportunities: The Gaelic revival and Irish society, 1893–1910* (Syracuse: Syracuse University Press, 2008).

11 In 1900, Peadar Ó Laoghaire's *Tadhg Saor*, staged in County Cork, was the first play produced in Irish.

12 Breandán S. Mac Aodha, 'Was This a Social Revolution?', in Seán Ó Tuama (ed.), *The Gaelic League Idea* (Cork: Mercier Press, 1972), p. 21.

13 Reverend Eugene O'Growney, *Simple Lessons in Irish*, published in five parts (Dublin: Gaelic League, 1894).

14 O'Casey, *Autobiographies*, 2, p. 171.

15 Ibid., p. 178. In this case, a house in Merrion Square in 1905 usually meant a back room in a tenement.

16 O'Casey, *Autobiographies*, 3, p. 66.

17 Proinsias Mac Aonghusa, 'Seán O'Casey and the Gaelic League', *Féile Zozimus*, vol. 3, pp. 11–28.

18 Ibid., p. 19.

19 Ibid., p. 18; see also O'Casey, *Autobiographies*, 3, pp. 147–9.

20 O'Casey, *Autobiographies*, 3, p. 66.

21 O'Casey, *Letters*, 1, p. 909.

22 O'Casey, *Autobiographies*, 3, p. 147.

23 See Leaslaoí Ó Briain, 'What! Have a Service in Erse and in St. Patrick's? Cumann Gaelach na hEaglaise – 90 Years Young', *Search*, vol. 27, no. 1, Spring 2004, pp. 5–11.

24 O'Casey, *Autobiographies*, 3, p. 6.

25 Quoted in Tomás Ó Fiaich, 'The Great Controversy', in Ó Tuama (ed.), *The Gaelic League Idea*, p. 71.

26 Quoted in *Wolfe Tone Annual 1944* (Dublin, 1945: refused publication by the censor in 1944 and published at end of war in 1945), p. 48.

27 William Delaney SJ, *Irish University Education* (London: John Murray, 1904).

28 Ó Fiaich, 'The Great Controversy', in Ó Tuama (ed.), *The Gaelic League Idea*, p. 72.

29 Lucy McDiarmid, *The Irish Art of Controversy* (Dublin: The Lilliput Press, 2005), p. 54.

30 O'Casey, *Autobiographies*, 3, p. 134. Arthur Griffith founded the Sinn Féin party in 1905.

31 Ibid., pp. 130–43.

32 P.J. Matthews, *Revival* (Cork: Cork University Press in association with Field Day Publications, 2003), p. 27.

33 O'Casey, *Letters*, 1, p. 920.

34 Sean O'Casey, *The Peasant and Irish Ireland*, 6 July 1907.

35 Sean O'Casey, *Irish Opinion*, 9 March 1918, and *Feathers from a Green Crow: Sean O'Casey, 1903–1925*, Robert Hogan (ed.) (London: Macmillan, 1963), p. 36.

36 Sean O'Casey, *The Irish Statesman*, 29 November 1924 and *Feathers from a Green Crow*, p. 264.

37 See Dónall Ó Corcora, *What's This About the Gaelic League?* (Dublin: Conradh na Gaedhilge, 1956).

38 James Connolly, *Workers' Republic*, vol. 1, no. 7, 1 October 1898.

39 Quoted in Mac Aonghusa, 'Sean O'Casey and the Gaelic League', p. 11.

40 *The End of the Beginning* was also based on the children's book *Gone Is Gone: Or the story of the man who wanted to do housework* by Wanda Gág.

41 O'Casey, *Letters*, 2, p. 397. Even after his departure for England O'Casey retained his proficiency in Irish: see letters to *Inniú*, 2 December 1955 and *Feasta*, August 1960.

42 Ibid., p. 94. The following plays by O'Casey were translated into Irish and produced by An Taibhdhearc in Galway: *Sgáil an Óglaigh* (*The Shadow of a Gunman*) (1940), *An Céacta is an Réaltaí* (*The Plough and the Stars*) (1942), *Punt ar Éileamh* (*A Pound on Demand*) (1952), *Juno agus an Phéacóg* (*Juno and the Paycock*) (1963). See Heinz Kosok, *Plays and Playwrights from Ireland in International Perspective* (Trier: WVT, 1995), pp. 180–6.

43 Declan Kiberd, *The Irish Times*, 10 August 1999.

44 After the First World War, American, Irish and then Caribbean writers boldly remade the world literary system long dominated by Paris and London. See Joe Cleary, *Modernism, Empire, World Literature* (Cambridge: Cambridge University Press, 2021).

45 R.V. Comerford, 'Isaac Butt and the Home Rule Party 1870–7', in W.E. Vaughan (ed.), *A New History of Ireland*, vol. vi (Oxford: Oxford University Press, 2010), pp. 21–2.

46 Owen McGee, 'Fred Allen (1861–1937): Republican, Methodist, and Dubliner', *Dublin Historical Record*, vol. lvi, no. 2, Autumn 2003, pp. 205–16.

47 See Jacqueline R. Hill, 'Artisans, Sectarianism, and Politics in Dublin, 1828–1848, for a discussion of the Protestant working class in Dublin', *Saothar*, vol. 7, 1981, pp. 12–27.

48 Earnán de Blaghd, *Trasna na Bóinne* (Dublin: Sáirséal agus Dill, 1957).

49 Quoted in Marnie Hay, *Bulmer Hobson and the Nationalist Movement in Twentieth-Century Ireland* (Manchester: Manchester University Press, 2009), p. 101.

50 Ibid., chapter 5.

51 O'Casey, *Autobiographies*, 3, p. 164.

52 O'Casey, *Letters*, 1, p. 697.

53 Ibid.

54 Ibid.

55 Martin B. Margulies, *The Early Life of Sean O'Casey* (Dublin: Dolmen Press, 1970), p. 73.

56 O'Casey, *Autobiographies*, 3, p. 162.

CHAPTER 4: A PROMETHEUS IN DUBLIN

1 O'Casey, *Autobiographies*, 3, p. 187.

2 Theo Dorgan, 'Larkin through the Eyes of Writers', in Donal Nevin (ed.), *James Larkin: Lion of the fold* (Dublin: Gill & Macmillan, 1998), pp. 102–9.

3 Quoted in Donal Nevin, *National Library of Ireland SIPTU Tribute to James Larkin* (Dublin: Gill & Macmillan, 1997), p. 24.

4 ITGWU rulebook 1909, quoted in Dermot Keogh, *The Rise of the Irish Working Class* (Belfast: Appletree Press, 1982), p. 139.

5 Sean O'Casey, original typescript (in possession of author), date unknown.

6 Robert G. Lowery, 'Sean O'Casey and the Irish Worker', in Robert G. Lowery (ed.), *O'Casey Annual*, no. 3 (London: Macmillan, 1984), pp. 33–114.

7 O'Casey, *Autobiographies*, 3, p. 187.

8 Francis Devine, *Organising History: A centenary of SIPTU* (Dublin: Gill & Macmillan 2009), pp. 5–9.

9 O'Casey, *Autobiographies*, 3, p. 190.

10 Emmet O'Connor, 'Syndicalism, Industrial Unionism, and Nationalism in Ireland', in S. Hirsch and L. Van der Walt (eds), *Anarchism and Syndicalism in the Colonial and Postcolonial World, 1870–1940*, vol. 1 (Leiden: Brill Publishers, 2011), pp. 193–226.

11 Susan Cannon Harris, 'Red Star versus Green Goddess: Sean O'Casey's *The Star Turns Red* and the politics of form', *The Princeton University Library Chronicle*, vol. 68, nos 1–2, Winter 2007, pp. 357–98.

12 *Freeman's Journal*, 6 March 1913.

13 Leon Trotsky, 'Where Is Britain Going?', *Collected Writings and Speeches on Britain* (London: New Park Publications, 1974), p. 8.

14 G.W. Alcock, *Fifty Years of Railway Trade Unionism* (London: Co-operative Printing Society, 1922), p. 427.

15 Quoted in Conor McCabe, 'The Context and Course of the Irish Railway Disputes of 1911', *Saothar*, vol. 30, 2005, p. 25.

16 Letter from a railway worker who is a supporter of Sinn Féin. He refused to join the ASRS because it was a British union; he accepts that his mates call him a scab, but he wants Sinn Féin to set up an Irish trade union: *The Peasant and Irish Ireland*, 6 July 1907.

17 Jim Kavanagh, 'My Friend O'Casey', *The Seán O'Casey Review*, vol. 2, no. 1, Fall 1975, pp. 58–60.

18 See O'Casey, *Letters*, 1, pp. 10–13 for details.

19 O'Casey, *Irish Worker*, 8 June 1912.

20 Ibid., 1 March 1913.

21 John Newsinger, 'Irish Labour in a Time of Revolution', *Socialist History*, no. 22, 2002, pp. 1–31.

22 James Larkin, *Irish Worker*, 27 May 1911.

23 O'Casey, *Irish Freedom*, March 1913.

24 O'Casey, *Irish Worker*, 10 May 1913.

25 The Second Socialist International was an organisation of socialist and labour parties formed in July 1889 in Paris where delegations from twenty countries participated.

26 Kieran Allen, *The Politics of James Connolly* (London: Pluto Press, 1990), p. 172.

27 O'Casey, *Irish Worker*, 7 March 1914. O'Casey's tone and closing line are very similar to the famous speech in the House of Commons by Oliver Cromwell on 20 April 1653 demanding the dissolution of the Long Parliament. Cromwell's speech ends with, 'In the name of God, go.'

28 A. Patrick Wilson (Euchan), *Irish Worker*, 1 February 1913. See also, for details of dispute, O'Casey, *Letters*, 1, pp. 13–27.

29 Wilson (Euchan), *Irish Worker*, 1 February 1913.

30 Jim Larkin, quoted in Donal Nevin (ed.), *Trade Union Century* (Cork: Mercier Press, 1994), p. 180.

31 O'Casey, *Irish Worker*, 8 February, 22 February 1913.

32 Ibid., 8 March 1913.

33 Ibid., 22 February 1913.

34 James Larkin, *Irish Worker*, 27 May 1911. William Wordsworth had hoped to launch a radical newspaper in 1793. In a letter he outlined his hopes for the paper: 'I know the multitude walk in darkness; I would put a lantern in each man's hand to guide him.'

35 John de Courcy Ireland gave me this account of the time he lived with Larkin in the late 1930s (April 1999).

36 O'Casey, *The Irish Times*, 31 January 1947.

37 See Emmet Larkin, *James Larkin: Irish labour leader, 1876–1947* (London: Routledge & Kegan Paul, 1965), pp. 76–82 for details. Also, Robert G. Lowery, 'Sean O'Casey and the Irish Worker', *O'Casey Annual*, no. 3 (London: Macmillan, 1984), p. 35.

38 Robert G. Lowery is to be commended for his work in indexing the *Irish Worker*, and indeed his Annotated Index of the six volumes of Sean O'Casey's autobiographies, painstakingly put together before the advent of computer search programmes. I met with Robert Lowery, and had access to his personal O'Casey archive, which is now in the Boston College Library (Boston, USA). See Robert G. Lowery, 'Sean O'Casey and the Irish Worker', *O'Casey Annual*, no. 3 (London: Macmillan, 1984), pp. 33–114.

39 Lowery, 'Sean O'Casey and the Irish Worker', p. 92.

40 O'Casey, *Autobiographies*, 3, p. 83. Darwin's theory of natural selection appears in a comic exchange between the Covey and Fluther in *The Plough and the Stars* (London: Macmillan, 1926), pp. 15–17.

41 O'Casey, *Autobiographies*, 2, p. 122.

42 See Manus O'Riordan, *Liberty Hall as a Cultural Centre: The early years* (Dublin: SIPTU, 2002).

43 O'Casey, *Autobiographies*, 3, p. 101.

44 Ibid., p. 143. See also *Irish Worker*, 14 December 1912, where O'Casey writes, 'The [Gaelic] League is worse now even than it was.'

45 See *An Phoblacht*, 20 June 1936, where it was first published.

46 William Martin Murphy: a former member of parliament and prominent businessman owner of the Independent Group of newspapers and the Dublin United Tram Company.

47 Quoted in Dermot Keogh, *The Rise of the Irish Working Class: The Dublin trade union movement and labour leadership, 1890–1914* (Belfast: Appletree Press, 1982), p. 186.

48 Pádraig Yeates, *Lockout, Dublin 1913* (Dublin: Gill & Macmillan, 2000).

49 O'Casey, *Autobiographies*, 3, pp. 212–13.

50 O'Casey, *Irish Worker*, 27 September 1913.

51 *The Irish Times*, 10 December 1913.

52 Ronald Ayling, 'Feathers Flying', *The Dubliner*, Spring 1964, p. 54.

53 Robert Hogan (ed.), *Feathers from the Green Crow: Sean O'Casey, 1905–1925* (London: Macmillan, 1963), p. 43.

54 In the first draft the chapter was headed 'Red Prometheus'. NLI, *Autograph Notebook of Sean O'Casey (1927–1964).*

55 *The Toiler*, 4 April 1914. During the dispute, *The Toiler* denounced supporters of Larkin in an attempt to destroy the ITGWU. They slandered Larkin on a regular basis claiming he was the son of the hated informer James Carey, from the time of the Fenians (1883). See John Newsinger, '"The Curse of Larkinism": Patrick McIntyre, *The Toiler* and the Dublin lockout of 1913', *Éire-Ireland*, vol. xxx, no. 3, Fall 1995, pp. 90–102.

56 C. Desmond Greaves, *Sean O'Casey: Politics and art* (London: Lawrence & Wishart, 1979), p. 54.

57 O'Casey, *Irish Worker*, 18 October 1913; see also O'Casey, *Letters*, 1, p. 31.
58 O'Casey, *Letters*, 1, p. 29 (n. 1).
59 See O'Casey, *Irish Worker*, 26 November 1913.
60 The attack by the police on striking workers on 31 August 1913, which came to be known as 'Bloody Sunday'.
61 O'Casey, *Irish Worker*, see 13, 20 December 1913 and 24 January 1914 issues.
62 Ibid., 10 January 1914.
63 Sean O'Casey, November 1920, original handwritten manuscript (in possession of author).
64 O'Casey, *Letters*, 1, p. 99.
65 Ibid., p. 97.
66 Ibid., p. 98.
67 C. Desmond Greaves, *The Irish Transport and General Workers' Union* (Dublin: Gill & Macmillan, 1982), p. 316.
68 It is unclear if the Ministry of Justice in the First Dáil and then the Free State took any action to secure Larkin's release. Larkin's denunciation of the Anglo Irish treaty may have been the reason for this inaction. National Archives, *Cabinet Papers, 1923*, S. 2,009.
69 R.M. Fox, 'James Larkin and His Work', *The Gael*, 31 October 1921.
70 Francis Devine, *Organising History: A centenary of SIPTU* (Dublin: Gill & Macmillan, 2009), pp. 168–72.
71 John Reed was a socialist and a writer best known for his book about the Russian Revolution, *Ten Days that Shook the World* (New York: Boni & Liveright, 1919). Joe Hill (Hillström), an organiser for the Industrial Workers of the World in America, was executed in 1915 for a crime he did not commit during a strike.
72 O'Casey was also friends with R.M. Fox, the labour historian, who had visited Russia in 1921. So, one can assume O'Casey was reasonably well informed about the USSR.
73 Liam Mellows, *Jail Programme* (1922), based on notes Mellows had smuggled out of jail after being captured by the Irish Free State. Mellows outlined a ten-point republican socialist programme that he hoped the movement might adopt. Peadar O'Donnell, Frank Ryan and George Gilmore were founder members of the Republican Congress, a left-wing split from the IRA in 1934. In their later phase they were involved with the Communist International and the International Brigades in Spain. NLI: Liam Mellows, *Jail Programme*, Irish Labour Party.
74 James Larkin, *Irish Worker*, 8 September 1923.
75 Sean O'Casey, *The Star Turns Red* (London: Macmillan, 1940), p. 99.
76 Lady Gregory, *Journals*, 2 vols, Daniel J. Murphy (ed.) (Gerrards Cross: Colin Smythe, 1978–88), vol. 1, p. 584.
77 O'Casey, *Letters*, 1, p. 148.
78 Theresa Moriarty, 'Delia Larkin: Relative obscurity', in Nevin (ed.), *James Larkin*, p. 437.
79 O'Casey, *Letters*, 1, p. 122.
80 See correspondence with Jack Carney in O'Casey, *Letters*.
81 Emmet O'Connor, *James Larkin* (Cork: Cork University Press, 2002), p. 100.
82 The Irish Labour Party sat on the fence over Spain. In a pamphlet edited by William Norton, the Labour Party leader equated Nazism with Stalinism: *Cemeteries of Liberty: Communist and fascist dictatorships* (Dublin: Labour Party, 1937).
83 O'Casey, *Letters*, 2, p. 396.
84 Sean O'Casey, *Plebs*, March 1942.
85 Sean O'Casey, *The Irish Times*, 31 January 1947.
86 O'Casey, *Letters*, 2, p. 447. Sean T. O'Kelly was president of Ireland, and John Charles McQuaid was archbishop of Dublin.

87 Sean O'Casey, *Irish Democrat*, February 1946.
88 R.M. Fox, *James Connolly: The forerunner* (Tralee: The Kerryman, 1946).
89 O'Casey, *Letters*, 2, p. 436.
90 Ibid., p. 234.
91 Ibid., p. 359.
92 Ronald Ayling, 'Seeds for Future Harvest', *Irish University Review*, vol. 10, no. 1, Spring 1980, pp. 25–40.
93 The Rocliffe family were neighbours of O'Casey in Hawthorn Terrace. They worked in the print trade and were members of St Barnabas, the same church as O'Casey. I have not been able to establish whether there is any connection with the play.
94 Richard Davies and W.J. McCormack, 'Sean O'Casey's Unpublished Correspondence with Raissa Lomonovska, 1925–1926', *Irish Slavonic Studies*, no. 5, 1984, pp. 181–7.
95 Sean O'Casey, *Red Roses for Me* (London: Macmillan, 1942), p. 134.
96 O'Casey, *Letters*, 4, p. 310.
97 Horst Höhne, 'Brecht vs. O'Casey, or Brecht & O'Casey', in Robert G Lowery (ed.), *O'Casey Annual*, no. 3 (London: Macmillan, 1984), pp. 1–32.
98 Bertolt Brecht, *The Days of the Commune* (London: Methuen, 1978).
99 O'Casey, *Red Roses for Me*, p. 151.
100 John Brannigan, 'Seán O'Casey and Brendan Behan: Aesthetics, democracy and the voice of labour', in Michael Pierse (ed.), *A History of Working-Class Writing* (Cambridge: Cambridge University Press, 2018), pp. 289–302.

CHAPTER 5: THE ROAD TO 1916

1 The origin of the quote was Churchill's infamous speech in Belfast's Ulster Hall when he declared 'Ulster will fight, and Ulster will be right'; he was the first British politician to play the 'Orange card'.
2 *An Claidheamh Soluis*, 1 November 1913.
3 Bulmer Hobson, *A Short History of the Irish Volunteers*, vol. 1 (only one volume published) (Dublin: Three Candle Press, 1918), p. 27.
4 Marnie Hay, *Bulmer Hobson and the Nationalist Movement in Twentieth-Century Ireland* (Manchester: Manchester University Press, 2009), p. 144.
5 Quoted in Kenneth Griffith and Timothy O'Grady, *Curious Journey* (Cork: Mercier Press, 1998), p. 21.
6 P. O Cathasaigh (Seán O'Casey), *The Story of the Irish Citizen Army* (Dublin: Maunsel, 1919), p. 55.
7 Quoted in Pádraig Yeates, *Lockout: Dublin 1913* (Dublin: Gill & Macmillan, 2000), p. 394.
8 Larkin would later claim that the idea of a citizen army arose during the Cork dock workers' strike in 1908, when the strikers were equipped with red armlets and long staves.
9 D.R. O'Connor Lysaght, 'The Irish Citizen Army: 1913–1916', *History Ireland*, vol. 14, no. 2, March/April 2006, p. 21.
10 Martin Margulies, *The Early Life of Sean O'Casey* (Dublin: Dolmen Press, 1970), p. 56.
11 O'Casey, *Irish Worker*, 24 January 1914.
12 Ibid.
13 James MacGowan, *Irish Worker*, 7 February 1914.
14 O'Casey, *Irish Worker*, 21 February 1914.
15 Ibid.
16 MacGowan, *Irish Worker*, 28 February 1914.
17 O'Casey, *Irish Worker*, 7 March 1914.
18 R.M. Fox, *The History of the Irish Citizen Army* (Dublin: James Duffy, 1944), p. 66.

19 See L. Fogarty, *James Fintan Lalor* (Dublin: Talbot Press, 1918), p. 59.
20 Quoted in Donal Nevin, *James Connolly: A full life* (Dublin: Gill & Macmillan, 2005), p. 554.
21 O Cathasaigh (Seán O'Casey), *The Story of the Irish Citizen Army*, p. 71. Fox in *The History of the Irish Citizen Army* said that this clause was proposed by Constance Markievicz, p. 64.
22 O'Casey, *Autobiographies*, 3, p. 225.
23 O'Casey, *The Story of the Irish Citizen Army*, pp. 69–70.
24 Recruiting poster for Irish Citizen Army designed by Seán O'Casey, *The Seán O'Casey Review*, vol. 2, no. 2, Spring 1976, p. 103.
25 O'Casey, *Irish Worker*, 2 May 1914.
26 *William O'Brien Papers*, NLI, MS 15673/2.
27 See C. Desmond Greaves in *Sean O'Casey: Politics and art* (London: Lawrence & Wishart, 1979), n. 15, p. 81.
28 O'Casey, *Autobiographies*, 3, p. 227.
29 Ibid.
30 Bulmer Hobson, *Ireland Yesterday and Tomorrow* (Tralee: Anvil Press, 1968), p. 70.
31 O'Casey, *Autobiographies*, 3, p. 268.
32 None of these articles or letters have survived.
33 Leo Keohane, *Captain Jack White: Imperialism, anarchism and the Irish Citizen Army* (Newbridge: Irish Academic Press, 2014).
34 James Connolly, *Workers' Republic*, 8 April 1916.
35 O'Casey, *The Story of the Irish Citizen Army*, p. 56.
36 Lindie Naughton, *Markievicz: A most outrageous rebel* (Dublin: Merrion Press, 2016).
37 O'Casey, *Autobiographies*, 3, p. 212.
38 Sean O'Casey, *The Star Turns Red* (London: Macmillan, 1940), p. 152.
39 O'Casey, *Autobiographies*, 3, p. 213.
40 Ibid., pp. 212–13.
41 *William O'Brien Papers*, NLI, MS 15,673 (2). Rosamond Jacob also had a poor opinion of Markievicz: 'She revolted me the way she talked about politics.' Quoted in Leeann Lane, *Rosamond Jacob: Third person singular* (Dublin: UCD Press, 2010), p. 65.
42 O'Casey, *The Story of the Irish Citizen Army,* p. 44.
43 Ibid., p. 46.
44 Ibid., p. v.
45 Sean O'Casey, *Feathers from a Green Crow 1905–1925*, Robert Hogan (ed.) (London: Macmillan, 1963), p. 177.
46 O'Casey, *The Story of the Irish Citizen Army,* p. 7.
47 Hobson, *A Short History of the Irish Volunteers.*
48 W.P. Ryan, *The Irish Labour Movement* (Dublin: Talbot Press, 1919).
49 Brian O'Neill, *Easter Week* (New York: International Publishers, 1936).
50 ICA Council Minute Book 1919–20, Irish Labour History Museum and Archives. I am grateful to Brian Hanley for this information.
51 Eimar O'Duffy, *The Irish Statesman*, 12 July 1919, p. 72.
52 Fox, *The History of the Irish Citizen Army*, pp. 227–32.
53 O'Connor Lysaght, 'The Irish Citizen Army', p. 16.
54 Frank Robbins, *Under the Starry Plough* (Dublin: Academy Press, 1977).

CHAPTER 6: THE 1916 RISING

1 James Connolly, *Forward*, 15 August 1914.
2 Sean O'Casey, Robert Hogan (ed.), *Feathers from the Green Crow 1905–1925* (London: Macmillan, 1963), p. 132.

3 O'Casey, *Autobiographies*, 4, p. 12.
4 O'Casey, *Autobiographies*, 3, p. 245.
5 James Connolly, *Workers' Republic*, 22 January 1916.
6 C. Desmond Greaves, *The Life and Times of James Connolly* (London: Lawrence & Wishart, 1961), pp. 314–16.
7 William Shakespeare, 'Two Gentlemen of Verona', in *Complete Works* (London: Macmillan, 2007), p. 64.
8 Greaves, *The Life and Times of James Connolly*, p. 403.
9 For a perspective on the role played by socialists and labour activists in the rising, see '1916 Special Issue', *Saothar*, vol. 41, 2016.
10 John O'Connor, *The 1916 Proclamation* (Dublin: Anvil Books, 1986).
11 For details see Sean Enright, *Easter Rising 1916: The trials* (Dublin: Merrion Press, 2014).
12 Quoted in Kieran Allen, *James Connolly: Revolutionary socialist* (Dublin: Bookmarks, 2006), p. 3.
13 See James Connolly, *The Re-Conquest of Ireland* (Dublin: ITGWU, 1916).
14 James Connolly, *Irish Worker*, 8 August 1914.
15 See O'Casey, *Letters*, 3, p. 346.
16 Christopher Murray, *Seán O'Casey: Writer at work* (Dublin: Gill & Macmillan, 2004), p. 103.
17 Sean O'Casey, *The Plough and the Stars* (London: Macmillan, 1926), p. 95.
18 Martin Margulies, *The Early Life of Sean O'Casey* (Dublin: Dolmen Press, 1970), p. 71.
19 Between 1946 and 1949 O'Casey lobbied both publicly and privately on behalf of Irish prisoners in English jails. He also sent letters and books to those in prison. See NLI, MS 37,963.
20 T.A. Jackson was a leading member of the Communist Party in Britain. Hugh Delargy was a Labour Party MP from an Irish background. Krishna Menon led the overseas wing of the Indian independence movement, campaigning within the United Kingdom to win public support for Indian independence.
21 Sean O'Casey, review of Sean O'Callaghan, *The Easter Lily* (London: Allan Wingate, 1956), in *Tribune*, 22 February 1957.
22 Sean O'Casey, *The Sean O'Casey Review*, vol. 1, no. 1, Fall 1974, p. 11.
23 O'Casey, *Letters*, 1, p. 65.
24 O'Casey, *Autobiographies*, 4, p. 15.
25 O'Casey, *The Story of the Irish Citizen Army* (Dublin: Maunsel, 1919), p. 64. Sheehy Skeffington was murdered while in custody in Portobello barracks by a British army officer more than two weeks before the execution of Connolly.
26 Quoted in Jason Knirck, *Women of the Dáil* (Dublin: Irish Academic Press, 2006), p. 65.
27 O'Casey, *The Story of the Irish Citizen Army*, p. 64.
28 Connolly, *The Re-Conquest of Ireland*, p. vii.
29 O'Casey, *The Story of the Irish Citizen Army*, p. 67.
30 O'Casey, *Letters*, 1, p. 62.
31 V.I. Lenin, 'The Right of Nations to Self-Determination', *Lenin's Collected Works* (Moscow: Progress Publishers, 1972), vol. 20, pp. 393–454.
32 The Dublin Steam Packet strike, in October 1915 when workers trained as a defence force to protect their pickets, was an example of what could have been achieved with a more open and politicised mobilisation of the forces that looked to Connolly and the ITGWU for leadership. For an account of the strike, and a selection of Connolly's articles on the strike in the *Workers' Republic*, see D.R. O'Connor Lysaght, *The Steam Packet Company Strike* (Dublin, 2014).

33 William Irwin Thompson, *The Imagination of an Insurrection: Dublin, Easter 1916* (New York: Harper Colophon Books, 1967), chapter 4.
34 See also Florence O'Donoghue, 'Plans for the 1916 Rising', *University Review* (Dublin), vol. 3, no. 1, 1963, pp. 3–21.
35 Quoted in David Thornley, 'Patrick Pearse', *Studies: An Irish quarterly review*, vol. lv, no. 217, Spring 1966, pp. 10–20.
36 Quoted in Emmet O'Connor, *Big Jim Larkin: Hero or wrecker?* (Dublin: UCD Press, 2015), p. 176.

CHAPTER 7: A WRITER AT LAST: 1917–22

1 O'Casey, *Letters*, 1, p. 74.
2 Ibid., p. 78.
3 John Boyle O'Reilly (1844–90), a poet, journalist and writer. As a young man in Ireland, he was a member of the IRB, for which he was transported to Western Australia. Having escaped to the United States, he became a prominent spokesperson for the Irish community through his editorship of the Boston newspaper *The Pilot*, and as a writer and lecturer.
4 O'Casey, *Letters*, 1, p. 74
5 Ibid., pp. 69, 71.
6 Sean O'Casey, *Irish Worker*, 15 November 1913.
7 Sean Ó Cathasaigh, *Songs of the Wren, nos 1 & 2* (Dublin: Fergus O'Connor, 1918). See also Sean O'Casey, Robert Hogan (ed.), *Feathers from the Green Crow 1905–1925* (London: Macmillan, 1963), pp. 131–52.
8 A popular anthology, *Poems of To-Day: Third series* (London: Macmillan, 1938), pp. 120–2, published two of his poetic pieces from his play *Within the Gates.*
9 F.S.L. Lyons, 'The New Nationalism, 1916–1918', in W.E. Vaughan (ed.), *A New History Of Ireland*, vol. vi (Oxford: Oxford University Press, 2010), pp. 225–59.
10 Seán Ó Lúing, *I Die in a Good Cause* (Cork: Mercier Press, 2017), p. 104.
11 Ibid., p. 61.
12 O'Casey, *Feathers from the Green Crow*, p. 158.
13 Ibid., p. 171.
14 O'Casey, *Letters*, 1, p. 64.
15 Editorial, *Irish Opinion*, 8 December 1917.
16 Sean O'Casey, 'Juno and the Paycock', in *Two Plays* (London: Macmillan, 1925), p. 104.
17 *Irish Opinion*, 8 December 1918.
18 Ibid., 16 March 1918.
19 Ibid.
20 O'Casey, *Letters*, 1, p. 69.
21 Ibid., p. 82, where he mentions an English socialist newspaper, *Satire.*
22 *The Irish Times*, 24 April 1918.
23 O'Casey, *Letters*, 1, p. 95.
24 Charles Townshend, 'The Irish Railway Strike of 1920: Industrial action and civil resistance in the struggle for independence', *Irish Historical Studies*, vol. 21, no. 83, March 1979, pp. 265–82. See also Henry Somerville, 'The Political Impotence of British Labour', *Studies: An Irish quarterly review*, vol. x, no. 37, March 1921, pp. 1–18, for a contemporary account of the failure of British-based unions to support their Irish colleagues.
25 See Conor Kostick, *Revolution in Ireland: Popular militancy 1917 to 1923* (Cork: Cork University Press, 2009).
26 Donal Ó Drisceoil, *Peadar O'Donnell* (Cork: Cork University Press, 2001), chapter 2.
27 Ernie O'Malley, *No Surrender Here: The Civil War papers of Ernie O'Malley 1922–1924* (Dublin: The Lilliput Press, 2007), p. 152.

28 A. de Blácam, 'Thoughts on Labour Policy in Ireland', *Studies: An Irish quarterly review*, vol. x, no. 40, December 1921, pp. 599–600.

29 Gavin Foster, 'The Social Basis of the Civil War Divide', in John Crowley, Donal Ó Drisceoil and Mike Murphy (eds), *Atlas of the Irish Revolution* (Cork: Cork University Press, 2017), pp. 665–7.

30 Brian Hanley, 'The Treaty: Victory or defeat?', *History Ireland*, vol. 29, no. 6, November/December 2021, p. 15.

31 O'Casey, *Autobiographies*, 4, p. 51.

32 O'Casey, *Letters*, 1, p. 82.

33 Ibid., p. 72.

34 Ibid., p. 67.

35 O'Casey, *Autobiographies*, 4, p. 96.

36 Ibid., p. 88.

37 Adrian Hoare, *The Red and the Green: The lives of Frank Ryan* (Dingle: Brandon Books, 2004), p. 25.

38 Robert Goode Hogan and Richard Burnham, *The Years of O'Casey 1921–1926: A documentary history* (Newark, DE: University of Delaware Press, 1992), p. 240.

CHAPTER 8: THE NEW DRAMA

1 Quoted in Colbert Kearney, *The Glamour of Grammar* (Westport, CT: Greenwood Press, 2000), p. 36.

2 William Halpin, http://eastwallforall.ie/?p=972 (accessed 15 July 2017).

3 Ibid.

4 O'Casey, *Autobiographies*, 2, p. 131.

5 Letter from O'Casey to Saros Cowasjee, in Christopher Murray, *Seán O'Casey: Writer at work* (Dublin: Gill & Macmillan, 2004), p. 93.

6 R.M. Fox, *The Irish Times*, 1 December 1964.

7 Murray, *Seán O'Casey*, p. 93; also Paul O'Brien, 'Sean O'Casey and the Abbey Theatre: A conflicted relationship', in Patrick Lonergan and Riana O'Dwyer (eds), *Echoes Down the Corridor* (Dublin: Carysfort Press, 2007), pp. 69–80.

8 Emmet O'Connor, *A Labour History of Ireland* (Dublin: Gill & Macmillan, 1992), p. 68.

9 James Plunkett, 'Big Jim: A loaf on the table, a flower in the vase', in Donal Nevin (ed.), *James Larkin: Lion of the fold* (Dublin: Gill & Macmillan, 1998), pp. 110–15. See also Jim Larkin, *Workers' Republic*, 14 August 1914: 'All forms of social relaxation – dancing, instrumental and vocal music, billiards, roulette, all forms of athletic effort are encouraged – boxing, swimming, etc. Educational facilities of all kinds are provided. We teach the Gaelic, French and German languages. We have our dramatic and choral societies … we have our own park of sixteen acres whereon we hold sports and gatherings every week-end.'

10 Robert Brustein, *The Theatre of Revolt* (Boston: Little, Brown, 1962), p. 9.

11 See Elizabeth Mannion, *The Urban Plays of the Early Abbey Theatre* (Syracuse: Syracuse University Press, 2014).

12 This was the forerunner of the Abbey Theatre.

13 Nelson O'Ceallaigh Ritschel, 'The Alternative Aesthetic: The theatre of Ireland's urban plays', in Stephen Watt, Eileen Morgan and Shakir Mustafa (eds), *A Century of Irish Drama* (Bloomington: Indiana University Press, 2000), p. 18.

14 Frederick Ryan – for a selection of his writings, see Bill McCamley and Manus O'Riordan (eds), *Socialism Democracy and the Church* (Dublin: Labour History Workshop, 1984).

15 Frederick Ryan, 'The Laying of the Foundations', in Robert Hogan and James Kilroy (eds), *Lost Plays of the Irish Renaissance* (Dixon, CA: Proscenium Press, 1970), pp. 23–37.

16 Mannion, *The Urban Plays of the Early Abbey Theatre*, pp. 173–95.

17 See Christopher Murray, 'Shaw's Ibsen and the Idea of an Irish Theatre', in Ross Dixon and Irina Ruppo Malone (eds), *Ibsen and Chekhov on the Irish Stage* (Dublin: Carysfort Press, 2012), pp. 23–36.

18 Ben Levitas, 'Plumbing the Depths: Irish realism and the working class from Shaw to O'Casey', *Irish University Review*, vol. 33, no. 1, Spring/Summer 2003, pp. 133–49.

19 Christopher Morash, *A History of Irish Theatre: 1660–2000* (Cambridge: Cambridge University Press, 2002), p. 153.

20 The Irish Workers' Dramatic Company was founded in 1912 by Delia Larkin and Helena Maloney. See Lauren Arrington, 'Theatre of Dissent: The historical imagination of the Irish Workers' Dramatic Company', in Christopher Collins and Mary Caulfield (eds), *Ireland, Memory and Performing the Historical Imagination* (London: Palgrave Macmillan, 2014), pp. 101–17.

21 *The Irish Times*, 4 November 1914.

22 See Levitas, 'Plumbing the Depths', n. 52, p. 149.

23 Robert Hogan, Richard Burnham and Daniel P. Poteet, *The Abbey Theatre: The rise of the realists 1910–1915* (Dublin: Dolmen Press, 1979), p. 342.

24 *The Irish Times*, 12 December 1917.

25 A number of associated Clarion clubs and societies (cycling, rambling, handicrafts, field, drama and choral societies) were created, including the People's Theatre, Newcastle-upon-Tyne, which began life in 1911 as the Newcastle Clarion Drama Club, and premiered two of O'Casey's post-Second World War plays.

26 Quoted in Nevin, *James Larkin: Lion of the fold*, p. 488.

27 Emmet O'Connor, *Syndicalism in Ireland* (Cork: Cork University Press, 1988), p. 10.

28 Quoted in Manus O'Riordan, *Liberty Hall as a Cultural Centre: The early years* (Dublin: SIPTU, 2002), p. 10.

29 Delia Larkin, *Irish Worker*, 16 November 1912.

30 O'Casey, *Letters*, 1, p. 147.

31 *The Workers' Republic*, 19 February 1916.

32 R.M. Fox, *The History of the Irish Citizen Army* (Dublin: James Duffy, 1944), p. 107.

33 See James Moran, *Four Irish Rebel Plays* (Dublin: Irish Academic Press, 2007). Also, Nelson O'Ceallaigh Ritschel, *Shaw, Synge, Connolly, and Socialist Provocation* (Gainesville: University Press of Florida, 2012), pp. 198–213.

34 Moran, *Four Irish Rebel Plays*, pp. 16–17.

35 Francis Sheehy Skeffington, *The Workers' Republic*, 8 April 1916.

36 Keith Jeffery, *Ireland and the Great War* (Cambridge: Cambridge University Press, 2000), p. 7.

37 James Connolly, *The Workers' Republic*, 5 February 1916.

38 Sean O'Casey, quoted in Moran, *Four Irish Rebel Plays*, p. 23.

39 In Moran's introduction he controversially states in relation to James Connolly's play *Under Which Flag?* that O'Casey in *The Plough and the Stars* 'went on to reverse the message of *Under Which Flag?* by revealing that, whatever banner leads people into battle, political commitments that result in violence are always corrupting and lamentable rather than valiant and praiseworthy': *Four Irish Rebel Plays*, p. 23.

40 O'Casey, *Letters*, 1, p. 697.

41 Nicholas Grene, *The Politics of Irish Drama* (Cambridge: Cambridge University Press, 1999), p. 22.

42 Bernard Shaw, *John Bull's Other Island* (London: Constable, 1930), p. 14.

43 See O'Ceallaigh Ritschel, *Shaw, Synge, Connolly, and Socialist Provocation*, p. 150.

44 Bernard Shaw, *The Matter with Ireland*, Dan H. Laurence and David H. Greene (eds), (New York: Hill & Wang, 1962), p. 110.

45 Stanley Weintraub, 'The Making of an Irish Rebel', *Éire-Ireland*, vol. v, no. 4, Winter 1970, pp. 9–27.
46 O'Casey, *Letters*, 1, p. 697.
47 Saros Cowasjee, *Sean O'Casey: The man behind the plays* (Edinburgh: Oliver & Boyd, 1965), p. 253.
48 O'Casey, *Autobiographies*, 4, p. 30.
49 O'Casey, *Letters*, 1, p. 87.
50 See Bernard Shaw, *Prefaces* (London: Constable, 1934). The prefaces are some of the most astute pamphleteering since the time of Jonathan Swift.
51 Peter James Harris, *Sean O'Casey: Letters and autobiographies* (Trier: WVT, 2004), p. 49.
52 O'Casey, *Autobiographies*, 3, p. 174.
53 Sean O'Casey, 'A Whisper about Bernard Shaw', in *The Green Crow* (London: W.H. Allen, 1957), p. 179.
54 Shaw developed a modified form of evolutionary theory based on the ideas of the French scientist Jean-Baptiste Lamarck, which he called creative evolution. At its simplest, creative evolution postulates that organisms can evolve by force of will and they can pass on these changes to their offspring.
55 Sean O'Casey, 'The Silver Tassie', in *Collected Plays*, vol. 2 (London: Macmillan, 1958), p. 103.
56 Sean O'Casey, 'Author Interprets *Within the Gates*', *The Daily Princetonian* (Boston), 10 January 1935.

CHAPTER 9: DISMANTLING THE MYTH

1 Kieran Allen, 'The 1916 Rising: Myth or reality?', *Irish Marxist Review*, no. 14, 2016, p. 3.
2 Ernie O'Malley, *On Another Man's Wound* (London: Rich & Cowan, 1936), p. 311.
3 Diarmaid Ferriter, programme for *The Plough and the Stars*, Abbey Theatre, 2010, p. 7.
4 Desmond Slowey, *The Radicalization of Irish Drama 1600–1900* (Dublin: Irish Academic Press, 2008), p. 234.
5 Ibid.
6 Sean O'Casey, *The Harvest Festival* (Gerrards Cross: Colin Smythe, 1980), p. 65.
7 Ibid., p. 15.
8 Ibid., p. 30.
9 Rosa Luxemburg, http://www.anu.edu.au/polsci/marx/contemp/pamsetc/socfrombel/sfb_5.htm. (accessed 15 March 2015).
10 O'Casey, *Letters*, 1, p. 94. According to Shivaun O'Casey, her father 'thought *The Crimson in the Tricolour* a good play full of youthful energy that had gone from him now' (letter from Shivaun O'Casey to author).
11 Quoted in Christopher Murray, *Seán O'Casey: Writer at work* (Dublin: Gill & Macmillan, 2004), p. 132.
12 Colbert Kearney, *The Glamour of Grammar: Orality and politics and the emergence of Sean O'Casey* (Westport, CT: Greenwood Press, 2000), p. 42.
13 O'Casey, *Letters*, 2, p. 33.
14 Lady Gregory, *Journals*, 2 vols, Daniel J. Murphy (ed.) (Gerrards Cross: Colin Smythe, 1978–88), vol. 1, p. 307.
15 O'Malley, *On Another Man's Wound*.
16 Joe Cleary, *Outrageous Fortune* (Dublin: Field Day Publications, 2007), p. 144.
17 John Millington Synge, *The Playboy of the Western World* (Dublin: Maunsel, 1907).
18 Sean O'Casey, 'The Shadow of a Gunman', in *Two Plays* (London: Macmillan, 1925), p. 157.
19 P.S. O'Hegarty, *The Irish Statesman*, vol. 2, no. 13, 7 June 1924, p. 399.
20 See Bernice Schrank, *Sean O'Casey: A research and production sourcebook* (Westport, CT: Greenwood Press, 1996), p. 66.

21 Ronald Ayling, *Sean O'Casey's Theatre of War* (Vernon, BC: Kalamalka Press, 2004), p. 29.
22 Maureen Malone, *The Plays of Sean O'Casey* (Carbondale: Southern Illinois University Press, 1969), p. 24.
23 Ayling, *Sean O'Casey's Theatre of War*, pp. 30–1.
24 O'Casey, *Letters*, 4, p. 191.
25 Elizabeth Mannion, 'Different C/Kathleens', paper delivered at IASIL Conference, Prague, 2015.
26 Gabriel Fallon, *Sean O'Casey: The man I knew* (London: Routledge & Kegan Paul, 1965), p. 14.
27 Christopher Murray, 'Sean O'Casey's *The Cooing of the Doves*: A one-act play rediscovered', *The Princeton University Library Chronicle*, vol. 68, nos 1–2, Winter 2007, pp. 327–56.
28 Ibid., p. 354.
29 Ibid., p. 352.
30 Sean O'Casey, 'The Seamless Coat of Kathleen', *Poblacht na hÉireann*, 29 March 1922.
31 O'Casey, *Letters*, 1, p. 101.
32 Sean O'Casey, *Feathers From a Green Crow 1905–1925*, Robert Hogan (ed.) (London: Macmillan, 1963), p. 288.
33 Ibid., p. 280.
34 Bernard Shaw, *John Bull's Other Island* (London: Constable, 1909), p. 18.
35 Murray, 'Sean O'Casey's *The Cooing of the Doves*', p. 333.
36 O'Casey, *Letters*, 1, p. 92. John Moore, who lived with his family in the flat above O'Casey on North Circular Road, was the victim of a faulty will drawn up by a schoolmaster. This incident provided a sub-plot for *Juno and the Paycock*. The false legacy or reversal of fortune was a staple of Victorian melodrama.
37 O'Casey, *Autobiographies*, 4, p. 120.
38 Fallon, *Sean O'Casey*, p. 19.
39 Victoria Stewart, *About O'Casey: The playwright and the work* (London: Faber & Faber, 2003), p. 110.
40 Peadar O'Donnell, in James Plunkett, *The Gems She Wore* (London: Arrow Books, 1978), p. 161.
41 Rosamond Jacob, *Diary*, NLI, MS 32,582, vol. 45, 7 March 1924.
42 Sean O'Casey, 'Juno and the Paycock', in *Two Plays* (London: Macmillan, 1925), p. 4.
43 Ibid., p. 22.
44 Bertolt Brecht, *Mother Courage and Her Children*, John Willett (tr.) (London: Methuen, 1980).
45 Jack Mitchell, *The Essential O'Casey* (New York: International Publishers, 1980), p. 55. While Mitchell's book is the most comprehensive and extensive analysis of O'Casey's drama from a left-wing perspective, he is on occasions over-reductive and prescriptive in judging O'Casey's characters by his own Marxist standards.
46 Herbert Goldstone, *In Search of Community* (Cork: Mercier Press, 1972), p. 39.
47 O'Casey, 'Juno and the Paycock', in *Two Plays*, p. 110.
48 Ibid.
49 Patrick H. Pearse, *Collected Works of Pádraic H. Pearse: Plays, stories, poems* (Dublin: Phoenix, 1924), p. 333.
50 O'Casey, 'Juno and the Paycock', p. 111. O'Casey would have been aware of Yeats' poem 'Easter 1916' where, in a heroic and uplifting way, hearts are turned to stone in a rebellion that 'changed utterly' the course of Irish history.
51 O'Casey, 'Juno and the Paycock', p. 111.
52 Ibid., p. 113.

53 Ronald Ayling, 'History and Artistry in Sean O'Casey's Trilogy', *Theoria*, no. 31, October 1971, p. 8.
54 Sean O'Casey, interview with Rupert Croft-Cooke, 'The Real Sean O'Casey', *Theatre World* (London), October 1926.
55 The Irregulars were the republican forces that opposed the Free State forces during the Civil War which began in 1922.
56 John Crowley in Stewart, *About O'Casey*, p. 101.
57 O'Casey, 'Juno and the Paycock', p. 71.

CHAPTER 10: THE PLOUGH IS HITCHED TO THE STARS

1 C.C. Barfoot, 'By Way of Introduction: Saint Joan', in C.C. Barfoot and Rias van den Doel (eds), *Ritual Remembering: History, myth and politics in Anglo-Irish drama* (Amsterdam & Atlanta GA: Rodopi, 1995), p. 10.
2 Seamus Deane, *Small World: Ireland, 1798–2018* (Cambridge: Cambridge University Press, 2021), p. 264.
3 Roland Barthes, *Mythologies*, Annette Lavers (tr.) (New York: Farrar, Straus & Giroux, 1972). See also Adrian Caesar, *Dividing Lines: Poetry, class and ideology in the 1930s* (Manchester: Manchester University Press, 1991), introduction.
4 Editorial, *The Irish Times*, 11 May 2000.
5 Fintan O'Toole, *The Irish Times*, 22 November 2002.
6 Seán Holmes, quoted in Peter Crawley interview, *The Irish Times*, 16 March 2016.
7 Seán O'Faoláin, quoted in Diarmaid Ferriter, *Between Two Hells: The Irish Civil War* (London: Profile Books, 2021), p. 144.
8 Seán O'Faoláin, *The Irish Times*, 17 February 1966.
9 Quoted by Brooks Atkinson, *New York Times*, 16 May 1926.
10 Geraldine Dillon, 'Irish Republican Brotherhood', *University Review* (Dublin), vol. 2, no. 8, 1961, pp. 23–36.
11 Kevin Whelan, 'The Revisionist Debate in Ireland', *Boundary 2*, vol. 3, no. 1, Spring 2004, pp. 179–205.
12 See George Lyons, *An t-Óglác*, 24 April 1926.
13 This was also a point that Peadar O'Donnell made in his book on the Spanish Civil War. Reacting against the concept of wars being 'fought between devils and angels', he wrote that 'Spaniards are like the rest of us, brave and cowardly by turns'. *Salud! An Irishman in Spain* (Dublin: Friends of the International Brigades in Ireland, 2020), p. 10.
14 Thomas McCarthy, Bureau of Military History, *Witness Statement 307*.
15 Michael Foy and Brian Barton, *The Easter Rising* (Stroud: Sutton Publishing, 2004), p. 131.
16 Sean O'Casey, *The Plough and the Stars* (London: Macmillan, 1926), pp. 121, 128. Fluther's protest at the uneven odds carries more than an echo of the protest made by John Dillon MP in the House of Commons on 11 May 1916 against the executions of the leaders of the rising. Dillon said: 'It would be a damned good thing for you if your soldiers were able to put up as good a fight as did these men in Dublin: three thousand against twenty thousand with machine-guns and artillery.' (*HC Deb*, 11 May 1916, vol. 82, cc. 952).
17 Bernice Schrank, 'Sean O'Casey and the Dialectics of Violence', in Danine Farquharson and Sean Farrell (eds), *Shadows of the Gunmen: Violence and culture in modern Ireland* (Cork: Cork University Press, 2008), pp. 38–62.
18 Tom Irwin, *The Voice of Labour*, 20 February 1926.
19 'A Tale of Easter Week', *Banba*, vol. 2, no. 6, April 1922, pp. 468–72.
20 Ibid., p. 468.
21 O'Casey, *The Plough and the Stars*, p. 114.
22 Amos Oz, *Judas* (London: Chatto & Windus, 2016), p. 207.

23 Peadar O'Donnell, quoted in Michael McInerney, *Peadar O'Donnell: Irish social rebel* (Dublin: O'Brien Press, 1974), p. 197.

24 James Moran, *Staging the Easter Rising: 1916 as theatre* (Cork: Cork University Press, 2005), pp. 33, 34.

25 See Pádraic H. Pearse, *Collected Works: Political writings and speeches* (Dublin: Phoenix, 1924), p. 333.

26 O'Casey, *The Plough and the Stars*, typescript with additions, NLI, *O'Casey Papers*, Collection List 75, MS 29,407. See also James Moran, 'Class During the Irish Revolution: British soldiers, 1916 and the abject body', in Michael Pierse (ed.), *A History of Working-Class Writing* (Cambridge: Cambridge University Press, 2018), p. 160.

27 See Joost Augusteijn, 'Patrick Pearse: Proto-fascist or mainstream European thinker?', *History Ireland*, vol. 18, no. 6, November/December 2010, p. 34; Kevin Myers, 'Myths of Ireland's Easter Rising', *The Dorchester Review*, vol. 6, no. 1, Spring/Summer 2016, pp. 23–31; Liam Collins, 'Rebel Pearse was no gay blade but had autistic temperament', *Irish Independent*, 9 August 2006.

28 Quoted in Harry Browne review of Terence Brown, 'The Irish Times: 150 years of influence', in *The Sunday Times*, Culture Section, 19 April 2015, p. 32.

29 Pearse, 'The Sovereign People' (1916), in *Collected Works: Political writings and speeches*, p. 350.

30 Pearse, '*From a Heritage*' (October 1913), in *Collected Works: Political writings and speeches,* p. 177.

31 O'Casey, *Autobiographies*, 3, p. 235.

32 Ibid., p. 242.

33 See Raymond J. Porter, 'O'Casey and Pearse', in Robert G. Lowery (ed.), *Essays on Sean O'Casey's Autobiographies* (New York and London: Macmillan, 1981), pp. 89–102.

34 O'Casey, *The Plough and the Stars*, p. 59.

35 Micheál Ó hAodha, 'The First Production', Abbey Theatre programme for *The Plough and the Stars*, 1976. Ethel Mannin was a novelist and political activist.

36 Robert G. Lowery, *A Whirlwind in Dublin: The Plough and the Stars riots* (Westport, CT: Greenwood Press, 1984), p. 11.

37 Anne Horniman was a benefactor of the Abbey but withdrew her financial support when the theatre refused to shut as a mark of respect to the late King Edward VII in 1910.

38 Lady Gregory, *Journals*, 2 vols, Daniel J. Murphy (ed.) (Gerrards Cross: Colin Smythe, 1978–88), vol. 2, p. 42.

39 Thomas Sheridan was playing at the Smock Alley Theatre in Dublin in January 1747. Edward Kelly, a student at Trinity College, climbed on to the stage and then proceeded to the dressing rooms where he tried to rape one of the actresses. Sheridan stopped the play, went back, confronted Kelly and had him arrested. Kelly's friends banded together and two nights later ransacked the theatre. Seven of the rioters including Kelly were indicted for riot.

40 See *The Irish Statesman*, 20 February 1926, 6 March 1926.

41 Arthur Griffith, *Sinn Féin*, 2 February 1907.

42 For a discussion on this see Timothy Hays, *The Review: A journal of undergraduate student research*, http://fisherpub.sjfc.edu/ur/vol1/iss1/5 (accessed 21 January 2021).

43 *The Irish Times*, 9 February 1926.

44 Joseph Holloway, *Joseph Holloway's Abbey Theatre: A selection from his unpublished journals* (Carbondale: Southern Illinois Press, 1967), p. 252. Holloway was a devoted playgoer who kept a journal note of every play that he attended up to his death in 1944.

45 Ibid.

46 Garry O'Connor, *Sean O'Casey: A life* (London: Hodder & Stoughton, 1988), p. 198. The twenty-year-old Samuel Beckett was also in the audience that night.

47 Sighle Humphreys, republican activist and socialist, https://www.dib.ie/biography/humphreys-sighle-mary-ellen-sighle-bean-ui-dhonnchadha-a4157 (accessed 25 November 2022).
48 Dorothy Macardle, writer and activist. She reviewed the 1931 production of *The Plough and the Stars* as containing 'a cynical disparagement of the Irish struggle', *Irish Press*, 22 September 1931. See Leeann Lane, *Dorothy Macardle* (Dublin: UCD Press, 2019), pp. 119–20.
49 *The Irish Times*, 12 February 1926.
50 Holloway, *Joseph Holloway's Abbey Theatre*, p. 254.
51 Shelah Richards, extract from an unpublished autobiography. See programme for Abbey Theatre production of *The Plough and the Stars*, 1976.
52 Holloway, *Joseph Holloway's Abbey Theatre*, p. 253.
53 *The Catholic Bulletin*, March 1926, pp. 242–50.
54 *Evening Herald*, 12 February 1926.
55 Liam O'Flaherty, *The Informer* (London: Jonathan Cape, 1925).
56 O'Casey, *Letters*, 1, p. 167.
57 Hanna Sheehy Skeffington, *Hanna Sheehy Skeffington: Suffragette and Sinn Féiner*, Margaret Ward (ed.) (Dublin: UCD Press, 2017), p. 259. See also *Irish Citizen*, September 1919 for review of O'Casey pamphlet on ICA.
58 Sean O'Casey, *Irish Independent*, 20 February 1926.
59 Liam O'Flaherty, *The Irish Statesman*, 20 February 1926, p. 767.
60 Brian Trench, 'The Radical Club', *History Ireland*, vol. 27, no. 5, September/October 2019, p. 44.
61 Ibid., p. 46.
62 Tom Irwin, *Voice of Labour*, 13 February 1926.
63 *The Irish Statesman*, 15 February 1926.
64 The entire correspondence and the quotes following concerning the disturbances are to be found in Lowery, *A Whirlwind in Dublin*.
65 Report of debate, *Irish Independent*, 2 March 1926.
66 Ibid.
67 Máire Comerford, *Memoir* (UCD Archives), chapter 21, pp. 1–2. Robert Johnston's nationalist play *The Old Land* (1903) was condemned for having a scene set in a public house.
68 *Irish Independent*, 2 March 1926.
69 Ibid.
70 All the above quotes are from the report of the meeting in the *Irish Independent*, 2 March 1926.
71 Holloway, *Joseph Holloway's Abbey Theatre*, p. 266.
72 Owen Sheehy Skeffington in O'Casey, *Letters*, 1, n. 2, p. 179.
73 Hollywood has not been kind to O'Casey either. John Ford's adaption of *The Plough and the Stars* (1936) was given the full Hollywood treatment. In O'Casey's play Jack Clitheroe is killed and Nora goes insane, but in Ford's film version Jack and Nora survive unscathed. See Adrian Frazier, 'Barry Goes to Hollywood', *The Dublin Review*, no. 15, Summer 2004, pp. 68–86.
74 See *The Irish Times*, 10 November 1947, pp. 4, 5.
75 Seán O'Faoláin, quoted in Ronald Ayling, *Sean O'Casey* (Nashville: Aurora, 1970), p. 194.

CHAPTER 11: THE TEMPTATIONS OF FAME: 1926–36

1 NLI, *O'Casey Papers*, Collection List 75, MS 37,944 27, April to May 1926.
2 *The Irish Times*, 12 June 1926.

3 The Garrick Club was founded in London in 1831 as a 'gentlemen's club' drawing its membership from the theatrical and artistic world. It remains an exclusive and men-only club to this day (though a number of pending legal actions may change policy).
4 O'Casey, *Letters*, 1, p. 186.
5 NLI, *O'Casey Papers*, Collection List 75, MS 46,725.
6 Constance Vaughan, 'O'Casey Explains Himself', *Daily Sketch*, 24 March 1926.
7 Sean O'Casey, in Victoria Stewart (ed.), *About O'Casey: The Playwright and the work* (London: Faber & Faber, 2003), p. 25.
8 Interview with O'Casey, *Daily Sketch*, 6 March 1926.
9 See Jeffrey Skelley (ed.), *The General Strike, 1926* (London: Lawrence & Wishart, 1976).
10 O'Casey, *Letters*, 1, p. 192.
11 NLI, *O'Casey Papers*, Collection List 75, MS 37,993, 21 February 1927, 10 March 1927.
12 O'Casey, *Letters*, 1, p. 202.
13 Sean O'Casey, *Liverpool Post and Mercury*, 2 June 1926.
14 O'Casey, *Letters*, 1, p. 202, and O'Casey, *Autobiographies*, 5, p. 58.
15 O'Casey, *Autobiographies*, 5, p. 63.
16 O'Casey, *Letters*, 2, p. 938.
17 Ibid.
18 Sean O'Casey, *Irish Worker*, 21 February 1914.
19 O'Casey, *Letters*, 1, p. 313.
20 Shivaun O'Casey (interview with author, 2 June 2010).
21 O'Casey, *Autobiographies*, 5, p. 16.
22 Ibid., pp. 78–91, most likely the home of Lord and Lady Londonderry in London.
23 Ramsay MacDonald, in O'Casey, *Letters*, 1, p. 444.
24 Joseph Holloway in Robert Hogan and Michael J. O'Neill (eds), *Joseph Holloway's Abbey Theatre: A selection from his unpublished journals* (Carbondale: Southern Illinois University Press, 1967), pp. 270–1.
25 Ian Kershaw, *Making Friends with Hitler* (London: Penguin, 2005), p. 24.
26 O'Casey must have been aware of the reactionary politics of Lord Londonderry. O'Casey's friend Jack Carney wrote for *Spanish News* (a London-based paper supporting the Spanish Republic during the Civil War). In the issue of 5 February 1937 in a series headed 'Enemies of Spain', they exposed Lord Londonderry's support for 'Hitler and his lieutenants', and also featured an article by Jack Carney, 'What Frank Ryan Means to Ireland'.
27 Kershaw, *Making Friends with Hitler*, chapter 1.
28 https://first100years.org.uk/nancy-astor-viscountess-astor/ (accessed 20 August 2021).
29 O'Casey, *Letters*, 1, p. 749.
30 O'Casey, *Letters*, 2, p. 153.
31 NLI, *O'Casey Papers*, Collection List 75, MS 37,943, 16 June 1962, 6 March 1964.
32 Marie White, *The South Atlantic Quarterly*, vol. 53, 1954, p. 156.
33 Robert Burns, 'The Silver Tassie', https://www.scottishpoetrylibrary.org.uk/poem/silver-tassie/ (accessed 20 August 2020).
34 Perhaps as a tribute to Charles Stewart Parnell, the football club is called 'Avondale', the name of the Parnell family home in Wicklow.
35 Wilfred Owen, 'Disabled', *The Collected Poems* (London: Chatto & Windus, 1971), p. 67.
36 Sean O'Casey, 'The Silver Tassie' (stage version), IV, 103, in *Collected Plays*, vol. 2 (London: Macmillan, 1949).
37 O'Casey, *Autobiographies*, 5, p. 31.
38 See O'Casey, 'The Silver Tassie' (stage version).
39 See Carol Kleiman, *Sean O'Casey's Bridge of Vision: Four essays on structure and perspective* (Toronto: University of Toronto Press, 1982), p. 133, n. 3.

40 Ed Mulhall, 'From Somme to Silver Tassie: Seán O'Casey & the contested legacy of 1916', https://www.rte.ie/centuryireland/index.php/articles/from-somme-to-silver-tassie-sean-ocasey-the-contested-legacy-of-1916 (accessed 20 March 2018).
41 O'Casey, 'The Silver Tassie' (stage version), II, p. 35.
42 Brenna Katz Clarke and Harold Ferrar, *The Dublin Drama League 1919–1941* (Dublin: Dolmen Press, 1979), p. 16.
43 Denis Johnston, 'An Appreciation', *The Daily Telegraph*, 11 March 1926.
44 O'Casey, 'Green Goddess of Realism', *The Flying Wasp* (London: Macmillan, 1937), pp. 111–27.
45 Susan Cannon Harris, 'Red Star versus Green Goddess: Sean O'Casey's *The Star Turns Red* and the politics of form', *The Princeton University Library Chronicle*, vol. 68, nos 1–2, Winter 2007, p. 392.
46 Ronald Ayling, *Continuity and Innovation in Sean O'Casey's Drama* (Salzburg: Universität Salzburg, 1976), p. 141.
47 Richard Sheppard, 'German Expressionism', in Malcolm Bradbury and James McFarlane (eds), *Modernism: A guide to European literature 1890–1930* (London: Penguin, 1919), pp. 274–91.
48 Huntley Carter, *The New Spirit in the Cinema* (London: Shaylor, 1930).
49 I am grateful to Brendan Duddy SJ for this information on O'Casey's knowledge of German and Soviet film. Brendan Duddy, lecture, *Sean O'Casey, Ernst Toller, and Medieval Theatre*, Free University of Ireland, 21 May 2010.
50 Shivaun O'Casey (letter from Shivaun O'Casey to author).
51 See Ernst Toller, *Seven Plays* (London: John Lane The Bodley Head, 1935).
52 Ernst Toller, quoted in Martin Kane, *Weimar Germany and the Limits of Political Art* (Fife: Hutton Press, 1987), p. 93.
53 Joachim Fischer, 'Ernst Toller and Ireland', in Richard Dove and Stephen Lamb (eds), *German Writers and Politics 1918–1939* (London: Palgrave Macmillan, 1992), p. 192.
54 See Erwin Piscator, *The Political Theatre* (London: Eyre Methuen, 1963), p. x.
55 Ernst Toller, *Letters from Prison* (London: John Lane The Bodley Head, 1935), p. 253.
56 Quoted in Ayling, *Continuity and Innovation in Sean O'Casey's Drama*, p. 109.
57 O'Casey, *New Statesman*, 9 February 1935, p. 184.
58 In the mid to late 1930s in Britain the Workers' Theatre Movement, Left Book Club, Unity Theatre and the literary and artistic movements associated with them, for a brief period, provided the potential for such a movement (see chapter 12).
59 Erwin Piscator, in Michael Patterson, *The Revolution in German Theatre 1900–33* (London: Routledge & Kegan Paul, 1981), p. 130.
60 Richard Allen Cave, 'Johnston, Toller and Expressionism', in Joseph Ronsley (ed.), *Denis Johnston: A retrospective* (Gerrards Cross: Colin Smythe, 1981), p. 80.
61 Fischer, 'Ernst Toller and Ireland', pp. 192–206.
62 Kleiman, *Sean O'Casey's Bridge of Vision*, p. 5.
63 O'Casey, *Letters*, 1, p. 230.
64 Ibid., p. 235.
65 Terry Phillips, *Irish Literature and the First World War* (Bern: Peter Lang, 2015), pp. 152–63. See also Walter Benjamin, who wrote in 'Experience and Poverty' (1933): 'Wasn't it noticed at the time how many people returned from the front in silence?', quoted in *London Review of Books*, 17 June 2021, p. 33.
66 O'Casey, *Letters*, 1, p. 284. See also https://www.atlasofplaces.com/essays/experience-and-poverty/ (accessed 1 August 2022).
67 Ibid., pp. 225–336.
68 Ibid., p. 451.

69 Seán O'Faoláin, 'The Silver Tassie Staged', *The Irish Statesman*, 19 October 1929, pp. 134–5.
70 Clifford Odets, 'The Parish and the World of O'Casey', *New York Times Book Review*, 5 February 1950, p. 5.
71 *Irish Independent*, 29 August 1935.
72 Father M.H. Gaffney, *The Standard*, 16 August 1935. See also O'Casey, *Letters*, 1, pp. 418, 576.
73 O'Casey, *Letters*, 1, p. 579.
74 Myles na gCopaleen (Brian O'Nolan), *The Irish Times*, 3 October 1951. Brian O'Nolan is better known as the novelist Flann O'Brien, author of *At Swim-Two-Birds* (London: Longmans, Green, 1939). Whether O'Nolan was being deliberately provocative or just contrarian for the sake of controversy is hard to say.
75 Sean O'Casey, *Within the Gates* (London: Macmillan, 1933). See also Jack Mitchell, *A Study of the Twelve Major Plays of Sean O'Casey* (New York: International Publishers, 1980), pp. 126–48.
76 Sean O'Casey, *The Flying Wasp* (London: Macmillan, 1937), p. 48.
77 Robert Hogan, *The Experiments of Sean O'Casey* (London: St. Martin's Press, 1960), p. 77.
78 *New York Times*, 2 February 1969.
79 Robert G. Lowery and Patricia Angelin (eds), *My Very Dear Sean* (Madison, NJ: Fairleigh Dickenson University Press, 1985), p. 34.
80 George Nathan, *The American Spectator*, December 1934.
81 Lowery and Angelin, *My Very Dear Sean*, p. 35.
82 *New York American*, 23 October 1934.
83 *Daily Worker* (USA), 27 October 1934.
84 *Daily Express*, 7 February 1934.
85 Lowery and Angelin, *My Very Dear Sean*, p. 34.
86 Bernice Schrank, *Sean O'Casey: A research and production handbook* (Westport, CT: Greenwood Press, 1966), p. 79.
87 Christopher Murray, *Seán O'Casey: Writer at work* (Dublin: Gill & Macmillan, 2004), p. 233.

CHAPTER 12: RISE O' THE RED STAR

1 O'Casey, *Autobiographies*, 5, p. 75.
2 O'Casey, *Autobiographies*, 3, p. 245.
3 O'Casey, *Letters*, 1, p. 781.
4 There is a problem about what to call Russia in the twentieth century. Before 1917 it was known as the Russian Empire. From about 1920 to 1991 it was officially known as the Soviet Union or the USSR. By the 1930s it was an empire under the control of the Stalinist bureaucracy, where all vestiges of workers' power or soviets had disappeared. I have used the terms Russia, Soviet Union or the USSR where it is appropriate, and where it was the term that O'Casey used.
5 O'Casey, *Autobiographies*, 4, p. 128. However, the Russian, critic and writer Korney Chukovsky was not impressed. He deemed the plays 'to be offensive to the dignity of working people': Richard Davies and W.J. McCormack, 'Sean O'Casey's Unpublished Correspondence with Raissa Lomonovska, 1925–6', *Irish Slavonic Studies*, no. 5, 1984, p. 182.
6 Sean O'Casey, *Lenin*, Berg Collection, New York Public Library. O'Casey added a handwritten note on the typed manuscript: 'For International Literature Magazine, Moscow, February 1960'.
7 David Krause, 'The Paradox of Ideological Formalism: Art vs. ideology', *The Massachusetts Review*, vol. 28, no. 3, Autumn 1987, pp. 516–24.
8 Saros Cowasjee, *Sean O'Casey: The man behind the plays* (Edinburgh: Oliver & Boyd, 1965), p. 169.

9 Barry McLoughlin and Emmet O'Connor, *In Spanish Trenches* (Dublin: UCD Press, 2020).
10 O'Casey, *Letters*, 1, p. 642.
11 Ibid., p. 676.
12 Sean O'Casey, *The Black Flag of Fascism*, Berg Collection, New York Public Library, n.d.
13 Frank Ryan, in Fearghal McGarry, *Irish Politics and the Spanish Civil War* (Cork: Cork University Press, 1999), p. 49.
14 Frank Ryan, *Irish Independent*, 14 December 1936.
15 O'Casey, *Letters*, 1, p. 646.
16 Ibid., p. 803.
17 Eileen O'Casey, *Sean* (London: Macmillan, 1971), p. 156.
18 O'Casey, *Letters*, 1, p. 656.
19 O'Casey, *Letters*, 2, p. 870.
20 W.H. Auden and Stephen Spender, *Authors Takes Sides* (London: Left Review, 1937).
21 What Ryan was doing in Germany has been a subject of controversy. A number of historians have tried to sully his reputation by accusing him of collaboration with the Nazi regime during the war. For a discussion on these matters see Enda Staunton, 'Frank Ryan & Collaboration: A reassessment', *History Ireland*, Autumn 1997, pp. 49–51. See also McLoughlin and O'Connor, *In Spanish Trenches*, chapter 9. James Moran has suggested that the character of the communist commander who is killed by the fascists in *The Star Turns Red* was based on Frank Ryan. See James Moran, *The Theatre of Seán O'Casey* (London: Bloomsbury Methuen Drama, 2013), p. 99.
22 O'Casey, *Letters*, 2, pp. 870, 879.
23 O'Casey, *Letters*, 1, p. 762.
24 See George Orwell, *Homage to Catalonia* (London: Secker & Warburg, 1938). Also *Revolutionary History*, vol. 4, nos 1–2, 1992 and McLoughlin and O'Connor, *In Spanish Trenches*, chapter 4.
25 Harry Pollitt, *Daily Worker*, 17 March 1937.
26 O'Casey, *Letters*, 2, p. 1120.
27 George Orwell, *The Observer*, 28 October 1945.
28 Quoted in Kevin Kirrane, 'Orwell's Ireland', *The Irish Review*, nos 36–7, Winter 2007, p. 26.
29 Sean O'Casey, *Autobiographies*, 6, p. 101. See also Arthur Mitchell, 'George Orwell and Sean O'Casey', *History Ireland*, vol. 6, no. 3, Autumn 1998, pp. 44–6.
30 Jack Mitchell, *A Study of the Twelve Major Plays of Sean O'Casey* (New York: International Publishers, 1980), p. 149.
31 O'Casey, *Letters*, 1, p. 655.
32 Ibid., p. 154.
33 Sean O'Casey, *The Star Turns Red* (London: Macmillan, 1940), p. 2.
34 O'Casey, *Letters*, 4, p. 279.
35 Shivaun O'Casey (letter to author).
36 Formed in the 1930s, the semi-fascist Army Comrades Association, later known as the National Guard and modelled on Mussolini's fascists in Italy, was also known as the Blueshirts from the colour of their tunic. In August 1936, the *Irish Independent* called for the formation of a committee to support Franco's fascists in Spain. This led to the formation of the Irish Christian Front with Patrick Belton the organisation's president.
37 Sean O'Casey, programme note, *The Star Turns Red*, Unity Theatre, 1946.
38 See Sean O'Casey, *Collected Plays*, vol. 2 (London: Macmillan, 1952), p. 240.
39 O'Casey, *The Star Turns Red*, p. 94.
40 Francis Devine, *Organising History: A centenary of SIPTU* (Dublin: Gill & Macmillan, 2009), chapter 10.

41 O'Casey, *The Star Turns Red*, p. 98.
42 Ibid., p. 184.
43 O'Casey, *Letters*, 1, p. 775.
44 For an interesting discussion on O'Casey and the politics of *The Star Turns Red*, though I have problems with some of her interpretations of Irish labour history, see Susan Cannon Harris, 'Red Star versus Green Goddess: Sean O'Casey's *The Star Turns Red* and the politics of form', *The Princeton University Library Chronicle*, vol. 68, nos 1–2, Winter 2007, pp. 357–98.
45 Roland G. Rollins, 'Sean O'Casey's *The Star Turns Red*: A political prophecy', *Mississippi Quarterly*, vol. xvi, 1963, p. 75.
46 Randall Swingler, *Daily Worker*, 23 March 1940.
47 O'Casey, *Letters*, 1, p. 795.
48 See Heinz Kosok, *Plays and Playwrights from Ireland in International Perspective* (Trier: WVT, 1995), pp. 172–9.
49 See letter to Richard Madden, Sean O'Casey, *Letters*, 1, p. 817.
50 George Strauss, *Tribune*, 13 September 1940. See also O'Casey, *Letters*, 1, pp. 868–73.
51 Barbara Nixon, 'Plays about Trade Unionism', *Left Review*, vol. 1, no. 2, November 1934, p. 42.
52 Unity circular (in possession of author).
53 Bernard Shaw was not a supporter of Unity Theatre, despite the fact that they produced many of his plays.
54 Unity manifesto (in possession of author).
55 Colin Chambers, *The Story of Unity Theatre* (London: Lawrence & Wishart, 1989), p. 27.
56 The Popular Front was a broad coalition of left-wing, and radical, liberal and even conservative forces united in the fight against fascism.
57 Sean O'Casey, *New Theatre*, no. 3, January 1938.
58 Ibid., no. 4, February 1938.
59 See Paul O'Brien, 'Writers of the Left: Politics and culture in Ireland in the 1930s', in Francis Devine, Fintan Lane and Niamh Puirséil (eds), *Essays in Irish Labour History* (Dublin: Irish Academic Press, 2008), pp. 210–14.
60 Quoted in Winifred Bannister, *James Bridie and His Theatre* (London: Rockliff, 1955), p. 193.
61 Correspondence regarding Unity Theatre Club, NLI, *O'Casey Papers*, Collection List 75, MS 38,049–52.
62 During the 1940s O'Casey's plays were a standard in the repertoire of the Unity Theatre group in Australia and New Zealand. Rachel Barrowman, *A Popular Vision: The arts and the left in New Zealand 1930–1950* (Wellington: Victoria University Press, 1991), p. 221.
63 Ewan MacColl, in Raphael Samuel, Ewan MacColl and Stuart Cosgrove, *Theatres of the Left: 1880–1935* (London: Routledge & Kegan Paul, 1985), p. 226.
64 Chambers, *The Story of Unity Theatre*, p. 138.
65 Ibid., p. 206.
66 O'Casey, *Letters*, 1, p. 837. O'Casey had met Peter Newmark in 1936 at a lecture he gave to the Shirley Society in Cambridge University. They corresponded and met on several occasions. As well as politics, they shared an interest in the theatre.
67 Quoted in Steve Nicholson, *British Theatre and the Red Peril* (Exeter: University of Exeter Press, 1999), p. 169.
68 James Agate, *The Sunday Times* (London), 17 March 1940.
69 O'Casey, *Letters*, 2, p. 342.
70 Ibid., p. 398.
71 Ibid.
72 O'Casey, *Letters*, 2, p. 366.

73 Ibid., p. 368.
74 Ibid., p. 1039.
75 Sean O'Casey, in J.B.S. Haldane (ed.), *Hands off the Daily Worker* (London: Daily Worker, 1940), p. 15.
76 J.B.S. Haldane, Sean O'Casey, J. Owen and R. Page Arnot, *The Case for the Daily Worker* (London: Marston Print Company, 1941).
77 O'Casey, *Letters*, 2, p. 67.
78 See Eileen O'Casey's letter to Brooks Atkinson, 10 October 1967, NLI, *O'Casey Papers*, Collection List 75, MS 37,919/11.
79 O'Casey, *Letters*, 3, p. 466.
80 Ronald Ayling and Michael J. Durkan (eds), *Sean O'Casey: A bibliography* (Seattle: University of Washington Press, 1998). They list sixty-one articles in Russian periodicals, in addition to dozens of articles that appeared in translation in the former Eastern bloc countries.

CHAPTER 13: THE LITERARY POPULAR FRONT: 1936–56

1 Frank Gloversmith (ed.), *Class, Culture and Social Change: A new view of the 1930s* (Brighton, Sussex/Atlantic Highlands, NJ: Harvester Press/Humanities Press, 1980).
2 Liam O'Flaherty, Leslie Daiken and R.M. Fox published books and articles arising from their visit to the USSR. See Katrina Goldstone, *Irish Writers and the Thirties* (New York & London: Routledge, 2021).
3 E.P. Thompson, quoted in Gertrude Himmelfarb, *The New History and the Old* (Cambridge, MA: Harvard University Press, 2004), p. 102.
4 Leslie Daiken described the 1930s as 'one long continuum of agitprop'. See Goldstone, *Irish Writers and the Thirties*, p. 48, where she describes the extensive political life and activities of Irish left-wing writers in London during that decade.
5 Gollancz had written to O'Casey in 1935 offering to publish his autobiography if he was not already committed to his existing publisher. This would have potentially given O'Casey access to the extensive Left Book Club readership. NLI, *O'Casey Papers*, Collection List 75, MS 37,882.
6 Sean O'Casey, *Left Review*, vol. 3, no. 16, May 1938, p. 961.
7 O'Casey, *Letters*, 3, p. 314.
8 Eileen O'Casey's letter to Brooks Atkinson, 10 October 1967, NLI, *O'Casey Papers*, Collection List 75, MS 37,919/11.
9 Andrei Zhdanov (1896–1948) was a member of the Politburo and led the assault on 'cosmopolitanism' which left the cultural world in shambles. Whether out of fear or cowardice, artists in the USSR and elsewhere competed to appear the most servile to the party; and those who did not fell silent. By 1947 Zhdanov's hold on cultural production in the USSR was almost total. In 1956 Nikita Khrushchev denounced Stalin's cultural policies, 'especially the cultural policies imposed on Leningrad through Zhdanov, as cruel and senseless. You can't regulate the development of literature, art, and culture with a stick, or by barking orders': www.spartucus-educational.com (accessed 20 May 2022).
10 O'Casey, *Letters*, 3, p. 112.
11 See Stephen Spender, *The Thirties and After* (London: Palgrave Macmillan, 1978), pp. 13–82. Also, Stephen Spender, 'Writers and Manifestoes', *Left Review*, vol. 1, no. 5, February 1935, pp. 145–50. Leslie Daiken, the Irish poet and activist, in his introduction to *Goodbye, Twilight: Songs of the struggle in Ireland* (London: Lawrence & Wishart, 1936) was undoubtedly influenced by the socialist realism concepts: 'The cultured studentry fostered pessimism. Futility, or more often an inconsequential groping in the dark for a new bourgeois aesthetic drove the most sensitive poets away from "politics" (i.e. Ireland: and all

its problems) to Paris, where the soul of Joyce ever presides as a source of inspiration to all thorough-going isolationists' (p. xii).

12 O'Casey, *Letters*, 2, p. 234.

13 Sean O'Casey, 'Censorship', *The Bell*, vol. 9, no. 5, February 1945, pp. 401–7.

14 Martin McCarthy, *Stalin and Stalinism* (Harlow: Pearson Longman, 2008), p. 51.

15 In January 1922, Sean McAteer along with the writer Liam O'Flaherty and about 200 unemployed workers occupied the Concert Room of the Rotunda in Dublin as a protest against the treatment of the unemployed by the newly formed Free State government. In Russia, Pat Breslin worked on the English language newspaper *Moscow News*.

16 Barry McLaughlin, *Left to the Wolves* (Dublin: Irish Academic Press, 2007).

17 For details see ibid., pp. 168–96.

18 T.A. Jackson, 'The Moscow Trial', *Left Review*, vol. 3, no. 2, March 1937, p. 15.

19 R. Page Arnot and Tim Buck, *Fascist Agents Exposed in the Moscow Trials* (London: Communist Party of Great Britain, 1938), p. 1.

20 J.R. Campbell, *Daily Worker*, 5 March 1938.

21 O'Casey, *Letters*, 1, pp. 705–22.

22 Ibid., p. 712.

23 Ibid., p. 718.

24 Ibid., p. 719.

25 See for instance 'The Case of Leon Trotsky' (Report of Dewey Commission, 1937), https://www.marxists.org/archive/trotsky/1937/dewey/index.htm (accessed 15 April 2018).

26 O'Casey, *Letters*, 1, p. 915. Peadar O'Donnell also defended the Russian invasion of Finland and shared the view that nothing in the newspapers about Russia could be believed. See Goldstone, *Irish Writers and the Thirties*, p. 172.

27 Quoted in Richard Greeman, 'Victor Serge and the Novel of Revolution', *Socialism* (Brussels), nos 226/7, July/October 1991.

28 See O'Casey, *Autobiographies*, 6, p. 94.

29 Sean O'Casey, *Oak Leaves and Lavender* (London: Macmillan, 1946), pp. 65–7.

30 O'Casey, *Autobiographies*, 6, p. 94.

31 See Leon Trotsky, *The Revolution Betrayed* (New York: Pathfinder Press, 1937).

32 In June 1953, workers in East Berlin rose in protest against government demands to increase productivity. Within days, nearly a million people joined the protests and began rioting across East German cities and towns.

33 Eric Hobsbawm, *Interesting Times: A twentieth-century life* (London: Allen Lane, 2002), p. 201.

34 See Peter Fryer, *Hungarian Tragedy* (London: New Park Publications, 1986) for an account of events.

35 Sean O'Casey, Berg Collection, New York Public Library.

36 Sean O'Casey, *Behind the Green Curtains, Figuro in the Night, The Moon Shines on Kylenamoe* (London: Macmillan, 1961).

37 O'Casey, *Letters*, 3, p. 349. While he was in New York in 1934, O'Casey was invited to speak at a local synagogue, where he spoke about the 'curious resemblances existing between the Jews and the Irish', *Autobiographies*, 5, p. 201.

38 Sean O'Casey, a note attached to Niall O'Casey's letter to his father regarding the events in Hungary. See Eileen O'Casey, *Sean* (London: Macmillan, 1971), p. 251.

39 Niall O'Casey, quoted in Eileen O'Casey, *Sean*, p. 250. J.R. Campbell, who was the editor of the *Daily Worker*, played a similar role in defending the USSR during the treason trials of 1938.

40 Eileen O'Casey, *Sean*, p. 251.

41 David Krause, in O'Casey, *Letters*, 3, p. 236.

42 Manus O'Riordan, 'Sean O'Casey and O'Riordan's on the 1956 Hungarian Uprising', *Irish Foreign Affairs*, December 2016.
43 *Daily Worker*, 25 October 1956.
44 Fryer, *Hungarian Tragedy*, p. 9.
45 O'Casey, Letters, 3, p. 341.
46 Ibid., p. 291.
47 Hobsbawm, *Interesting Times*, p. 217.
48 Jean Paul Sartre quoted by Elizabeth Day, *The Observer*, review section, 13 April 2008, p. 25.
49 O'Casey, *Letters*, 3, p. 635.
50 O'Casey, *The Green Crow* (London: W.H. Allen, 1957), p. 225. Harold Laski was one of Britain's most influential intellectual spokespersons for communism. Rajani Palme Dutt was a leading theoretician of the Communist Party of Great Britain.
51 W.J. Wetherby, 'Figures in the Shadows', *The Guardian*, 10 September 1959.
52 Sean O'Casey, quoted in Victoria Stewart, *About O'Casey: The playwright and the work* (London: Faber & Faber, 2003), p. 57.
53 O'Casey, *Letters*, 3, p. 158.
54 Ibid., pp. 157, 261. See also David Krause, 'The Paradox of Ideological Formalism: Art vs. ideology', *The Massachusetts Review*, vol. 28, no. 3, Autumn 1987, pp. 516–24.
55 Shivaun O'Casey (letter to author). The first two volumes of O'Casey's autobiography were published in the USSR in 1957, and in 1961 a volume of seven plays.
56 *The Seán O'Casey Review*, vol. 7, 1981, p. 22.
57 Sean O'Casey, *The Anglo-Soviet Journal* (London), vol. 7, no. 1, Spring 1946, p. 39.
58 See Wiktor Woroszylski, *The Life of Mayakovsky* (London: Victor Gollancz, 1972), pp. 413–25.
59 O'Casey, *The Anglo-Soviet Journal*, p. 39. O'Casey may have seen this groundless accusation in *Left Review*, vol. 2, no. 15, December 1936, p. 111.
60 For details of HUAC investigations and the impact on the left in America, see Howard Zinn, *A People's History of the United States: From 1492 to the present* (Harlow: Longman, 1996), pp. 420–8.
61 O'Casey, *Letters*, 2, p. 784.
62 NLI, *O'Casey Papers*, Collection List 75, MS 37,970.
63 O'Casey, *Letters*, 2, p. 996. Barrows Dunham was the author of *Giant in Chains* (Boston: Little, Brown & Company, 1953), a study of American values and democracy that was influenced by philosophical Marxism.
64 NLI, *O'Casey Papers*, Collection List 75, MS 38,114/1.
65 See Christopher Murray, *Seán O'Casey: Writer at work* (Dublin: Gill & Macmillan, 2004), p. 511 (n. 62).
66 Herbert Goldstone, 'O'Casey in '74: Or has everything been said?', *The Seán O'Casey Review*, vol. 1, no. 1, Fall 1974, p. 9.
67 David Krause, *Sean O'Casey: The man and his work* (London: MacGibbon & Kee, 1960), p. 160.
68 O'Casey, *Letters*, 1, p. 842.
69 NLI, *O'Casey Papers*, Collection List 75, MS 37,807–38,173, MS L93.
70 See John Irwin letter to O'Casey, NLI, *O'Casey Papers*, Collection List 75, MS 37,938, and O'Casey, *Letters*, 2, p. 29.
71 See NLI, *O'Casey Papers*, Collection List 75, MS 37,942.
72 British National Archives, FO1110/189. The *Guardian* review section, 21 June 2003, also printed the list of names. The list included Liam O'Flaherty, Bernard Shaw and Peadar O'Donnell. Orwell noted that Shaw cannot be trusted because he is 'reliably pro-Russian on all major issues' and that O'Casey is 'very stupid'.

73 Gjon Mili, *Life Magazine*, 9 October 1964.
74 Saros Cowasjee, *The Irish Times*, 25 July 1959.
75 See NLI, *O'Casey Papers*, Collection List 75, MS 37,981, MS 38,003, MS 38,004, for examples.
76 O'Casey, *Letters*, 2, p. 802.
77 Ibid., p. 1108. O'Casey was extremely annoyed when he saw the title given by the editor to an article of his on religion, 'Clericalism Gone Loony', *Daily Worker*, 20 March 1945.
78 E.P. Thompson, *The Making of the English Working Class* (London: Victor Gollancz, 1963), p. 12.
79 Michael Harrington, *The Vast Majority* (New York: Simon & Schuster, 1977), p. 175.
80 Leopold Trepper, quoted in *London Review of Books*, 21 November 2019, p. 17. A period of political liberalisation in the Czechoslovak Socialist Republic in January 1968, under Alexander Dubček, continued until August 1968, when the Soviet Union and other Warsaw Pact members invaded the country to suppress the regime.
81 See Andy Croft (ed.), *A Weapon in the Struggle* (London: Pluto Press, 1998).

CHAPTER 14: WAR AND IMPERIALISM

1 Charles Grimes, 'Bernard Shaw's Theory of Political Theatre: Difficulties from the vantages of postmodern and modern types of self', *SHAW: The annual of Bernard Shaw studies*, vol. 22, 2001, pp. 117–30.
2 Michael Feingold, *The Village Voice*, 5 March 2007.
3 David Krause, *Sean O'Casey: The man and his work* (London: MacGibbon & Kee, 1960).
4 Ibid., pp. 66–80.
5 Gabriel Fallon, *Sean O'Casey: The man I knew* (London: Routledge & Kegan Paul, 1965), pp. 68, 72.
6 Jules Koslow, *The Green and the Red: Sean O'Casey – The man and his plays* (New York: Golden Griffin Books, 1950), p. 42.
7 Sean O'Casey, 'O'Casey in a Hungarian Costume', in Ronald Ayling (ed.), *Blasts and Benedictions* (London: Macmillan, 1967), p. 136.
8 V.I. Lenin, 'The Right of Nations to Self-Determination', *Collected Works*, 45 vols (Moscow: Progress Publishers, 1972), vol. 20, pp. 393–454.
9 Erwin Piscator, *The Political Theatre* (London: Eyre Methuen, 1963).
10 See also James Moran, who re-examined O'Casey's attitude to violence for political ends in light of a later play, *Oak Leaves and Lavender*. Moran demonstrates that O'Casey was ready to endorse military action if such action advanced 'the cause of the left', in 'Conflicting Counter-Hegemonies? The dramaturgy of James Connolly and Sean O'Casey', *Kritika Kultura*, nos 21–2, 2013–14, http://kritikakultura.ateneo.net (accessed 20 October 2022).
11 Bernice Schrank, 'The Politics of O'Casey's War Plays', in C.C. Barfoot and Rias van den Dole (eds), *Ritual Remembering: History, myth and politics in Anglo-Irish drama* (Amsterdam & Atlanta, GA: Rodopi, 1995), p. 75. See also Bernice Schrank, 'Sean O'Casey and the Dialectics of Violence', in Danine Farquharson and Sean Farrell (eds), *Shadows of the Gunmen: Violence and culture in modern Ireland* (Cork: Cork University Press, 2008), pp. 38–62.
12 W.B. Yeats, 'The Man and the Echo', in *Collected Poems* (London: Macmillan, 1950), p. 393.
13 Lenin, *Collected Works*, vol. 9, p. 169.
14 Ronald Ayling, *Sean O'Casey's Theatre of War* (Vernon, BC: Kamalalka Press, 2004).
15 John Jordan, 'A World in Chassis', *University Review* (Dublin), vol. 1, no. 4, Spring 1955, pp. 21–8.
16 T.A. Jackson, *The Workers' Weekly*, 24 June 1928.

17 Christopher Murray, 'O'Casey at War', in Kathleen Devine (ed.), *Modern Irish Writers and the Wars* (Gerrards Cross: Colin Smythe, 1999), pp. 81–101.

18 Sean O'Casey, *Oak Leaves and Lavender* (London: Macmillan, 1946), p. 84.

19 Ibid., p. 132. Frederick Douglass' emancipation speech (1857): 'Those who profess to favor freedom and yet deprecate agitation are men who want crops without plowing up the ground; they want rain without thunder and lightning. They want the ocean without the awful roar of its many waters', https://www.blackpast.org/african-american-history/1857-frederick-douglass-if-there-no-struggle-there-no-progress/ (accessed 24 May 2019).

20 Ibid., p. 70.

21 O'Casey, *Letters*, 2, p. 80.

22 Eric Hobsbawm, *Interesting Times: A twentieth-century life* (London: Allen Lane, 2002), chapter 10.

23 See Donny Gluckstein, *A People's History of the Second World War* (London: Bookmarks, 2012) for debate on the class nature of the war.

24 Maroula Joannou, 'Sylvia Townsend Warner in the 1930s', in Andy Croft (ed.), *A Weapon in the Struggle: The cultural history of the Communist Party in Britain* (London: Pluto Press, 1998), p. 98.

25 Hobsbawm, *Interesting Times*, p. 153.

26 O'Casey, *Letters*, 2, p. 814.

27 Sean O'Casey, 'What Are Our War Aims?', *Picture Post*, 11 November 1939.

28 O'Casey, *Letters*, 2, p. 891.

29 Interview with Nancy Ross on 21 June 2010 by author. Nancy Ross worked as Eileen's secretary in London after Sean O'Casey's death. Eileen had worked in the theatre with Nancy's mother. Nancy spoke about Seán's great 'sense of humanism'. She also said that Eileen disliked Garry O'Connor's biography of Seán because she felt 'that O'Connor had betrayed Seán', in the way that he portrayed him.

30 Quoted in Christopher Murray, *Seán O'Casey: Writer at work* (Dublin: Gill & Macmillan, 2004), p. 269.

31 O'Casey, *Letters*, 2, p. 95.

32 Ibid., p. 130.

33 See Clair Wills, *That Neutral Island* (London: Faber & Faber, 2007) for an account of Irish neutrality during the Second World War.

34 Sean O'Casey, 'Ireland Should Be Against the War', *Irish Freedom*, January 1940.

35 As part of the treaty in 1921 Britain retained three ports in the Free State for military use. The treaty ports were returned to Irish control in 1938.

36 Sean O'Casey, *Irish Freedom*, January 1941.

37 O'Casey, *Letters*, 2, p. 144.

38 Sean O'Casey, 'There Go the Irish', in Leslie Daiken (ed.), *They Go, the Irish* (London: Nicholson & Watson, 1944), pp. 7–24. See O'Casey, *Blasts and Benedictions*, p. 252. Wing Commander Brendan Finucane, DSO, DFC, was an Irish Second World War Royal Air Force fighter pilot and flying ace, who was killed in action in 1942.

39 O'Casey, *Blasts and Benedictions*, pp. 245–61.

40 Sean O'Casey, *Irish Democrat*, June 1945.

41 See Eric Hobsbawm, *Age of Extremes: The short twentieth century, 1914–1991* (London: Abacus, 1995), chapter 8.

42 Ibid., pp. 228, 230.

43 O'Casey, *Letters*, 2, p. 725.

44 Ibid., p. 708.

45 Ibid., p. 869.

46 https://hatfulofhistory.wordpress.com/2013/03/21/the-communist-party-and-the-campaign-for-nuclear-disarmament (accessed 1 December 2019).
47 Sean O'Casey and seventeen others, *Irish Democrat*, June 1952.
48 NLI, *O'Casey Papers*, Collection List 75, MS 37,967, MS 37,970.
49 O'Casey, *Letters*, 3, p. 111.
50 Ibid., p. 36.
51 Published in *Manchester Guardian*, 31 July 1957. See also O'Casey, *Letters*, 3, p. 454.
52 Seamus Heaney, *The Government of the Tongue* (London: Faber & Faber, 1988), p. 107.

CHAPTER 15: RELIGION, GENDER AND IDENTITY

1 See Hanns Otto Münsterer, *The Young Brecht*, Tom Kuhn and Karen Leeder (tr.) (London: Libris, 1992), pp. 33, 77.
2 Vivien Mercier, 'Decline of a Playwright: The riddle of Sean O'Casey', *Commonweal* (New York), no. lxiv, 13 July 1956, pp. 366–8.
3 Bessie Burgess in *The Plough and the Stars* and the Grigsons in *The Shadow of a Gunman*.
4 Kenneth Milne, 'The Stripping of the Assets', in Kenneth Milne (ed.), *Christ Church Cathedral* (Dublin: Four Courts Press, 2010), p. 338.
5 See Bryan Whelan for history of St Barnabas parish, www.facebook.com/eastwallhistory (accessed 25 November 2022).
6 Hansard, *HC Deb, 04 July 1904, vol. 137, cc. 482–3.*
7 David Krause, 'Towards the End', in Sean McCann (ed.), *The World of Sean O'Casey* (London: Four Square Books, 1966), pp. 137–57.
8 Sean O'Casey, 'Sound the Loud Trumpet', *The Peasant and Irish Ireland*, 25 May 1907.
9 Sean O'Casey, Robert Hogan (ed.), *Feathers from the Green Crow 1905–1925* (London: Macmillan, 1963), p. 6.
10 *The Catholic Bulletin* (Dublin), March 1926, pp. 242–50.
11 *The Standard* (Dublin), 30 August 1935, p. 3.
12 Jack Mitchell, *The Essential O'Casey* (New York: International Publishers,1980), p. 169.
13 Conrad A. Balliett, 'The Lives – and Lies – of Maud Gonne', *Éire-Ireland*, vol. xiv, no. 3, Fall 1979, p. 33.
14 Sister Mary Carew, NLI, *O'Casey Papers*, Collection List 75, MS 37,973.
15 In 1938, George Thomson, the Blasket Island scholar, translated the *Book of Common Prayer* into Irish. O'Casey was pleased that a Marxist had done the translation.
16 Seán O'Casey, NLI, *O'Casey Papers*, Collection List 75, MS 37,911–13.
17 Father Michael Gallaher SJ, NLI, *O'Casey Papers*, Collection List 75, MS 37,913.
18 Sean O'Casey, 'Dowzard: The hector of the quays', *Irish Worker*, 20 December 1913.
19 Bernard Benstock, *Paycock and Others* (Dublin: Gill & Macmillan, 1976), p. 248.
20 Desmond MacCarthy, quoted in David Krause, 'Introduction', in Sean O'Casey, *Cock-a-Doodle Dandy* (Washington DC: Catholic University of America, 1991), p. 5.
21 Sean O'Casey, 'The Star Turns Red', in *Collected Plays*, vol. 2 (London: Macmillan, 1952), pp. 20, 22, 77.
22 https://www.vatican.va/content/leo-xiii/en/encyclicals/documents/hf_l-xiii_enc_15051891_rerum-novarum.html (accessed 10 March 2022).
23 O'Casey, *Autobiographies*, 5, p. 116. See also Pádraig Yeates, '"To Leaven Trades Unionism with Catholic Social Principles is the Dream I Cherish", Father Thomas Dowling OSFC', *Saothar*, no. 46, 2021, pp. 41–52.
24 Sean O'Casey, 'Study Course for a Vatican Recruit', in *The Pope, The People, and Politics* (London: People's Press Printing Society, 1948), p. 3. No relation to Dr Douglas Hyde of the Gaelic League and former president of Ireland.

25 Dermot Keogh and Andrew McCarthy, 'The Catholic Church and the Writing of the 1937 Constitution', *History Ireland*, vol. 13, no. 3, May/June 2005, pp. 36–41.

26 Karl Marx, *Critique of Hegel's Philosophy of Right*, Introduction, https://www.marxists.org/archive/marx/works/1843/critique-hpr/intro.htm (accessed 20 July 2019).

27 Sean O'Casey, 'Juno and the Paycock' in *Two Plays* (London: Macmillan, 1925), p. 31.

28 See William Morris, 'A Dream of John Ball', *Commonweal*, 13 November 1886 to 22 January 1887.

29 Sean O'Casey, '*The Plough and the Stars* in Retrospect', *The Seán O'Casey Review*, vol. 2, no. 2, Spring 1976, p. 157.

30 James Larkin, 'Murder Most Foul', *International Socialist Review* (New York), December 1916.

31 O'Casey, *Letters*, 4, p. 105. Cardinal Mindszenty was jailed by the Hungarian communist state after a 'show trial' in 1949 and released by the new regime during the Hungarian Revolution in 1956. *Behind the Green Curtains* (London: Macmillan, 1961) explores the moral cowardice of the Irish intellectual and liberal class and was a cutting riposte to those writers and intellectuals who had failed to support O'Casey during the controversy over *The Drums of Father Ned*.

32 David Krause, 'The Paradox of Ideological Formalism: Art vs. ideology', *The Massachusetts Review*, vol. 28, no. 3, Autumn 1987, pp. 516–24.

33 Sean O'Casey, 'A Crow for *Cock-a-Doodle Dandy*', *Articles on Catholicism*, Berg Collection, New York Public Library.

34 Mayor Mansfield, *Boston Globe*, 18 January 1935.

35 *The Harvard Crimson*, 25 January 1935, p. 2.

36 Robert G. Lowery, interviewed by author, 24 October 2004, New York.

37 O'Casey, *Letters*, 2, pp. 660–1.

38 Robert G. Lowery, *A Whirlwind in Dublin* (Westport, CT: Greenwood Press, 1984), p. 34.

39 W.B. Yeats, 'The Controversy over the *Playboy*', *The Arrow*, vol. 1, no. 3, 23 February 1907, p. 2.

40 National Archives, Dublin, Letter, 17 April 1934 (S 8,208). See also Lionel Pilkington, *Theatre and the State in Twentieth-Century Ireland* (London: Routledge & Kegan Paul, 2001), pp. 118–19 for further details.

41 Jack Mitchell, *The Essential O'Casey* (New York: International Publishers, 1980), pp. 149–50.

42 Mary Papke, '*Juno and the Paycock* as a Larkinite Stage Parable', *The Seán O'Casey Review*, vol. 3, no. 2, Spring 1977, pp. 105–16.

43 O'Casey, *Letters*, 1, p. 169.

44 Sean O'Casey, *The Plough and the Stars*, I, 32 (London: Macmillan, 1926). He returned to the theme of domestic work in his one-act comedy *The End of the Beginning*, where Lizzie sets her husband a challenge – to swap places with her and do the housework for a day – with disastrous results. Sean O'Casey, *Five Irish Plays* (London: Macmillan, 1935), pp. 343–80.

45 Ronald Ayling, 'Introduction', in *O'Casey: The Dublin trilogy* (London: Macmillan, 1985), p. 24.

46 Sean O'Casey, *The Bishop's Bonfire*, III (London: Macmillan, 1955).

47 Elizabeth Hazlehurst, 'O'Casey Frozen Out By Feminists', *Times Change*, no. 17, Spring/Summer 1999, p. 17.

48 O'Casey, *Letters*, 4, p. 163. This was a point also made by Cathy Airth: 'although critics have discussed the political content and implications of O'Casey's works in depth, there does not seem to have been as much attention paid to gender'. See Cathy Airth, 'Making the Least of Masculine Authority: Sean O'Casey's *Paycock* and *Plough and the Stars*', *Canadian Journal of Irish Studies*, vol. 32, no. 2, Fall 2006, p. 42.

49 Sean O'Casey, *Under a Colored Cap* (London: Macmillan, 1963), p. 55.
50 O'Casey, *The Irish Worker*, 11 April 1914.
51 Sam Sacks, 'Sean O'Casey's Women', *New York Review of Books*, 29 October 2013.
52 Victoria White, *Irish Examiner*, 21 April 2016.
53 Susan Cannon Harris, *Irish Drama and the Other Revolutions* (Edinburgh: Edinburgh University Press, 2017), p. 14.
54 Heather Laird, 'Writing Working-Class Women', in Michael Pierse (ed.), *A History of Working-Class Writing* (Cambridge: Cambridge University Press, 2018), p. 124.
55 Michael Pierse, 'The Shadow of Sean O'Casey: O'Casey, commitment and writing Dublin's working class', *Saothar*, vol. 35, 2010, pp. 69–85. See also Sarah L. Townsend, 'Walking the "Thorny Way": Pressures and predicaments of womanhood in Sean O'Casey's three Dublin plays', unpublished BA thesis, University of Michigan, 2002. Also Marianne Peyronnet, 'Was Sean O'Casey a Feminist Playwright?', *Times Change*, no. 12, Winter 1997/8, p. 23.
56 Rosie Hackett was a founder member of the Irish Women Workers' Union, She was active during the 1913 lockout, and took part in the 1916 Rising as part of the Irish Citizen Army contingent.
57 Seán O'Casey, interview with Don Ross, *New York Herald Tribune*, 16 November 1958.
58 Benstock, 'The Heroine as Hero', *Paycock and Others*, chapter 5.
59 Sinéad McCoole, *No Ordinary Women* (Dublin: O'Brien Press, 2016); Margaret Ward, *Unmanageable Revolutionaries* (London: Pluto Press, 1993); Roy Foster, *Vivid Faces* (London: Allen Lane, 2014).
60 Dorothy Macardle, *The Irish Republic* (London: Victor Gollancz, 1937).
61 Dorothy Macardle, quoted in Marie Bashford-Synnott, 'Annie M.P. Smithson: Romantic novelist, revolutionary nurse', *Dublin Historical Record*, vol. lxiv, no. 1, Spring 2011, p. 59. However, her letters to de Valera in the post-war period would indicate that her relationship with him 'was anything but one of alienation in the last decade of her life'. Leeann Lane, *Dorothy Macardle* (Dublin: UCD Press, 2019), p. 246.
62 *Irish Press*, 25 December 1958.
63 Lane, *Dorothy Macardle*, p. 246,
64 Foster, *Vivid Faces*, p. 152.
65 Belgrave Road in Rathgar was home to so many middle-class revolutionaries that it was known as 'Rebel Road'.
66 Friedrich Engels, *The Origin of the Family, Private Property and the State* (London: Lawrence & Wishart, 1942), p. 59.
67 See Angela Burke, et al., (eds), *The Field Day Anthology of Irish Writing: Irish women's writing and traditions* (Cork: Cork University Press in association with Field Day, 2002), vol. 5, p. 123. Margaret O'Callaghan links O'Casey to P.S. O'Hegarty as writers who articulated 'the trope of the nationalist harridan or "the fury"' as a way of dismissing women's political involvement on 'both sides in the Civil War divide, and in other political formations, after independence'. O'Casey was certainly critical of many of the middle-class women in the nationalist movement, but his portrayal of working-class women in the Dublin plays is regularly praised for their strength of character and their resolve in difficult circumstances. O'Casey's critique about class also makes some interesting observations about gender.
68 P.S. O'Hegarty, *The Victory of Sinn Féin* (Dublin: Talbot Press, 2015), pp. 39, 73.
69 Máire Comerford, quoted in Foster, *Vivid Faces*, p. 73.
70 James Connolly, *The Re-Conquest of Ireland* (Dublin: Maunsel, 1922), pp. 292–3.
71 The Murphy and Ryan Reports into the abuse of children and women in church-run institutions were published in 2009.
72 Shivaun O'Casey, *Irish Independent*, 3 October 2004.
73 O'Casey, *Letters*, 2, p. 171.

74 Letters from Miss Sheila O'Neill (1945–58), a Catholic factory worker in London, concerning religion and politics, the Catholic Church, communism and Russia. Also contains letters from her spiritual adviser, Father Cuthbert Cary Elwes SJ, and a copy of one of his sermons: NLI, *O'Casey Papers*, Collection List 75, MS 38,106. See also correspondence with dissident priest Dr John V. Simcox regarding his argument on the Catholic hierarchy, communism and Catholicism: MS 37,917/1–7. See also O'Casey, *Letters*, 2, pp. 687, 702, 714, 716, 735, 738, 739.

75 Shivaun O'Casey, *Irish Independent*, 3 October 2004.

76 Eileen O'Casey, NLI, *Eileen O'Casey Papers*, Collection List 137, MS 44,699/1, 44,762/1.

77 Eileen O'Casey, *Sean* (London: Macmillan, 1971), pp. 110–11.

78 Sean O'Casey, 'I Wanna Woman', *Cavalcade*, December 1961.

79 Sean O'Casey, 'The Job', *Scene*, August 1961.

80 Sean O'Casey, 'The Bald Primaqueera', *Atlantic Monthly*, September 1965, pp. 69–74. See also Sean O'Casey, *Blasts and Benedictions*, Ronald Ayling (ed.) (London: Macmillan, 1967), pp. 63–76.

81 Cannon Harris, *Irish Drama and the Other Revolutions*, p. 209.

CHAPTER 16: THE SHADOW OF THE VATICAN: 1950–64

1 O'Casey, *Letters*, 2, p. 797. In *The Bishop's Bonfire*, the character of Manus is named after the O'Riordans' son.

2 NLI, *O'Casey Papers*, Collection List 75, MS 37,971.

3 O'Casey, *Letters*, 4, p. 260. Kathleen Brady won 1,484 votes (3.4 per cent) in the 1961 general election in Carlow.

4 NLI, *O'Casey Papers*, Collection List 75, MS 38,117.

5 NLI, *Patrick Galvin Papers*, MS 49,654/43.

6 NLI, *O'Casey Papers*, Collection List 75, MS 38,117.

7 Ibid.

8 Patrick Galvin. See O'Casey, *Letters*, 2, p. 1074.

9 Dr John O'Brien (ed.), *The Vanishing Irish: The enigma of the modern world* (London: W.H. Allen, 1954).

10 Seamus Kelly, *The Irish Times*, 14 December 1949.

11 O'Casey, *Letters*, 2, pp. 659, 661.

12 J.H. Whyte, *Church and State in Modern Ireland* (Dublin: Gill & Macmillan, 1971), p. 214.

13 The fallout also led to the demise of Clann na Poblachta. In the immediate aftermath, seven branches disaffiliated, along with Dr Browne and a number of TDs. The party was dissolved in 1965.

14 See John Cooney, *John Charles McQuaid* (Dublin: O'Brien Press, 1999) on how McQuaid exercised enormous power over all aspects of government, education, hospitals and institutions of the state.

15 NLI, *O'Casey Papers*, Collection List 75, MS 38,005, letter from Sheila Greene, editor of *The Irish People*, October 1946. For O'Casey's reply, see O'Casey, *Letters*, 2, p. 402.

16 O'Casey, *Letters*, 2, p. 794.

17 Ibid., p. 849.

18 Donald Douglas, *Daily Worker*, 29 May 1953.

19 James Moran, 'Conflicting Counter-Hegemonies? The Dramaturgy of James Connolly and Sean O'Casey', *Kritika Kultura*, nos 21–2, 2013–14, https://ajol.ateneo.edu/kk (accessed 6 January 2023).

20 A famous line from W.B. Yeats' poem 'September 1913', utilised by Brinsley MacNamara in *The Clanking of the Chains* (Dublin: Maunsel, 1920), p. 2. This book is a pitiless exposure of

the verbal patriots who belittle every noble endeavour until it succeeds. MacNamara had an influence on a generation of Irish writers who 'had made the village their world'.

21 Quoted in Maurice Moynihan, 'On Language and the Irish Nation', in *Speeches and Statements by Éamon de Valera: 1917–1973* (Dublin: Gill & Macmillan, 1980), p. 466.

22 Even if O'Casey was prepared to offer *Cock-a-Doodle Dandy* to the Abbey, it is unlikely they could produce it, not only because the Abbey audience that O'Casey wrote for, but also the actors, were gone.

23 Best exemplified by Gabriel García Márquez, *One Hundred Years of Solitude* (New York: Harper & Row, 1970). First published in Spanish in 1967. Brecht and, to a lesser extent, O'Casey were reaching out to the genre before it was widely understood in Europe.

24 James Stephens, *The Crock of Gold* (London: Macmillan, 1912).

25 Sean O'Casey, *Cock-a-Doodle Dandy* (London: Macmillan, 1949), p. 100.

26 Doris daRin, *Sean O'Casey* (New York: Frederick Ungar Publishing, 1976), p. 141.

27 O'Casey, *Cock-a-Doodle Dandy*, p. 100.

28 Seamus Kelly, *The Irish Times*, 14 December 1949.

29 Quoted in daRin, *Sean O'Casey*, p. 138.

30 See Christopher Murray, *Seán O'Casey: Writer at work* (Dublin: Gill & Macmillan), p. 355.

31 O'Casey, *Letters*, 3, 27 March 1955, p. 94.

32 *The Standard*, 18 February 1955.

33 Ibid., 25 February 1955.

34 NLI, *O'Casey Papers*, Collection List 75, MS 37,937.

35 Ibid., (RUC were the Royal Ulster Constabulary, widely believed to be a sectarian and oppressive police force in Northern Ireland).

36 Sean O'Casey, *The Bishop's Bonfire* (London: Macmillan, 1955), pp. 54–5.

37 Ibid., p. 77.

38 Edna O'Brien, *Encore* (London), vol. vi, September/October 1961, p. 42.

39 O'Casey, *Letters*, 2, p. 124.

40 Gabriel Fallon, 'Roses With Thorns', *The Standard*, 28 June 1946. In *Red Roses for Me*, a statue of Our Lady of Eblana goes missing and then reappears restored and repainted in what appears to be a miracle, causing consternation among the local Catholic population. Several Irish critics, including Fallon, said that O'Casey was demeaning their religion and beliefs.

41 Gabriel Fallon, *Sean O'Casey: The man I knew* (London: Routledge & Kegan Paul, 1965), p. 174.

42 Ibid., p. 203.

43 An Tóstal Festival ran from 1953 to 1958 as a celebration of Irish life and culture.

44 Simpson was left with legal costs of £2,600. See Gerard Whelan and Carolyn Swift, *Spiked: Church–state intrigue and The Rose Tattoo* (Dublin: New Island Books, 2002) for details.

45 O'Casey, *Letters*, vol. 3, p. 439.

46 Despite the fact that McClelland had the script vetted by a priest to ensure it contained nothing objectional, Archbishop McQuaid opposed the production.

47 Quoted in E.H. Mikhail and John O'Riordan (eds), *The Sting and the Twinkle: Conversations with Sean O'Casey* (London: Macmillan, 1974), p. 115.

48 O'Casey, *Letters*, 3, p. 445, n. 1.

49 Ibid., p. 456.

50 Ibid., p. 529.

51 Shivaun O'Casey (letter to author).

52 See Peter Murray, 'Belting the Irish State with US Croziers: Theatre, tourism, UN policy and church–state relations, 1957–58', http://mural.maynoothuniversity.ie/2294 (accessed 10 February 2019).

53 O'Casey, *Letters*, 3, p. 530.

54 Seán O'Casey, *The Irish Times*, 17 February 1958.
55 Quoted in Murray, *Seán O'Casey*, p. 397. As late as 1963 the lord chamberlain in Britain banned the production of O'Casey's *Figuro in the Night* at an Irish festival in London.
56 O'Casey, *Letters*, 3, p. 627.
57 NLI, *O'Casey Papers*, Collection List 75, MS 37,971. Sybil le Brocquy was an Irish playwright and patron of the arts.
58 David Krause, *Sean O'Casey: The man and his work* (London: MacGibbon & Kee, 1960), pp. 202–24.
59 Quoted in Victoria Stewart, *About O'Casey: The playwright and the work* (London: Faber & Faber, 2003), p. 122.
60 Fintan O'Toole, Catherine Marshall and Eibhear Walshe (eds), *Modern Ireland in 100 Artworks* (Dublin: Royal Irish Academy, 2016), p. 111.
61 Sean O'Casey, 'Not Waiting For Godot', *Encore* (London), March 1956.
62 Shivaun O'Casey, *The Irish Times*, 12 October 2011.
63 O'Casey, *Letters*, 4, p. 231.
64 Sean O'Casey, 'The People and the Theatre', *Theatre Today* (London), no. 1, 1946, pp. 13–16.
65 Quoted in Susan Cannon Harris, 'Red Star versus Green Goddess: Sean O'Casey's *The Star Turns Red* and the politics of form', *The Princeton University Library Chronicle*, vol. 68, nos 1–2, Winter 2007, pp. 357–98.
66 Sean O'Casey, *Commonwealth Review*, January 1946.
67 Arnold Wesker was influenced by O'Casey's work and dramatic style and had read his autobiography.
68 Sean O'Casey, 'Mr. Wesker's March Past', *Blasts and Benedictions* (London: Macmillan, 1967), p. 62.
69 Arnold Wesker, quoted in O'Casey, 'Mr Wesker's March Past', p. 60, n. 1.
70 Quoted in Murray, *Seán O'Casey*, p. 434.

CHAPTER 17: KNOCKING ON THE DOOR

1 Brooks Atkinson, in Robert G. Lowery (ed.), *Essays on Sean O'Casey's Autobiographies* (London: Macmillan, 1981), p. xiii.
2 Quoted in Lowery, *Essays on Sean O'Casey's Autobiographies*, p. xiii.
3 Sean McCann, *The World of Sean O'Casey* (London: Four Square Books, 1966), p. 9.
4 Ibid., pp. 235, 236.
5 See Robert G. Lowery, *Sean O'Casey's Autobiographies: An annotated index* (Westport, CT: Greenwood Press, 1983); Lowery (ed.), *Essays on Sean O'Casey's Autobiographies*; Michael Kenneally, *Portraying the Self* (Gerrards Cross: Colin Smythe, 1988); Peter James Harris, *Sean O'Casey: Letters and autobiographies* (Trier: WVT, 2004); Robert G. Lowery, 'The Autobiographies of Sean O'Casey', *Research Studies* (USA), vol. xxxvii, no. 2, June 1969, pp. 122–9.
6 See Anthony Butler and David Krause, 'A Storm in the Fair City', *The Seán O'Casey Review*, vol. 3, no. 2, Spring 1977, pp. 127–43. See also essays in McCann, *The World of Sean O'Casey*.
7 St John Ervine, *The Spectator*, 2 November 1945.
8 Tony Butler, *Evening Herald*, 1 April 1980.
9 Sean O'Casey, in Patrick O'Connor, 'Theatre', *The Furrow*, vol. 12, no. 10, October 1965, p. 632.
10 Sean O'Casey, *The Bishop's Bonfire* (London: Macmillan, 1955), p. 117.
11 O'Casey, *Letters*, 1, p. 441.
12 Kenneally, *Portraying the Self*, p. 14.
13 See the work of Claude Levi-Strauss, Roland Barthes and Paul de Man on texts and their meaning.

14 O'Casey, *Autobiographies*, 4, p. 98.

15 Padraic Colum, 'Sean O'Casey's Narratives', in Ronald Ayling (ed.), *Sean O'Casey: Modern judgements* (London: Aurora Publishers, 1969), pp. 220–7.

16 O'Casey, *Autobiographies*, 4, p. 102.

17 Ibid., p. 51. The 'Tommies' were regular British army units who were more disciplined and less feared than the 'Black and Tans', an irregular auxiliary police force who acted with brutality and impunity towards the local population.

18 Kenneally, *Portraying the Self*, p. 16.

19 Samuel Beckett, *The Letters of Samuel Beckett*, 4 vols (Cambridge: Cambridge University Press, 2009–16), vol. iv, p. 592.

20 Granville Hicks, 'The More You Shout, the Less I Hear', *The New Republic*, 22 October 1956, p. 17.

21 David Krause, 'The Maiming of O'Casey', *The Seán O'Casey Review*, vol. 3, no. 2, Spring 1977, p. 130.

22 See Christopher Murray, *Seán O'Casey: Writer at work* (Dublin: Gill & Macmillan, 2004), pp. 52, 53, 55.

23 Seamus Deane (ed.), The *Field Day Anthology of Irish Writing*, 3 vols (Derry: Field Day Publications, 1991), vol. 3, p. 456. See also James Simmons, 'Sean O'Casey: The autobiographies', *Threshold*, no. 33, Winter 1983, p. 37, where he describes the autobiographies as being 'back with the failed literary ambition that spoils so many of the plays'.

24 Nicholas Grene, *The Politics of Irish Drama* (Cambridge: Cambridge University Press, 1999), p. 113.

25 O'Casey, *Autobiographies*, 4, p. 268.

26 Gabriel Fallon, *Sean O'Casey: The man I knew* (London: Routledge & Kegan Paul, 1965), p. 1.

27 O'Casey, *Letters*, 2, p. 939.

28 David Krause, *A Self-Portrait of the Artist as a Man: Sean O'Casey's letters* (Dublin: Dolmen Press, 1968), p. 37.

29 Desmond Rushe, *New York Times*, 13 July 1970.

30 O'Casey, *Letters*, 2, p. viii.

31 O'Casey, *Letters*, 4, p. 104.

32 See Harris, *Sean O'Casey's Letters and Autobiographies*.

33 O'Casey, *Letters*, 3, p. 427. Cardinal József Mindszenty of Hungary was arrested in 1948 and convicted of treason. He was sentenced to life imprisonment by the Communist People's Court.

34 O'Casey, *Letters*, 2, p. 133. Michael Colgan was a trade union official and independent senator first elected in 1943. TD (Teachta Dála) is a member of the Irish parliament.

35 Ibid., p. 598.

CHAPTER 18: POLITICS, ART AND LITERATURE

1 Quoted in Terry Eagleton, *Marxism and Literary Criticism* (London: Routledge, 1989), p. 3.

2 See Ciaran Brady (ed.), *Interpreting Irish History* (Dublin: Irish Academic Press, 1994). Also Máirín Ní Dhonnchadha and Theo Dorgan (eds), *Revising the Rising* (Derry: Field Day, 1991).

3 Roy Foster, *Modern Ireland: 1600–1972* (London: Allen Lane, 1988), pp. 477–93. For critique of Foster's book see Seamus Deane, 'Wherever Green Is Read', in Máirín Ní Dhonnchadha and Theo Dorgan (eds), *Revising the Rising*, pp. 91–105.

4 Joe Cleary, *Outrageous Fortune* (Dublin: Field Day Publications, 2007), p. 235.

5 G.J. Watson, quoted in David Krause, 'The Paradox of Ideological Formalism: Art vs. ideology', *The Massachusetts Review*, vol. 28, no. 3, Autumn 1978, pp. 516–24.

6 Cleary, *Outrageous Fortune*, p. 235.

7 Seamus Deane, 'Irish Politics and O'Casey's Theatre', *Threshold*, no. 24, Spring 1973, p. 11.

8 Nicholas Grene, *The Politics of Irish Drama* (Cambridge: Cambridge University Press, 1999), p. 150. See also Rónán McDonald, *Tragedy and Irish Literature: Synge, O'Casey, Beckett* (Basingstoke: Palgrave, 2002), pp. 94–6.

9 Field Day was founded in 1980 in Derry as a cultural and intellectual response to the political crisis in Northern Ireland. Playwright Brian Friel and actor/director Stephen Rea set out to identify and develop a new audience for theatre. Field Day also established a publishing company. Since the mid-1990s, Field Day has become synonymous with the development of Irish Studies.

10 Declan Kiberd, 'The Elephant of Revolutionary Forgetfulness', in Ní Dhonnchadha and Dorgan (eds), *Revising the Rising*, p. 18.

11 C. Desmond Greaves, *Sean O'Casey: Politics and art* (London: Lawrence & Wishart, 1979).

12 See O'Casey, *Letters*, 1, p. 60.

13 David Flood, Letter, *The Irish Times*, 17 July 2017: 'In 1877, the Irish National Foresters was founded by members who were expelled [from the British Ancient Order of Foresters] for having become involved in the amnesty campaign [for Irish prisoners]. It expanded rapidly to have a total of 1,000 branches and 250,000 members worldwide ... The Foresters in their ceremonial garb were a familiar sight to Irish people of the day at "national" events such as Bodenstown, Ivy Day (for Parnell's memory) or the funeral of O'Donovan Rossa.'

14 Sean O'Casey, *The Plough and the Stars* (London: Macmillan, 1926), p. 57.

15 Kiberd, 'The Elephant of Revolutionary Forgetfulness', p. 18.

16 Declan Kiberd, *Irish Classics* (London: Granta Books, 2001), p. 484.

17 Ibid.

18 Ibid., p. 488.

19 Cleary, *Outrageous Fortune*, p. 144.

20 See a series of essays that discuss O'Casey from a working-class perspective in Michael Pierse (ed.), *A History of Working-Class Writing* (Cambridge: Cambridge University Press, 2018). Also James Moran, *The Theatre of Seán O'Casey* (London: Bloomsbury Methuen Drama, 2013), and Susan Cannon Harris, *Irish Drama and Other Revolutions* (Edinburgh: Edinburgh University Press, 2017).

21 See Jack Mitchell, *The Essential O'Casey* (New York: International Publishers, 1980).

22 Greaves, *Sean O'Casey*, p. 69.

23 Ibid., pp. 91, 138.

24 Jack Mitchell, 'Sean O'Casey: Politics and art', in Robert G. Lowery (ed.), *O'Casey Annual*, no. 1 (New Jersey: Humanities Press, 1982), pp. 195–211.

25 Raymond Williams, *Drama: From Ibsen to Eliot* (London: Chatto & Windus, 1952), pp. 169–74.

26 Quoted in Jack Lindsay, '*The Plough and the Stars* Reconsidered', *The Seán O'Casey Review*, vol. 2, no. 2, Spring 1976, pp. 186–95. Francis Mulhern is associate editor of *New Left Review* (London).

27 Raymond Williams, *Drama from Ibsen to Brecht* (London: Chatto & Windus, 1968), p. 147.

28 See Moran, *The Theatre of Seán O'Casey*, pp. 181–2.

29 Hunam Yun, 'Appropriations of Irish drama by modern Korean nationalist theatre: A focus on the influence of Sean O'Casey in a colonial context', unpublished PhD thesis, University of Warwick, 2010. Hunam Yun's discussion of Irish drama in the Korean theatre under colonialism raises the question of why particular cultures at particular stages of their political existence appropriate foreign texts as a means of facilitating discourses that would otherwise be prohibited.

30 Catherine O'Leary, 'Translating the Armed Struggle: Alonso Sastre and Sean O'Casey in Spain', *Translation Studies*, vol. 11, no. 1, 2018, pp. 47–65.
31 Lara Marlowe, *The Irish Times*, 4 June 2002.
32 Sirklau Aaltonen, 'Time Sharing on Stage', *Topics in Translation: 17* (Clevedon: Multilingual Matters Ltd, 2002).
33 *Irish Worker*, 26 September 1931. In 1929 O'Casey had turned down the offer of a German production of *Juno and the Paycock*.
34 See Regina Heidenreich-Krawschak, 'Critical Reception of Sean O'Casey in Berlin since 1953', *The Seán O'Casey Review*, vol. 5, no. 1, Fall 1978, pp. 55–68.
35 James Moran, *The Theatre of Seán O'Casey* (London: Bloomsbury Methuen Drama, 2013), pp. 178–9; also *The Guardian*, 3 August 2009.
36 Ibid., p. 180.
37 Nesta Jones, *File on O'Casey* (London: Heinemann, 1988), p. 48.
38 Hans-Georg Simmgen, 'O'Casey Stage Productions in the German Democratic Republic', in Micheál Ó hAodha (ed.), *The O'Casey Enigma* (Cork: Mercier Press, 1980), pp. 70–80.
39 For details of German productions see Manfred Pauli, *Sean O'Casey: Drama, poesie, wirklichkeit* (Berlin: Henschelverlag, 1977).
40 Bertolt Brecht, *The Messingkauf Dialogues*, John Willett (tr.) (London: Methuen, 1974), p. 32.
41 https://www.marxists.org/archive/lukacs/works/theory-novel/preface.htm (accessed 10 August 2020).
42 Sean O'Casey, 'The Bald Primaqueera', *The Atlantic Monthly*, September 1965, pp. 69–74. See also Sean O'Casey in Ronald Ayling (ed.), *Blasts and Benedictions* (London: Macmillan, 1967), pp. 63–76.
43 Sean O'Casey, 'Thoughts from O'Casey', in E.H. Mikhail and John O'Riordan (eds), *The Sting and the Twinkle* (London: Macmillan, 1974), p. 165.
44 See Robert Murphy, 'Sean O'Casey and the Bald Primaqueera', *James Joyce Quarterly*, vol. viii, no. 1, Fall 1970, pp. 96–110.
45 Lukács' attack on modernism, particularly in *Studies in European Realism*, is more complex and politically nuanced than the crude dogmatic denunciation of modernism that emerged from the USSR in the 1930s. His concept of 'critical realism' was a response to the rise of fascism in the 1930s and the 'Cold War' era of the 1950s. See Georg Lukács, *Studies in European Realism* (London: Hillway Publishing, 1950) and *The Historical Novel* (London: Merlin Press, 1962).
46 David Gilchrist, *Socialist Review* (London), no. 402, May 2015.
47 Steve Nicholson, *British Theatre and the Red Peril* (Exeter: University of Exeter Press, 1999), p. 103.
48 Walter Benjamin, in Hannah Arendt (ed.), *Illuminations* (New York: Harcourt, Brace & World, 1968), pp. 47–8.
49 Beginning in May 1968, a period of civil unrest occurred throughout France, which included demonstrations, general strikes and occupations of factories and universities. The protests inspired a movement for civil and political rights across the world.
50 In an interview in 1977, Heaney reflected on the relationship between the emergence of the Northern Irish group of poets and the 'Troubles': 'The root of the troubles may have something in common with the root of the poetry': *The Crane Bag*, vol. 1, no. 1, Spring 1977, pp. 61–7.
51 Sean O'Casey, *The Sting and the Twinkle* (London: Macmillan, 1974). Sean O'Casey, *Blasts and Benedictions* (London: Macmillan, 1967).
52 Sean O'Casey, *Notebook 15*, Berg Collection, New York Public Library.

53 Alick West, *One Man in His Time* (London: Allen & Unwin, 1969), p. 132.

54 Patrick Deane (ed.), *History in Our Hands* (London: Leicester University Press, 1998), p. 384.

55 Ernst Toller, quoted in Martin Kane, *Weimar Germany and the Limits of Political Art* (Fife: Hutton Press, 1987), p. 120.

56 Malcolm Bradbury and James McFarlane, 'The Name and Nature of Modernism', in Malcolm Bradbury and James McFarlane (eds), *Modernism: A guide to European literature 1890–1930* (London: Penguin, 1991), p. 20.

57 Gorky, Radek, Bukharin, Zhdanov and others, *Soviet Writers' Congress 1934* (London: Lawrence & Wishart, 1977), chapter 7. Socialist realism literature was defined as 'realist in content, socialist in politics and affirmative in tone'. See Robert Lowery, 'Sean O'Casey and Socialist Realism', in Harold Bloom (ed.), *Sean O'Casey* (New York: Chelsea House Publishers, 1987), p. 91. See also Amabel Williams-Ellis, 'Soviet Writers Conference', *Left Review*, vol. 1, no. 2, November 1934, p. 26 for her report on Radek's speech. She dismissed Erich Maria Remarque's anti-war novel *All Quiet on the Western Front*, because 'nowhere does he make any protest against the slaughter'. For an assessment of Joyce's reintegration into post-Stalinist Russian literary life, see Emily Tall, 'The Joyce Centenary in the Soviet Union: Making way for *Ulysses*', *James Joyce Quarterly*, vol. 21, no. 2, Winter 1984, pp. 107–22.

58 See Edward Ahern, *Marx and Modern Fiction* (New Haven & London: Yale University Press, 1989), chapter 1.

59 O'Casey, *Letters*, 4, p. 298.

60 Sean O'Casey, 'The Theatre and the Politician', *Commonwealth Review* (London), January 1946.

61 Alan Simpson, 'Staging O'Casey's Plays', *The Seán O'Casey Review*, vol. 5, no. 2, Spring 1979, pp. 134–7.

62 See Steven Griffith, *Theatre Journal*, vol. 44, no. 1, March 1992, pp. 97–9.

63 Peter Crawley, 'Culture Shock: *The Plough and the Stars* is back. Must be time for a riot', *The Irish Times*, 18 March 2016. Fergus Linehan wrote that the 1991 Hynes production was offering 'yesterday's avant-garde' and that the use of 'Brecht's alienation effect ... was a total failure', *The Irish Times*, 11 May 1991.

64 *New York Times*, 2 February 1969.

65 Quoted in Victoria Stewart, *About O'Casey: The playwright and the work* (London: Faber & Faber, 2003), p. 98.

66 Brian Friel, *Seán O'Casey Review*, vol. 4, no. 2, Spring 1978, p. 87.

67 Robert G. Lowery (ed.), *Essays on O'Casey's Autobiographies* (Totowa, NJ: Barnes & Noble Books, 1981), p. xiii.

68 The Eighth Amendment (1983) to the Irish constitution prohibited abortion. The 2018 referendum repealed this amendment and permitted abortion to be legalised in defined circumstances.

69 ANU Theatre Group, *The Lost O'Casey*, Abbey Theatre, Dublin, September 2018 was based on O'Casey's forgotten play *Nannie's Night Out*.

70 José Lanters, '"Dragging Our Hidden Slums into the Centre of the Footlights": Homelessness, addiction, and audience discomfort in Sean O'Casey's *Nannie's Night Out* and ANU's *The Lost O'Casey*', *New Hibernia Review*, vol. 25, no. 2, Summer/Samhradh 2021, pp. 60–75.

71 Christina Reid, *Joyriders* and *Tea in a China Cup* (London: Methuen, 1987). *Joyriders* was first produced at the Tricycle Theatre (London) in 1986.

72 RTÉ Television, 18 and 25 June 2020. Unfortunately, due to Covid 19, the performance at the Abbey Theatre was cancelled.

73 Dr Austin Carroll, programme notes for ANU production *The Lost O'Casey*, ANU and the Abbey Theatre, 2018.

74 Victor Merriman, 'O'Casey's Postcolonial Dramaturgy', in James Moran, *The Theatre of Seán O'Casey* (London: Bloomsbury Methuen Drama, 2013), pp. 214–26.

EPILOGUE

1 *The Irish Times*, 15 March 1960. Ed Sullivan, the host of *Toast of the Town*, used the red-baiting magazine *Counterattack* to determine whether a guest should be invited on to his show or not.

2 For details see Christopher Murray letter, *The Irish Times*, 30 January 2012.

3 O'Casey, *Letters*, 4, p. 111.

4 Ibid., p. xvii.

5 NLI, *O'Casey Papers*, Collection List 75, MS 37,899.

6 He has since been honoured by the Seán O'Casey Bridge over the River Liffey and the Seán O'Casey Community Centre in the East Wall district of Dublin. In 2020 Dublin City Council proposed buying his former home, 422 North Circular Road, for use as homeless accommodation. If the sale goes ahead the house will be called the 'Seán O'Casey House', a fitting memorial that O'Casey would surely have approved of.

7 *The Seán O'Casey Review*, vol. 7, 1981, p. 8.

8 NLI, *O'Casey Papers*, Collection List 75, MS 37,930, MS 37,968.

9 Father Edward Daly was the priest, in the famous photograph from 1972, waving a white handkerchief on Bloody Sunday in Derry.

10 O'Casey, *Letters*, 4, p. 508.

11 Tomás Mac Anna, 'The Old Man Said "Truflais"', *The Seán O'Casey Review*, vol. 5, no. 1, Fall 1978, pp. 51–4.

12 Walter Macken, *Recall the Years* (Abbey Archives), July 1966.

13 Sean O'Casey, *New York Times*, 12 March 1950.

14 Bernard Benstock, 'The Plough Behind, the Stars Ahead', *The Seán O'Casey Review*, vol. 3, no. 2, Spring 1977, pp. 149–54.

15 O'Casey, *Letters*, 2, p. 789.

16 From the text of the 1916 Proclamation.

17 Ernst Toller, 'Masses and Man', *Seven Plays* (London: John Lane, 1935) and Georg Kaiser, *Gas II* (New York: Frederick Ungar Publishing, 1963).

18 Karl Liebknecht, https://www.marxists.org/history/etol/newspape/laboraction-ny/1943/vol07no04/liebknecht.htm. (accessed 20 April 2015).

19 O'Casey, *Letters*, 4, p. 310.

Bibliography

ARCHIVES AND LIBRARIES

Boston College Library (Boston, USA)

Robert G. Lowery, Seán O'Casey Archive

British Museum Library

Seán O'Casey holdings
Bernard Shaw holdings
Newspaper Archive

Church of Ireland Representative Church Body Library

St Barnabas Church holdings

Harvard University Library Archives

Newspaper files, including *The Boston Globe* and *The Harvard Crimson*
Alumni files

Irish Church Missions

Box 7,254

Irish Labour History Museum and Archives

ICA Council Minute Book 1919–20
ITGWU holdings
Socialist and communist newspapers and publications

Marx Memorial Library, London

Communist Party publications
Spanish Civil War holdings

National Archives of Ireland

Cabinet Papers, 1923, S. 2009, 1934, S. 8,208

National Library Ireland

Leslie Daiken papers
Patrick Galvin papers
Joseph Holloway papers
Rosamond Jacob papers, MS 32,582
Irish Labour Party papers
Newspaper holdings
William O'Brien papers, MS 15673/2
Eileen O'Casey papers, Collection List 137, MS 44,699–758
Seán O'Casey papers, Collection List 75, MS 37,807–38,173
Hanna Sheehy Skeffington papers

New York Public Library

Berg Collection, Lady Gregory papers
Berg Collection, Seán O'Casey papers
Berg Collection, Lennox Robinson papers

Paul O'Brien Archive

Seán O'Casey papers, letters, etc.

University College Dublin Archive

Máire Comerford, *Memoir*
Mulcahy papers

Victoria and Albert Museum Library

Unity Theatre Archive

Working Class Movement Library (Salford)

British socialist and Labour Party publications
Communist Party Archive

DIGITAL ARCHIVES

1901 and 1911 Irish Census
Bureau of Military History, Witness Statements and Pension Records
Dáil Debates
East Wall History Group

Hansard
Marxists Internet Archive
Seán O'Casey Festival Archive

NEWSPAPERS AND PERIODICALS

(Irish unless otherwise stated)

An Phoblacht
An tÓglác
Banba
Boundary
Commonweal (New York)
Commonwealth Review (London)
Daily News (London)
Daily Sketch (London)
Daily Worker (London)
Dana
Dublin Historical Record
Éire-Ireland (USA)
Encore (London)
Evening Herald
Féile Zozimus
Feminist Review (London)
Forward (Glasgow)
Freeman's Journal
History Ireland
Horizon (London)
International Literature Magazine (Moscow)
Irish Citizen
Irish Democrat
Irish Examiner
Irish Freedom
Irish Historical Studies
Irish Independent
Irish Opinion
Irish Press
Irish Review
Irish Slavonic Studies
Irish Statesman
Irish University Review
Irish Worker
James Joyce Quarterly (USA)
Left Review (London)
Life Magazine (USA)
Manchester Guardian (Manchester)
New Statesman (London)
New Theatre (London)
New York Herald Tribune (USA)
New York Post (USA)
New York Times (USA)
O'Casey Annual (London)
Picture Post (London)
Plebs (Glasgow)
Princeton University Library Chronicle (USA)
Revolutionary History (London)
Saothar
Scene (USA)
Sinn Féin
Socialism (Brussels)
Socialist History (London)
Socialist Review (London)
Spanish News (London)
Studies
The Anglo-Soviet Journal (London)
The Annual of Bernard Shaw Studies (USA)
The Arrow
The Atlantic (USA)
The Bell
The Capuchin Annual
The Catholic Bulletin

The Crane Bag
The Daily Princetonian (USA)
The Daily Telegraph (London)
The Dublin Magazine
The Furrow
The Guardian (London)
The Harvard Crimson (USA)
The Irish Commonwealth
The Irish Review
The Irish Times
The Massachusetts Review (USA)
The Nation (USA)
The New Republic
The New York Review of Books (USA)
The Observer (London)
The Seán O'Casey Review (USA)
The South Atlantic Quarterly (USA)
The Spectator (London)
The Standard
The Sunday Times (London)
The Village Voice (USA)
The Workers' Republic
The Workers' Weekly
Theatre Journal (USA)
Theatre World (London)
Threshold
Times Change
Times Educational Supplement (London)
University Review
Voice of Labour
Wolfe Tone Annual
Workers' Republic

PRIMARY TEXTS: WORKS BY SEÁN O'CASEY

(Published by Macmillan, London, unless otherwise stated)

Autobiographies

I Knock at the Door, vol. 1 (1939)
Pictures in the Hallway, vol. 2 (1942)
Drums under the Window, vol. 3 (1945)
Inisfallen Fare Thee Well, vol. 4 (1949)
Rose and Crown, vol. 5 (1952)
Sunset and Evening Star, vol. 6 (1954)
Pan Books edition, vols 1–6 (London: Pan Books, 1971–3)

Letters

The Letters of Sean O'Casey, David Krause (ed.), vol. 1 (New York: Macmillan, 1975)
The Letters of Sean O'Casey, David Krause (ed.), vol. 2 (New York: Macmillan, 1980)
The Letters of Sean O'Casey, David Krause (ed.), vol. 3 (Washington, DC: Catholic University of America Press, 1989)
The Letters of Sean O'Casey, David Krause (ed.), vol. 4 (Washington, DC: Catholic University of America Press, 1992)

Plays

Two Plays: Juno and the Paycock and *The Shadow of a Gunman* (1925)
The Plough and the Stars (1926)

The Silver Tassie (1928)
Within the Gates (1933)
Windfalls: Stories, poems and plays (1934). Includes *The End of the Beginning, A Pound on Demand*
Five Irish Plays (1935)
Purple Dust (1940)
The Star Turns Red (1940)
Red Roses for Me (1942)
Oak Leaves and Lavender (1946)
Cock-a-Doodle Dandy (1949)
Collected Plays, vols 1 & 2 (1949)
Collected Plays, vols 3 & 4 (1951)
The Bishop's Bonfire (1955)
Five One-Act Plays: The End of the Beginning, A Pound on Demand, Hall of Healing, Bedtime Story, Time to Go (1958)
The Drums of Father Ned (1960)
Behind the Green Curtains, Figuro in the Night, The Moon Shines on Kylenamoe (1961)
The Harvest Festival (Gerrards Cross: Colin Smythe, 1980)
Collected Plays, 5 vols (1984)

Other

The Story of Thomas Ashe (Dublin: Fergus O'Connor, 1917)
Songs of the Wren, nos 1–2 (Dublin: Fergus O'Connor, 1918)
The Story of the Irish Citizen Army (Dublin: Maunsel, 1919)
Windfalls: Stories, poems and plays (1934)
The Flying Wasp (1937)
The Green Crow (London: W.H. Allen, 1957)
Feathers from the Green Crow: Sean O'Casey 1905–1925, Robert Hogan (ed.) (1963)
Under a Colored Cap (1963)
Blasts and Benedictions (1967)
The Sting and the Twinkle, E.H. Mikhail and John O'Riordan (eds) (1974)
Niall: A lament (London & New York: Calder/Riverrun Press, 1991)

BIBLIOGRAPHIES AND INDEXES

Ayling, Ronald and Michael J. Durkan (eds), *Sean O'Casey: A bibliography* (Seattle: University of Washington Press, 1998)
All-Union State Library of Foreign Literature, *Sean O'Casey: Bibliographic index* (Moscow: Book Publishing House, 1964)
Lowery, Robert G., *Sean O'Casey's Autobiographies: An annotated index* (Westport, CT: Greenwood Press, 1983)

Mikhail, E.H., *Sean O'Casey and His Critics: An annotated bibliography, 1916–1982* (New Jersey: Scarecrow Press, 1985)
—, in Robert G. Lowery (ed.), 'Sean O'Casey: An annual bibliography', *O'Casey Annual*, vols. 1–4 (London: Macmillan, 1982–85)
Schrank, Bernice, *Sean O'Casey: A research and production sourcebook* (Westport, CT: Greenwood Press, 1996)

SECONDARY TEXTS

Aaltonen, Sirklau, *Topics in Translation: 17* (Clevedon: Multilingual Matters Ltd., 2002)
Aaron, Daniel, *Writers on the Left* (New York: Harcourt, Brace & World, 1961)
Adams, Davis and Katie Brittain, *Federico Lorca & Sean O'Casey: Powerful voices in the wilderness* (Salzburg: Universität Salzburg, 1978)
Ahern, Edward, *Marx and Modern Fiction* (New Haven and London: Yale University Press, 1989)
Airth, Cathy, 'Making the Least of Masculine Authority: Sean O'Casey's "Paycock" and "Plough and the Stars"', *Canadian Journal of Irish Studies*, vol. 32, no. 2, Fall 2006, pp. 42–7
Alcock, G.W., *Fifty Years of Railway Trade Unionism* (London: Co-operative Printing Society, 1922)
Allen, Kieran, *The Politics of James Connolly* (London: Pluto Press, 1990)
—, *James Connolly: Revolutionary socialist* (Dublin: Bookmarks, 2006)
—, *Ireland's Revolutionary Tradition* (London: Pluto Press, 2016)
Allen Cave, Richard, 'Johnston, Toller and Expressionism', in Joseph Ronsley (ed.), *Denis Johnston: A retrospective* (Gerrards Cross: Colin Smythe, 1981), pp. 78–104
Arnot, R. Page and Tim Buck, *Fascist Agents Exposed in the Moscow Trials* (London: Communist Party of Great Britain, 1938)
Arrington, Lauren, 'Theatre of Dissent: The historical imagination of the Irish Workers' Dramatic Company', in Christopher Collins and Mary Caulfield (eds), *Ireland, Memory and Performing the Historical Imagination* (London: Palgrave Macmillan, 2014), pp. 101–17
Arvon, Henri, *Marxist Aesthetics* (London: Cornell University Press, 1973)
Atkinson, Brooks, *Broadway* (London: Cassell, 1970)
—, in Robert, G. Lowery (ed.), *Sean O'Casey from Times Past* (New Jersey: Barnes & Noble Books, 1982)
Auden, W.H. and Stephen Spender, *Authors Take Sides* (London: Left Review, 1937)
Augusteijn, Joost (ed.), *Ireland in the 1930s* (Dublin: Four Courts Press, 1999)
—, 'Patrick Pearse: Proto-fascist or mainstream European thinker?', *History Ireland*, vol. 18, no. 6, November/December 2010, pp. 34–7

Ayling, Ronald, 'Feathers Flying', *The Dubliner*, Spring 1964, pp. 54–67

—, *Sean O'Casey* (Nashville: Aurora, 1970)

—, 'History and Artistry in Sean O'Casey's Trilogy', *Theoria*, no. 31, October 1971, pp. 1–13

—, *Continuity and Innovation in Sean O'Casey's Drama* (Salzburg: Universität Salzburg, 1976)

—, 'Seeds for Future Harvest', *Irish University Review*, vol. 10, no. 1, Spring 1980, pp. 25–40

—, *O'Casey: The Dublin trilogy* (London: Macmillan, 1985)

—, *Sean O'Casey's Theatre of War* (Vernon, BC: Kalamalka Press, 2004)

Baldick, Chris, *The Oxford English Literary History: The modern movement*, vol. 10 (Oxford: Oxford University Press, 2004)

Ballagh, Robert, 'What Anniversaries Tell Us', *History Ireland*, vol. 24, no. 2, March/April 2016, pp. 10–11

Balliett, Conrad A., 'The Lives – and Lies – of Maud Gonne', *Éire-Ireland*, vol. xiv, no. 3, Fall 1979, pp. 17–43

Bannister, Winifred, *James Bridie and His Theatre* (London: Rockliff, 1955)

Barfoot, C.C., 'By Way of Introduction: Saint Joan', in C.C. Barfoot and Rias van den Doel (eds), *Ritual Remembering: History, myth and politics in Anglo-Irish drama* (Amsterdam & Atlanta, GA: Rodopi, 1995), pp. 1–14

Barrowman, Rachel, *A Popular Vision: The arts and the left in New Zealand 1930–1950* (Wellington: Victoria University Press, 1991)

Barthes, Roland, *Mythologies*, Annette Lavers (tr.) (New York: Farrar, Straus & Giroux, 1972)

Bashford-Synnott, Marie, 'Annie M.P. Smithson: Romantic novelist, revolutionary nurse', *Dublin Historical Record*, vol. lxiv, no. 1, Spring 2011, pp. 47–68

Beckett, Samuel, *The Letters of Samuel Beckett*, 4 vols (Cambridge: Cambridge University Press, 2009–16)

Benjamin, Walter, *Illuminations*, Hannah Arendt (ed.) (New York: Harcourt, Brace & World, 1968), pp. 47–8

Benning, Tim, *The Romantic Revolution* (London, Weidenfeld & Nicolson, 2010)

Benstock, Bernard, 'The Plough Behind, the Stars Ahead', *The Seán O'Casey Review*, vol. 3, no. 2, Spring 1977, pp. 149–55

—, *Paycock and Others* (Dublin: Gill &Macmillan, 1976)

Bentley, Eric, *The Modern Theatre* (London: Robert Hale, 1948)

—, *In Search of Theatre* (New York: Alfred A. Knopf, 1953)

—, *Theatre of War* (London: Eyre Methuen, 1972)

Bew, Paul, *Enigma: A new life of Charles Stewart Parnell* (Dublin: Gill & Macmillan, 2012)

Bloom, Harold (ed.), *Sean O'Casey* (New York: Chelsea House Publishers, 1987)

Blythe, Ernest, *The State and the Nation* (Dublin: Comhdháil Náisiúnta na Gaeilge, 1919)

Bort, Eberhard (ed.), *Commemorating Ireland* (Dublin: Irish Academic Press, 2004)
Boucicault, Dion, *Selected Plays* (Gerrards Cross: Colin Smythe, 1987)
Bowen, Desmond, *Paul Cardinal Cullen and the Shaping of Modern Irish Catholicism* (Dublin: Gill & Macmillan, 1983)
Bradbury, Malcolm and James McFarlane (eds), *Modernism: A guide to European literature 1890–1930* (London: Penguin, 1991)
Brady, Ciaran (ed.), *Interpreting Irish History* (Dublin: Irish Academic Press, 1994)
Brannigan, John, 'Aesthetics, Democracy and the Voice of Labour', in Michael Pierse (ed.), *A History of Working-Class Writing* (Cambridge: Cambridge University Press, 2018), pp. 289–302
Branson, Noreen and Margot Heinemann, *Britain in the Nineteen Thirties* (London: Weidenfeld & Nicolson, 1971)
Brecht, Bertolt, *Brecht on Theatre*, John Willett (ed.) (London: Methuen, 1974)
—, *The Messingkauf Dialogues*, John Willett (tr.) (London: Methuen, 1974)
—, *The Days of the Commune*, Clive Barker and Arno Reinfrank (tr.) (London: Methuen, 1978)
—, *Mother Courage and Her Children*, John Willett (tr.) (London: Methuen, 1980)
Brown, Malcolm, *The Politics of Irish Literature* (Seattle: University of Washington Press, 1973)
Brown, Terence, *Ireland: A social and cultural history 1922–1985* (London: Fontana, 1985)
Brustein, Robert, *The Theatre of Revolt* (Boston: Little, Brown, 1962)
Buckley, David, *James Fintan Lalor: Radical* (Cork: Cork University Press, 1990)
Burke, Angela, et al. (eds), *The Field Day Anthology of Irish Writing: Irish women's writing and traditions*, vols 4–5 (Cork: Cork University Press in association with Field Day, 2002)
Burns, Robert, 'The Silver Tassie', https://www.scottishpoetrylibrary.org.uk/poem/silver-tassie/
Butler, Anthony and David Krause, 'A Storm in the Fair City', *The Seán O'Casey Review*, vol. 3, no. 2, Spring 1977, pp. 127–43
Caesar, Adrian, *Dividing Lines: Poetry, class and ideology in the 1930s* (Manchester: Manchester University Press, 1991)
Cannon Harris, Susan, 'Red Star versus Green Goddess: Sean O'Casey's "The Star Turns Red" and the politics of form', *The Princeton University Library Chronicle*, vol. 68, nos 1–2, Winter 2007, pp. 357–98
—, *Irish Drama and the Other Revolutions* (Edinburgh: Edinburgh University Press, 2017)
Carlson, Julia, *Banned in Ireland: Censorship and the Irish writer* (London: Routledge, 1990)
Carter, Huntley, *The New Spirit in the Cinema* (London: Shaylor, 1930)
Carty, Xavier, *In Bloody Protest: The tragedy of Patrick Pearse* (Dublin: Able Press, 1978)

Caute, David, *The Illusion* (London: Andre Deutsch, 1971)
Chambers, Colin, *The Story of Unity Theatre* (London: Lawrence & Wishart, 1989)
Clark, Jon, Margot Heineman, David Margolies and Carole Snee, *Culture and Crisis in Britain in the 30s* (London: Lawrence & Wishart, 1979)
Cleary, Joe, *Literature, Partition and the Nation State* (Cambridge: Cambridge University Press, 2002)
—, *Outrageous Fortune* (Dublin: Field Day Publications, 2007)
—, *Modernism, Empire, World Literature* (Cambridge: Cambridge University Press, 2021)
Coates, W.P., *The Moscow Trial (April 1933)* (London: The Anglo-Russian Parliamentary Committee, 1933)
Collis, Maurice, *Nancy Astor* (London: Futura, 1982)
Colum, Padraic, 'Sean O'Casey's Narratives', in Ronald Ayling (ed.), *Sean O'Casey: Modern judgements* (London: Aurora Publishers, 1969), pp. 220–7
Connolly, James, *Labour in Ireland* (Dublin: Maunsel & Roberts, 1922)
—, *The Re-Conquest of Ireland* (Dublin: ITGWU, 1916)
—, *Between Comrades: Letters and correspondence 1889–1916*, Donal Nevin (ed.) (Dublin: Gill & Macmillan, 2007)
—, *James Connolly: Political writings 1893–1916*, Donal Nevin (ed.) (Dublin: SIPTU, 2011)
—, *Writings of James Connolly: Collected works*, Donal Nevin (ed.) (Dublin: SIPTU, 2011)
Coogan, Tim Pat, *Ireland in the Twentieth Century* (London: Hutchinson, 2003)
Cooney, John, *John Charles McQuaid* (Dublin: O'Brien Press, 1999)
Costello, Francis, *The Irish Revolution and its Aftermath* (Dublin: Irish Academic Press, 2003)
Coutts, Charlie, *Eye-Witness in Hungary* (London: Daily Worker Co-Operative Society, 1957)
Cowasjee, Saros, *Sean O'Casey: The man behind the plays* (Edinburgh: Oliver & Boyd, 1965)
Croft, Andy (ed.), *A Weapon in the Struggle* (London: Pluto Press, 1998)
Cruise O'Brien, Conor, *Writers and Politics* (New York: Pantheon Books, 1965)
Cunningham, Valentine, *British Writers of the Thirties* (Oxford: Oxford University Press, 1988)
Curran, Joseph M., 'The Decline and Fall of the IRB', *Éire-Ireland*, vol. x. no. 1, Spring 1975, pp. 14–23
Curry, James, *The Artist of the Revolution* (Cork: Mercier Press, 2012)
Curtis, Maurice, *A Challenge to Democracy: Militant Catholicism in modern Ireland* (Dublin: The History Press Ireland, 2010)
Daiken, Leslie (ed.), *They Go, the Irish* (London: Nicholson & Watson, 1944)
daRin, Doris, *Sean O'Casey* (New York: Frederick Ungar, 1976)

Davies, Richard and W.J. McCormack, 'Sean O'Casey's Unpublished Correspondence with Raissa Lomonovska, 1925–6', *Irish Slavonic Studies*, no. 5, 1984, pp. 181–91

Davitt, Michael, *Jottings in Solitary* (Dublin: UCD Press, 2003)

Dawson, Jerry, *Left Theatre* (Liverpool: Merseyside Writers, 1985)

Deane, Patrick (ed.), *History in Our Hands* (London: Leicester University Press, 1998)

Deane, Seamus, 'Irish Politics and O'Casey's Theatre', *Threshold*, no. 24, Spring 1973, pp. 5–16

—, 'Exemplary Dramatists: Yeats and O'Casey', *Threshold*, no. 30, Spring 1979, pp. 21–8

— (ed.), *The Field Day Anthology of Irish Writing*, vols 1–3 (Derry: Field Day Publications, 1991)

—, 'Wherever Green is Read', in Máirín Ní Dhonnchadha and Theo Dorgan (eds), *Revising the Rising* (Derry: Field Day, 1991), pp. 91–105

—, *Small World: Ireland, 1798–2018* (Cambridge: Cambridge University Press, 2021)

Deasy, Joseph, *Fiery Cross: The story of Jim Larkin* (Dublin: New Books, 1963)

De Barra, Caoimhín, *Gaeilge: A radical revolution* (Dublin: Currach Books, 2019)

de Blácam, A., 'Thoughts on Labour Policy in Ireland', *Studies: An Irish quarterly review*, vol. x, no. 40, December 1921, pp. 599–600

de Blaghd, Earnán, *Trasna na Bóinne* (Dublin: Sáirséal agus Dill, 1957)

Delaney, William SJ, *Irish University Education* (London: John Murray, 1904)

Delaney, William, *The Green and the Red* (San Jose: Writers Showcase, 2001)

Denning, Michael, *The Cultural Front* (London: Verso, 1997)

Devine, Francis and Manus O'Riordan, *James Connolly, Liberty Hall and the 1916 Rising* (Dublin: Irish Labour History Society, 2006)

—, *Organising History: A centenary of SIPTU* (Dublin: Gill & Macmillan, 2009)

—, *A Capital in Conflict: Dublin city and the 1913 lockout* (Dublin: Dublin City Council, 2013)

Devine, Kathleen, *Modern Irish Writers and the Wars* (Gerrards Cross: Colin Smythe, 1999)

Dewey Commission, *The Case of Leon Trotsky* at, https://www.marxists.org/archive/trotsky/1937/dewey/index.htm

Dietrich, Julia, *The Old Left* (New York: Twayne Publishers, 1996)

Dillon, Geraldine, 'Irish Republican Brotherhood', *University Review* (Dublin), vol. 2, no. 8, 1961, pp. 23–36

Dorgan, Theo, 'Larkin through the Eyes of Writers', in Donal Nevin (ed.), *Lion of the Fold* (Dublin: Gill & Macmillan, 1998), pp. 102–9

Douglass, Frederick, https://www.blackpast.org/african-american-history/1857-frederick-douglass-if-there-no-struggle-there-no-progress/

Doyle, Aidan, *A History of the Irish Language* (Oxford: Oxford University Press, 2015)

Dukore, Bernard (ed.), *Drama and Revolution* (New York: Holt, Rinehart & Winston, 1971)

Eagleton, Terry, *Heathcliff and the Great Hunger* (London: Verso, 1995)

—, *Crazy John and the Bishop* (Cork: Cork University Press, 1998)

Edwards, Gwynne, *Lorca: The theatre beneath the sand* (London: Marion Boyars, 1987)

Edwards, Ruth Dudley, *Patrick Pearse: The triumph of failure* (London: Gollancz, 1977)

Engels, Friedrich, *The Origin of the Family, Private Property and the State* (London: Lawrence & Wishart, 1942)

English, Richard, *Irish Freedom* (London: Pan Books, 2007)

Enright, Sean, *Easter Rising 1916: The trials* (Dublin: Merrion Press, 2014)

Ervine, St John, *The Spectator*, 2 November 1945

Esslin, Martin, *Brecht: A choice of evils* (London: Eyre & Spottiswoode, 1959)

Esslinger, Pat M., 'The Irish Alienation of Sean O'Casey', *Éire-Ireland*, vol. 1, no. 1, Spring 1965–6, pp. 18–25

—, 'Sean O'Casey and the 1913 Lockout', *Modern Drama*, May 1963, pp. 53–63

Ewen, Frederic, *Bertolt Brecht: His life, his art, his times* (New York: Citadel Press, 1992)

Fallon, Brian, *An Age of Innocence: Irish culture 1930–1960* (Dublin: Gill & Macmillan, 1998)

Fallon, Gabriel, *Sean O'Casey: The man I knew* (London: Routledge & Kegan Paul, 1965)

Fanon, Frantz, *The Wretched of the Earth* (New York: Grove Press, 1963)

Farquharson, Danine, 'Sexing the Rising: Men, sex, violence and Easter 1916', in Danine Farquharson and Sean Farrell (eds), *Shadows of the Gunman: Violence and culture in modern Ireland* (Cork: Cork University Press, 2008), pp. 63–78

Farrell, Mel, Jason Knirck and Ciara Meehan, *A Formative Decade: Ireland in the 1920s* (Sallins: Irish Academic Press, 2015)

Fay, Gerald, *The Abbey Theatre* (Dublin: Clonmore & Reynolds, 1958)

Ferriter, Diarmaid, *The Transformation of Ireland 1900–2000* (London: Profile Books, 2004)

—, *Between Two Hells: The Irish Civil War* (London: Profile Books, 1921)

Fischer, Joachim, 'Ernst Toller and Ireland', in Richard Dove and Stephan Lamb (eds), *German Writers and Politics 1918–39* (London: Palgrave Macmillan, 1992)

Fitz-Simon, Christopher, 'The Sir John T. Gilbert Commemorative Lecture, 2011', in *Mr J. Kennedy Miller's Very Capable Company of Irish Players* (Dublin: Dublin City Public Libraries, 2011)

Flannery, James W., *W.B. Yeats and the Idea of a Theatre* (New Haven: Yale University Press, 1989)

Fletcher, Ruth, 'Silences: Irish women and abortion', *Feminist Review*, no. 50, Summer 1995, pp. 44–66

Fogarty, L., *James Fintan Lalor* (Dublin: Talbot Press, 1918)
Foster, Gavin, 'The Social Basis of the Civil War Divide', in John Crowley, Donal Ó Drisceoil and Mike Murphy (eds), *Atlas of the Irish Revolution* (Cork: Cork University Press, 2017), pp. 665–7
Foster, Roy, *Modern Ireland 1600–1972* (London: Allen Lane, 1988)
—, *Vivid Faces* (London: Allen Lane, 2014)
Fox, R.M., *Green Banners* (London: Secker & Warburg, 1938)
—, *The History of the Irish Citizen Army* (Dublin: James Duffy, 1944)
—, *James Connolly: The forerunner* (Tralee: The Kerryman, 1946)
Frawley, Oona, *Irish Pastoral* (Dublin: Irish Academic Press, 2005)
Frazier, Adrian, *Behind the Scenes: Yeats, Horniman, and the struggle for the Abbey Theatre* (Berkley: University of California Press, 1990)
—, *George Moore, 1852–1933* (New Haven: Yale University Press, 2000)
—, 'Barry Goes to Hollywood', *The Dublin Review*, no. 15, Summer 2004, pp. 68–86
Fryer, Peter, *Hungarian Tragedy* (London: New Park Publications, 1986)
Gardiner, Juliet, *The Thirties* (London: Harper Press, 2010)
Genet, Jacqueline and Wynne Hellegouarec'h (eds), *Studies on Sean O'Casey* (Caen: Presses Universitaires de Caen, 1987)
Gilmore, George, *Labour and the Republican Movement* (Dublin: The United Irishman, 1966)
—, *The Irish Republican Congress* (Cork: Cork Workers Club, 1974)
Girvin, Brian, *The Emergency: Neutral Ireland 1939–1945* (London: Macmillan, 2006)
Gish, Nancy K., *Hugh MacDiarmid: The man and his work* (London: Macmillan, 1984)
Glahn, Philip, *Bertolt Brecht* (London: Reaktion Books, 2014)
Gloversmith, Frank (ed.), *Class, Culture and Social Change: A new view of the 1930s* (Brighton, Sussex/Atlantic Highlands, NJ: Harvester Press/Humanities Press, 1980)
Gluckstein, Donny, *Fighting on all Fronts: Popular resistance and the Second World War* (London: Bookmarks, 2015)
Goldstone, Herbert, *In Search of Community* (Cork: Mercier Press, 1972)
—, 'O'Casey in '74: Or has everything been said?', *The Sean O'Casey Review*, vol. 1, no. 1, Fall 1974, pp. 6–10
Goldstone, Katrina, *Irish Writers and the Thirties* (London: Routledge, 2021)
Goorney, Howard and Ewan MacColl, *Agit-Prop to Theatre Workshop* (Manchester: Manchester University Press, 1986)
Gorky, Radek, Bukharin, Zhdanov and others, *Soviet Writers' Congress 1934* (London: Lawrence & Wishart, 1977)
Grant, Adrian, *Irish Socialist Republicanism 1909–1936* (Dublin: Four Courts Press, 2012)
Greaves, C. Desmond, *Father O'Flanagan: Republican priest* (London: Connolly Association, n.d.)

—, *The Life and Times of James Connolly* (London: Lawrence & Wishart, 1976)

—, *Sean O'Casey: Politics and art* (London: Lawrence & Wishart, 1979)

—, *The Irish Transport and General Workers' Union* (Dublin: Gill & Macmillan, 1982)

Greeman, Richard, 'Victor Serge and the Novel of Revolution', *Socialism* (Brussels), nos 226–7, July/October 1991

Gregory, Lady Augusta, *Journals*, Daniel J. Murphy (ed.), 2 vols (Gerrards Cross: Colin Smythe, 1978–88)

Grene, Nicholas, 'Bernard Shaw: Socialist and playwright', *The Crane Bag*, vol. 7, no. 1, 1983, pp. 135–40

—, *The Politics of Irish Drama* (Cambridge: Cambridge University Press, 1999)

Griffith, Kenneth and Timothy O'Grady, *Curious Journey* (Cork: Mercier Press, 1998)

Grimes, Charles, 'Bernard Shaw's Theory of Political Theatre', *SHAW: The annual of Bernard Shaw studies*, vol. 22, 2001, pp. 117–30

Grotowski, Jerzy, *Towards a Poor Theatre* (London: Methuen, 1981)

Haldane, J.B.S., Sean O'Casey, J. Owen and R. Page Arnot, *The Case for the Daily Worker* (London: Marston Print Company, 1941)

Hall, Simon, *1956: The world in revolt* (London: Faber & Faber, 2016)

Hanley, Brian, 'The Treaty: Victory or defeat? *History Ireland*, vol. 29, no. 6, November/December 2021, pp. 14–15

Harrington, Michael, *The Vast Majority* (New York: Simon & Schuster, 1977)

Harris, Peter James, *Sean O'Casey: Letters and autobiographies* (Trier: WVT, 2004)

—, *From Stage to Page* (Oxford: Peter Lang, 2011)

Hay, Marnie, *Bulmer Hobson and the Nationalist Movement in Twentieth-Century Ireland* (Manchester: Manchester University Press, 2009)

Hays, Timothy, *The Review*: *A journal of undergraduate student research*, http://fisherpub.sjfc.edu/ur/vol1/iss1/5

Hazelhurst, Elizabeth, 'O'Casey Frozen out by Feminists', *Times Change*, no. 17, Spring/Summer 1999, pp. 17–19

Heaney, Seamus, *The Spirit Level* (London: Faber & Faber, 1975)

—, *The Crane Bag*, vol. 1, no. 1, Spring 1977, pp. 61–7

—, *The Government of the Tongue* (London: Faber & Faber, 1988)

Heidenreich-Krawschak, Regina, 'Critical Reception of Sean O'Casey in Berlin since 1953', *The Seán O'Casey Review*, vol. 5, no. 1, Fall 1978, pp. 55–68

Hickey, Des and Gus Smith, *A Paler Shade of Green* (London: Frewin, 1972)

Hicks, Granville, 'The More You Shout, the Less I Hear', *The New Republic*, 22 October 1956, p. 17.

Himmelfarb, Gertrude, *The New History and the Old* (Cambridge, MA: Harvard University Press, 2004)

Hitchens, Christopher, *Why Orwell Matters* (New York: Basic Books, 2002)

Hoar, Adrian, *The Red and the Green: The lives of Frank Ryan* (Dingle: Brandon, 2004)

Hobsbawm, Eric, *Interesting Times: A twentieth-century life* (London: Allen Lane, 2002)

—, *Age of Extremes* (London: Abacus, 1995)

Hobson, Bulmer, *A Short History of the Irish Volunteers*, vol. 1 (Dublin: Three Candle Press, 1918)

—, *Ireland Yesterday and Tomorrow* (Tralee: Anvil Press, 1968)

Hogan, Robert, *'Since O'Casey' and other Essays on Irish Drama* (Gerrards Cross: Colin Smythe, 1983)

Hogan, Robert, Richard Burnham and Daniel P. Poteet, *The Abbey Theatre: The rise of the realists 1910–1915* (Dublin: The Dolmen Press, 1979)

Hogan, Robert and James Kilroy (eds), *Lost Plays of the Irish Renaissance* (Dixon, CA: Proscenium Press, 1970)

Hogan, Robert and Richard Burnham, *The Years of O'Casey 1921–1926: A documentary history* (Delaware: University of Delaware Press, 1992)

Höhne, Horst, 'Brecht vs O'Casey, or Brecht & O'Casey', in Robert G. Lowery (ed.), *O'Casey Annual No. 3* (London: Macmillan Press, 1984), pp. 1–32

Holloway, Joseph, Robert Hogan and Michael J. O'Neill (eds), *Joseph Holloway's Abbey Theatre* (Carbondale: Southern Illinois University Press, 1967)

Hopkinson, Michael, *Green Against Green: The Irish Civil War* (Dublin: Gill & Macmillan, 2004)

Hunt, Hugh, *The Theatre and Nationalism in Ireland* (Swansea: University College of Swansea, 1974)

Hynes, Samuel, *The Auden Generation* (London: The Bodley Head, 1976)

Jackson, T.A., 'The Moscow Trial', *Left Review*, vol. 3, no. 2, March 1937, pp. 15–19

Jameson, Fredric, 'Reflections in Conclusion', in Theodor W. Adorno (ed.), *Aesthetics and Politics* (London: Verso, 1977), pp. 196–219

Jeffery, Keith, *Ireland and the Great War* (Cambridge: Cambridge University Press, 2000)

Joannou, Maroula, 'Sylvia Townsend Warner in the 1930s', in Andy Croft (ed.), *A Weapon in the Struggle: The cultural history of the Communist Party in Britain* (London: Pluto Press, 1998), pp. 89–105

Johnston, Denis, *The Dramatic Works of Denis Johnston*, 3 vols (Gerrards Cross: Colin Smythe, 1977–92)

Johnston, Kevin, *Home or Away; The Great War and the Irish revolution* (Dublin: Gill & Macmillan, 2010)

Johnston, Máirín, 'Priests and Proselytism in 19th Century Dublin', *Féile Zozimus*, vol. 1, 1992, pp. 61–6

Jones, Nesta, *File on O'Casey* (London: Heinemann, 1988)

Jordan, John, 'A World in Chassis', *University Review* (Dublin), vol. 1, no. 4, Spring 1955, pp. 21–8

Joyce, James, *Dubliners* (Harmondsworth: Penguin, 1965)

Kaiser, Georg, *Gas II* (New York: Frederick Ungar, 1963)

Kane, Martin, *Weimar Germany and the Limits of Political Art* (Fife: Hutton Press, 1987)

Katz Clarke, Brenna and Harold Ferrar, *The Dublin Drama League 1919–1941* (Dublin: The Dolmen Press, 1979)

Kavanagh, Jim, 'My Friend O'Casey', *The Seán O'Casey Review*, vol. 2, no. 1, Fall 1975, pp. 58–60

Kearney, Colbert, 'Brendan Behan and the Oral Tradition of Dublin City', *Féile Zozimus*, vol. 2, 1993, pp. 37–54

—, *The Glamour of Grammar* (Westport, CT: Greenwood Press, 2000)

Kearns, Kevin C., *Dublin Tenement Life* (Dublin: Gill & Macmillan, 1994)

Kee, Robert, *The Laurel and the Ivy* (London: Hamish Hamilton, 1994)

Kenneally, Michael, *Portraying the Self* (Gerrards Cross: Colin Smythe, 1988)

Kennedy, Sinéad, 'Marxism after Modernism: Anglo-American leftist theorisations of modernism in the later twentieth century', unpublished PhD thesis, Maynooth, 2007

Keogh, Dermot, *The Rise of the Irish Working Class* (Belfast: Appletree Press, 1982)

Keogh, Dermot, Finbarr O'Shea and Carmel Quinlan (eds), *The Lost Decade: Ireland in the 1950s* (Cork: Mercier Press, 2004)

Keogh, Dermot and Andrew McCarthy, 'The Catholic Church and the Writing of the 1937 constitution', *History Ireland*, vol. 13, no. 3, May/June 2005, pp. 36–41

Keohane, Leo, *Captain Jack White: Imperialism, anarchism and the Irish Citizen Army* (Newbridge: Irish Academic Press, 2014)

Kershaw, Ian, *Making Friends with Hitler* (London: Penguin, 2005)

Kiberd, Declan, 'The Elephant of Revolutionary Forgetfulness', in Máirín Ní Dhonnchadha and Theo Dorgan (eds), *Revising the Rising* (Derry: Field Day, 1991), pp. 1–20

—, 'W.B. Yeats: Endings and Beginnings: A review article', *Éire-Ireland*, vol. xxxii, nos 2–3, Summer/Fall 1997, pp. 183–91

—, *Irish Classics* (London: Granta Books, 2001)

Kilroy, Thomas (ed.), *Sean O'Casey: A collection of critical essays* (New Jersey: Prentice Hall, 1975)

King, Carla, *Michael Davitt: After the Land League 1882–1906* (Dublin: UCD Press, 2016)

Kirrane, Kevin, 'Orwell's Ireland', *The Irish Review*, nos 36–7, Winter 2007, pp. 14–32

Klaus, Gustav, *Strong Words, Brave Deeds* (Dublin: O'Brien Press, 1994)

Kleiman, Carol, *Sean O'Casey's Bridge of Vision: Four essays on structure and perspective* (Toronto: University of Toronto Press, 1982)

Knirck, Jason, *Women of the Dáil* (Dublin: Irish Academic Press, 2006)

Komesu, Okifumi and Masaru Sekine (eds), *Irish Writers and Politics* (Gerrards Cross: Colin Smythe, 1990)

Koslow, Jules, *The Red and the Green* (New York: Golden Griffin Books, 1949)

Kosok, Heinz, 'Unity Theatre and "The Star Turns Red"', *The Seán O'Casey Review*, vol. 6, 1980, pp. 68–74

—, *O'Casey: The dramatist* (Gerrards Cross: Colin Smythe, 1985)

—, *Plays and Playwrights from Ireland* (Trier: WVT, 1995)

Kostick, Conor, *Revolution in Ireland: Popular militancy 1917 to 1923* (Cork: Cork University Press, 2009)

Kramnick, Isaac and Michael Foot (eds), *The Tom Paine Reader* (London: Penguin Classics, 1987)

Krause, David, *Sean O'Casey: The man and his work* (London: MacGibbon & Kee, 1960)

—, 'Towards the End', in Sean McCann (ed.), *The World of Sean O'Casey* (London: Four Square Books, 1966), pp. 137–57

—, *A Self-Portrait of the Artist as a Man: Sean O'Casey's letters* (Dublin: Dolmen Press, 1968)

—, 'The Risen O'Casey: Some Marxist and Irish ironies', in Robert G. Lowery (ed.), *O'Casey Annual No. 3* (London: Macmillan, 1984), pp. 138–68

—, 'The Paradox of Ideological Formalism', *The Massachusetts Review*, vol. 28, no. 3, Autumn 1987, pp. 516–24

—, 'The Conscience of Ireland: Lalor, Davitt, and Sheehy Skeffington', *Éire-Ireland*, vol. xxiii, no. 1, Spring 1993, pp. 7–31

Krause, David and Robert G. Lowery (eds), *Sean O'Casey Centenary Essays* (Gerrards Cross: Colin Smythe, 1980)

Kurzweil, Edith and William Phillips (eds), *Writers and Politics: A Partisan Review reader* (Boston: Routledge & Kegan Paul, 1983)

Laird, Heather, 'Writing Working Class Irish Women', in Michael Pierse (ed.), *A History of Working-Class Writing* (Cambridge: Cambridge University Press, 2018), pp. 122–39

Lalor, James Fintan, *The Rights of Ireland* and *The Faith of a Felon*, James Connolly (ed.) (Dublin: Irish Socialist Republican Party, 1896)

Lane, Leeann, *Rosamond Jacob: Third person singular* (Dublin: UCD Press, 2010)

—, *Dorothy Macardle* (Dublin: UCD Press, 2019)

Lanters, José, '"Dragging Our Hidden Slums into the Centre of the Footlights": Homelessness, addiction, and audience discomfort in Sean O'Casey's "Nannie's Night Out" and ANU's "The Lost O'Casey"', *New Hibernia Review*, vol. 25, no. 2, Summer/Samhradh 2021, pp. 60–75

Larkin, Emmet, *James Larkin: Irish labour leader, 1876–1947* (London: Routledge & Kegan Paul, 1965)

Larkin, James, 'Murder Most Foul', *International Socialist Review* (New York), December 1916

Leddin, Jeffrey, *The 'Labour Hercules': The Irish Citizen Army and Irish republicanism 1913–1923* (Sallins: Irish Academic Press, 2019)

Leerssen, Joep, *Mere Irish and Fíor Ghael* (Cork: Cork University Press in association with Field Day, 1996)

Lenin, V.I., *Collected Works*, 45 vols (Moscow: Progress Publishers, 1964–70)

—, *Lenin on Ireland* (Dublin: New Books, 1970)

Le Roux, Louis N., *Life of P.H. Pearse*, Desmond Ryan (tr.) (Dublin: Phoenix Publishing Company, 1932)

Leslie, John, 'The Irish Question 1894', *Justice*, 24 March and 5 May 1894

Levitas, Ben, *The Theatre of Nation* (Oxford: Oxford University Press, 2002)

—, 'Plumbing the Depths: Irish realism and the working class from Shaw to O'Casey', *Irish University Review*, vol. 33, no. 1, Spring/Summer 2003, pp. 133–49

Lewis, Allan, *The Contemporary Theatre* (New York: Crown Publishers, 1971)

Liddell, J. (ed.), *Lenin's Struggle for a Revolutionary International*, 3 vols (New York: Monad, 1984)

Lieberman, Robbie, *My Song Is My Weapon* (Urbana: University of Illinois Press, 1989)

Lindsay, Jack, '"The Plough and the Stars" Reconsidered', *The Seán O'Casey Review*, vol. 2, no. 2, Spring 1976, pp. 186–95

Local Government Board of Ireland, 'Report of the Departmental Committee into Housing Conditions of the Working Classes in the City of Dublin' (CD 7273), Parliamentary Papers, vol. 19 (1914)

Lowery, Robert G. (ed.), *Essays on Sean O'Casey's Autobiographies* (London: Macmillan, 1981)

—, 'Sean O'Casey and the Irish Worker', in Robert G. Lowery (ed.), *O'Casey Annual No. 3* (London: Macmillan Press, 1984), pp. 33–114

—, *A Whirlwind in Dublin: The Plough and the Stars riots* (Westport: Greenwood Press, 1984)

—, 'Sean O'Casey and Socialist Realism', in Harold Bloom (ed.), *Sean O'Casey* (New York: Chelsea House Publishers, 1987), pp. 91–104

Lowery, Robert G. and Patricia Angelin (eds), *My Very Dear Sean* (Madison, NJ: Fairleigh Dickenson University Press, 1985)

Luddy, Maria, *Hanna Sheehy Skeffington* (Dundalk: Historical Association of Ireland, 1995)

—, *Prostitution and Irish Society 1880–1914* (Cambridge: Cambridge University Press, 2008)

Lukács, Georg, *Studies in European Realism* (London: Hillway Publishing, 1950)

—, *The Historical Novel* (London: Merlin Press, 1962)

Lunn, Eugene, *Marxism and Modernism* (Berkley: University of California Press, 1982)

Luxemburg, Rosa, http://www.anu.edu.au/polsci/marx/contemp/pamsetc/socfrombel/sfb_5.htm

Lyons, F.S.L., 'The Parnell Theme in Literature', in Andrew Carpenter (ed.), *Place, Personality and the Irish Writer* (Gerrards Cross: Colin Smythe, 1971), pp. 69–96

—, *Charles Stewart Parnell* (Oxford: Oxford University Press, 1977)

—, *Culture and Anarchy in Ireland 1890–1939* (Oxford: Oxford University Press, 1982)

—, 'The New Nationalism, 1916–1918', in W.E. Vaughan (ed.), *A New History of Ireland*, vol. 6 (Oxford: Oxford University Press, 1989), pp. 225–59

Mac Aodha, Breandán S., 'Was this a Social Revolution?', in Seán Ó Tuama (ed.), *The Gaelic League Idea* (Cork: Mercier Press, 1972), pp. 20–30

Mac Aonghusa, Proinsias, 'Sean O'Casey and the Gaelic League', *Féile Zozimus*, vol. 3, 1994, pp. 11–28

MacDiarmid, Hugh, 'Sláinte Chúramach, Seán', in Ronald Ayling (ed.), *Sean O'Casey* (Nashville: Aurora, 1970)

MacDonagh, Oliver, W.F. Mandle and Pauric Travers (eds), *Irish Culture and Nationalism 1750–1950* (New York: St Martin's Press, 1983)

MacNamara, Brinsley, *The Clanking of the Chains* (Dublin: Maunsel, 1920)

MacSiomóin, Tomás, 'The Colonised Mind: Irish language and society', in Daltún Ó Ceallaigh (ed.), *Reconsiderations of Irish History and Culture* (Dublin: Léirmheas, 1994), pp. 42–71

McCabe, Conor, 'The Context and Course of the Irish Railway Disputes of 1911', *Saothar*, vol. 30, 2005, pp. 21–32

McCann, Sean (ed.), *The World of Sean O'Casey* (London: Four Square, 1966)

McCarey, Peter, *Hugh MacDiarmid and the Russians* (Edinburgh: Scottish Academic Press, 1987)

McCarthy, Martin, *Stalin and Stalinism* (Harlow: Pearson Longman, 2008)

McCoole, Sinéad, *No Ordinary Women* (Dublin: O'Brien Press, 2016)

McDiarmid, Lucy, *The Irish Art of Controversy* (Dublin: The Lilliput Press, 2005)

McDonald, Rónán, *Tragedy and Irish Literature: Synge, O'Casey, Beckett* (Basingstoke: Palgrave, 2002)

McDonald, Rónán, 'Sean O'Casey's Dublin Trilogy: Disillusionment to delusion', in Shaun Richards (ed.), *The Cambridge Companion to Twentieth-Century Irish Drama* (Cambridge: Cambridge University Press, 2006), pp. 136–49

McGarry, Fearghal, *Irish Politics and the Spanish Civil War* (Cork: Cork University Press, 1999)

—, *Frank Ryan* (Dublin: Historical Society of Ireland, 2002)

—, 'The Military Bureau of History', *History Ireland*, vol. 19, no. 6, November/December 2011, pp. 26–9

—, *The Abbey Rebels of 1916* (Dublin: Gill & Macmillan, 2015)

—, 'Memory: Easter 1916 in 2016', *History Ireland*, vol. 24, no. 2, March/April 2016, pp. 46–9

McGee, Owen, 'Fred Allen (1861–1937): Republican, Methodist, and Dubliner', *Dublin Historical Record*, vol. lvi, no. 2, Autumn 2003, pp. 205–16

—, *Arthur Griffith* (Sallins: Merrion Press, 2015)

McGreevy, Ronan, *Was it for This?* (Dublin: Irish Times Books, 2016)

McGuire, Charlie, *Roddy Connolly and the Struggle for Socialism in Ireland* (Cork: Cork University Press, 2008)

McHugh, Roger, *Dublin 1916* (London: Arlington Books, 1966)

McInerney, Michael, *Peadar O'Donnell: Irish social rebel* (Dublin: O'Brien Press, 1974)

McLaughlin, Barry, *Left to the Wolves* (Dublin: Irish Academic Press, 2007)

McLoughlin, Barry and Emmet O'Connor, *In Spanish Trenches* (Dublin: UCD Press, 2020)

McMahon, Timothy G., *Grand Opportunity: The Gaelic revival and Irish society 1893–1910* (Syracuse: Syracuse University Press, 2008)

McNamara, Conor, 'Liam Mellows and the Irish Revolution', *History Ireland*, vol. 19, no. 4, July/August 2011, pp. 36–7

Malone, Andrew E., *The Irish Drama* (London: Constable, 1929)

Malone, Maureen, *The Plays of Sean O'Casey* (Carbondale, IL: Southern Illinois University Press, 1969)

Mannion, Elizabeth, *The Urban Plays of the Early Abbey Theatre* (Syracuse: Syracuse University Press, 2014)

—, 'Different C/Kathleens', paper delivered at IASIL Conference, Prague, 2015

Mansergh, Nicholas, *Ireland in an Age of Reform and Revolution* (London: Allen & Unwin, 1940)

Margolies, David (ed.), *Writing the Revolution* (London: Pluto Press, 1998)

Margulies, Martin, *The Early Life of Sean O'Casey* (Dublin: Dolmen Press, 1970)

Martin, F.X. (ed.), *The Irish Volunteers 1913–1915* (Dublin: James Duffy, 1963)

Márquez, Gabriel García, *One Hundred Years of Solitude* (New York: Harper & Row, 1970)

Marx, Karl and Friedrich Engels, *On Literature and Art* (Moscow: Progress Publishers, 1976)

Marx, Karl, *Critique of Hegel's Philosophy of Right*, https://www.marxists.org/archive/marx/works/1843/critique-hpr/intro.htm

Matthews, P.J., *Revival* (Cork: Cork University Press in association with Field Day, 2003)

Mercier, Vivien, 'Decline of a Playwright: The riddle of Sean O'Casey', *Commonweal*, no. lxiv, 13 July 1956, pp. 366–8.

Merriman, Victor, 'O'Casey's Postcolonial Dramaturgy', in James Moran, *The Theatre of Seán O'Casey* (London: Bloomsbury Methuen Drama, 2013), pp. 214–26

Metscher, Priscilla, *Republicanism and Socialism in Ireland* (Dublin: Connolly Books, 2016)

Miller, Arthur, *Echoes Down the Corridor* (New York: Viking, 2000)

Milne, Kenneth (ed.), *Christ Church Cathedral* (Dublin: Four Courts Press, 2010)
Milotte, Mike, *Communism in Modern Ireland* (Dublin: Gill & Macmillan, 1984)
Mitchell, Arthur, *Labour in Irish Politics 1890–1930* (Dublin: Irish University Press, 1974)
—, 'George Orwell and Sean O'Casey', *History Ireland*, vol. 6, no. 3, Autumn 1998, pp. 44–6
Mitchell, Jack, *The Essential O'Casey* (New York: International Publishers, 1980)
—, 'Sean O'Casey: Politics and art', in Robert G. Lowery (ed.), *O'Casey Annual*, no. 1 (New Jersey: Humanities Press, 1982), pp. 195–211
Moran, James, *Staging the Easter Rising: 1916 as theatre* (Cork: Cork University Press, 2005)
—, *The Theatre of Seán O'Casey* (London: Bloomsbury Methuen Drama, 2013)
—, *Four Irish Rebel Plays* (Dublin: Irish Academic Press, 2007)
—, 'Class During the Irish Revolution: British soldiers, 1916 and the abject body', in Michael Pierse (ed.), *A History of Working-Class Writing* (Cambridge: Cambridge University Press, 2018), pp. 153–67
—, 'Conflicting Counter-Hegemonies? The dramaturgy of James Connolly and Sean O'Casey', *Kritika Kultura*, nos 21–2, 2013–14, http://kritikakultura.ateneo.net
Morash, Christopher, *A History of Irish Theatre, 1601–2000* (Cambridge: Cambridge University Press, 2002)
—, 'The Road to God Knows Where: Can theatre be national?', in Nicholas Grene and Christopher Morash (eds), *Irish Theatre on Tour*, Irish Theatre Diaspora Series 1 (Dublin: Carysfort Press, 2005), pp. 101–15
Moriarty, Theresa, 'Delia Larkin: Relative obscurity', in Donal Nevin (ed.), *James Larkin: Lion of the fold* (Dublin: Gill & Macmillan, 1998), pp. 28–38
Morrissey, Mary, *The Rising of Bella Casey* (Dingle: Brandon, 2013)
Morrissey SJ, Thomas J., *William O'Brien: 1881–1968* (Dublin: Four Courts Press, 2007)
Moynihan, Maurice, *Speeches and Statements by Éamon de Valera: 1917–1973* (Dublin: Gill & Macmillan, 1980)
Mulhall, Ed., 'From Somme to Silver Tassie: Seán O'Casey and the contested legacy of 1916', https://www.rte.ie/centuryireland/index.php/articles/from-somme-to-silver-tassie-sean-ocasey-the-contested-legacy-of-1916
Münsterer, Hanns Otto, *The Young Brecht*, Tom Kuhn and Karen Leeder (tr.) (London: Libris, 1992)
Murphy, Brian P., *Patrick Pearse and the Lost Republican Ideal* (Dublin: James Duffy, 1991)
—, *The Catholic Bulletin and Republican Ireland* (Belfast: Athol Books, 2005)
Murphy, Paul, 'O'Casey and Class', in James Moran, *The Theatre of Seán O'Casey* (London: Bloomsbury Methuen Drama, 2013), pp. 227–38

Murphy, Robert, 'Sean O'Casey and the Bald Primaqueera', *James Joyce Quarterly*, vol. viii, no. 1, Fall, 1970, pp. 96–110

Murray, Christopher, *Twentieth-Century Irish Drama* (Manchester: Manchester University Press, 1997)

—, 'O'Casey at War', in Kathleen Devine (ed.), *Modern Irish Writers and the Wars* (Gerrards Cross: Colin Smythe, 1999), pp. 81–101

—, *Seán O'Casey: Writer at work* (Dublin: Gill & Macmillan, 2004)

—, 'Sean O'Casey's "The Cooing of the Doves": A one-act play rediscovered', *The Princeton University Library Chronicle*, vol. 68, nos 1–2, Winter 2007, pp. 327–56

—, 'Shaw's Ibsen and the Idea of an Irish Theatre', in Ros Dixon and Irina Ruppo Malone (eds), *Ibsen and Chekhov on the Irish Stage* (Dublin: Carysfort Press, 2012), pp. 23–36

Murray, Patrick, *Oracles of God: The Roman Catholic Church and Irish Politics* (Dublin: UCD Press, 2000)

Murray, Peter, 'Belting the Irish State with US Croziers: Theatre, tourism, UN policy and church–state relations, 1957–58', https://mural.maynoothuniversity.ie/2294/1/WP_Murray_Belting_Irish_State_with_Croziers.pdf

Myers, Kevin, 'Myths of Ireland's Easter Rising', *The Dorchester Review*, vol. 6, no. 1, Spring/Summer 2016, pp. 23–31

Naughton, Lindie, *Markievicz: A most outrageous rebel* (Dublin: Merrion Press, 2016)

Nevin, Donal, *James Larkin: Lion of the fold* (Dublin: Gill & Macmillan, 1998)

—, *Trade Union Century* (Cork: Mercier Press, 1994)

—, *James Connolly: A full life* (Dublin: Gill & Macmillan, 2005)

New Historical Express, https://hatfulofhistory.wordpress.com/2013/03/21/the-communist-party-and-the-campaign-for-nuclear-disarmament/

Newsinger, John, '"The Curse of Larkinism": Patrick McIntyre, *The Toiler* and the Dublin lockout of 1913', *Éire-Ireland*, vol. xxx, no. 3, Fall 1995, pp. 90–102

—, 'Sean O'Casey, Larkinism and Literature', *Irish Studies Review*, vol. 12, no. 3, 2004, pp. 283–92

—, 'Irish Labour in a Time of Revolution', *Socialist History*, no. 22, 2002, pp. 1–31

—, *Hope Lies in the Proles* (London: Pluto Press, 2018)

Ní Dhonnchadha, Máirín and Theo Dorgan, *Revising the Rising* (Derry: Field Day, 1991)

Nicholson, Steve, *British Theatre and the Red Peril* (Exeter: University of Exeter Press, 1999)

Nixon, Barbara, 'Plays about Trade Unionism', *Left Review*, vol. 1, no. 2, November 1934, pp. 42–3

Ó Briain, Leaslaoí, 'What! Have a Service in Erse and in St Patrick's? Cumann Gaelach na hEaglaise – 90 Years Young', *Search*, vol. 27, no. 1, Spring 2004, pp. 5–11

O'Brien, Dr John (ed.), *The Vanishing Irish: The enigma of the modern world* (London: W.H. Allen, 1954)

O'Brien, Joseph V., *Dear Dirty Dublin* (Berkeley: University of California Press, 1982)

O'Brien, Paul, 'Sean O'Casey and the Abbey Theatre: A conflicted relationship', in Patrick Lonergan and Riana O'Dwyer (eds), *Echoes Down the Corridor* (Dublin: Carysfort Press, 2007), pp. 69–80

—, 'Writers of the Left: Politics and culture in Ireland in the 1930s', in Francis Devine, Fintan Lane and Niamh Puirséil (eds), *Essays in Irish Labour History* (Dublin: Irish Academic Press, 2008), pp. 200–18

—, *The 1913 Lockout* (Dublin: PBPA, 2013)

O'Callaghan, Sean, *The Easter Lily* (London: Allan Wingate, 1956)

O'Casey, Eileen, *Cheerio Titan* (New York: Charles Scribner's Sons, 1989)

—, *Sean* (London: Macmillan, 1971)

O'Ceallaigh Ritschel, Nelson, 'The Alternative Aesthetic: The theatre of Ireland's urban plays', in Stephen Watt, Eileen Morgan and Shakir Mustafa (eds), *A Century of Irish Drama* (Bloomington: Indiana University Press, 2000), pp. 17–33

—, *Shaw, Synge, Connolly, and Socialist Provocation* (Gainesville: University Press of Florida, 2012)

—, *Bernard Shaw, Sean O'Casey, and the Dead James Connolly* (London: Palgrave Macmillan, 2021)

O'Connor, Emmet, *Syndicalism in Ireland* (Cork: Cork University Press, 1988)

—, *A Labour History of Ireland* (Dublin: Gill & Macmillan, 1992)

—, *Reds and the Green: Ireland, Russia and the Communist International 1919–1943* (Dublin: UCD Press, 2004)

—, 'Syndicalism, Industrial Unionism, and Nationalism in Ireland', in S. Hirsch and L. Van der Walt (eds), *Anarchism and Syndicalism in the Colonial and Postcolonial World, 1870–1940,* vol. 1 (Leiden: Brill Publishers, 2011), pp. 193–226

—, *Big Jim Larkin: Hero or wrecker?* (Dublin: UCD Press, 2015)

O'Connor, Garry, *Sean O'Casey: A life* (London: Hodder & Stoughton, 1988)

O'Connor, John, *The 1916 Proclamation* (Dublin: Anvil Books, 1986)

O'Connor, Joseph, *Even the Olives Are Bleeding* (Dublin: New Island Books, 1992)

O'Connor, Patrick, 'Theatre', *The Furrow*, vol. 12, no. 10, October 1965, pp. 631–3

O'Connor Lysaght, D.R., 'The Irish Citizen Army: 1913–1916', *History Ireland*, vol. 14, no. 2, March/April 2006, pp. 16–21

—, *The Steam Packet Company Strike* (Dublin: no imprint, 2014)

Ó Corcora, Dónall, *What's This About the Gaelic League?* (Dublin: Conradh na Gaedhilge, 1956)

Ó Cuív, Brian, *Irish Dialects and Irish-Speaking Districts* (Dublin: Dublin Institute for Advanced Studies, 1950)

O'Donnell, Peadar, *Salud! An Irishman in Spain* (Dublin: Friends of the International Brigades in Ireland, 2020)

O'Donoghue, Florence, 'Plans for the 1916 Rising', *University Review* (Dublin), vol. 3, no. 1, 1963, pp. 3–21

Ó Drisceoil, Donal, *Peadar O'Donnell* (Cork: Cork University Press, 2001)

O'Driscoll, Robert, *Theatre and Nationalism in 20th-Century Ireland* (Toronto: University of Toronto Press, 1971)

O'Faoláin, Seán, 'The Strange Case of Sean O'Casey', *The Bell*, vol. 6, no. 2, May 1943, pp. 112–21

Ó Fearaíl, Pádraig, *The Story of Conradh na Gaeilge* (Dublin: Conradh na Gaeilge, 1975)

Ó Fiaich, Tomás, 'The Great Controversy', in Seán Ó Tuama (ed.), *The Gaelic League Idea* (Cork: Mercier Press, 1972), pp. 63–75

O'Flaherty, Liam, *The Informer* (London: Jonathan Cape, 1925)

—, *The Assassin* (London: Jonathan Cape, 1928)

—, *Insurrection* (London: Gollancz, 1950)

O'Hegarty, P.S., *Irish Statesman*, vol. 2, no. 13, 7 June 1924, pp. 383–414

—, *The Victory of Sinn Féin* (Dublin: UCD Press, 2015)

O'Leary, Catherine, 'Translating the Armed Struggle: Alonso Sastre and Sean O'Casey in Spain', *Translation Studies*, vol. 11, no. 1, 2018, pp. 47–65

Ó Lúing, Seán, *I Die in a Good Cause* (Cork: Mercier Press, 2017)

O'Mahony, Sean, *The First Hunger Striker: Thomas Ashe 1917* (Dublin: The 1916–1921 Club in association with Elo Publications, 2001)

O'Malley, Ernie, *On Another Man's Wound* (London: Rich & Cowan, 1936)

O'Neill, Brian, *Easter Week* (New York: International Publishers, 1936)

O'Riordan, Manus, *Liberty Hall as a Cultural Centre: The early years* (Dublin: SIPTU, 2002)

—, 'Sean O'Casey and O'Riordans on the 1956 Hungarian Uprising', *Irish Foreign Affairs*, December 2016

Orwell, George, *Homage to Catalonia* (London: Secker & Warburg, 1938)

Orwell, George, Sonia Orwell and Ian Angus (eds), *The Collected Essays, Journalism and Letters*, 4 vols (New York: Harcourt, Brace & World, 1968)

O'Toole, Fintan, Catherine Marshall and Eibhear Walshe (eds), *Modern Ireland in 100 Artworks* (Dublin: Royal Irish Academy, 2016)

O'Toole, Fintan, *Judging Shaw* (Dublin: Prism, 2017)

Owen, Wilfred, *The Collected Poems* (London: Chatto & Windus, 1971)

Oz, Amos, *Judas* (London: Chatto & Windus, 2016)

Papke, Mary E., 'Sean O'Casey's Early Plays as Larkinite Parables', *The Seán O'Casey Review*, vol. 3, no. 2, Spring 1977, pp. 105–16

Patterson, Michael, *The Revolution in German Theatre 1900–1933* (London: Routledge & Kegan Paul, 1981)

Pearse, Patrick H., 'The Sovereign People', in *Collected Works of Pádraic H. Pearse: Political writings and speeches* (Dublin: Phoenix, 1924), pp. 335–72

—, *Collected Works of Patrick H. Pearse: Plays, stories, poems* (Dublin: Phoenix, 1924)

Peyronnet, Marianne, 'Was Sean O'Casey a Feminist Playwright?', *Times Change*, no. 12, Winter 1997–8, pp. 23–6

Phillips, Terry, *Irish Literature and the First World War* (Bern: Peter Lang, 2015)

Pierse, Michael, 'The Shadow of Sean O'Casey: O'Casey, commitment and writing Dublin's working class', *Saothar*, vol. 35, 2010, pp. 69–85

— (ed.), *A History of Irish Working-Class Writing* (Cambridge: Cambridge University Press, 2018)

Pilkington, Lionel, *Theatre and the State in Twentieth-Century Ireland* (London: Routledge & Kegan Paul, 2001)

Piscator, Erwin, *The Political Theatre* (London: Eyre Methuen, 1963)

Plunkett, James, *The Gems She Wore* (London: Arrow Books, 1978)

— 'Big Jim: A loaf on the table, a flower in the vase', in Donal Nevin (ed.), *James Larkin: Lion of the fold* (Dublin: Gill & Macmillan, 1998), pp. 110–15

Porter, Raymond J., 'O'Casey and Pearse', in Robert G. Lowery (ed.), *Essays on Sean O'Casey's Autobiographies* (New York & London: Macmillan, 1981), pp. 89–102

Prawer, S.S., *Karl Marx and World Literature* (Oxford: Oxford University Press, 1978)

Pritchett, V.S., *Midnight Oil* (New York: Random House, 1972)

Prunty, Jacinta, *Managing the Dublin Slums 1850–1922* (Dublin: Dublin City Public Libraries, 2004)

Reed, John, *Ten Days that Shook the World* (New York: Boni & Liveright, 1919)

Regan, John M., *The Irish Counter-Revolution 1921–1936* (Dublin: Gill & Macmillan, 2001)

Reid, Christina, *Joyriders* and *Tea in a China Cup* (London: Methuen, 1987)

Robbins, Frank, *Under the Starry Plough* (Dublin: Academy Press, 1977)

Robinson, Lennox (ed.), *The Irish Theatre* (London: Macmillan, 1939)

Roche, Anthony, *The Irish Dramatic Revival 1899–1939* (London: Bloomsbury, 2015)

Rollins, Roland G., 'Sean O'Casey's *The Star Turns Red*: A political prophecy', *Mississippi Quarterly*, vol. xvi, no. 2, Spring 1963, pp. 67–75

—, *Sean O'Casey's Drama* (Tuscaloosa, AL: University of Alabama Press, 1978)

Ronsley, Joseph (ed.), *Denis Johnston: A retrospective* (Gerrards Cross: Colin Smythe, 1981)

Rumph, E. and A.C. Hepburn, *Nationalism and Socialism in Twentieth-Century Ireland* (Liverpool: Liverpool University Press, 1977)

Rushe, Desmond, *The New York Times*, 13 July 1970

Ryan, Desmond, *Remembering Sion* (Dublin: Arthur Barker, 1934)

Ryan, Frederick, 'The Laying of the Foundations', in Robert Hogan and James Kilroy (eds), *Lost Plays of the Irish Renaissance* (Dixon, CA: Proscenium Press, 1970), pp. 23–37

—, Bill McCamley and Manus O'Riordan (eds), *Socialism, Democracy and the Church* (Dublin: Labour History Workshop, 1984)

Ryan, W.P., *The Irish Labour Movement* (Dublin: Talbot Press, 1919)

Said, Edward W., Steven Harris and Deborah Berke (eds), *Reflections on Exile* (London: Granta, 2001)

Samuel, Raphael, Ewan MacColl and Stuart Cosgrave, *Theatres of the Left 1880–1935* (London: Routledge & Kegan Paul, 1985)

Samuel, Richard and Thomas R. Hinton, *Expressionism in German Life, Literature and the Theatre (1910–1924)* (Cambridge: Heffer, 1939)

Schrank, Bernice, 'The Politics of O'Casey's War Plays', in C.C. Barfoot and Rias van den Doel (eds), *Ritual Remembering: History, myth and politics in Anglo-Irish drama* (Amsterdam & Atlanta, GA: Rodopi, 1995), pp. 75–84

—, 'Sean O'Casey and the Dialectics of Violence', in Danine Farquharson and Sean Farrell (eds), *Shadows of the Gunmen: Violence and culture in modern Ireland* (Cork: Cork University Press, 2008), pp. 38–62

Scrimgeour, James R., *Sean O'Casey* (Boston: Twayne Publishers, 1978)

Shaw, George Bernard, *Plays: Pleasant and unpleasant* (London: Constable, 1924)

—, *John Bull's Other Island* (London: Constable, 1909)

—, *The Matter with Ireland*, Dan H. Laurence and David H. Greene (eds) (New York: Hill & Wang, 1962)

—, *Collected Letters*, 4 vols, Dan H. Lawrence (ed.) (New York: Max Reinhardt, 1965–88)

Sheehy, Michael, *Is Ireland Dying?* (London: The Catholic Book Club, 1970)

Sheehy Skeffington, Andrée, *Skeff: A life of Owen Sheehy Skeffington 1909–1970* (Dublin: The Lilliput Press, 1991)

Sheehy Skeffington, Hanna, *Hanna Sheehy Skeffington: Suffragette and Sinn Féiner*, Margaret Ward (ed.) (Dublin: UCD Press, 2017)

Shelley, Percy Bysshe, *The Major Works* (Oxford: Oxford University Press, 2003)

Sheppard, Richard, 'German Expressionism', in Malcolm Bradbury and James McFarlane (eds), *Modernism: A guide to European literature 1890–1930* (London: Penguin, 1919) pp. 274–91

Shovlin, Frank, *The Irish Literary Periodical 1923–1958* (Oxford: Clarendon Press, 2003)

Simmgen, Hans-Georg, 'O'Casey Stage Productions in the German Democratic Republic', in Micheál Ó hAodha (ed.), *The O'Casey Enigma* (Cork: Mercier Press, 1980), pp. 70–80

Simpson, Alan, 'Staging O'Casey's Plays', *The Seán O'Casey Review*, vol. 5, no. 2, Spring 1979, pp. 134–7.

—, 'O'Casey and the East Wall Area in Dublin', *Irish University Review*, vol. 10, no. 1, Spring 1980, pp. 41–61

Skelley, Jeffrey (ed.), *The General Strike, 1926* (London: Lawrence & Wishart, 1976)

Slowey, Desmond, *The Radicalization of Irish Drama 1600–1900* (Dublin: Irish Academic Press, 2008)

Smith, Anthony D., *National Identity* (London: Penguin, 1991)

Smith, B.L., *O'Casey's Satiric Vision* (Kent, OH: Kent State University Press, 1978)

Smyth, Denis, *Cities in Revolt (Part 2)* (Belfast: North Belfast History Workshop, 1991)

Smyth, Gerry, *Decolonisation and Criticism* (London: Pluto Press, 1998)

Solomon, Maynard (ed.), *Marxism and Art* (New York: Alfred A. Knopf, 1973)

Somerville, Henry, 'The Political Impotence of British Labour', *Studies: An Irish quarterly review*, vol. 10, no. 37, March 1921, pp. 1–18

Spender, Stephen, 'Writers and Manifestoes', *Left Review*, vol. 1, no. 5, February 1935, pp. 145–50

—, *The Thirties and After* (London: Palgrave Macmillan, 1978)

Stanislavski, Constantin, *An Actor Prepares*, Elizabeth Reynolds Hapgood (tr.) (London: Methuen, 1980)

Stephens, James, *The Crock of Gold* (London: Macmillan, 1912)

Stewart, Victoria, *About O'Casey: The playwright and the work* (London: Faber & Faber, 2003)

Stradling, Robert A., *The Irish and the Spanish Civil War 1936–1939* (Manchester: Mandolin, 1999)

Strauss, E., *Irish Nationalism and British Democracy* (London: Methuen, 1951)

Synge, John Millington, *The Playboy of the Western World* (Dublin: Maunsel, 1907)

Tall, Emily, 'The Joyce Centenary in the Soviet Union: Making way for *Ulysses*', *James Joyce Quarterly*, vol. 21, no. 2, Winter 1984, pp. 107–22

Thompson, E.P., *The Making of the English Working Class* (London: Victor Gollancz, 1963)

Thompson, William Irwin, *The Imagination of an Insurrection* (New York: Harper Colophon Books, 1967)

Thornley, David, 'Patrick Pearse', *Studies: An Irish quarterly review*, vol. lv, no. 217, Spring 1966, pp. 10–20

Tóibín, Colm, *Lady Gregory's Toothbrush* (London: Picador, 2003)

Toller, Ernst, *Letters from Prison*, R. Ellis Roberts (tr.) (London: John Lane The Bodley Head, 1935)

—, *Seven Plays* (London: John Lane The Bodley Head, 1935)

Townsend, Sarah L., 'Walking the "Thorny Way": Pressures and predicaments of womanhood in Sean O'Casey's three Dublin plays', unpublished BA thesis, University of Michigan, 2002

Townshend, Charles, 'The Irish Railway Strike of 1920', *Irish Historical Studies*, vol. 21, no. 83, March 1979, pp. 265–82

—, *Easter 1916: The Irish rebellion* (London: Allen Lane, 2005)
—, *The Republic: The fight for Irish independence* (London: Allen Lane, 2013)
Trench, Brian, 'The Radical Club', *History Ireland*, vol. 27, no. 5, September/October 2019, pp. 43–6
Trotsky, Leon, *The Revolution Betrayed* (New York: Pathfinder Press, 1937)
—, 'Where Is Britain Going?', *Collected Writings and Speeches on Britain* (London: New Park Publications, 1974)
—, *Literature and Revolution* (London: Redwords, 1991)
Trotter, Mary, *Ireland's National Theaters* (Syracuse: Syracuse University Press, 2001)
Tytell, John, *The Living Theatre: Art, exile, and outrage* (London: Methuen, 1997)
Van Voris, Jacqueline, *Constance de Markievicz: In the cause of Ireland* (Manchester: Manchester University Press, 1967)
Vaughan, W.E. (ed.), *A New History of Ireland: Ireland under the union 1870–1921*, vol. 6 (Oxford: Oxford University Press, 1989)
Walsh, Maurice, *Bitter Freedom: Ireland in a revolutionary world 1918–1923* (London: Faber & Faber, 2015)
Ward, Margaret, *Unmanageable Revolutionaries* (London: Pluto Press, 1993)
Watt, Rev. Lewis, *A Handbook of 'Rerum Novarum'* (Oxford: Catholic Social Guild, 1941)
Watt, Stephen, Eileen Morgan and Shakir Mustafa, *A Century of Irish Drama* (Bloomington: Indiana University Press, 2000)
Watt, Stephen, *Joyce, O'Casey, and the Irish Popular Theater* (Syracuse: Syracuse University Press, 1991)
Weintraub, Stanley, 'The Making of an Irish Rebel', *Éire-Ireland*, vol. v, no. 4, Winter 1970, pp. 9–27
Welch, Robert, *Irish Writers and Religion* (Maryland: Barnes & Noble, 1992)
—, *The Abbey Theatre 1899–1999* (Oxford: Oxford University Press, 2003)
West, Alick, *A Good Man Fallen Among Fabians* (London: Lawrence & Wishart, 1950)
—, *One Man in His Time* (London: Allen & Unwin, 1969)
Whelan, Kevin, 'The Revisionist Debate in Ireland', *Boundary 2*, vol. 3, no. 1, Spring 2004, pp. 179–205
White, Marie, *The South Atlantic Quarterly*, vol. 53, 1954, p. 156
Whitehorn, Katherine, *Selective Memory* (London: Virago, 2008)
Whyte, J.H., *Church and State in Modern Ireland* (Dublin: Gill & Macmillan, 1971)
Willett, John, *The Theatre of Bertolt Brecht* (New York: New Directions Books, 1959)
Williams, Raymond, *Drama from Ibsen to Eliot* (London: Chatto & Windus, 1952)
—, *Drama from Ibsen to Brecht* (London: Chatto & Windus, 1968)
—, *Drama in Performance* (London: Pelican Books, 1972)

Wills, Clair, *That Neutral Island* (London: Faber & Faber, 2007)
—, *Dublin 1916: The siege of the GPO* (London: Profile Books, 2010)
Wilson, Donald Douglas, *Sean O'Casey's Tragi-comic Vision* (New York: Revisionist Press, 1976)
Winkler, Heinrich August, *The Age of Catastrophe* (New Haven: Yale University Press, 2015)
Wolfe, Bertram D., *Strange Communists I Have Known* (London: Allen & Unwin, 1966)
Woroszylski, Wiktor, *The Life of Mayakovsky* (London: Victor Gollancz, 1972)
Yeates, Pádraig, *Lockout: Dublin 1913* (Dublin: Gill & Macmillan, 2000)
—, *A City in Wartime: Dublin 1914–18* (Dublin: Gill & Macmillan, 2011)
—, '"To Leaven Trades Unionism with Catholic Social Principles is the Dream I Cherish", Father Thomas Dowling OSFC', *Saothar*, no. 46, 2021, pp. 41–52
Yeats, W.B., 'The Controversy over the *Playboy*', *The Arrow*, vol. 1, no. 3, 23 February 1907
—, *Collected Poems* (London: Macmillan, 1950)
Yun, Hunam, 'Appropriations of Irish Drama by Modern Korean Nationalist Theatre: A focus on the influence of Sean O'Casey in a colonial context', unpublished PhD thesis, University of Warwick, 2010
Zinn, Howard, *A People's History of the United States* (Harlow: Longman, 1996)

Index